How To Weld Scrap Metal Art

30 Easy Welding Projects

Written by
Barbie The Welder

Also Written By
Barbie The Welder

Horseshoe Crafts; More Than 30 Easy Projects You Can Weld At Home

The Inspiration Blueprint; How To Design And Create Your Inspired Life

The Artist's Guide To Branding, Marketing, & Selling Art Online

How To Weld Silverware Animals; 30 Metal Art Welding Projects

F*ck You Fuel; How To Turn Shit Into Sugar

Dedication

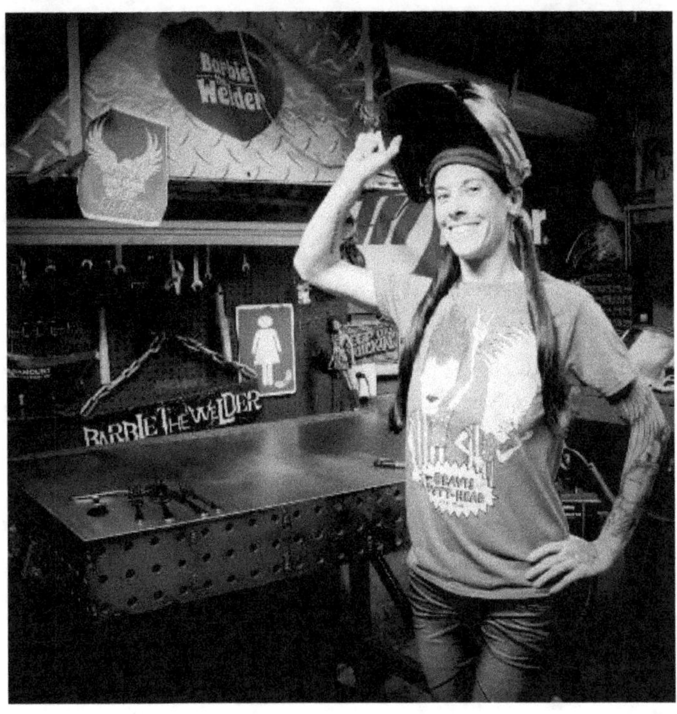

Dedicated to the artist who may not yet see themselves as one - may this book be the spark that ignites your creative soul. Play with possibility, push boundaries, dedicate yourself to craftsmanship, and have fun in the process!

Stay true live free,
Barbie The Welder

Table of Contents

Foreword

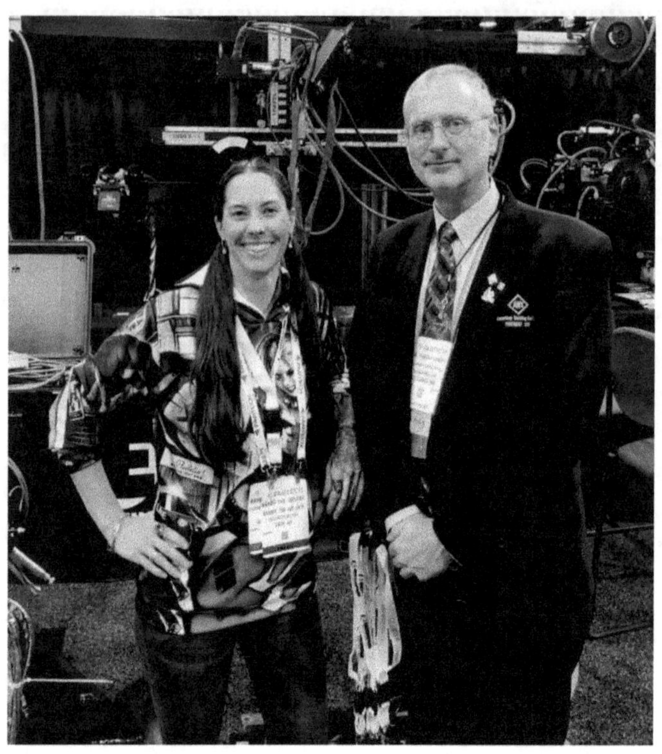

AsPresident of the American Welding Society (AWS) for 2019, our centennial year, I am often asked to support various efforts related to welding. While I am typically willing to do so in my personal life, I have to be careful to avoid any conflict of interest as AWS President. So, when Barbie Parsons, aka “Barbie the Welder”, asked me to write the foreword for this book, I was very interested to help, since I had heard many good things about her, but was also cautious. There was a need to learn more about Barbie’s background and to check with our corporate attorney to ensure no legal issues exist.

What did I discover? First, no legal concerns were found. What about Barbie? I completed web searches, watched her You-Tube videos, read reviews of her books and checked out her social media feeds. The first word that came to mind was **“WOW”**! Barbie is a professional welder, talented artist, prolific author, motivational speaker and successful entrepreneur. More importantly, she is a tireless advocate for AWS and the welding industry, **AND** is an influential role model for young women entering this field.

This book, entitled, How to Weld Scrap Metal Art, is the fourth in a series by Barbie. Like two of her previous books, this manuscript showcases Barbie’s artistic creativity and fabricating prowess. I like the fact that the book starts with a review of safety issues. It then continues with tips on MIG (GMAW) and TIG (GTAW) welding, a list of tools needed for the projects and ideas on finishing. The projects are rated with a degree of difficulty score for readers.

The other prior publication, The Inspiration Blueprint: How to Design and Create Your Inspired Life, chronicles Barbie's pathway from her upbringing to her early career and into her current successful business. Through sheer determination, Barbie pulled herself and her family up from poverty and welfare by training to become a welder, starting her own business and publishing four books. She has achieved popularity on par with rock stars, and her journey to success is simply inspirational.

This last point was really brought home to me during a visit to Knoxville in October where I spoke a meeting of the Northeast Tennessee Section of AWS. I arrived at the section meeting early and began to talk with student attendees. I played a large role in establishing the Diversity and Inclusion Committee at AWS and the developing our Future Leaders program aimed at having early career individuals from the welding industry participate in meetings of the AWS Board of Directors and other committees. As such, I make great efforts to engage with students and early career members at section meetings.

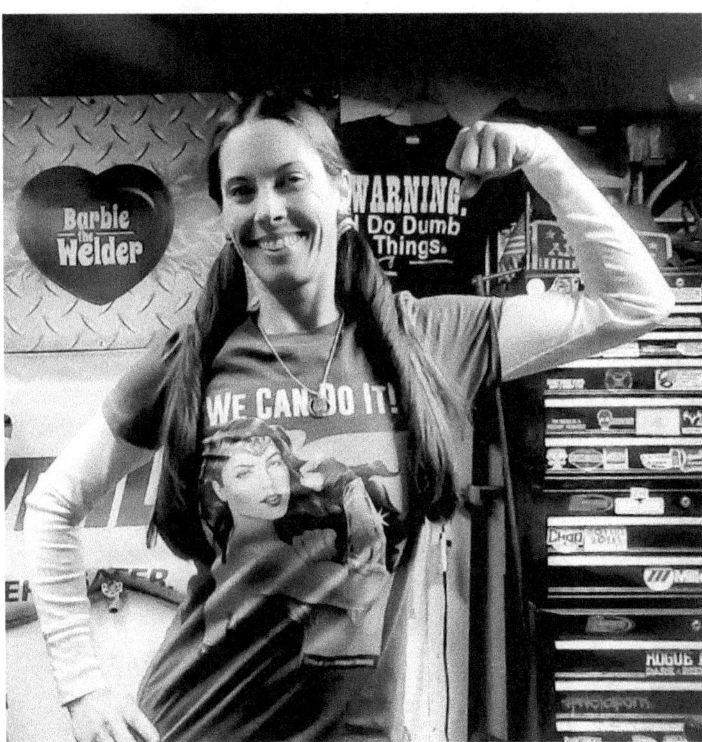

During one of the conversations, I met an impressive young woman named Grace. She had recently started her own welding and fabrication business. Given my recent emails with Barbie, I asked Grace if she had ever heard of Barbie. Her response: "Barbie is my hero, and I model my business after Barbie's just like in her YouTube videos". That was all I needed to become a big Barbie fan. I vowed that no matter how busy my schedule for the upcoming FabTech event and Board of Directors meeting in Chicago, I was going to meet Barbie the Welder in person. It is important to understand that the President's schedule is often double- and triple-booked that week, and that it is difficult for me to move about on the show floor without having to stop to talk with members. Nonetheless, I was able to make time meet Barbie face-to-face while at FabTech. She has an infectious smile, and is an engaging, delightful and humble person. I am grateful to become her friend.

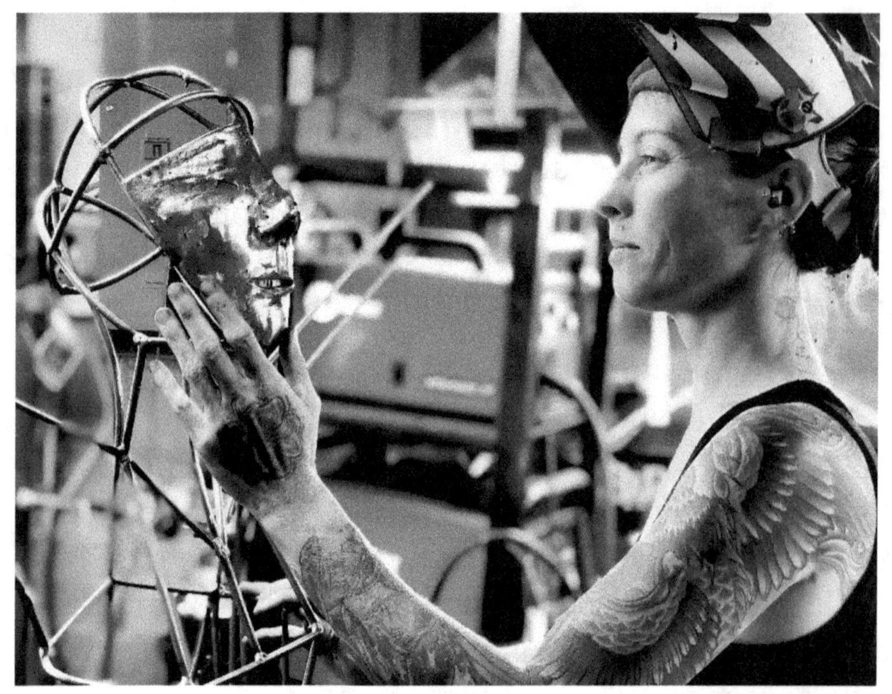

You will enjoy this book. Barbie is the perfect author for the book as her welding skills and fun personality jump right off the pages. It will teach you about art and about welding in exciting (and safe) ways. Be careful, you may also learn to become a better welder and entrepreneur along the way. I highly recommend this book to all in the welding industry. It will make a wonderful holiday present for all of the welders on your list. Weld on.

Tom

Dr. Thomas J. Lienert, FAWS, FASM, CWI

AWS 2019 President

Dear Artist

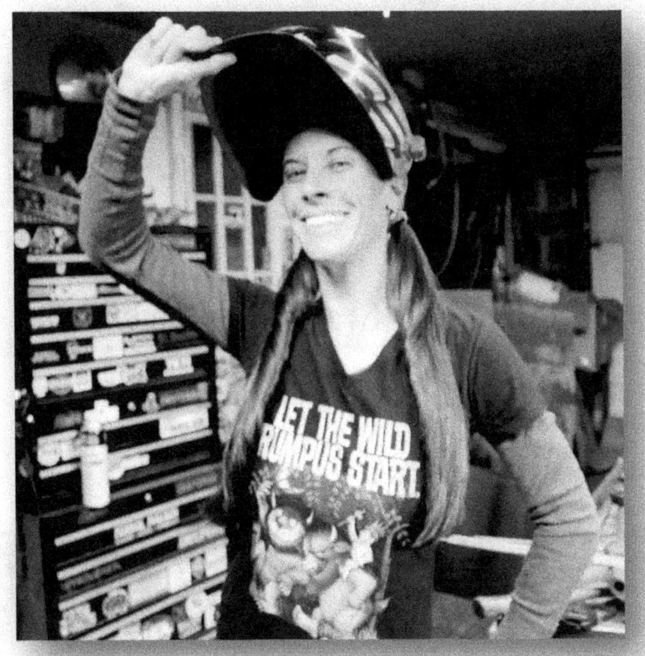

Scrap metal is fun to create with! It is inexpensive to buy, easy to find, and there is always plenty to create with! Try using different scrap pieces for these projects and see how it looks! Have fun and experiment, you are only limited by your imagination!
Scrap metal can be found at rummage sales, secondhand stores, the junk yard, and laying around your neighbors' garage, just make sure you ask first before you go welding their stuff up!

Making gifts for people instead of buying them is one of the most wonderful things in the world! You are giving someone something they can't get anywhere else, and that is made with love and one of a kind!

Ilove to see art and I hope you'll share your art with me! Tag #BarbieTheWelder on Instagram to share your beautiful creations with me!

Happy welding!

Barbie The Welder

How To Not Set Yourself On Fire!

Safety is no accident!

Welding,cutting, and grinding metal is extremely dangerous if you are not taking theproper precautions. Follow these steps to stay safe!

- Keepyour workareafree from clutter
- Keepany papers,flammable materials, and oily rags away from your workarea
- Makesure yourworkarea has the proper ventilation
- Havea fire extinguisher close by your work area when you are welding
- Always wear fireresistant clothing that fitproperly
- Always tie longhairback
- Make sure yourpantlegs are long enoughtocoverthe tops of your shoes/boots
- Protect yourfeetwithleather boots/steel toe shoes
- Always wearawelding helmet with the correctshadelens while welding

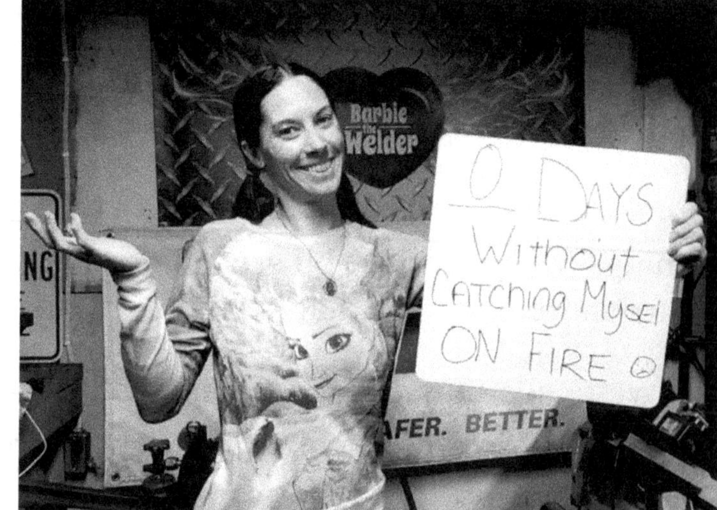

- Hearing protection,safety glasses, and a face shield should be worn each time you cutorhammer metal
- Always wearleathergloves to protect your hands and wrists as you work
- Always makesureanyone in the shop with you is also following these safety precautions

How To Stick Stuff Together

There are several welding processes that are used in the welding and art industries, but I will only speak for thetwoIuse,MIGandTIG. Both MIGandTIGarefantastic for creatingartandeach process has its advantages and disadvantages.

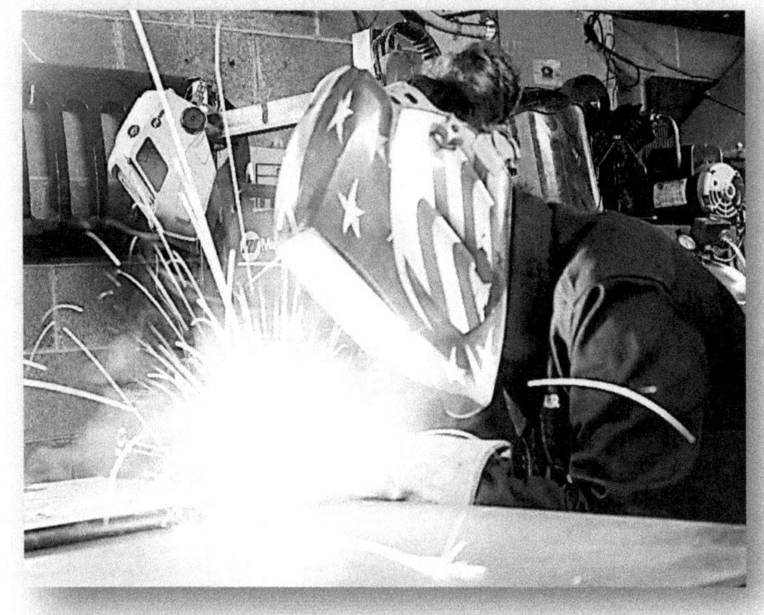

In myopinionMIGweldingis easier to learn, less expensive to get started,andweldsfaster, but whenusingittoweldyou will havemorecleaning.TIG welding takes more time to learn, butismoreprecise,you make smallercleanerwelds, and youhaveverylittleclean up.

When I weld silverware art, I use my MIG welder with 75/25 gas and .030 ER70s wire. Each welder has their own preferences as to what they use, what works for some might not work for others. Use what you are comfortable with. Welding is an art before you ever do anything else with it! If you are new to welding, like anything you try that is new, it will take time to learn your machine and improve your skills, have patience with yourself!

Setting up your welder correctly will give you the best results when welding. If you areMIGweldingthethicknessandtypeofmaterialyou'rewelding,the wire thicknessandwhetherornotyou'reusinggaswillalleffectthesettingsof your machine.IfyouareusingaTIGweldertocreateyourart,thethicknessof your material,tungstensize,andfillerrodsizewillalldetermineyourmachine settings. Each welder, whether MIG or TIG will have a basic parameter chart (machine settings) that is usually on the backside of the door. If the chart is not on themachinelookituponthemanufacture'swebsite.Thesesettingswill give youastartingpointwheretosetyourmachine,buttheymayneedtobe adjusted from here. If you are new to welding use practice pieces to tune in your machinebeforeyoustartweldingandcreatingart.Thereareatonof fantastic videos on YouTube that will help you properly set up your machine.

Having your settings correct for the job you are working on will make a big difference in your welding experience! For most of these welding projects you will be using small tack welds to weld your projects together. Tack welds are small dots of weld similar to the size and shape of candy dots, the rainbow color candy that come on a long strip of paper. (Yummy, now I want candy!) My favorite resource for any welding questions is Jody Collier, the man behind the Welding Tips and Tricks website and YouTube channel. Jody is an incredible wealth of information, the one the seasoned welders go to when they need answers! Website: WeldingTipsAndTricks.com YouTube: YouTube.com/user/WeldingTipsAndTricks Instagram: Instagram.com/Weldmonger

In addition to a welder and your imagination you will need a few tools to create these projects. Each project will tell you specifically what you will need.

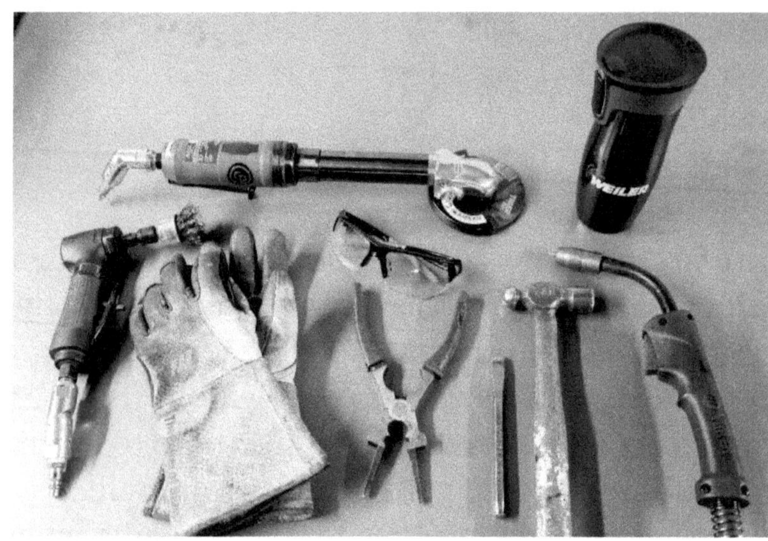

- Metal top work bench
- Wire brush
- Vise or clamp
- Hammer Chisel Punch Tape measure
- Whelpers or needle nose pliers
- Angle grinder or pneumatic grinder with a cut off wheel and sanding disk
- Clear coat spray or paint made for metal

When I started creating metal art, I didn't have much to work with and had to use my imagination and sometimes do things in an unconventional way. (I mostly still do!) If you don't have a metal bench you can put a sheet of 14-gauge steel between two sawhorses.

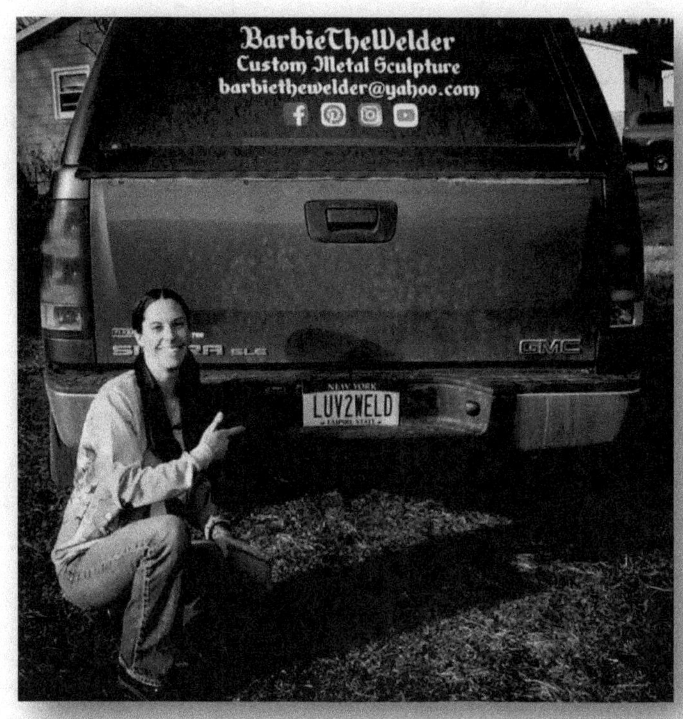

If you don't have an angle grinder with a cut off wheel and sanding disk you can bend the silverware back and forth until they break and then hand file any rough edges. There is always a workaround for any situation! When choosing silverware for your projects, stainless steel and steel silverware may be used, but silver-plated silverware cannot. Steel filler rod can be used to weld stainless steel silverware, but it must be clear coated when the project is finished to prevent rust.

Deburring, smoothing, and shaping: When you cut metal it leaves a burr, a sharp edge. Deburring something means to remove any sharp edges so that you can safely run your fingers over a piece of metal without getting cut. Smoothing and shaping refers to using a grinder to shape a piece to look like it was never cut. Each piece that you cut will need to be deburred and smoothed.

Clean Up and Finishing: When you are done welding your beautiful art, it is of utmost importance that you carefully clean it. Use a wire brush to clean any weld discoloration and a hammer and chisel to chip any weld spatter from your sculpture. Weld spatter can hurt someone when they pick up your masterpiece and cleaning any weld discoloration with a wire brush just looks better! Your attention to details will keep your art heads and shoulders above the crowd! Pride in craftsmanship always!!!! To finish my projects, I use a rattle can (spray paint) clear coat made for metal, it gives the sculpture a beautiful patina and keeps it from rusting.

Difficulty levels for the projects are shown in , one being the easiest and five the most difficult. If you are new to welding art start with the easier projects. Yes, I know, I am welder hear me roar! Lol, hear me out! When you start with the easier projects, are able to create them, and love what you create, you build confidence in yourself and will keep creating. If you start with the harder projects, you may get frustrated and give up something that will bring you and the people around you joy!

Alright Scrap Stars let's weld!

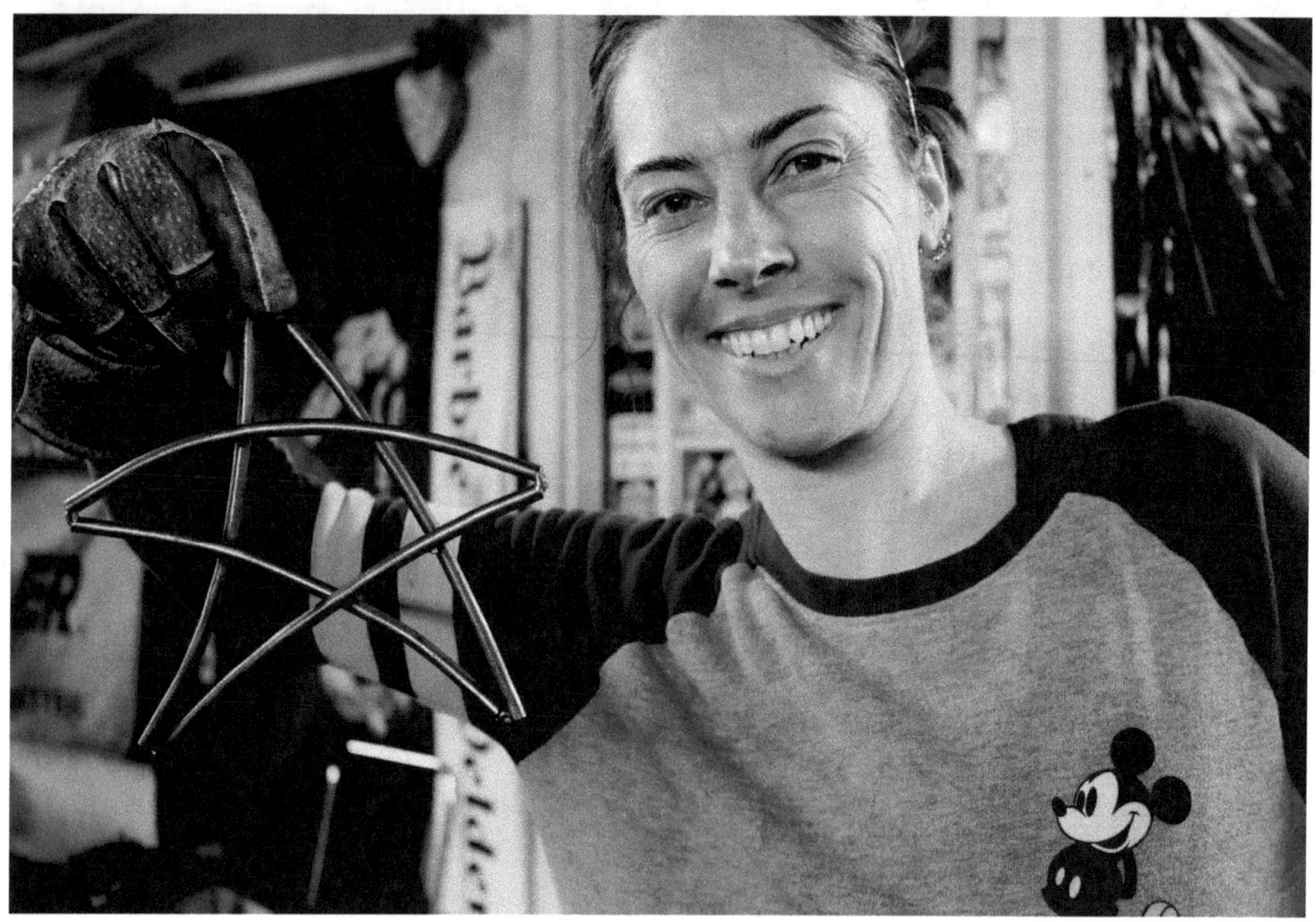

Keychains

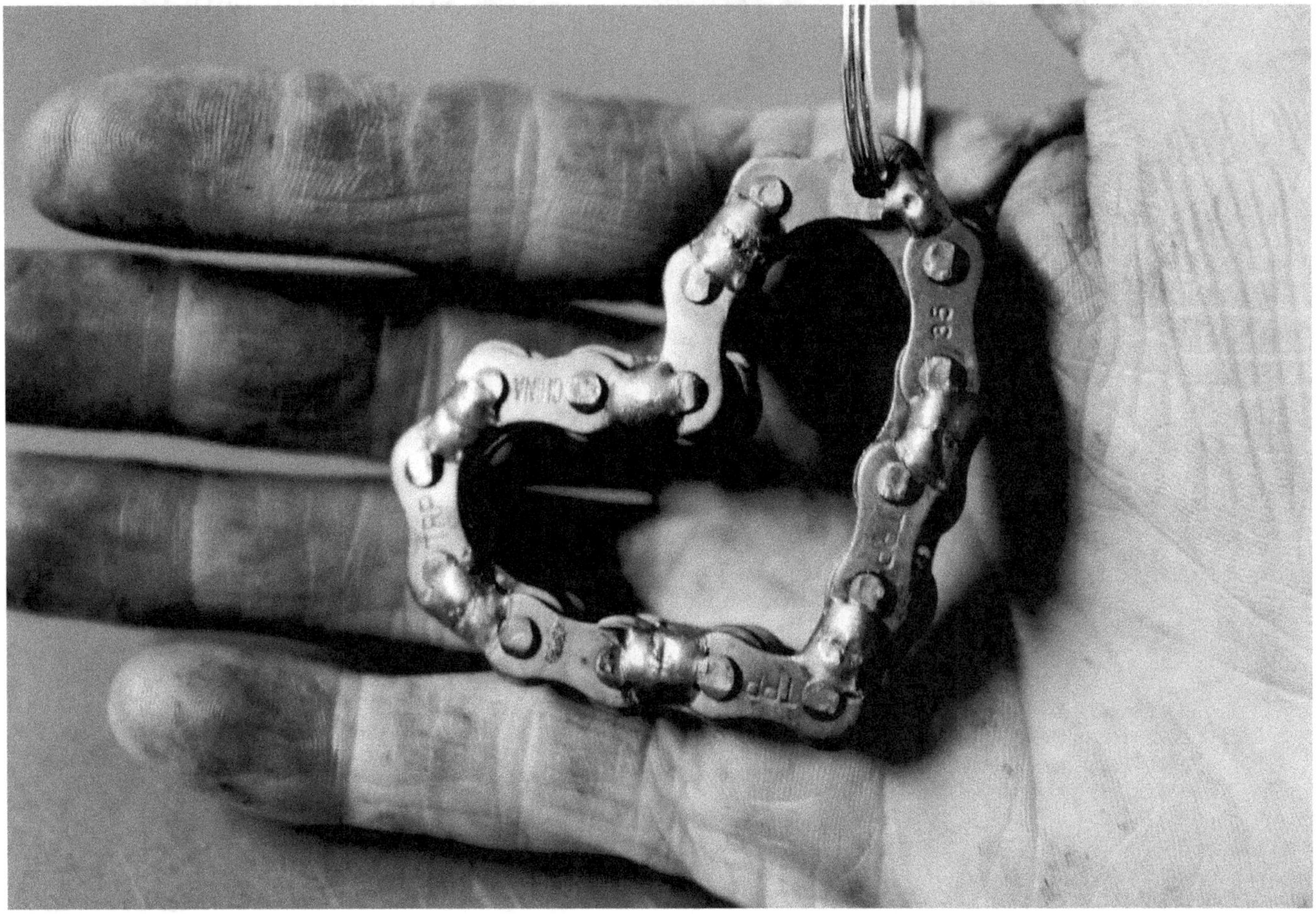

Difficulty

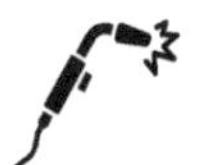

Materials

Roller chain from a bicycle or chainsaw

Tools

Wire brush
Grinder
Hammer and punch or chain breaker tool

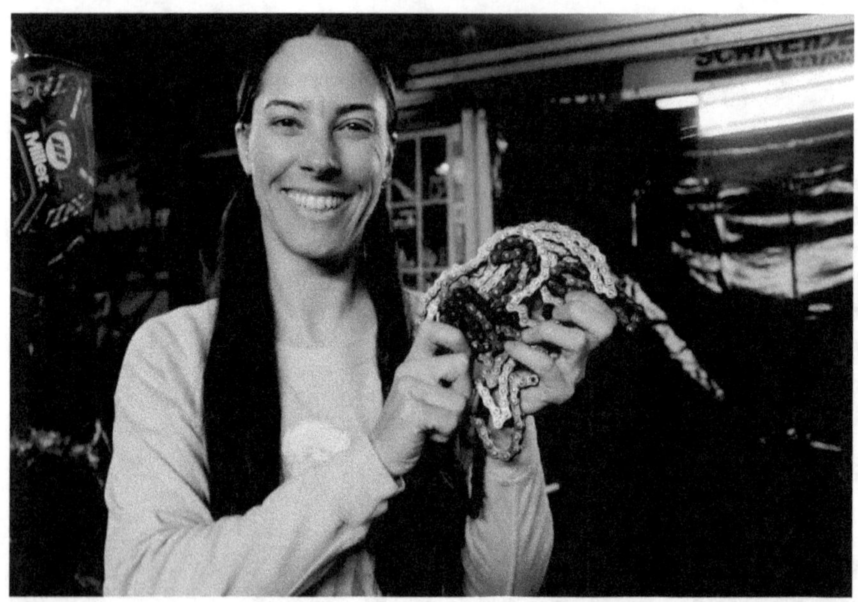

When you weld chain the grease burns out, so be very careful with the fumes and tiny fire! You'll see!
Clean the chain with a shop rag, you won't get all the grease out, but you can get most of it.

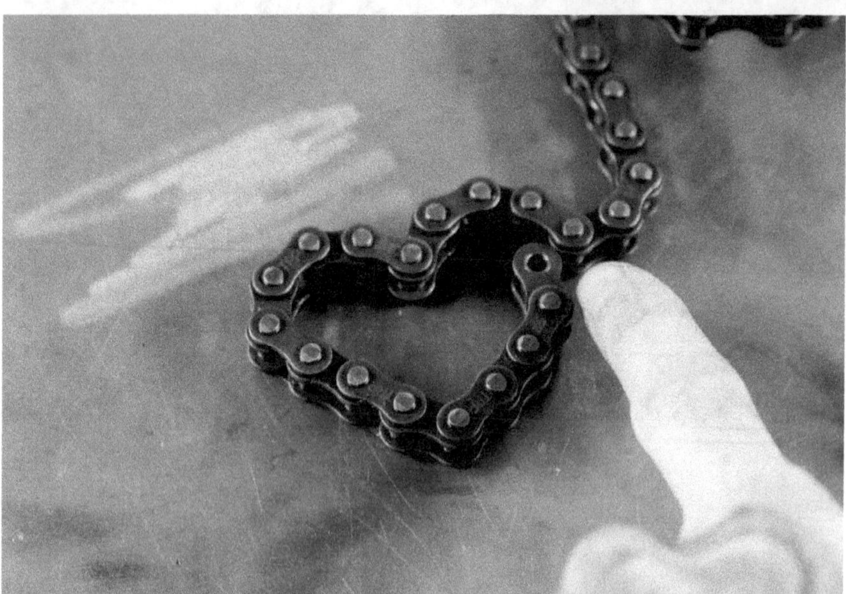

Choose the shape you want and lay out the design.
Mark the pin that will need to be removed.

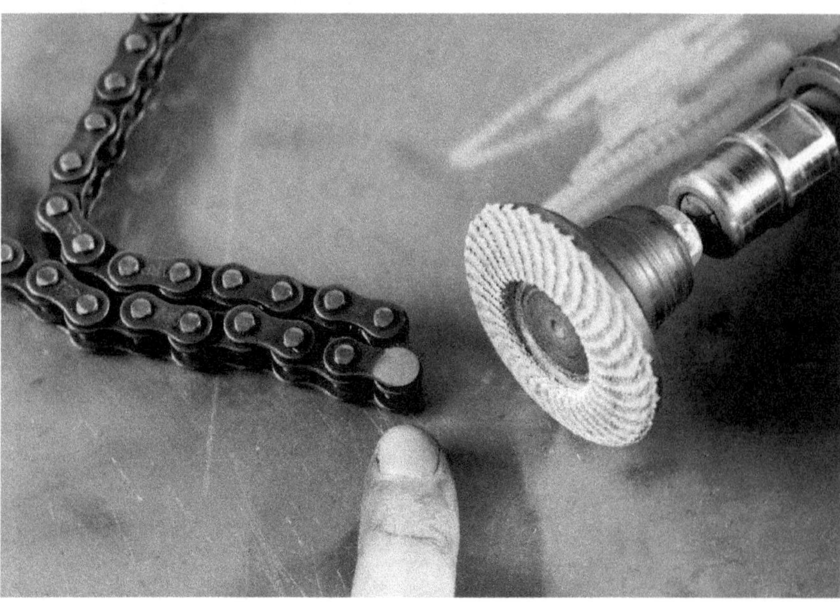

If you have a chain breaker tool use that to remove the pin.
If you don't have a chain breaker grind the pin down to the chain.

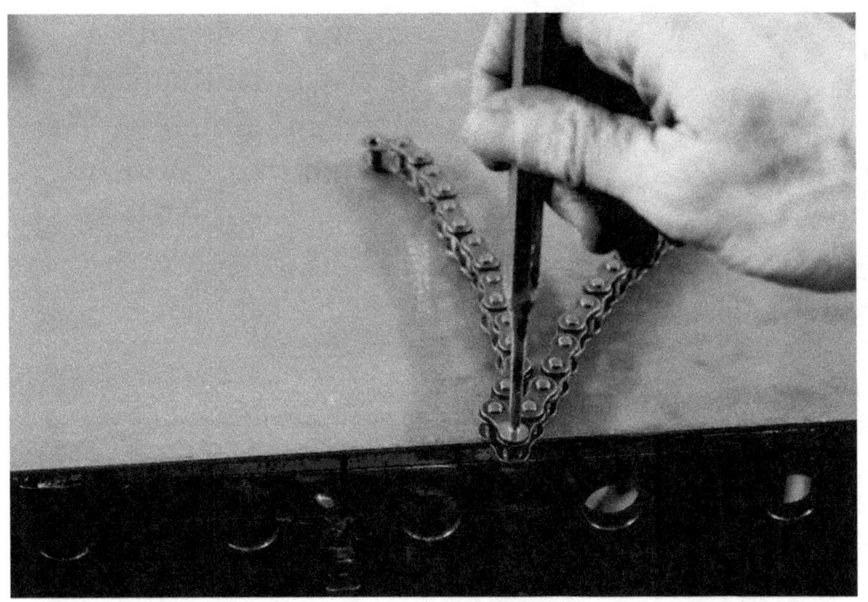

Hang the chain over the edge of the bench and use apunch and hammer to push the pin out.

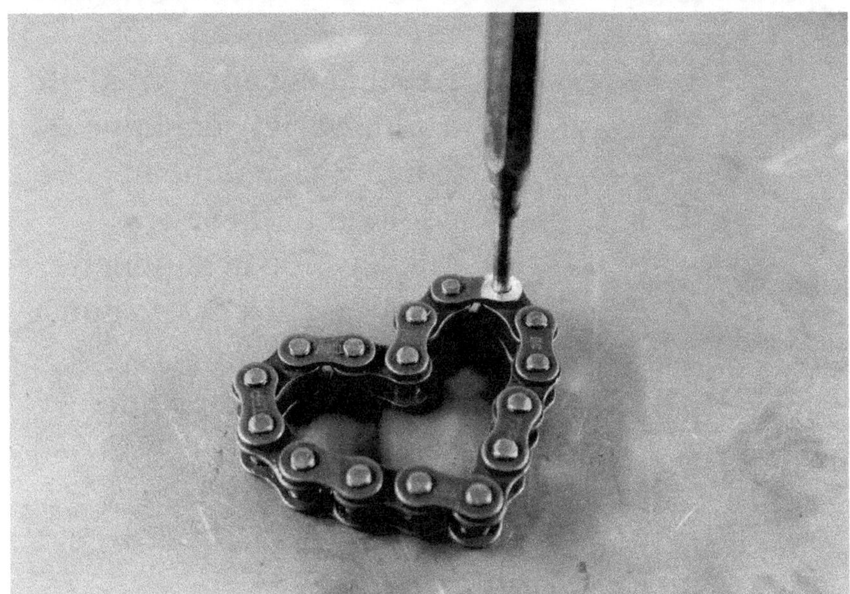

Lay out your design and use the punch to align the hole. Keep the punch in the hole while you're welding being very careful to not weld it in!

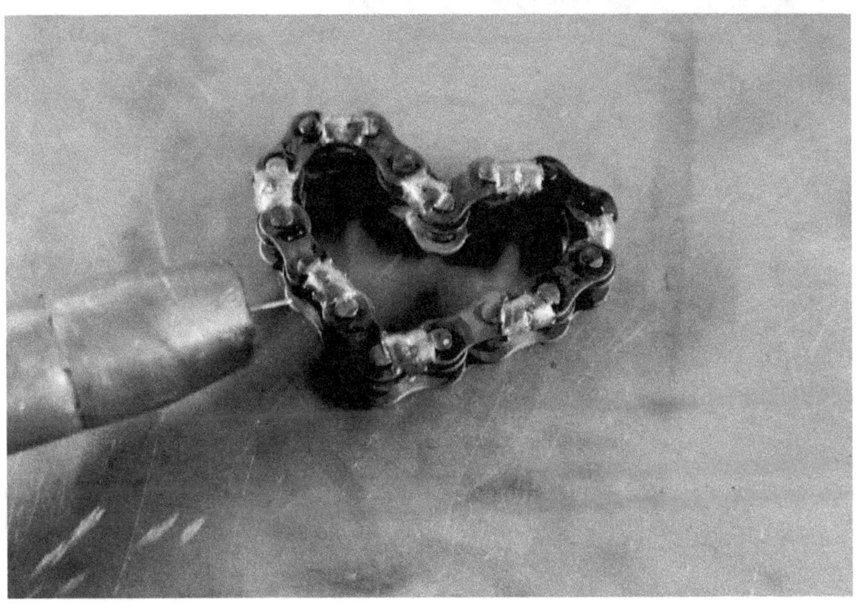

Weld each link to the next link.
Flip the keychain over and weld the other side.

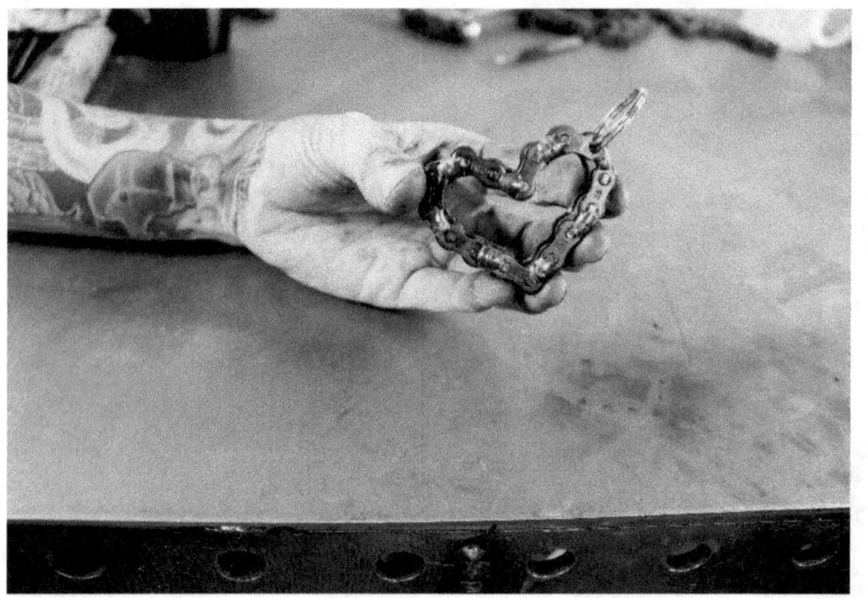

Clean the welds with a wire brush, chip any weld spatter, and finish with a clear coat to prevent rust.

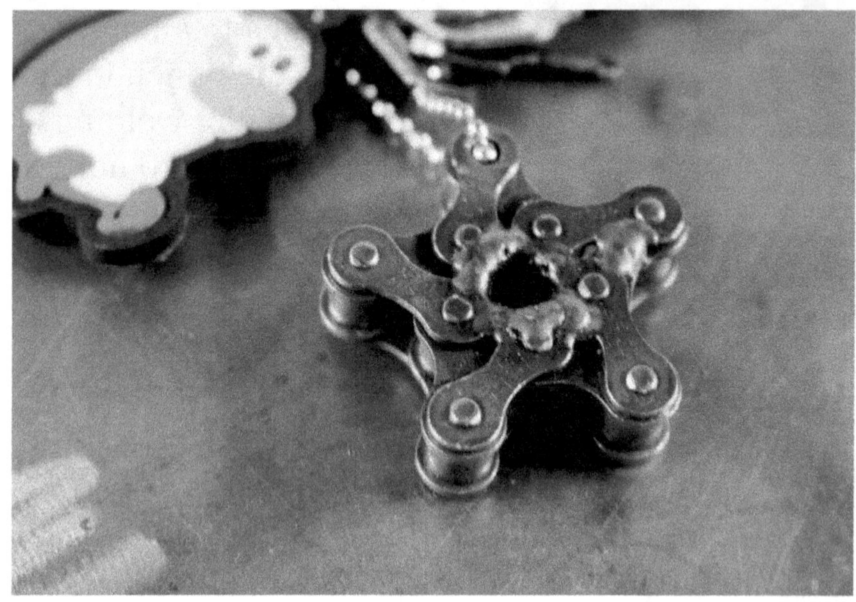

Keychains can be madein a wide variety of shapes. Some I have done in addition to these are Mickey Mouse silhouette, arrow, a stick figure,and a moon. Let your imagination run wildand design your own!

Star

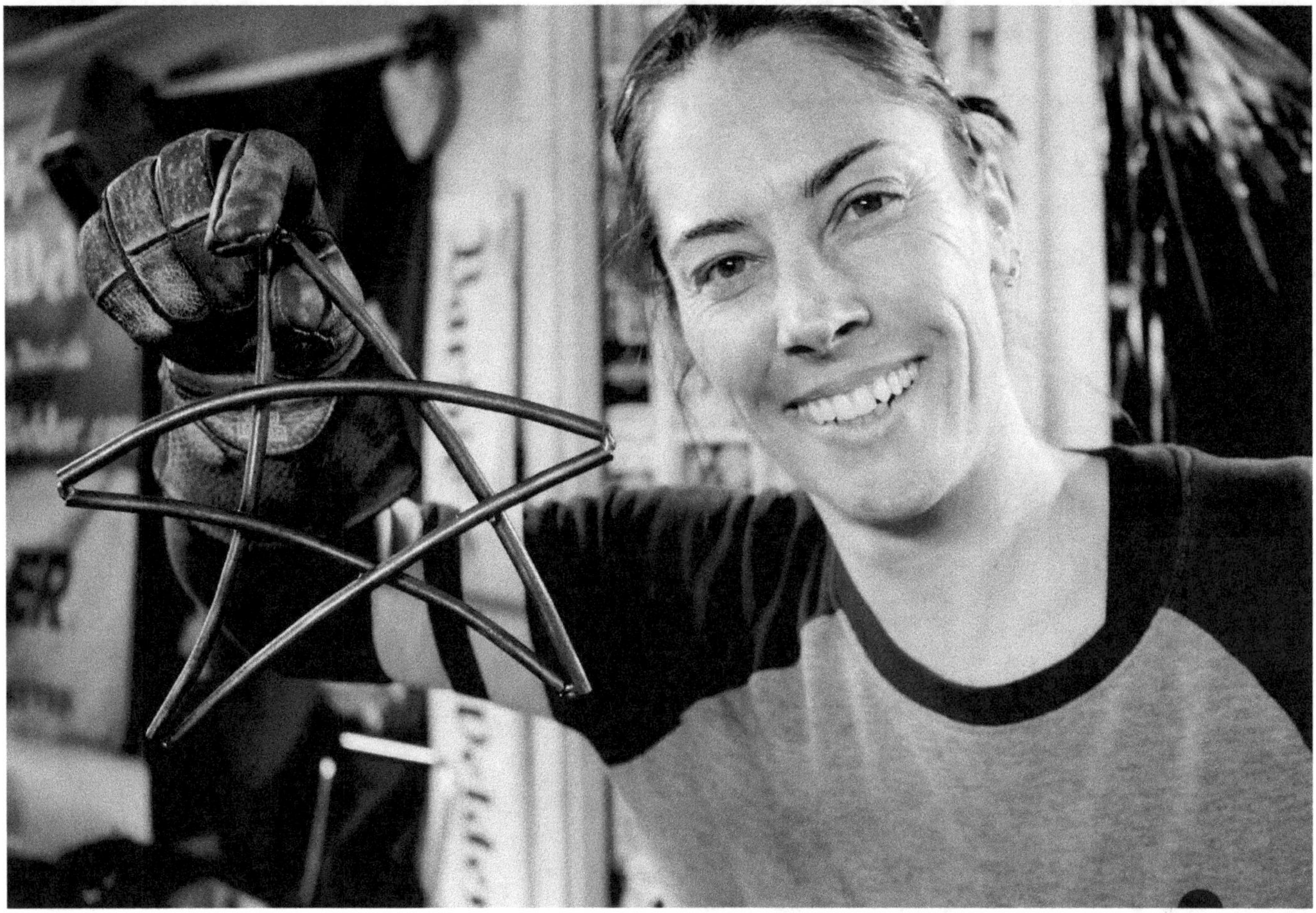

Difficulty

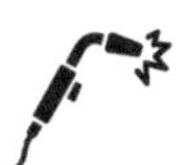

Materials

Round bar

Tools

Hammer
Wire brush
Grinder with cut off wheel and sanding disk

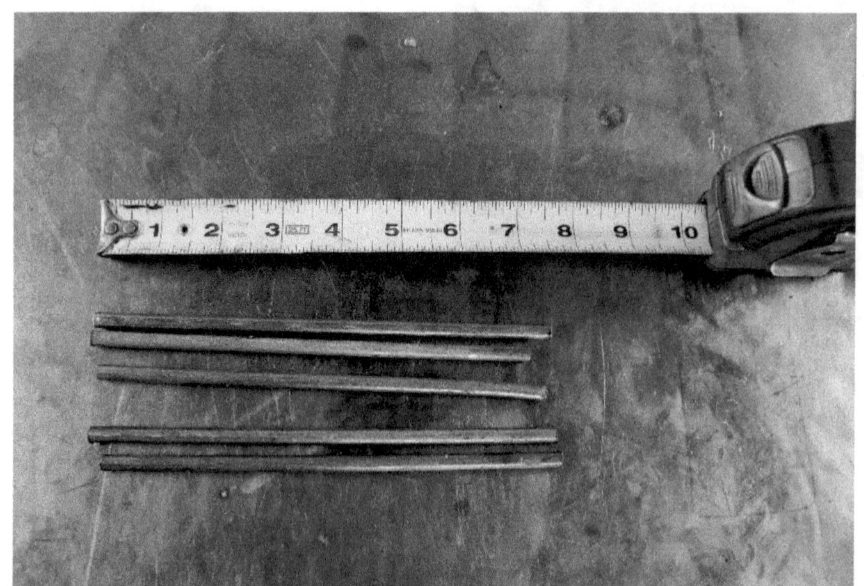

Mark and cut five pieces of round bar 8" long. (You can make a larger star by cutting your material longer or by using thicker round bar.

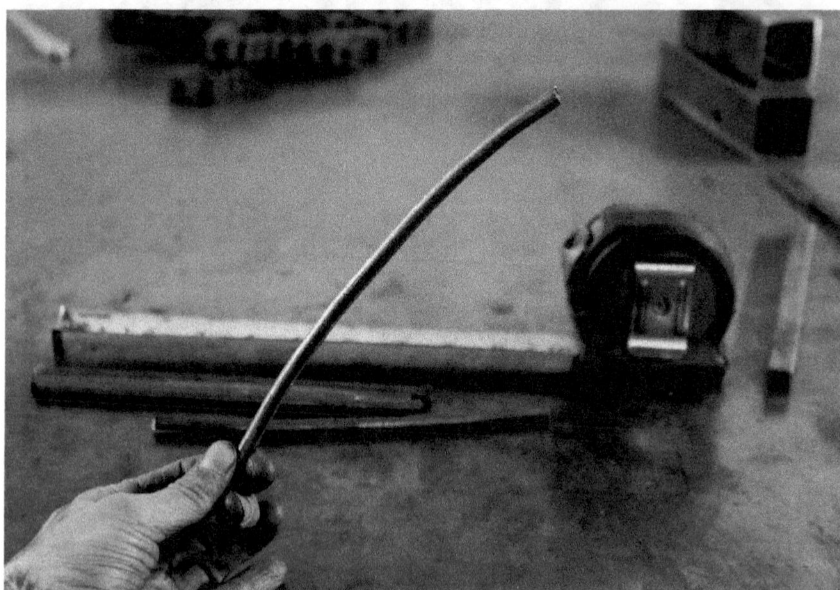

Curve each piece of round bar by clamping it and hammering it along the length.

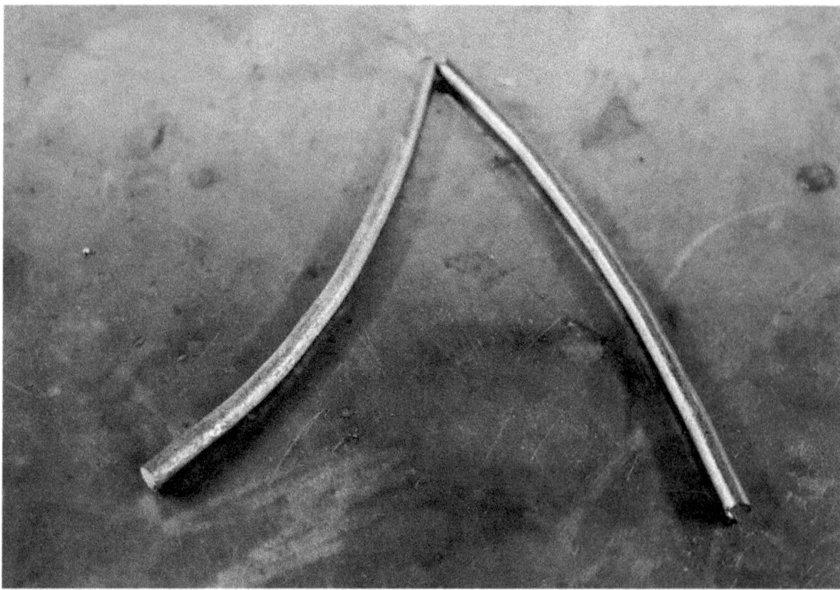

Lay out two pieces like this.

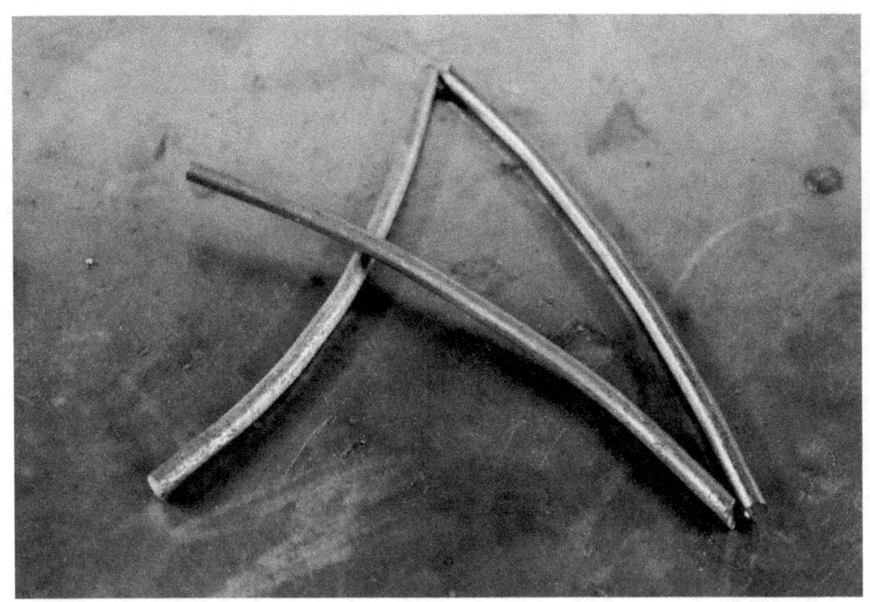

Place the third piece like this.

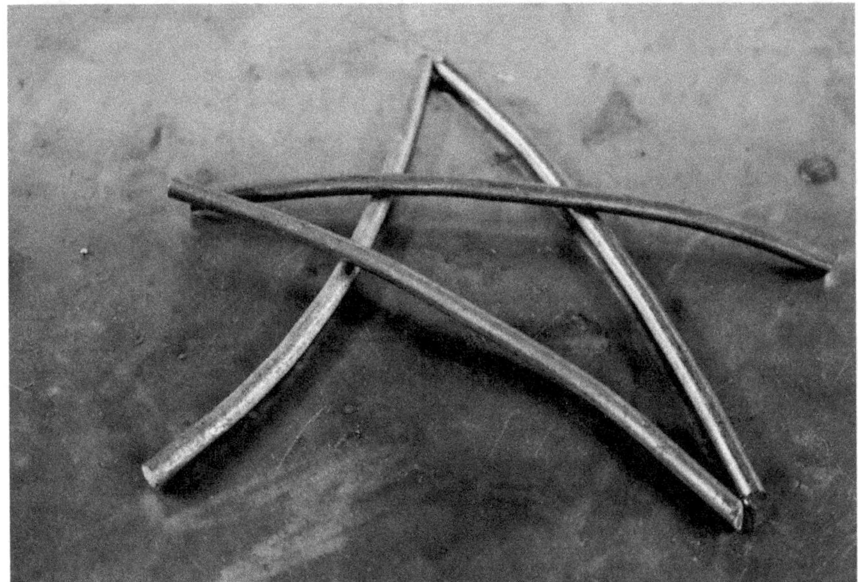

The fourth piece like this.

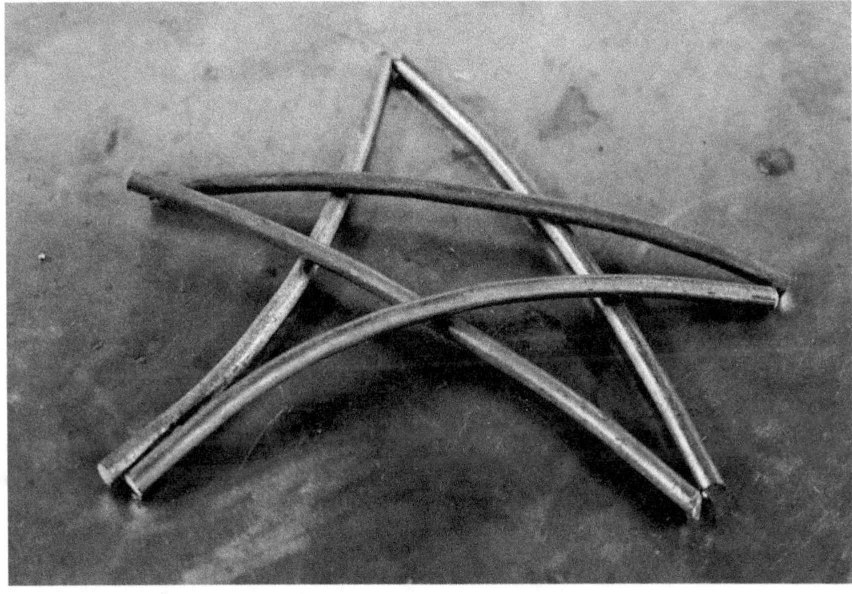

The final piece like this.

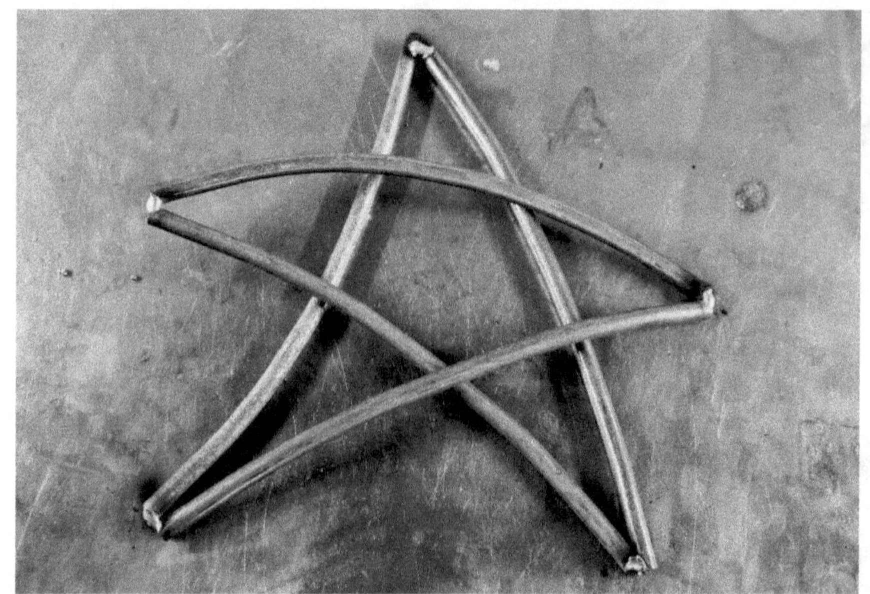

Adjust if necessary to get the shape you like.
Tack weld the round bar where the ends meet.

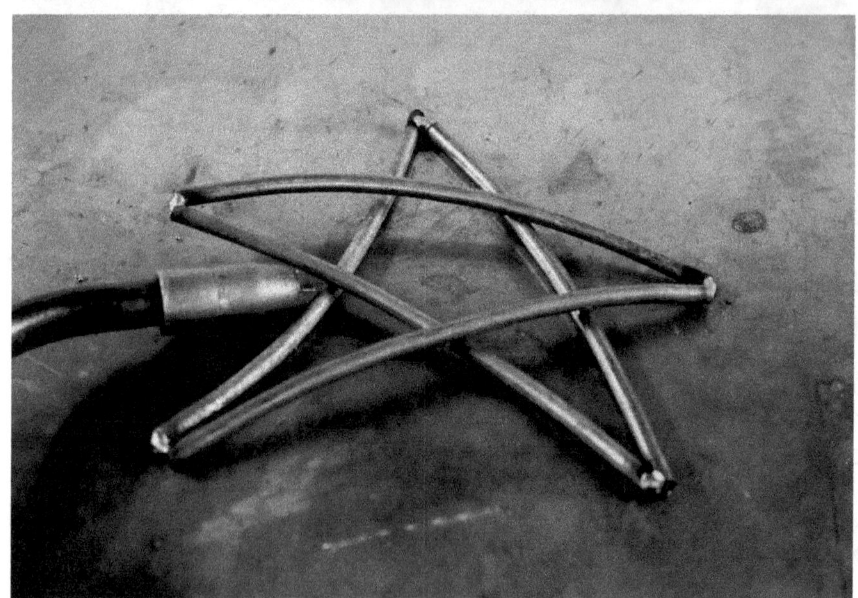

Weld the ends of the bars together where they touch.
Clean any weld discoloration with a wire brush and chip any weld spatter with a hammer and chisel.
Finish by painting or with a clear coat to prevent rusting.

Chain Heart or Star

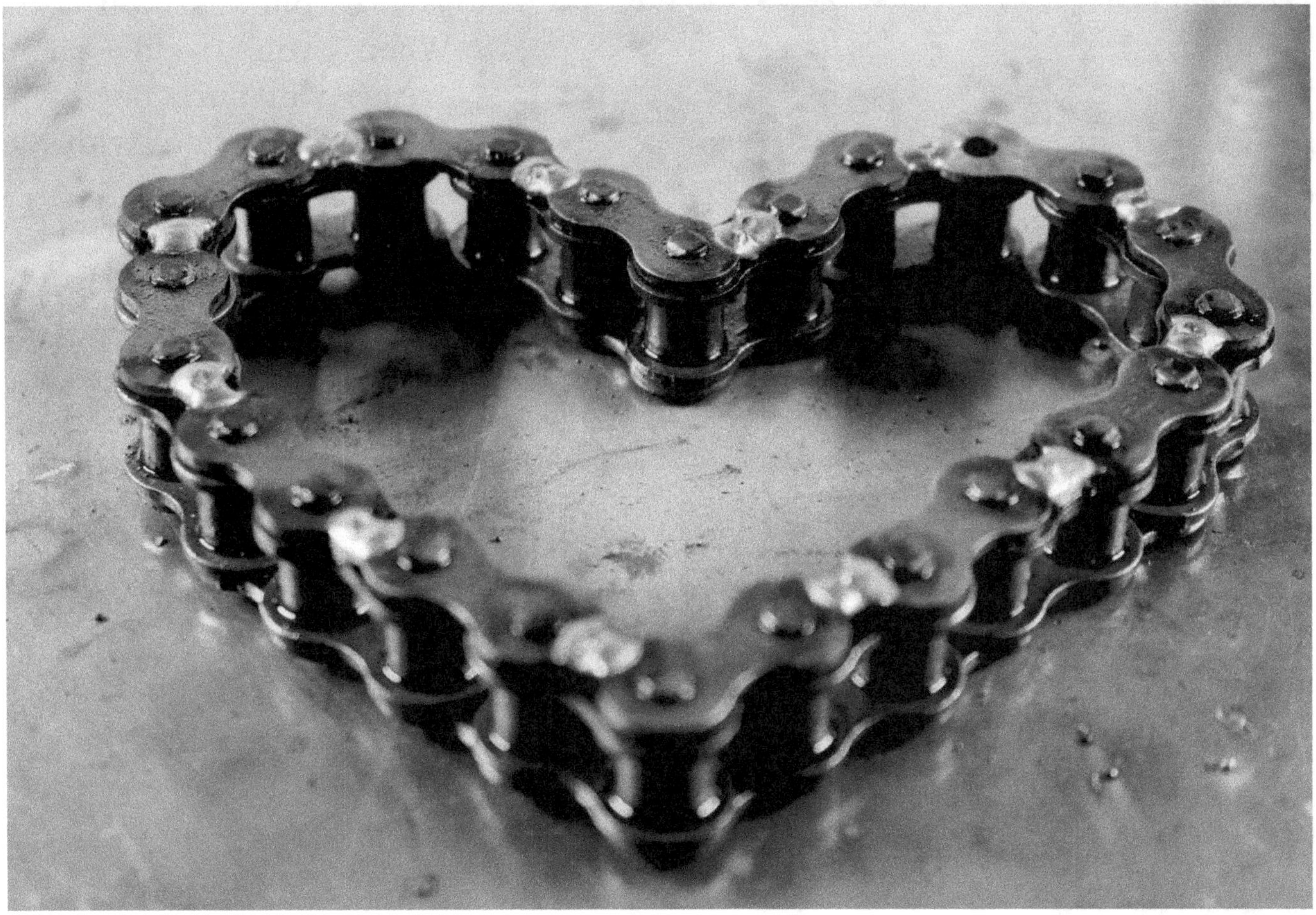

Difficulty

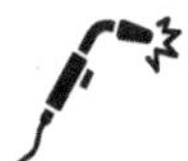

Materials

Large chain

Tools

Hammer
Chisel
Punch or chain breaker
Wire brush

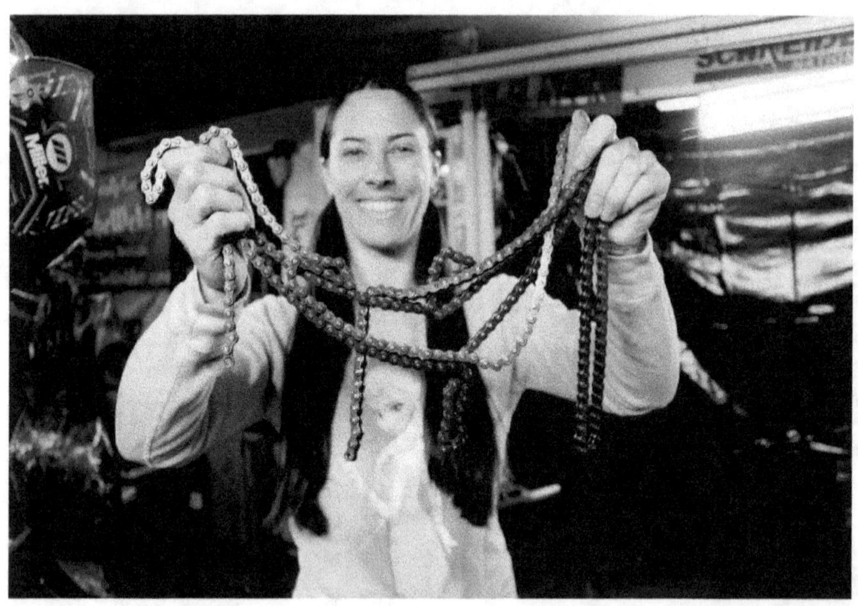

Clean the chain with a shop rag getting as much grease out as you can. When you weld chain grease will burn out of it, so be very careful with the fumes and tiny fire!

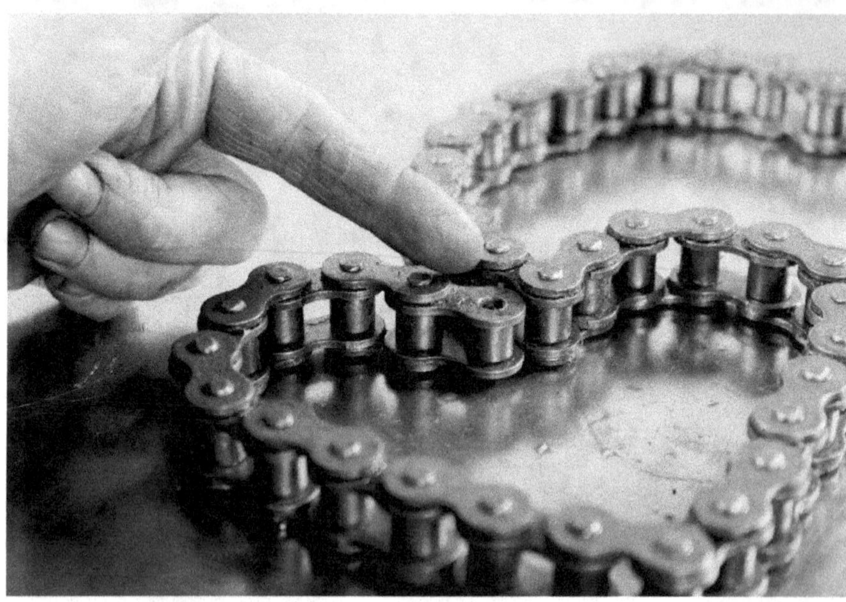

Shape the chain into a heart, or star or whatever shape you would like, and then choose the link that will be separated.

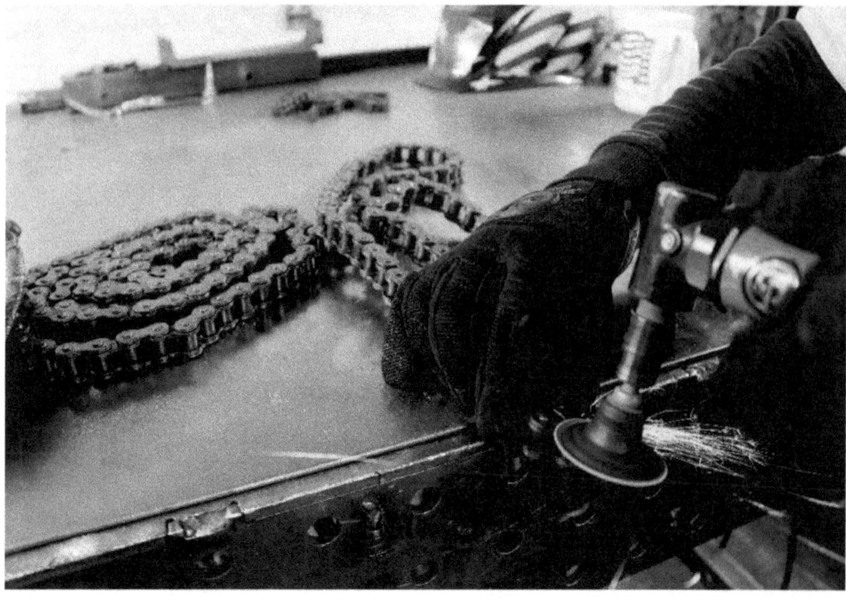

Use a chain breakto separate the chainifyou have one otherwisedo what I do, grind thetopof the pin down to thelink and then clamp thechain in a vise and hammerthe pin out.

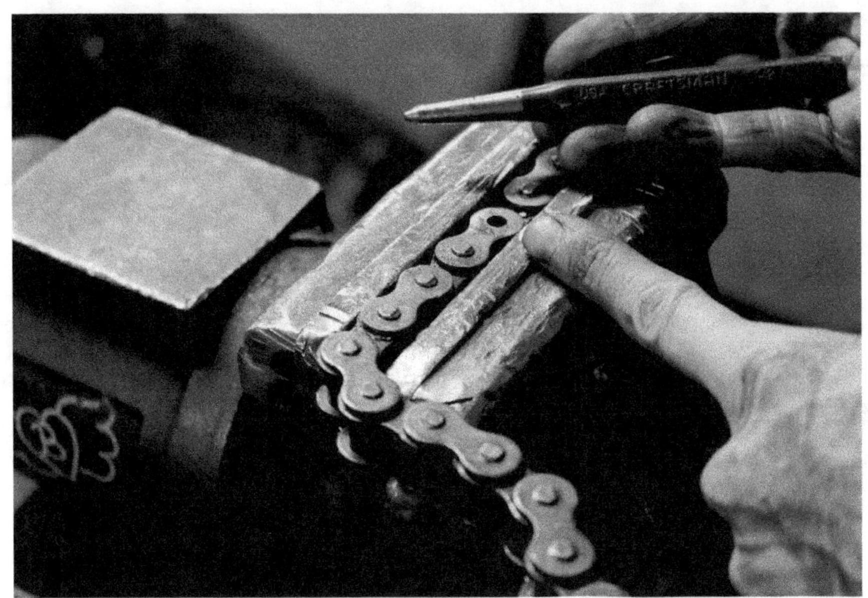

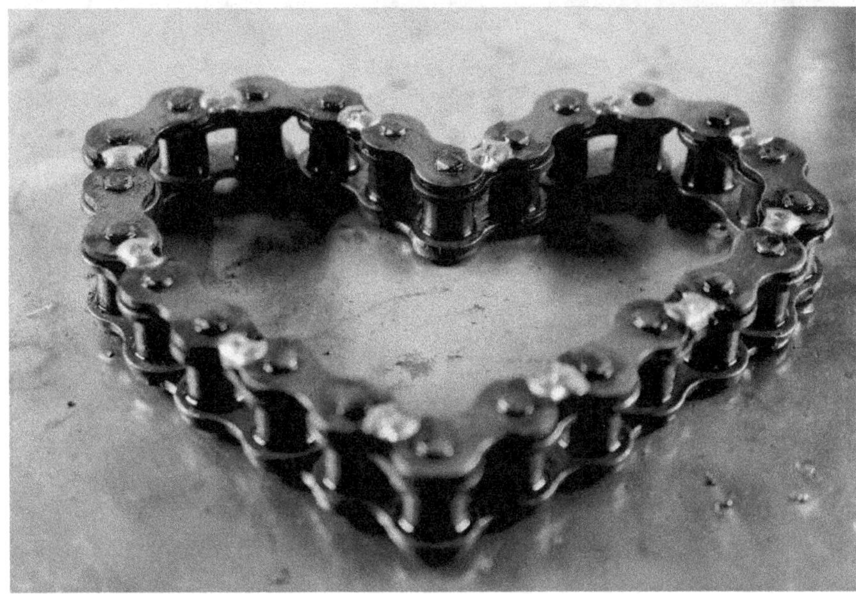

Shape the chainintothe shape you want,andtack weld each linktogether. For added strengthflipit over and weldtheother side.
Chip any spatterandclean any discoloration.
Clear coat to preventrust.

Business Card Holders

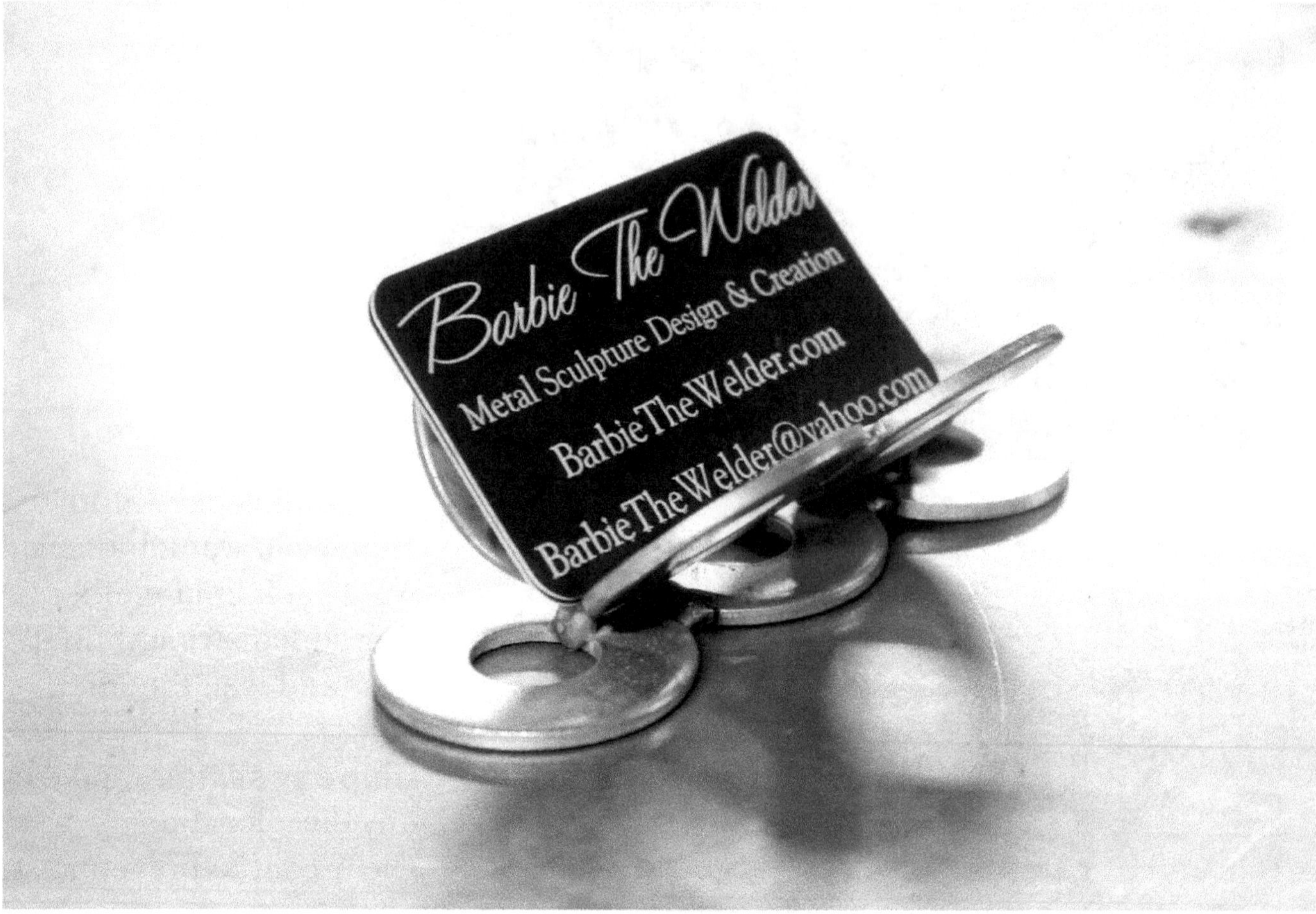

Difficulty

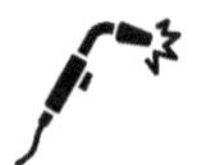

Materials

7large washers (Many different materials can be used for this project, simply use the same technique shown here with the materials of your choice.)

Tools

Wire brush

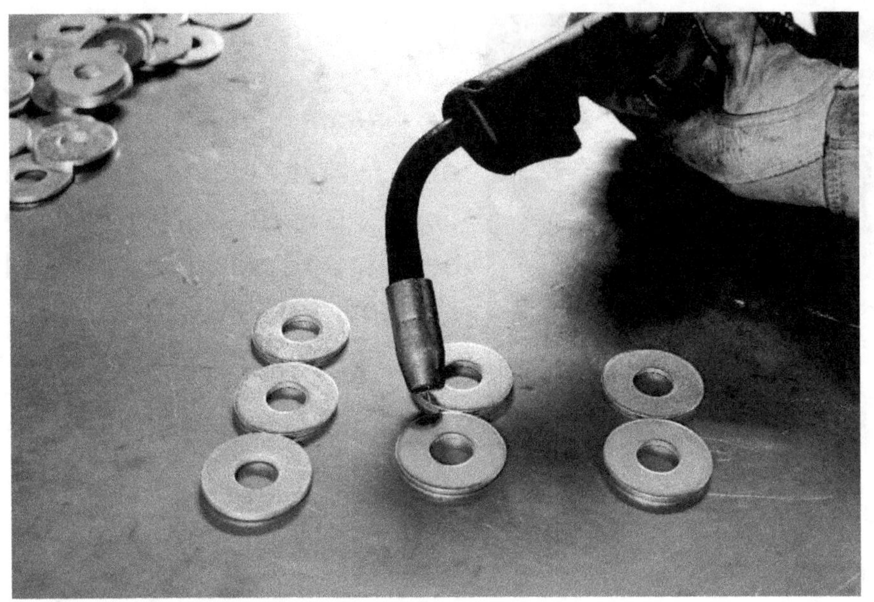

Lay the washers flat on your work bench as shown and weld them together using small tack welds.

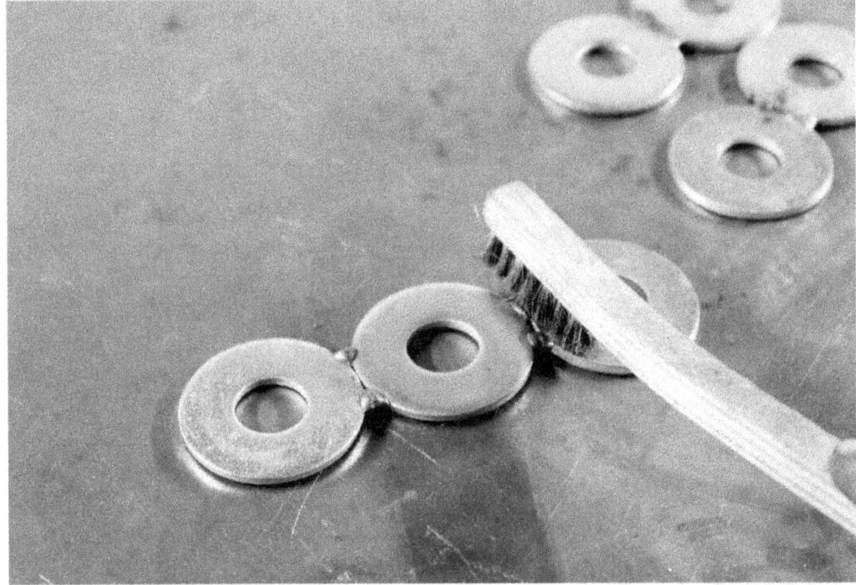

Clean the welds with a wire brush.

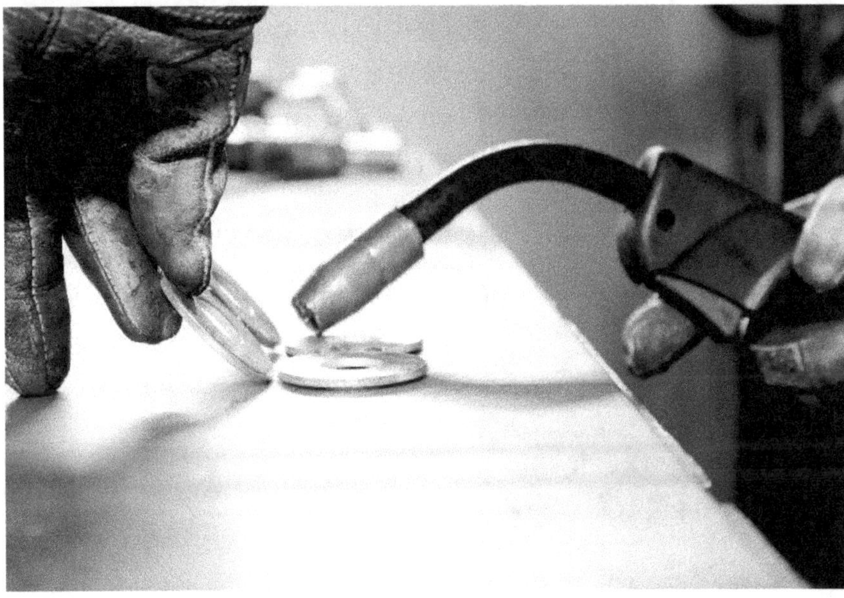

Hold the two sets of two washers up to each other at approximately a 45 degree angle and tack weld them together. Clean the welds and chip any weld spatter

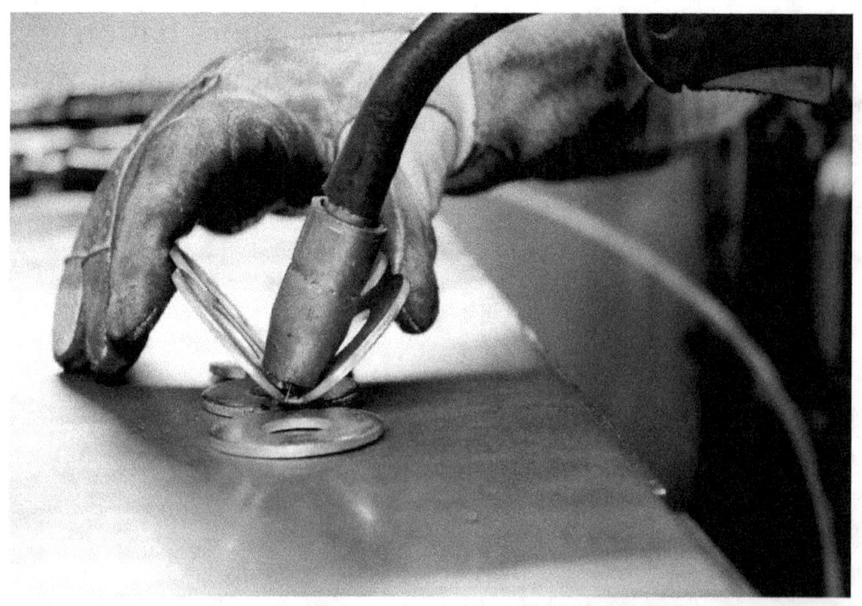

Hold that piece on the center of the set of three and weld it using two or three tack welds on both ends. Clean with a wire brush and chip any weld spatter. Finish with a clear coat to prevent rust.

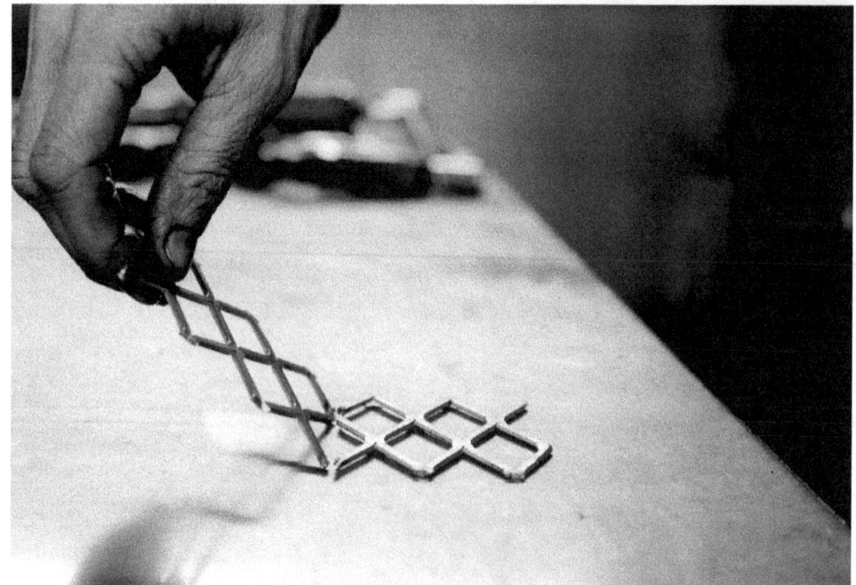

Here's the same project made with expanded metal.
Cut three pieces of material to the size of your business cards.
Smooth any burs or sharp edges with a sanding disk.
Hold two pieces together at a 45 degree angle and tack weld them together.

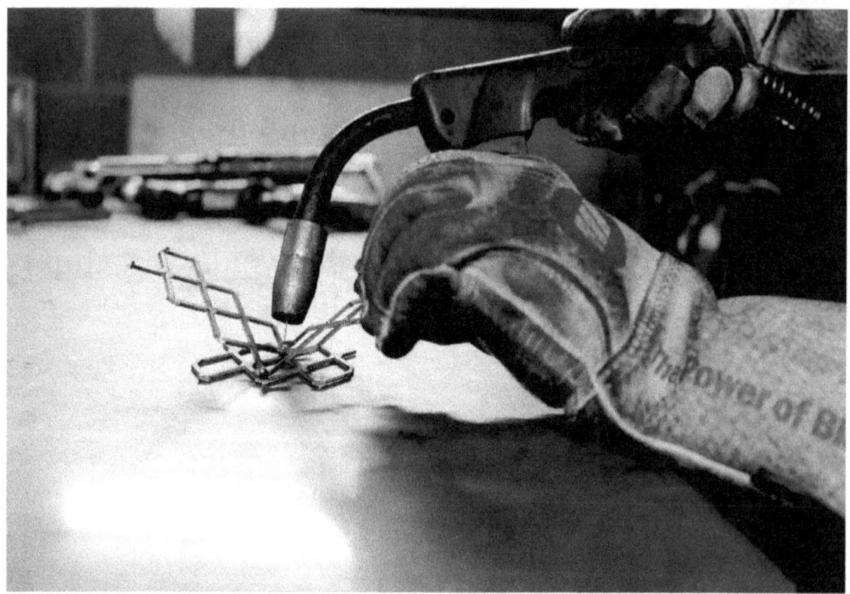

Hold those pieces on the center of the third and tack weld them on using small tack welds on each end.

Experiment with other materials using the same steps!

Scrap Heart

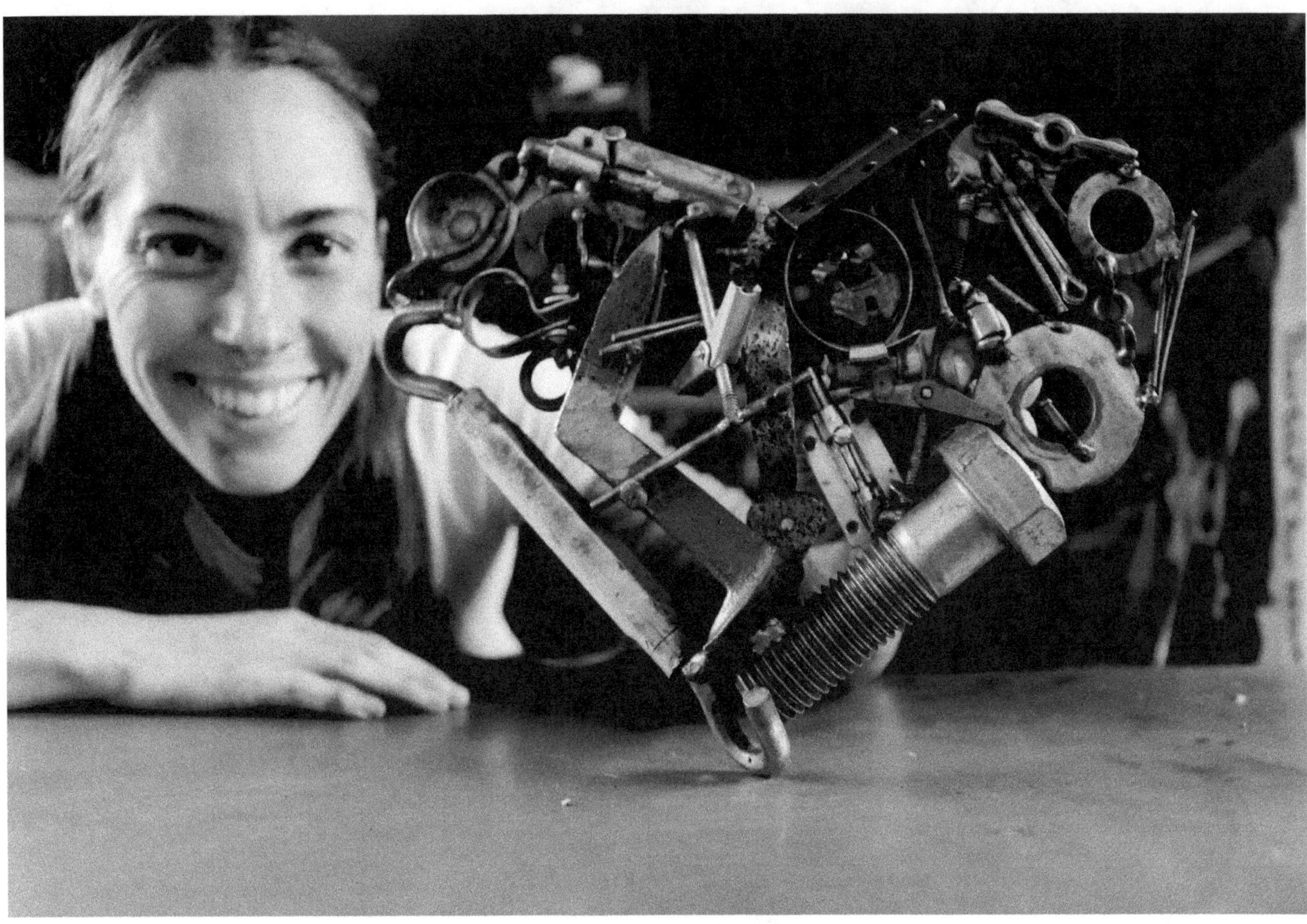

Difficulty

Materials
Randomshop scrapings like nuts, bolts, gears, locks, springs, and old tools

Tools:

Hammer
Chisel
Clear coat
Wire brush

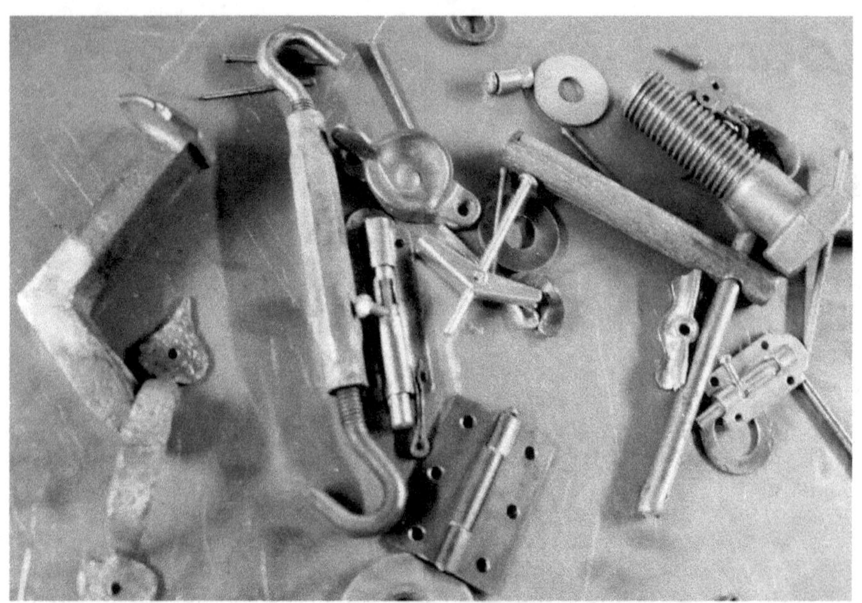

Choose random fun scrap metal.

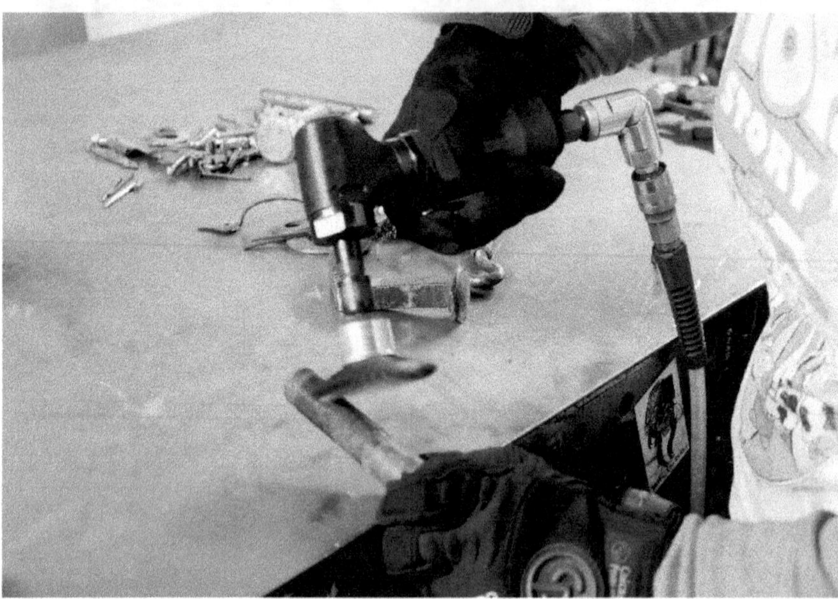

Use a wire brush or wheel to clean any rust from your materials.

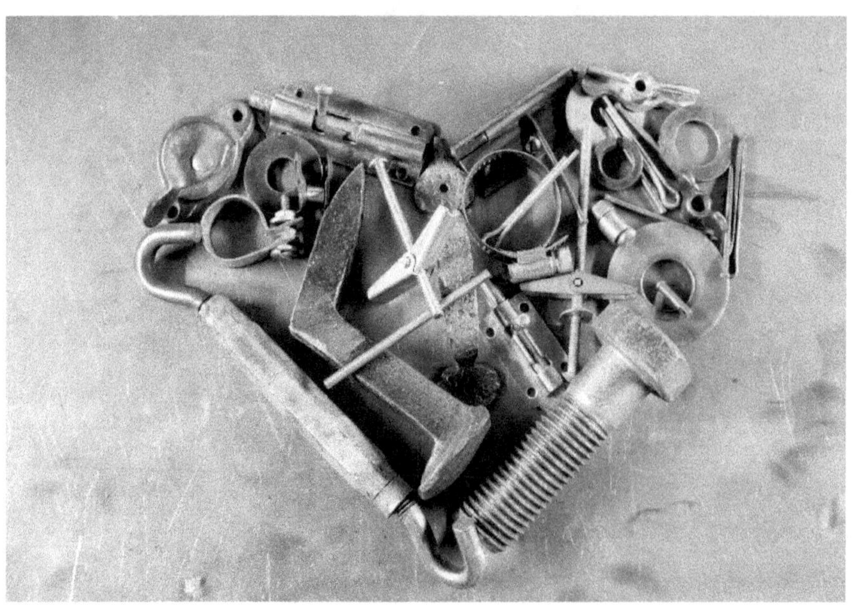

Lay your materials out in the shape you want. I chose a heart, but you can choose any shape. Make sure each piece is touching at least one other piece.

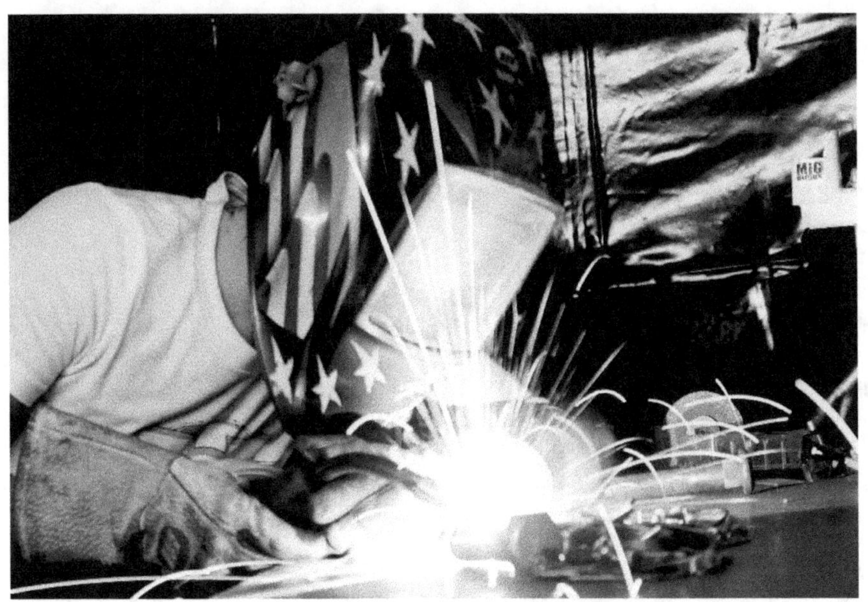

Weld your heart together by placing small tack welds where each piece meets another piece.

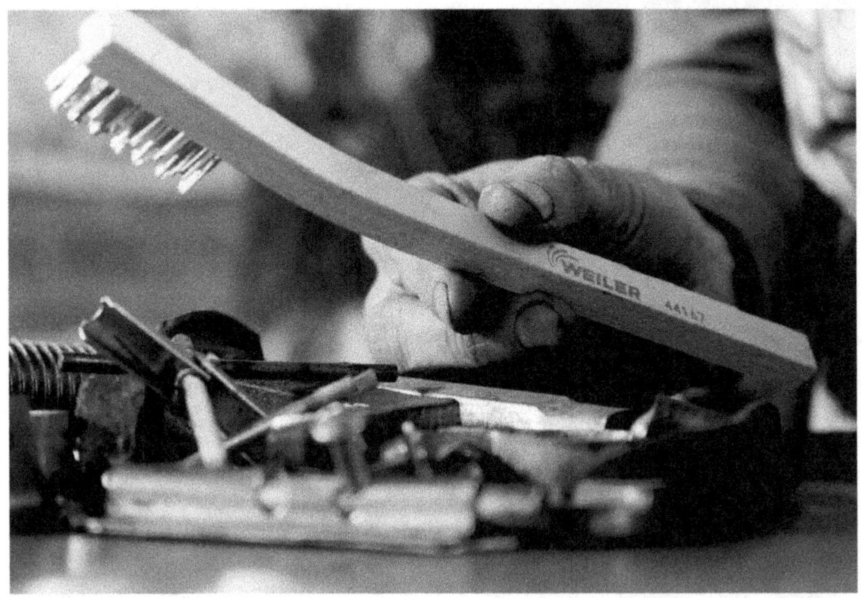

Clean each weld with a wire brush. Chip any weld spatter with a hammer and chisel.

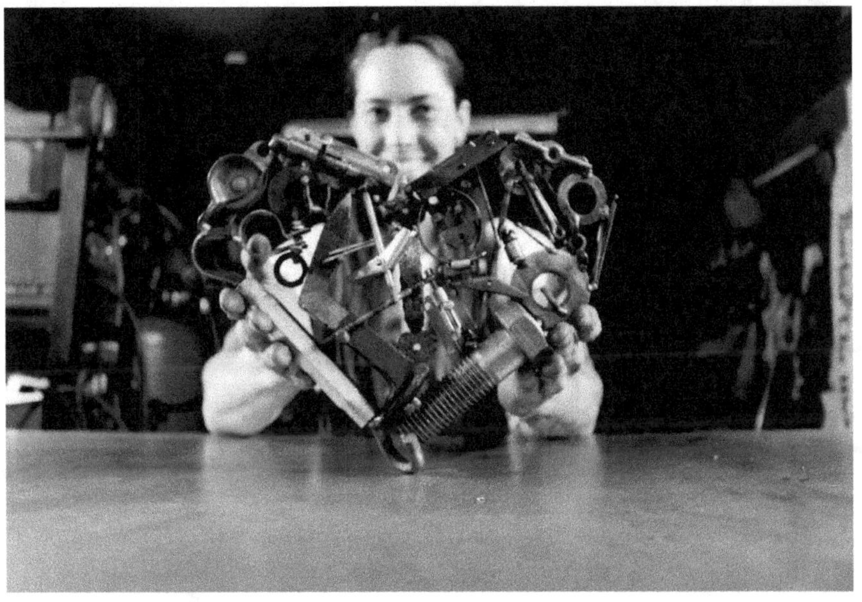

Finish with clear coat.

Snail

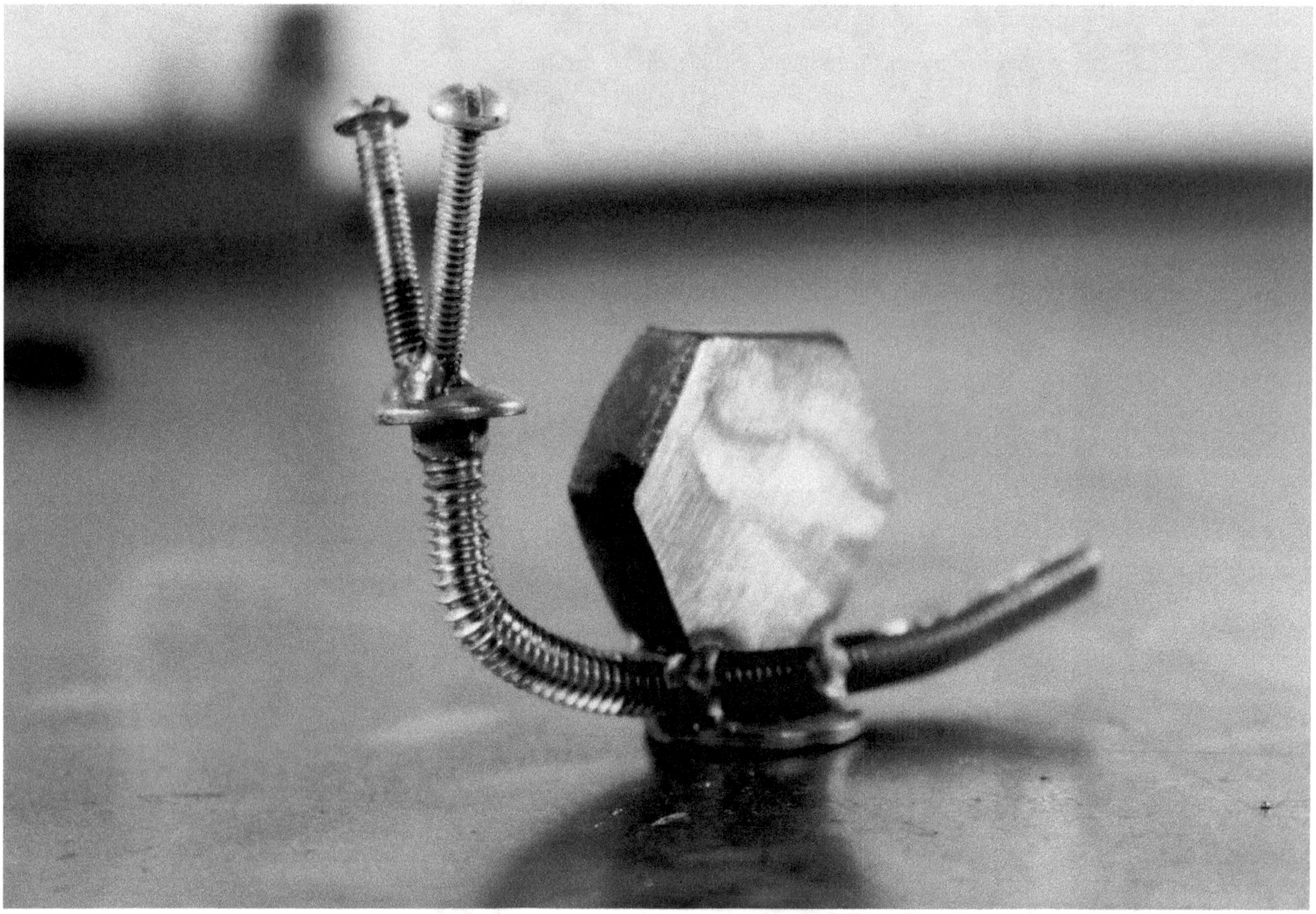

Difficulty

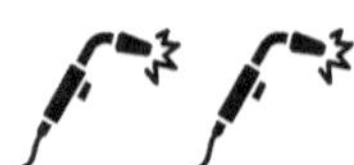

Materials

1large nut or bolt
1long thin bolt
2small thin bolts
1large washer

Tools

Hammer and chisel
Wire brush
Grinder with cutoff wheel and sanding disk

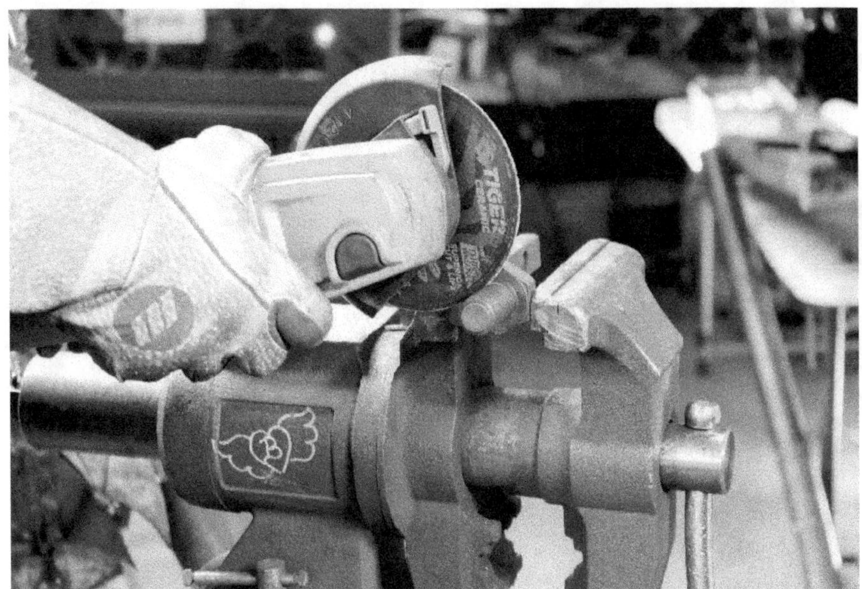

Clamp and cut the head off the large bolt. If you are using a large nut for the body skip this step!

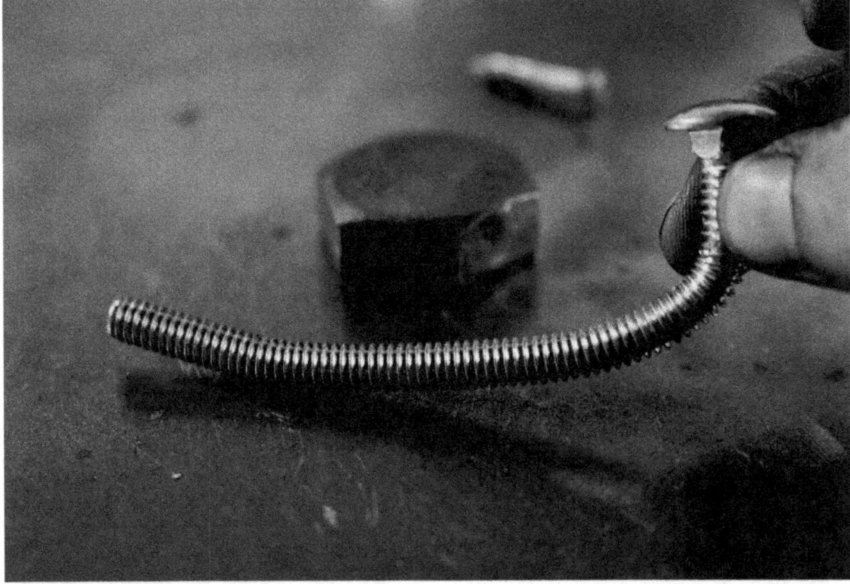

Clamp and curve the long thin bolt like this.

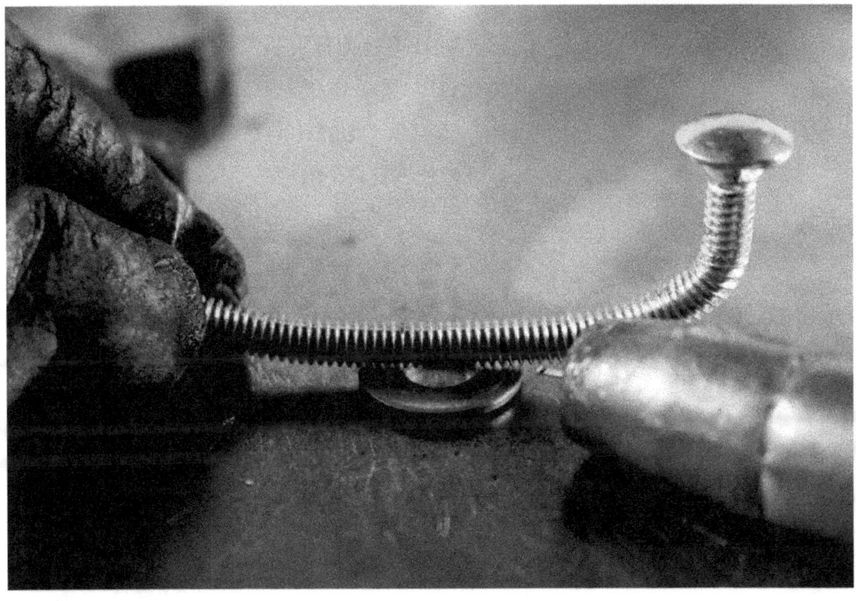

Hold the snail body on the washer base and carefully tack weld them together.

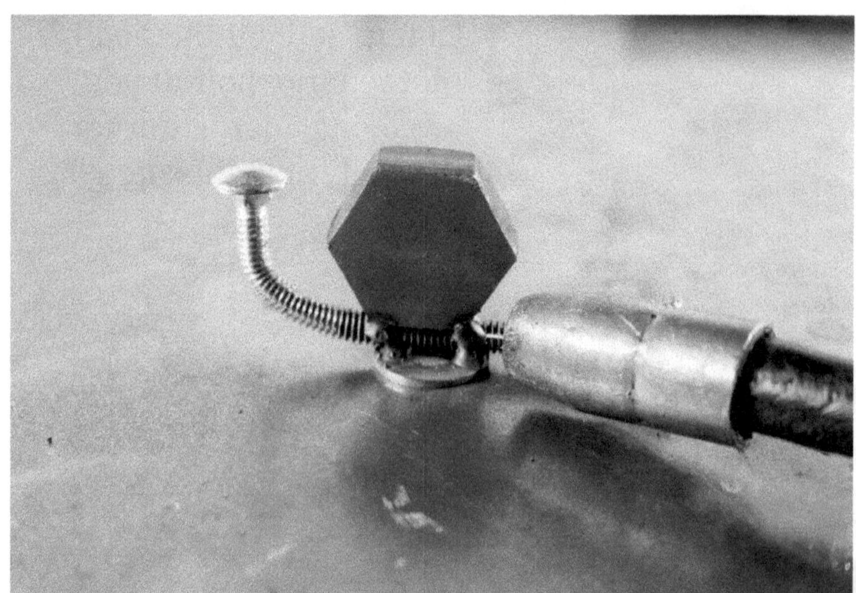

Weld the body on the back of the snail.

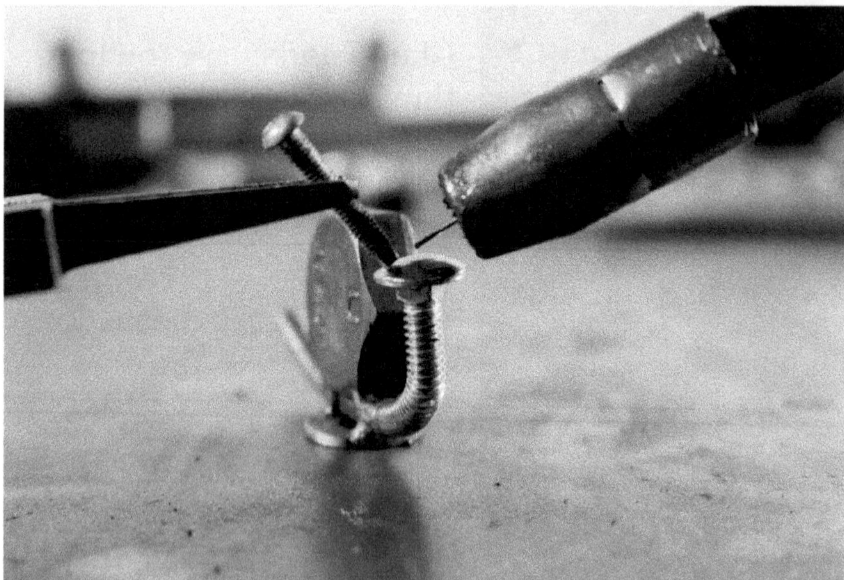

Hold and tack weld the small thin bolts to the head.

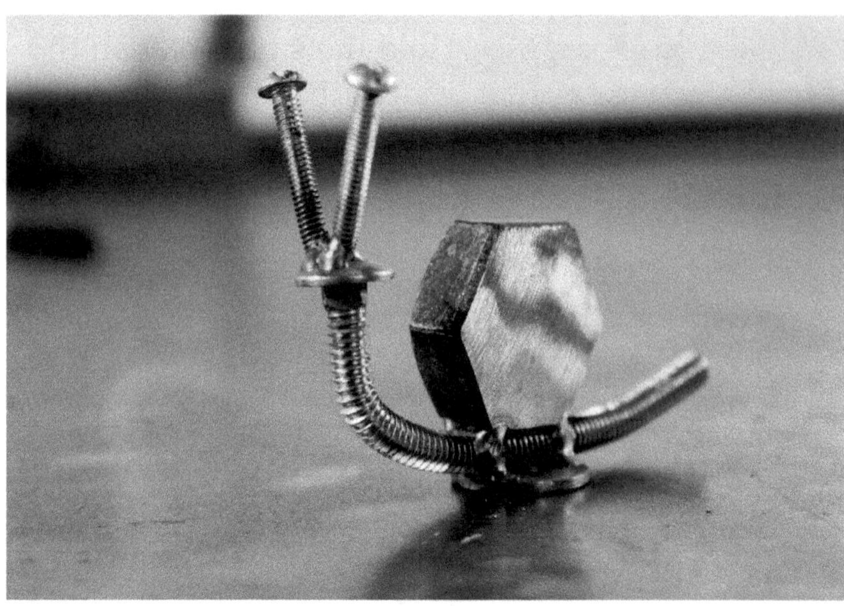

Clean any weld spatteror discoloration and finish with paint or clear coatto prevent rust. What a cutie!

Scrap Words

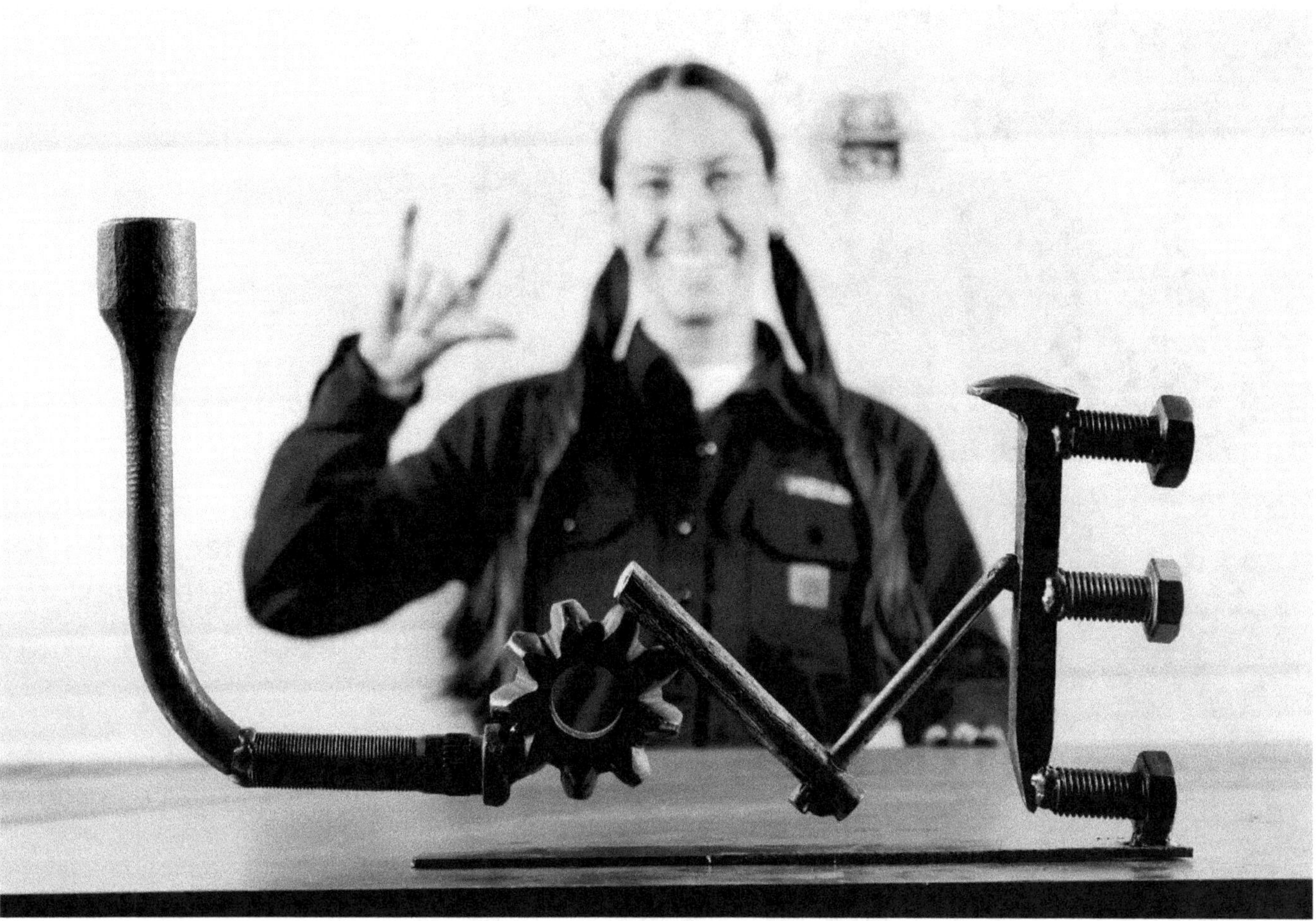

Difficulty

Materials
Random scrap. Once you decide what word you want to make look for shapes, for instance for the E I needed one long piece and three shorter pieces. Material for base unless you plan on wall hanging your sculpture.

Tools

Hammer and chisel
Wire brush
Grinder with cutoff wheel and sanding disk.

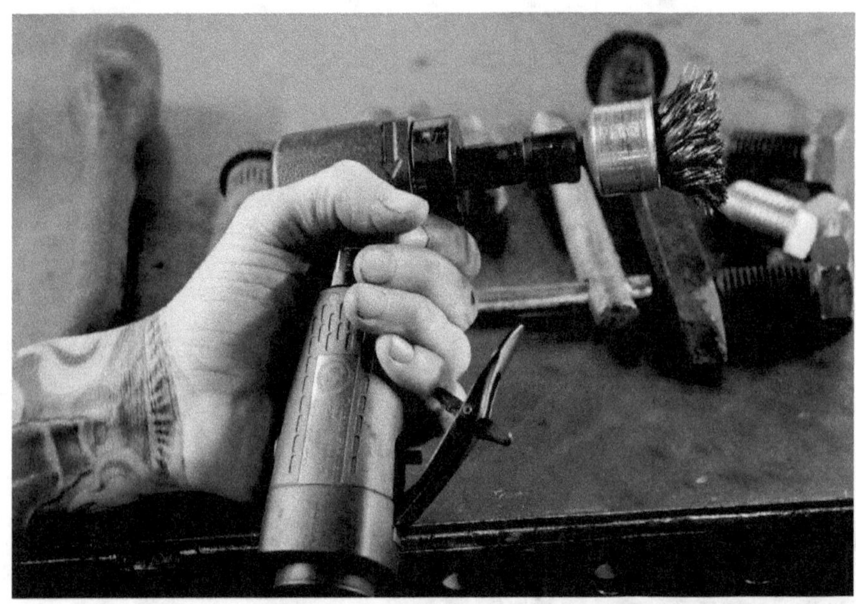

Remove rust from the scrap pieces with a wire brush or wheel.

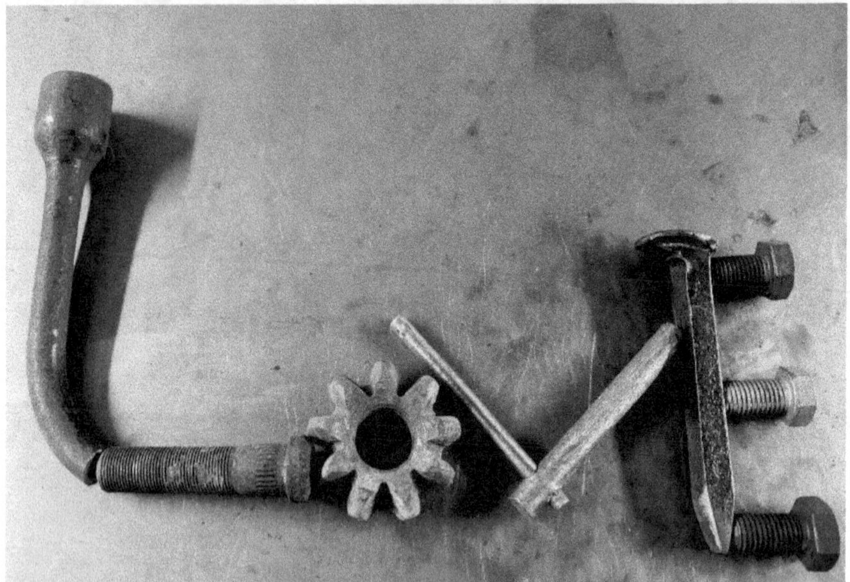

Lay out the word making sure each letter will be able to touch the letter next to it and look good.

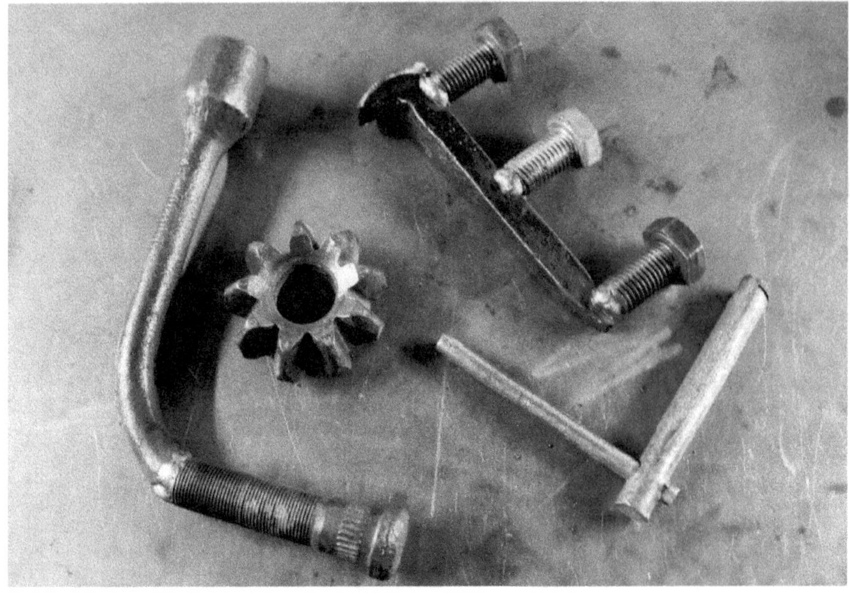

Weld the letters individually.

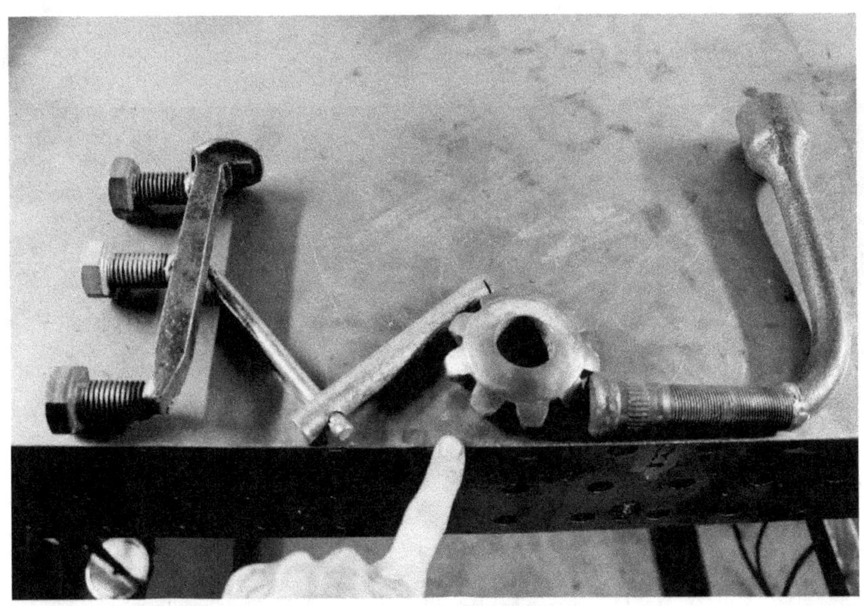

Using the edge of your workbench as a guide flip the letters over and line them up.

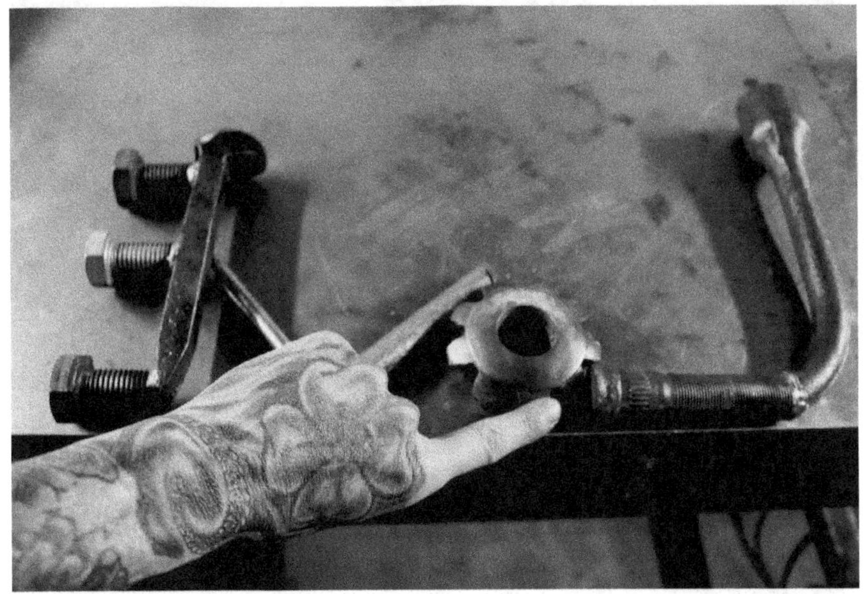

Weld each letter to the letter next to it.
Iweld mine from the back togive it a clean look.

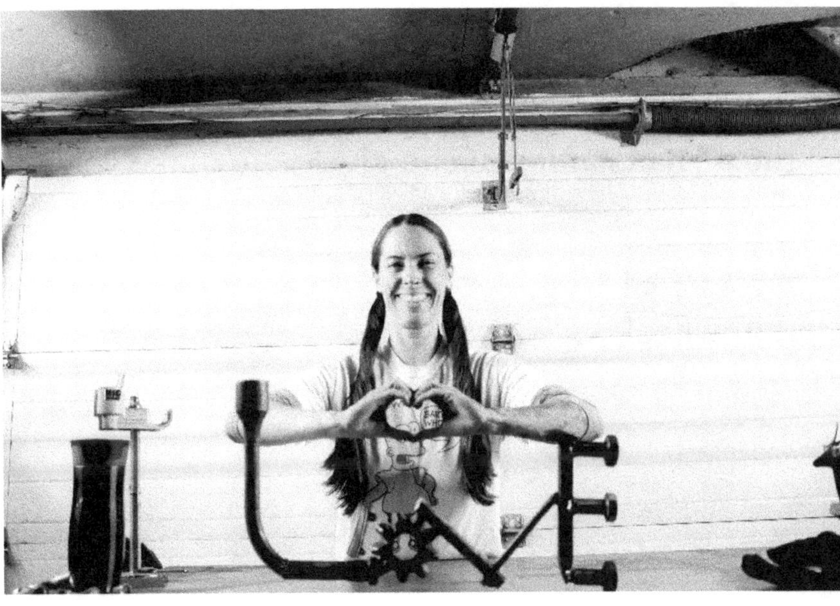

Weld the letters to the base, or if you choose to make it a wall hanging weld a couple washers to the back to use as hangers. I really liked how this looked only welded to the base by the E to make it float. Make this project your own!
Use clear coat finish to prevent rust.

Feather

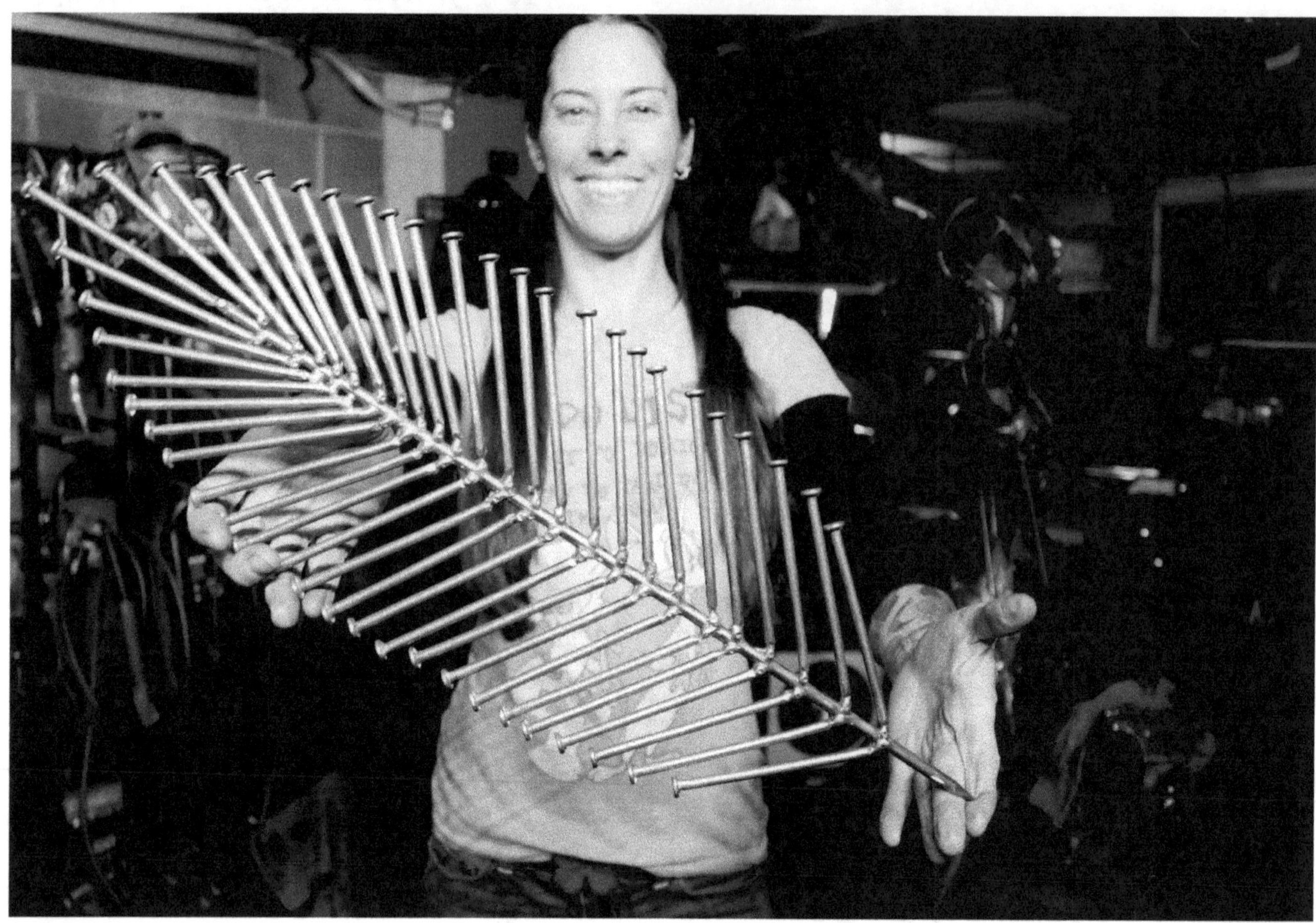

DifficultyLevel

Materials

18” of round bar (I choose 1/4’ round bar but you can choose whatever size you likedepending on the size of feather you will make.)
51 4” longnails (Again I choose the 4” nails and you can choose to make yours howeveryou like.)

Tools

Grinder with sandingdisk and cutoff wheel
Wire wheel or brush

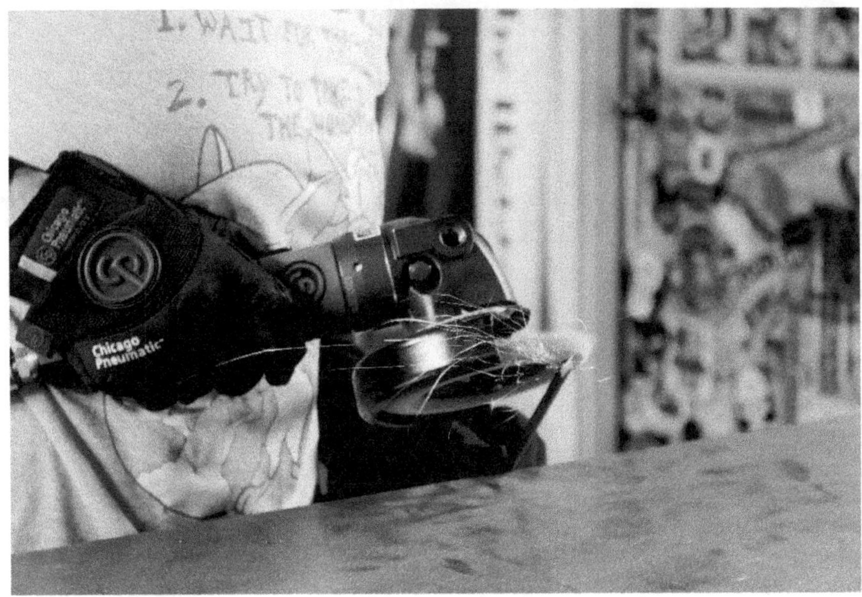

Grind a point into one end of your round bar like a pencil point.

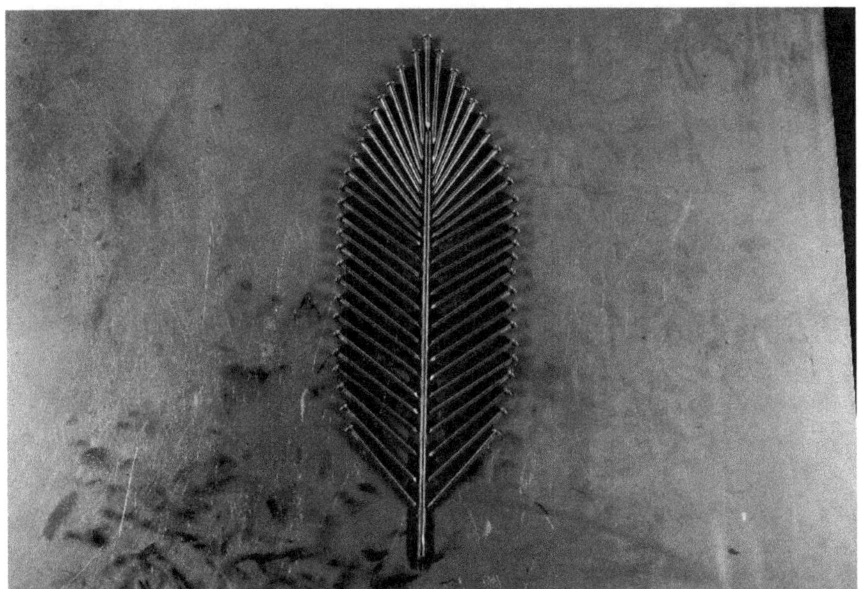

Lay the nails out in a position you like. Play around with the design until you love it. You can make your feather fatter or narrower. You can also choose to give your feather a curve if you first bend your round bar slightly

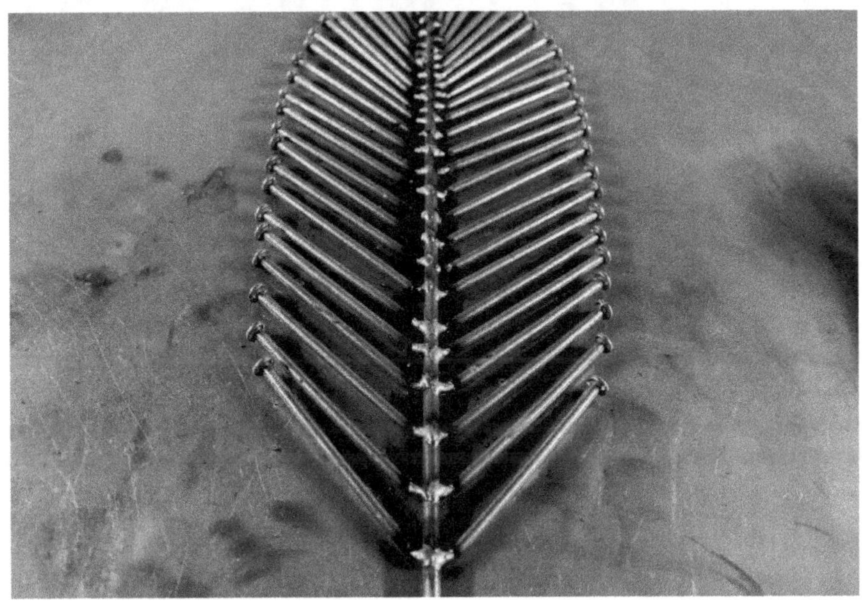

Tack weld each nail to the round bar. Flip your feather over and tack weld the back of each nail.

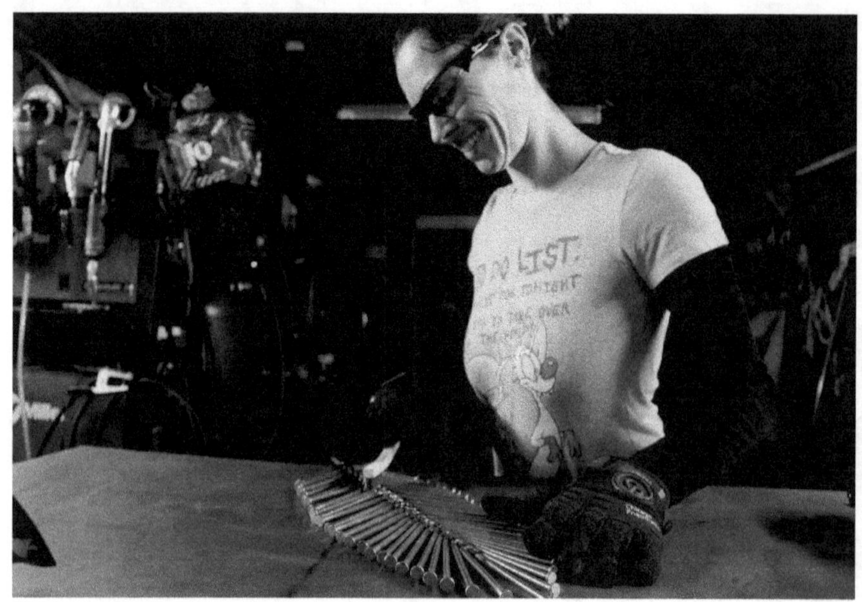

Clean the weld discoloration withawire brush and removeany weld spatter witha hammer and chisel. Clear coat the featherto protect it from rusting.

Bicycle

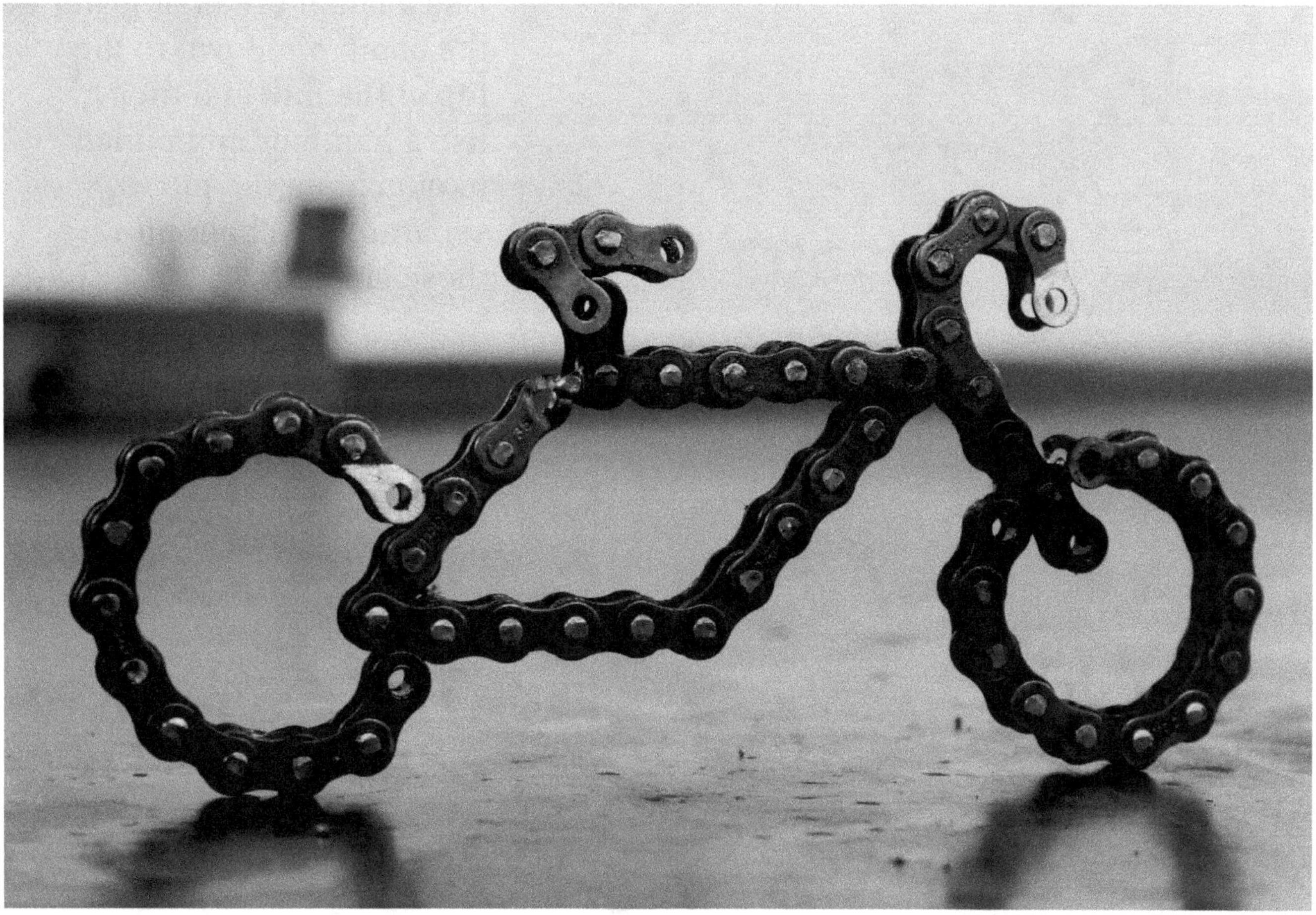

Difficulty

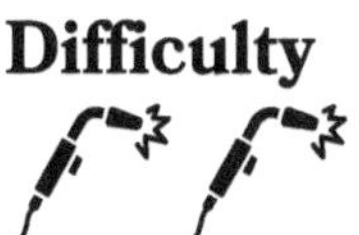

Materials

Chain

Tools

Hammer
Chisel
Punch or chain break
Wire brush

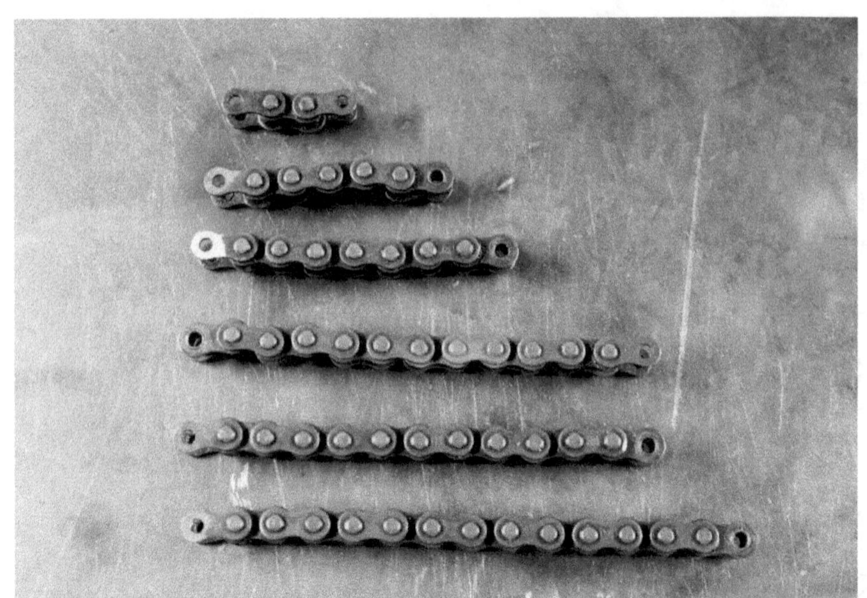

Clean the grease from the chain with a shop rag. Use a chain break or grind the chain pin down to the top of the link and then use a hammer and punch to punch out the pin to separate the chain into these sizes.

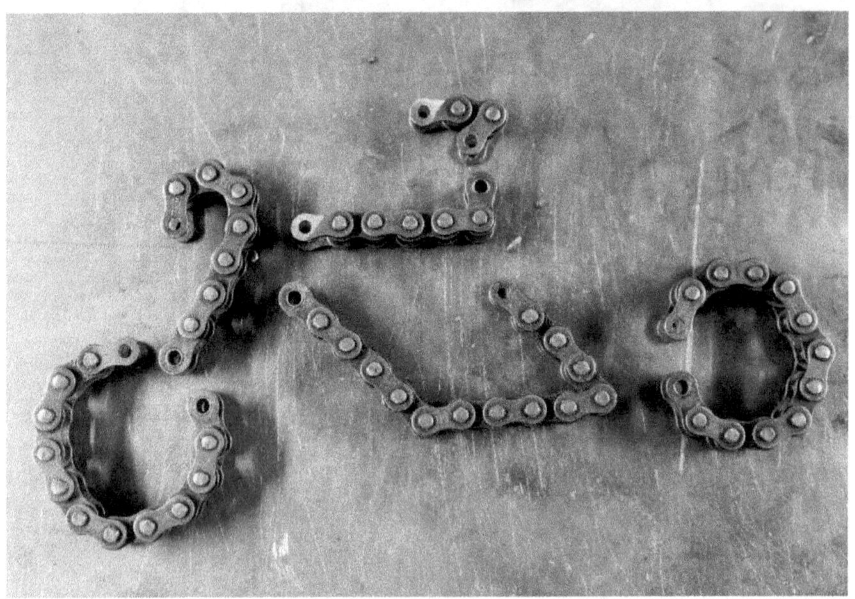

Shape the chain pieces into these shapes.

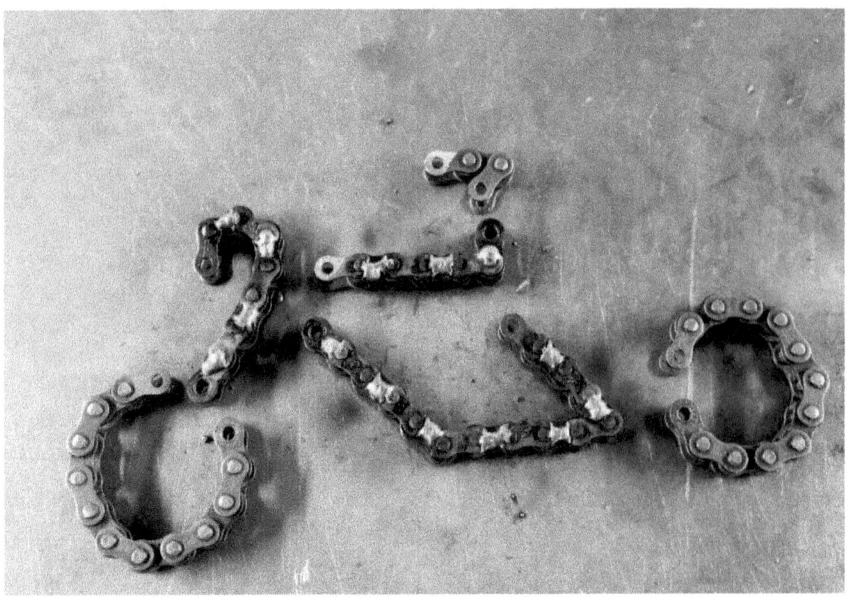

Tack weld each linktothe link next to it in the individual pieces. Donot weld the tires at thistime!

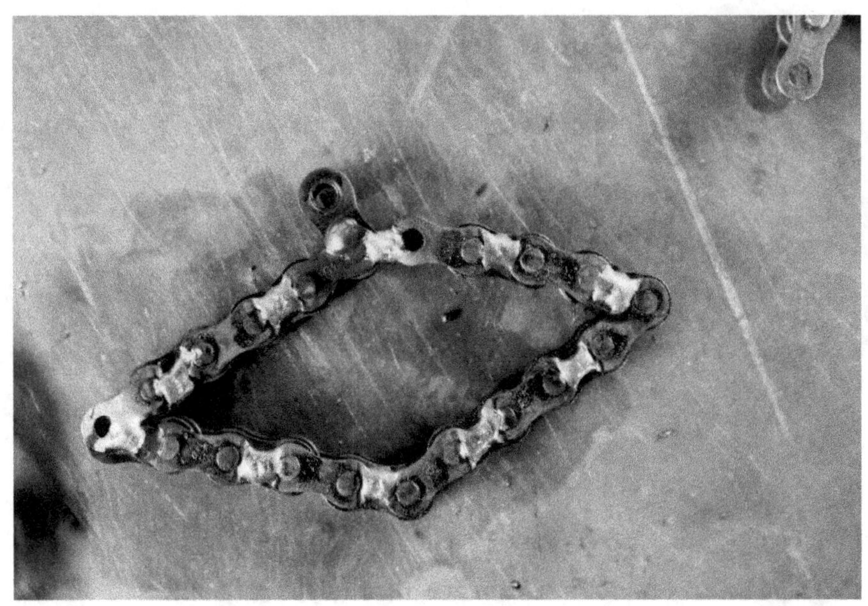

Tack weld these two pieces together to create the bike frame.

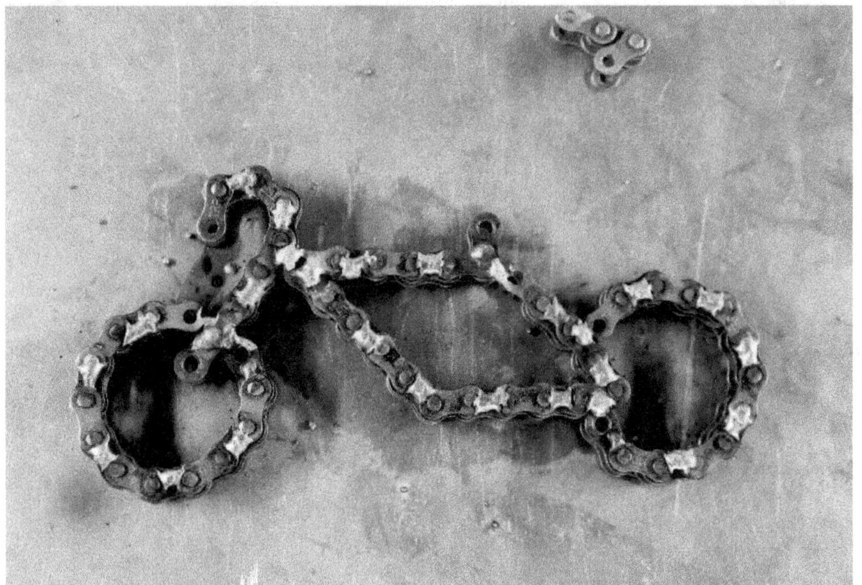

Weld the frame to the handlebars.
Weld the tires around the bottom on the handlebars and the back of the frame.
Weld the seat on.

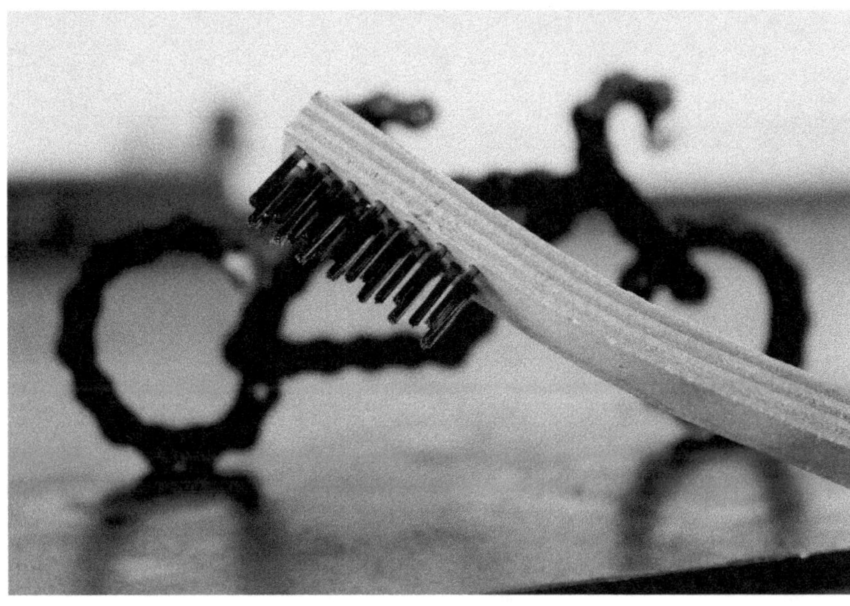

Clean the welds with a wire brush and chip any spatter with a hammerand chisel.
Finish with clear coatto prevent rust or paint.

Flowers

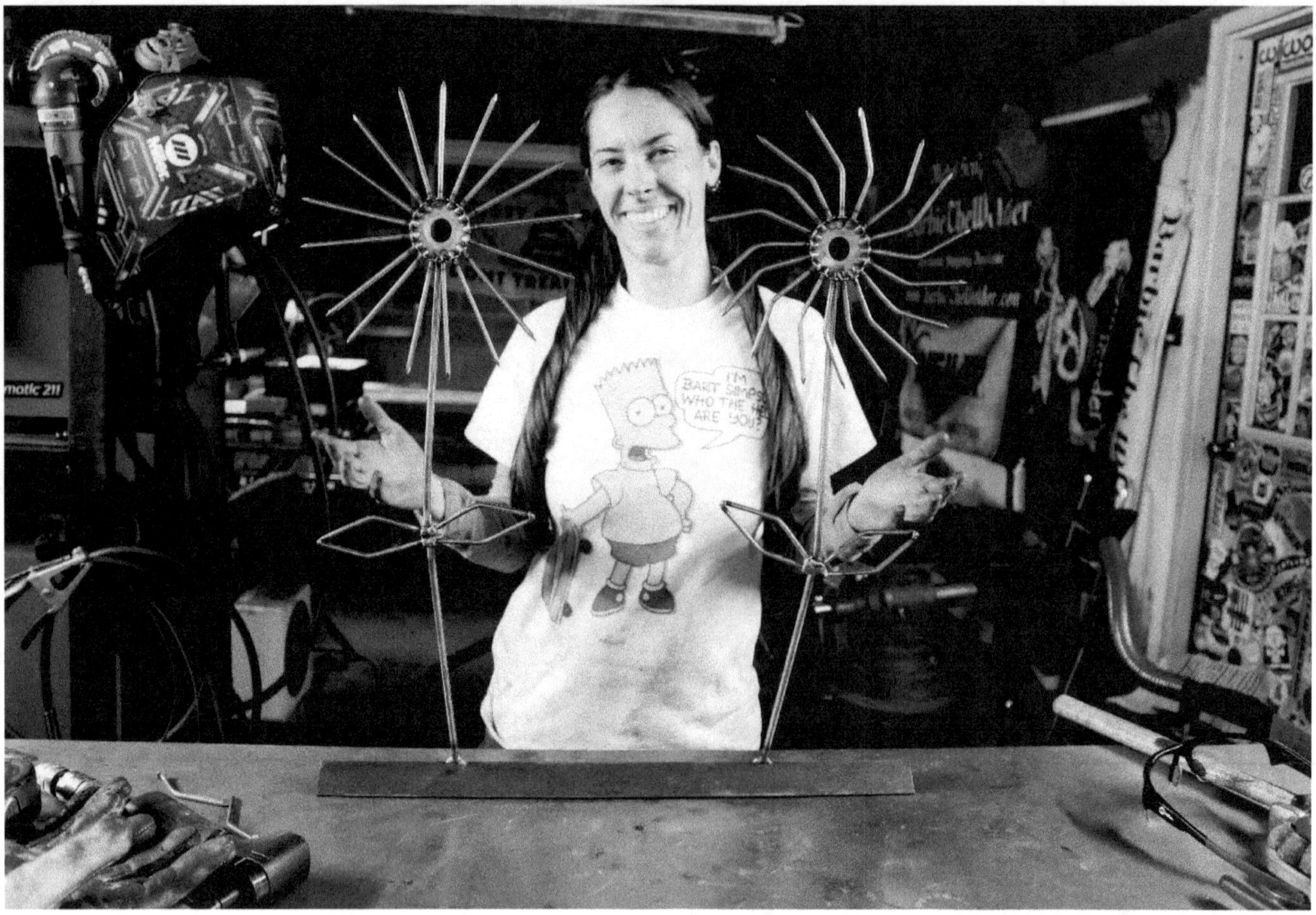

Difficulty

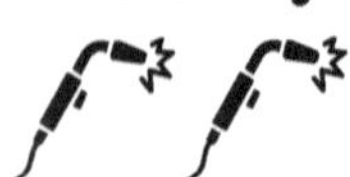

Materials

Angle iron or steel plate for the base
Round bar for stem
Nails or bolts for pedals and leaves
Washers or gears for center of flower

Tools

Hammer and chisel
Wire brush
Grinder with cutoff wheel

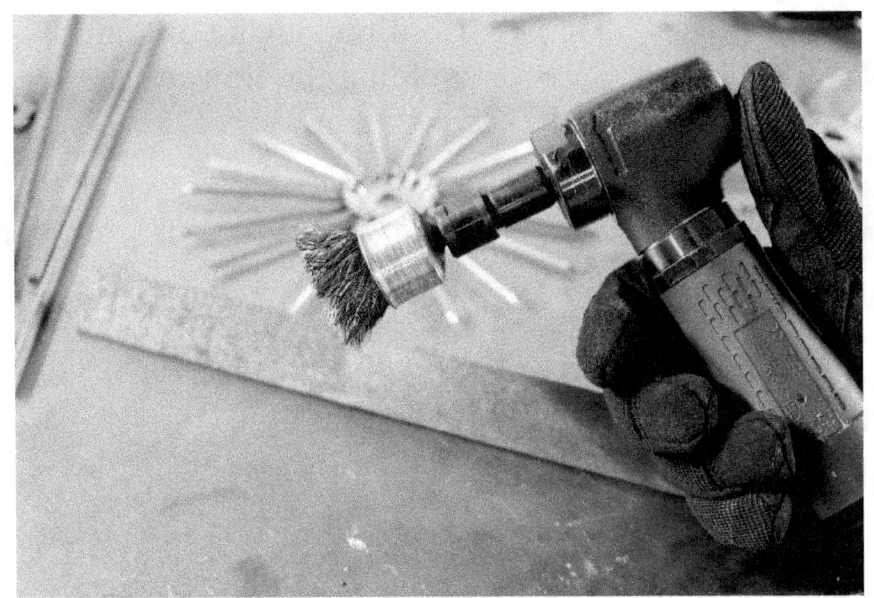

Clean any materials that are rusty and cut the material for the base

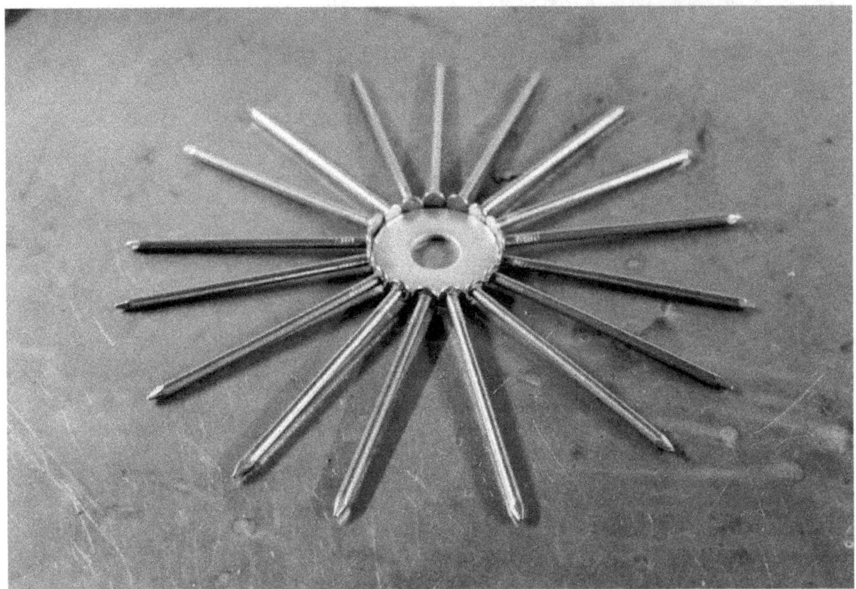

Lay out your flower. Ichoose a washer for the center of the flower and nails for the petals.

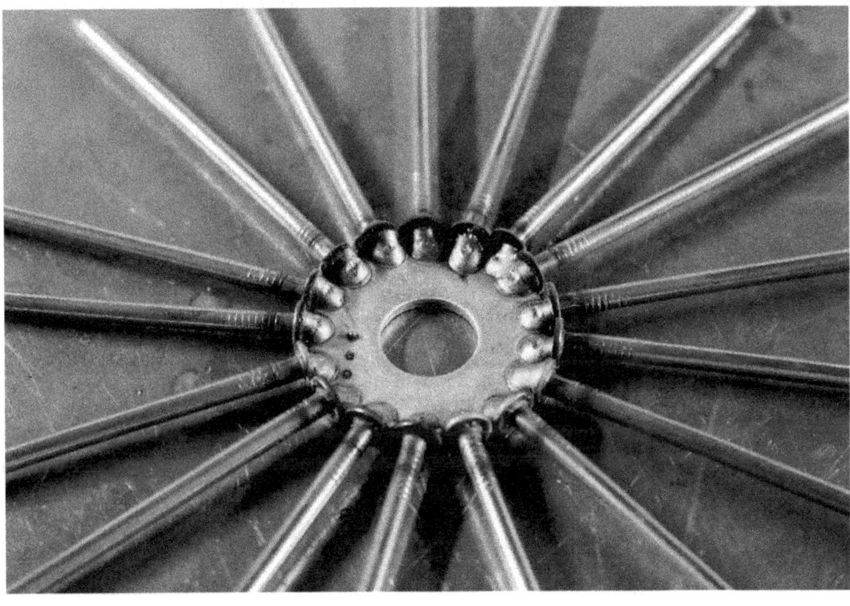

Tack weld the petals tothe center of the flower.

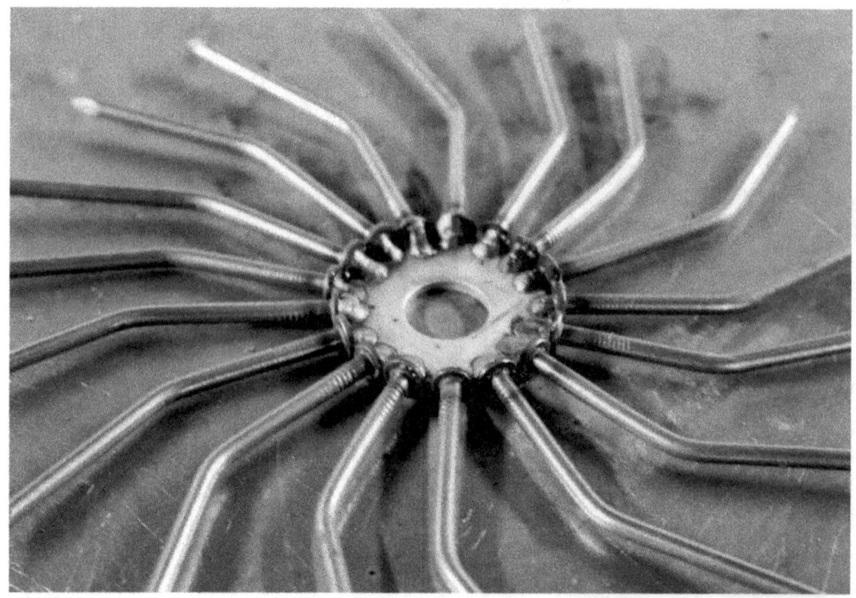

Continue laying out and welding the flowers.

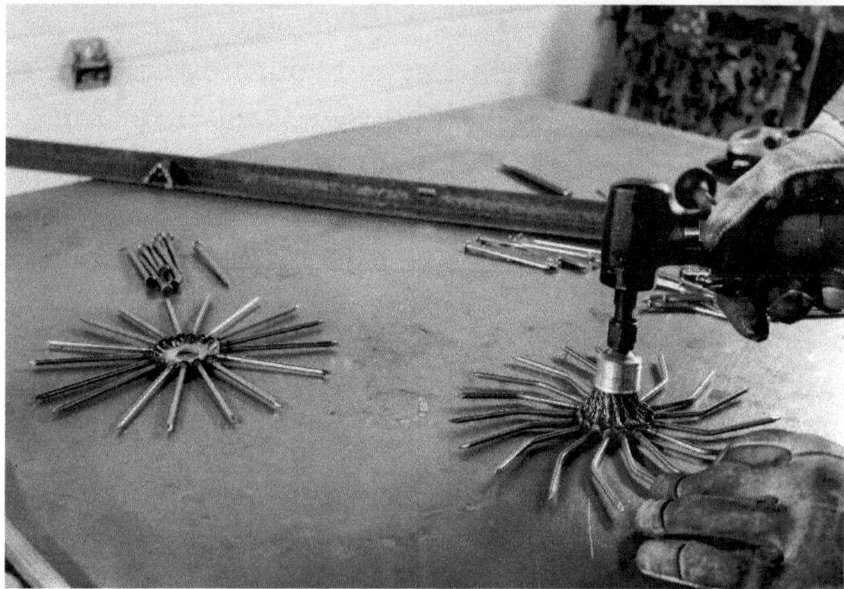

Clean the welds and chip any spatter.

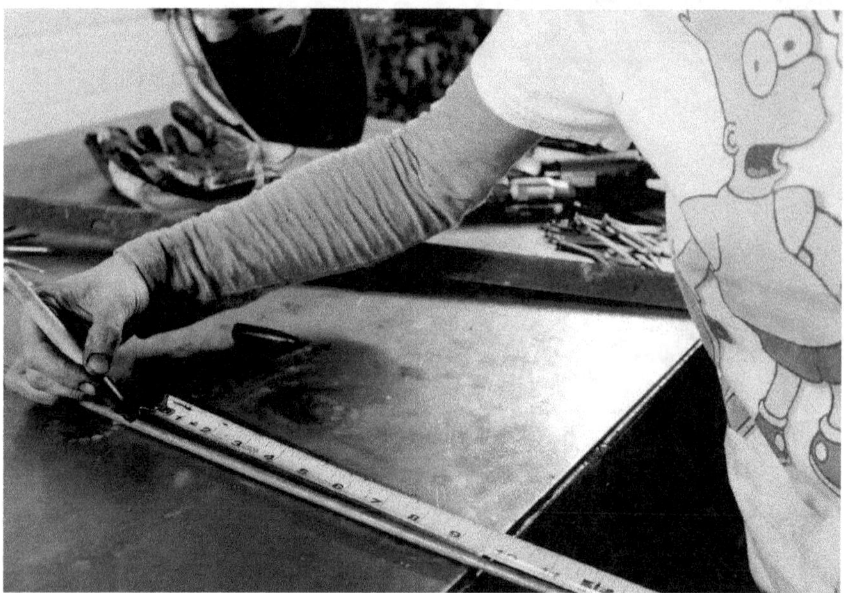

Mark the length of the stem.
I choose 1/4" round bar for my stem.

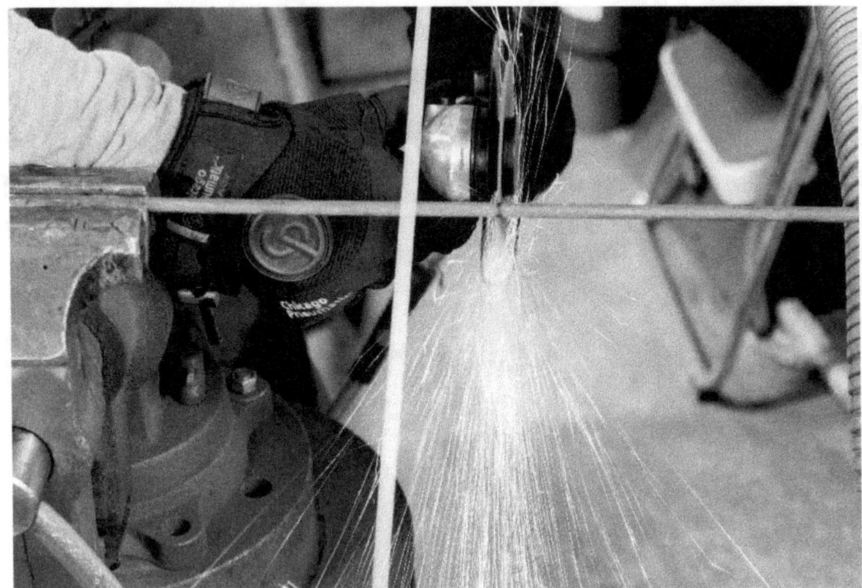

Clamp and cut the stem material.

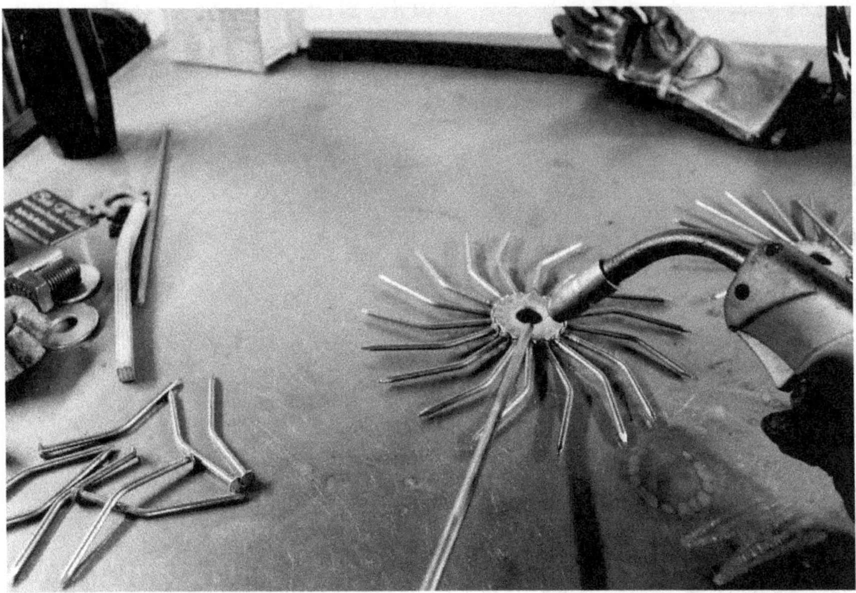

Tack weld the stems to the flowers.

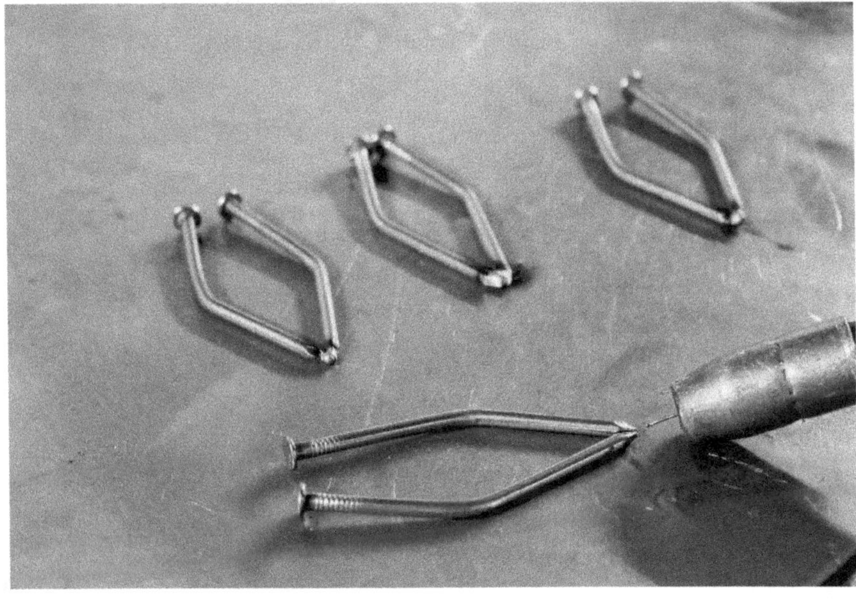

Create leaves for the flowers if you chooseto.

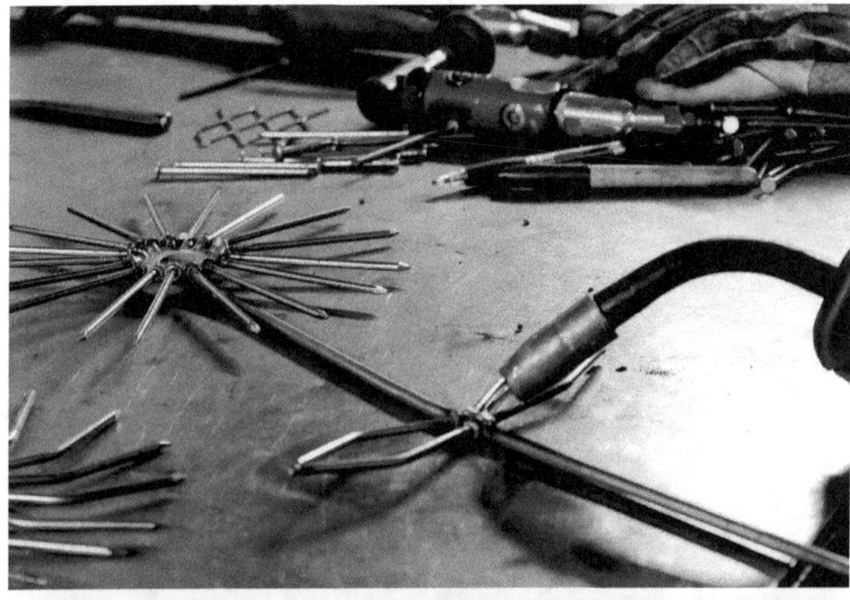

Weld the pedals to the stem.

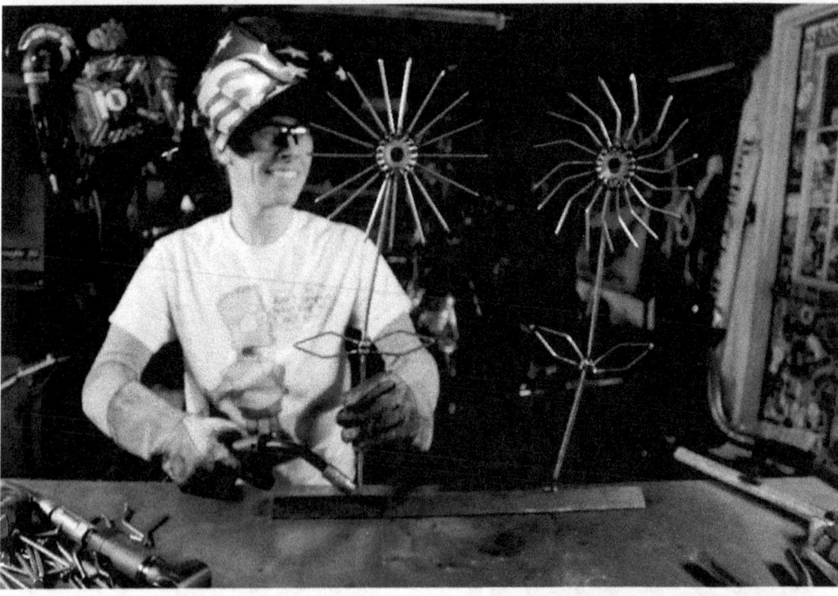

Weld the flowers to the base.

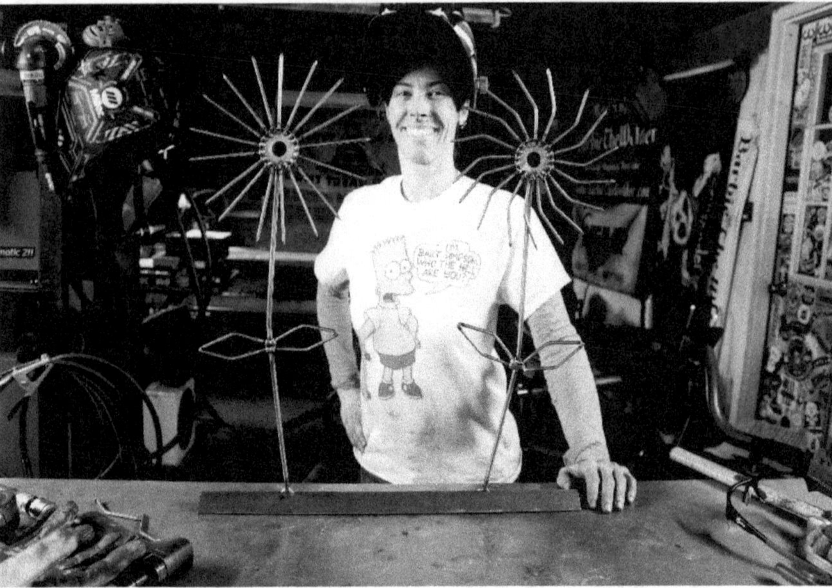

Clean welds with a wire brush and chip any weld spatter.
Finish with paint or clear coat to prevent rust.

Owl

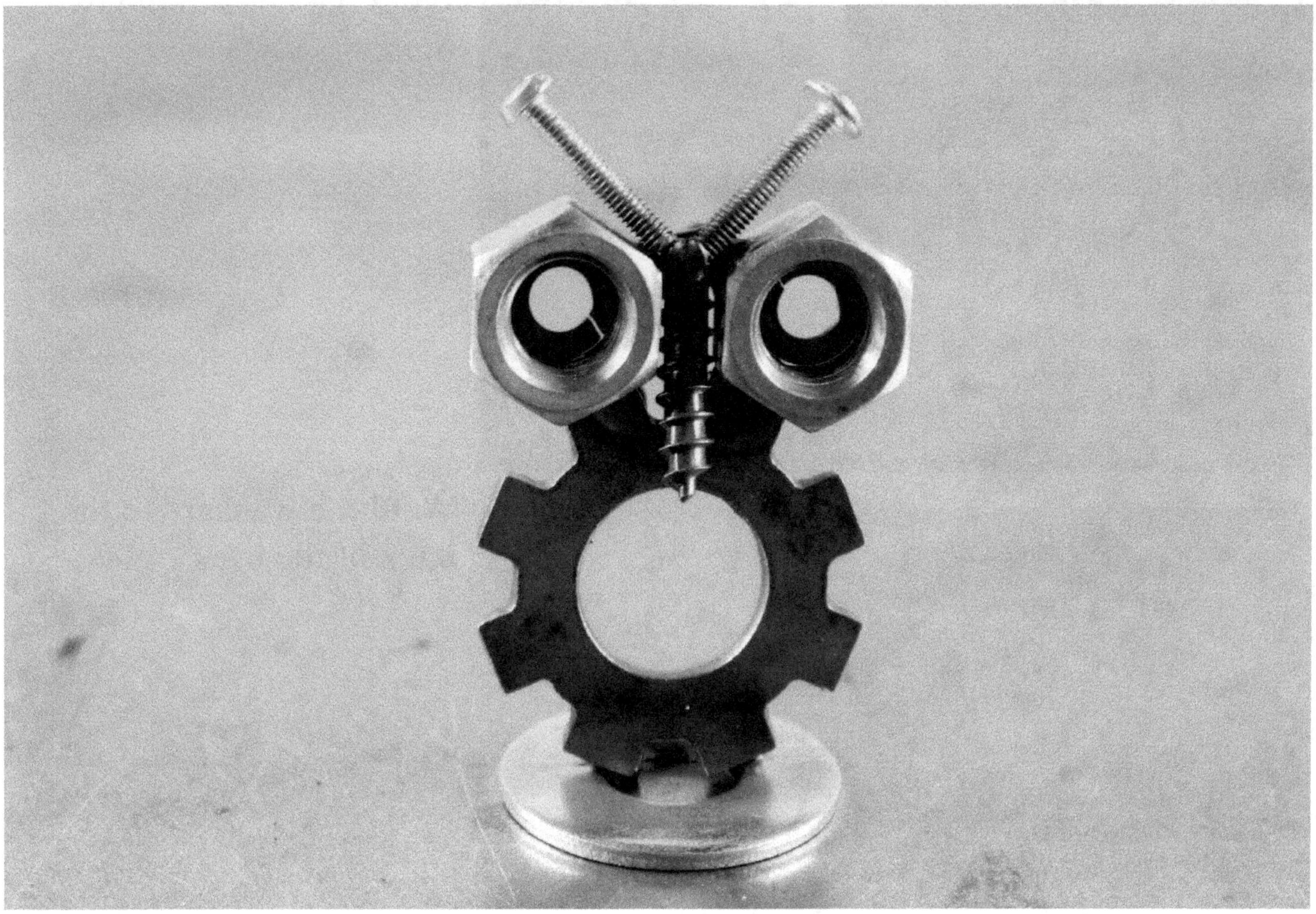

Difficulty

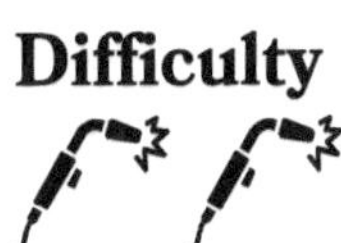

Materials Gear or large washer for the body Gear or large washer for the base 2 nuts for outside of eyes 2 washers for inside of eyes 2 bolts or screws for eyebrows 1 screw for beak

Tools

Pliers
Cut off wheel

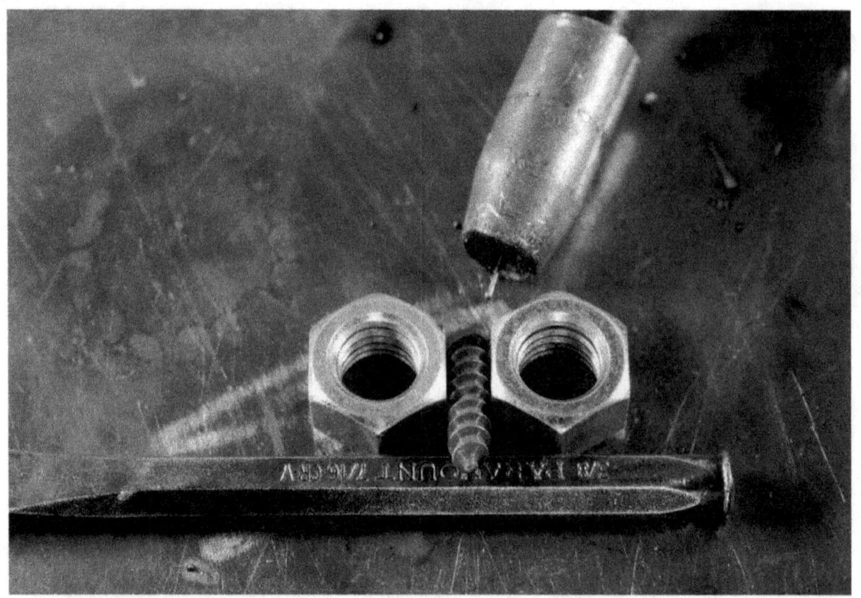

Cut the head off the screw you will use for the beak. Weld the beak to the two nuts.

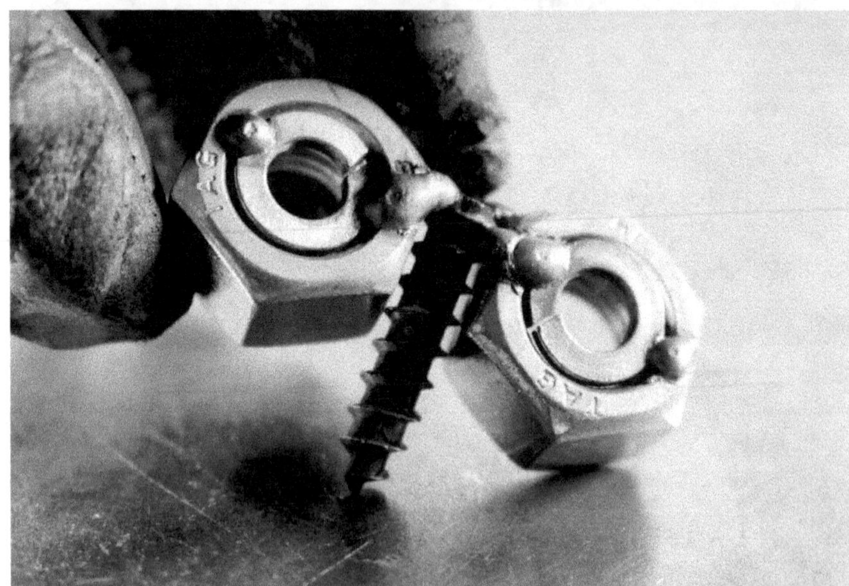

Weld the washers to the back of the eyes.

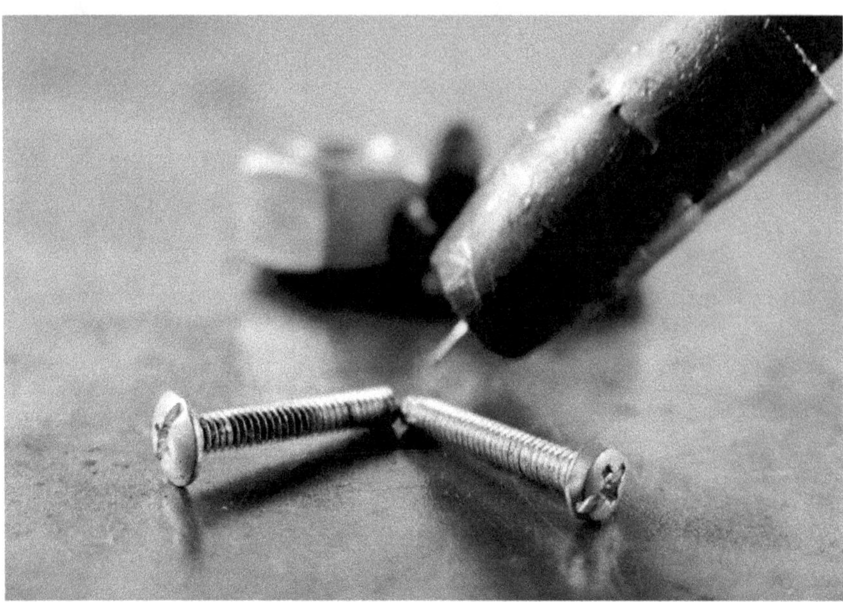

Gently tack weld the two screws together that you are using for eyebrows

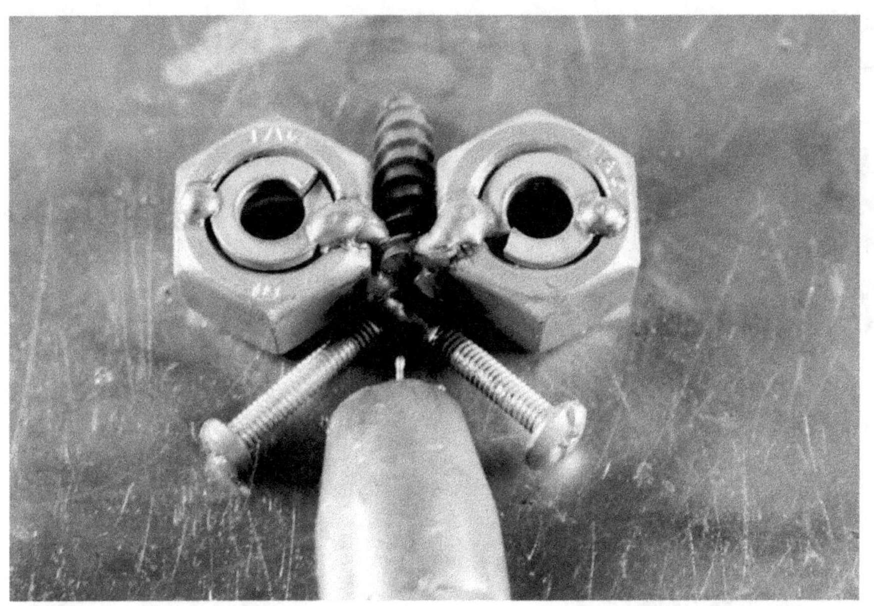

Tack weld the eyebrows to the head from the back.

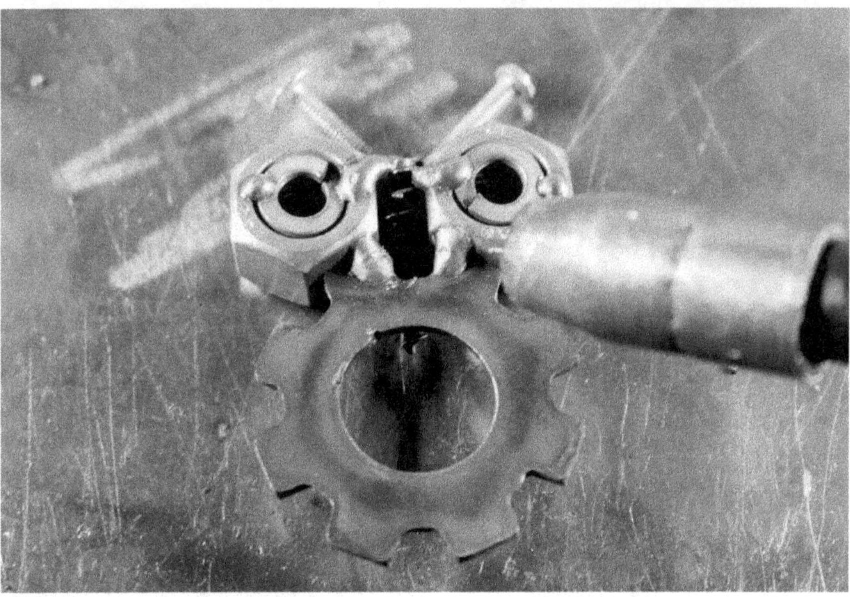

Tack weld the body onto the eyes from the back.

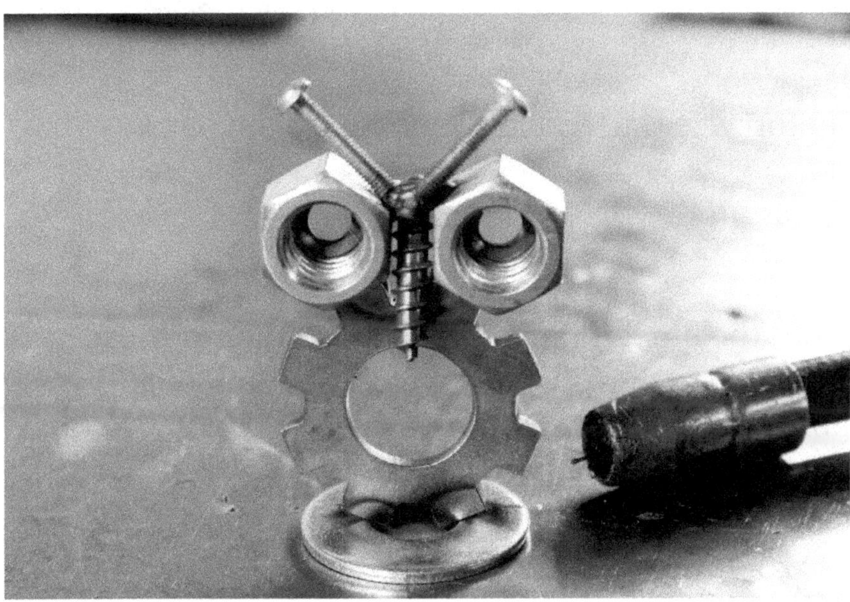

Tack weld the body on the base.
Clean any weld spatter and discoloration.
Clear coat finish to prevent rust.

Drink Coasters

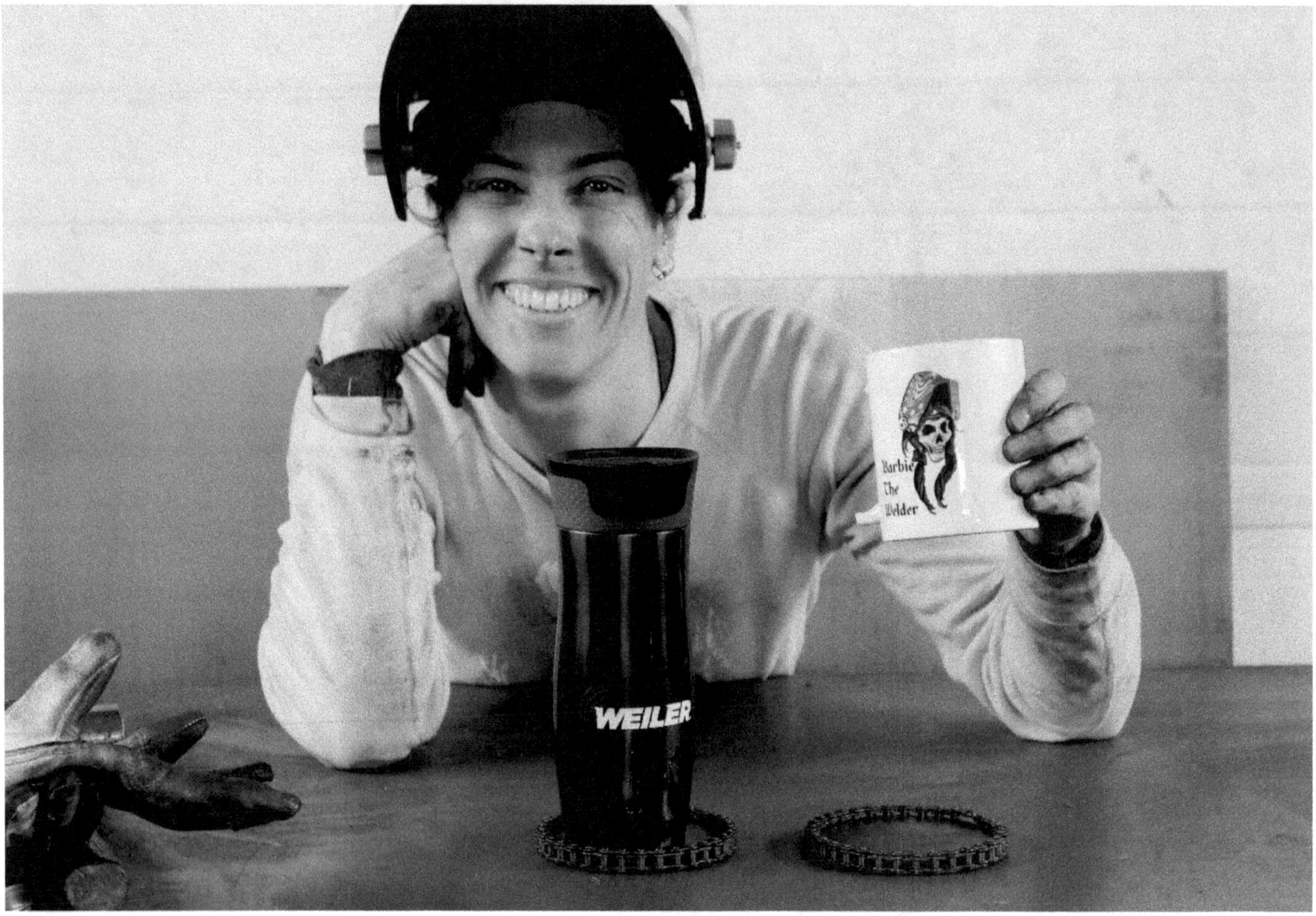

Difficulty

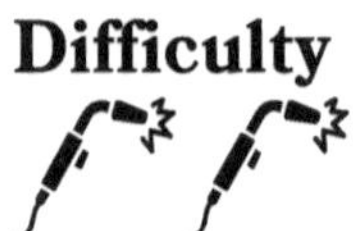

Materials

Roller chain from a bicycle or motorcycle (I used bicycle chain for the one shown.)
Scrap steel (18 gauge up to 1/8 plate)

Tools

Tin snips or a plasmacutter to cut the steel (If you don't have either of these you can cut the steelwith a cut off wheel and shape it with a sanding disk.)
Hammer and punchora chain breaker
Chisel

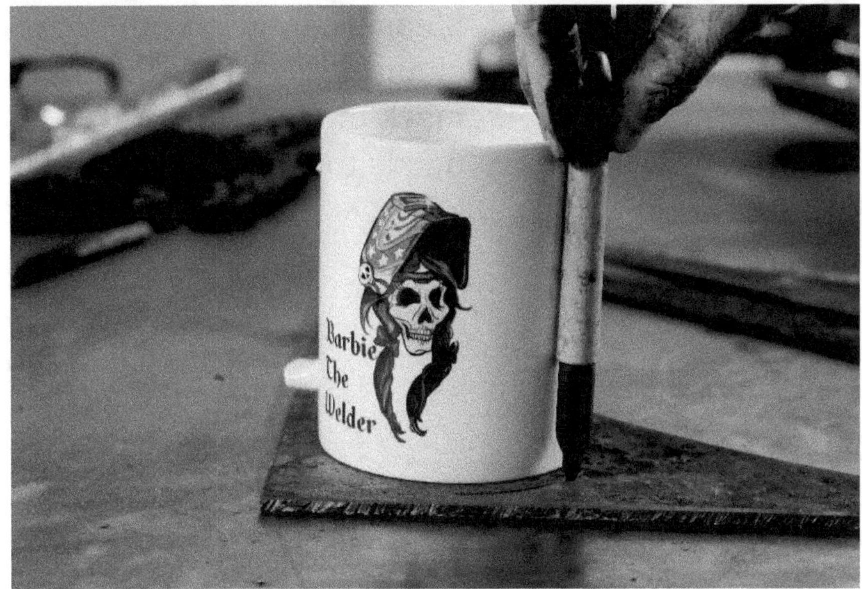

Trace around a coffee mug leaving an extra 1/4 inch all the way around. Ignore the broken handle on my favorite mug! This is why I work with metal and not glass!

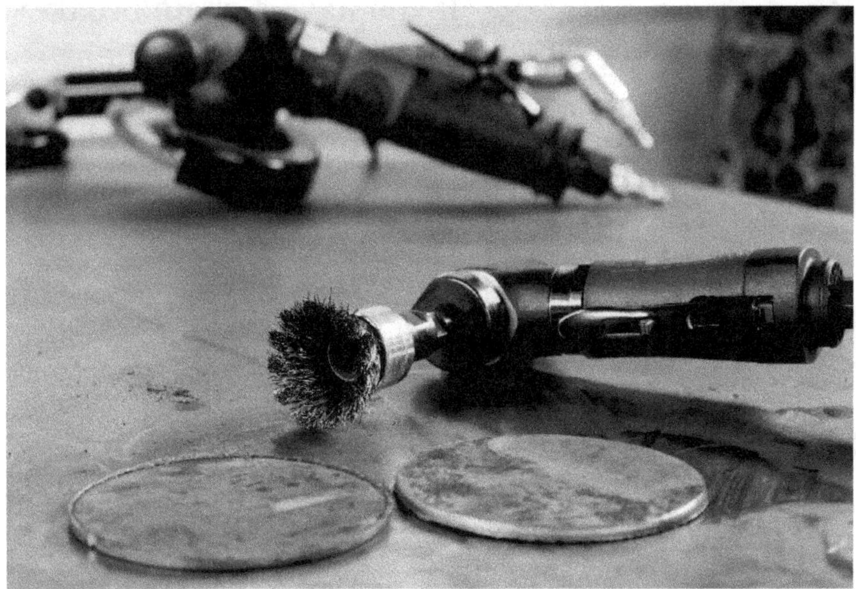

Cut one circle for each coaster.

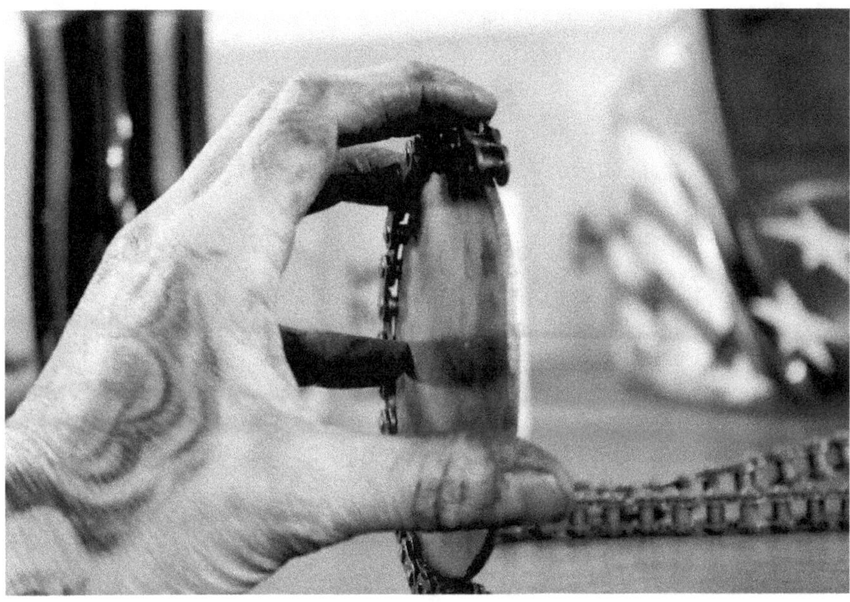

Place chain around the circle making sure the circle is trapped insideof the chain.

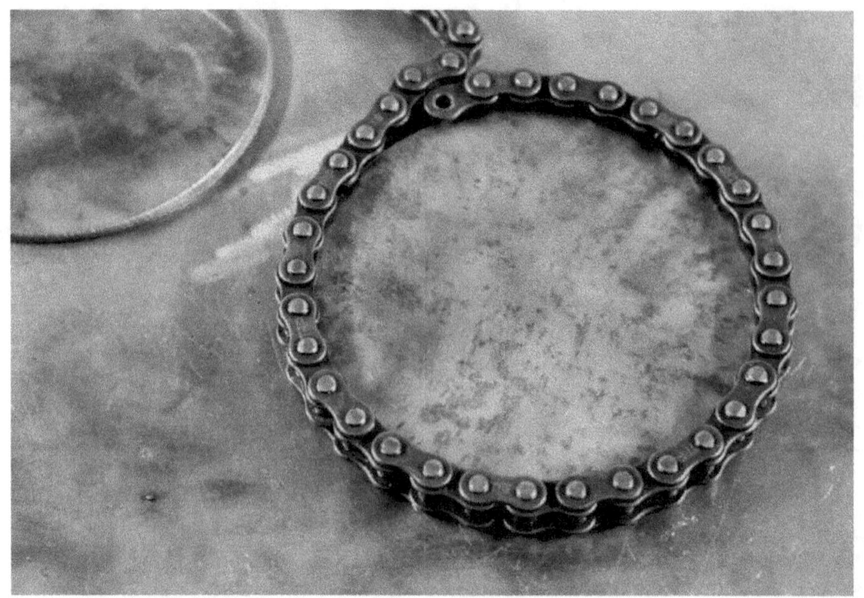

Measure how long the chain needs to be and then mark the link where it needs to be cut.

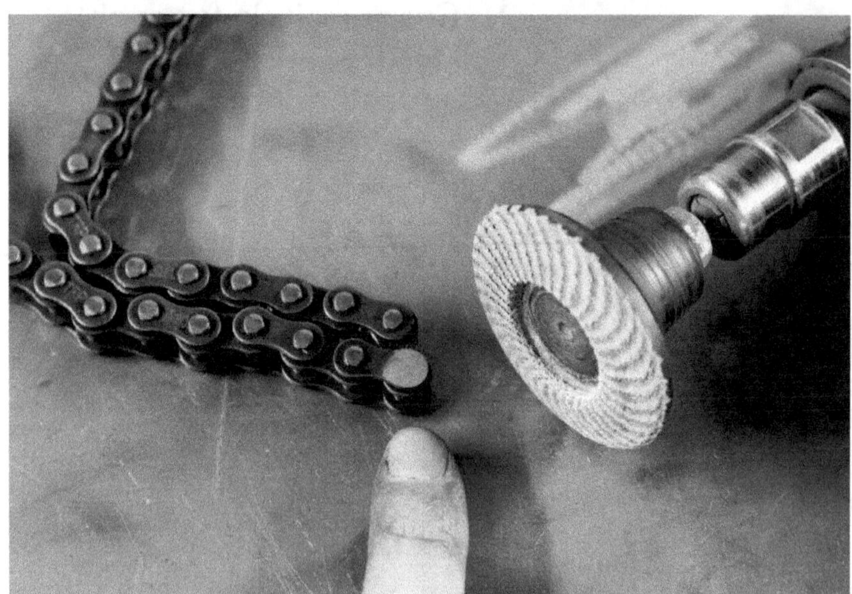

If you have a chain breaker use that to cut the chain otherwise grind the pin down to the top of the chain and then use a punch to hammer it out.

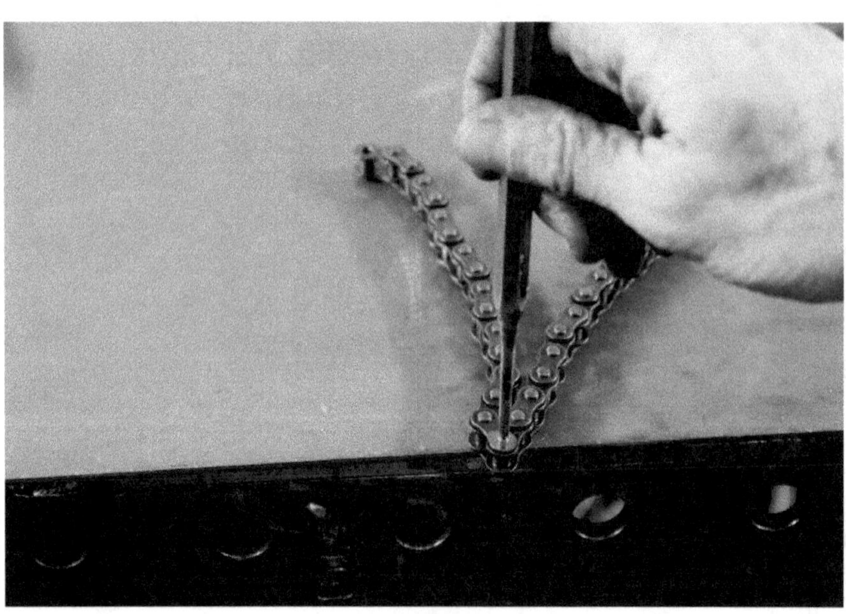

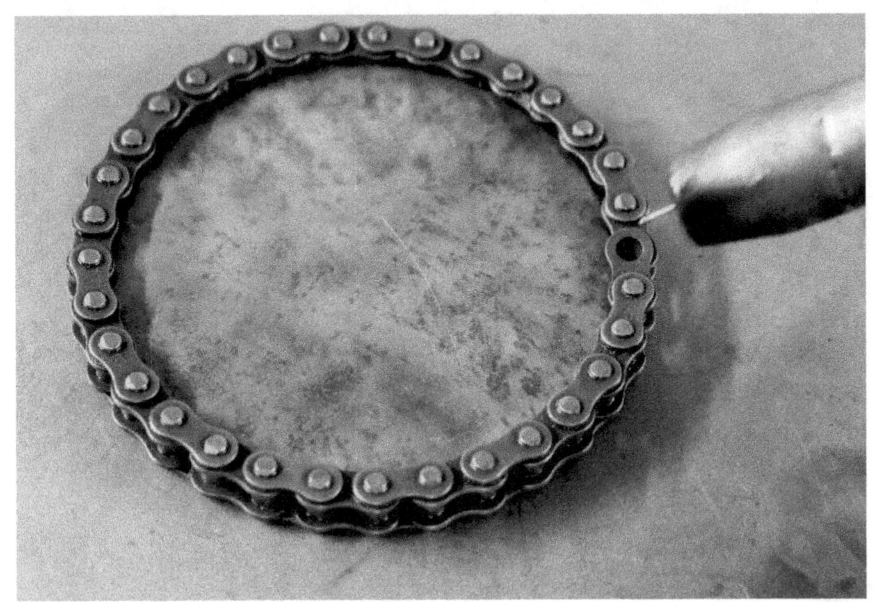

Hold the chain tight around the circle and place a tack weld where the two ends meet. Flip the coaster over and tack weld the chain link on the back where the two ends meet.

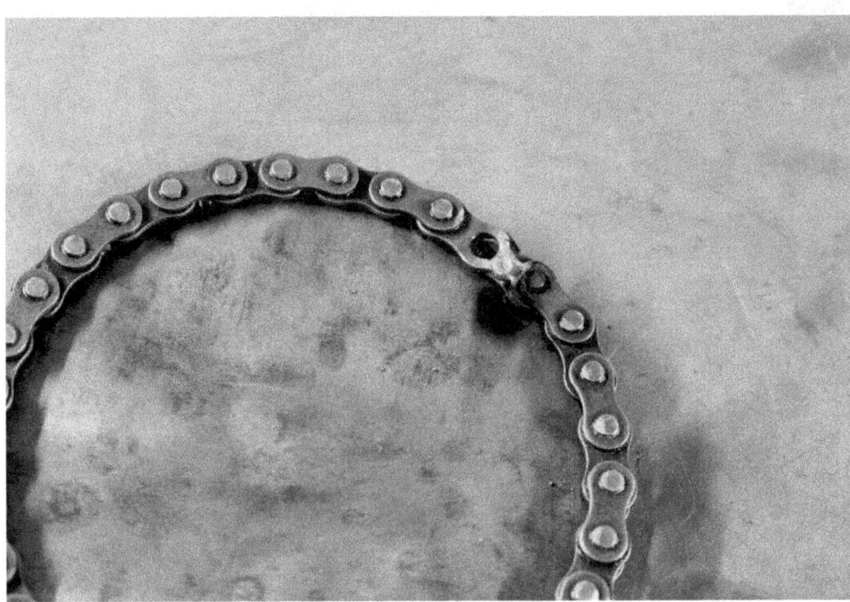

That one tack weld is all you need! The circle will move up and down inside the chain but is trappedby the links.

Chip any weld spatterand clean any weld discoloration with awire brush.

Clear coat to preventrust.

Try this project withlarge and small chain!

Bowl

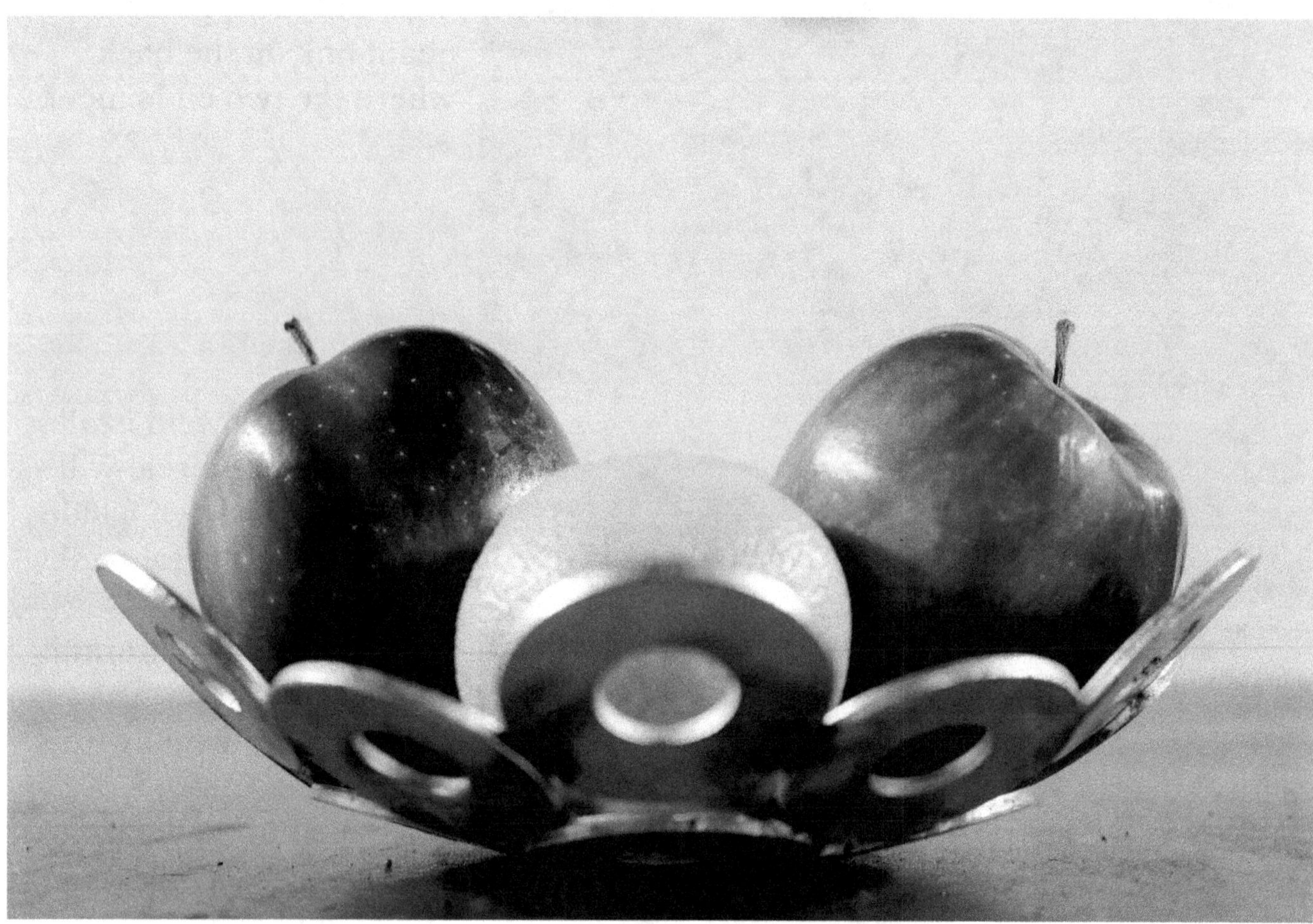

Difficulty

Materials
Washers (You can use various sizes, for this project I choose to use all the same size.)

Tools

Hammer and chisel

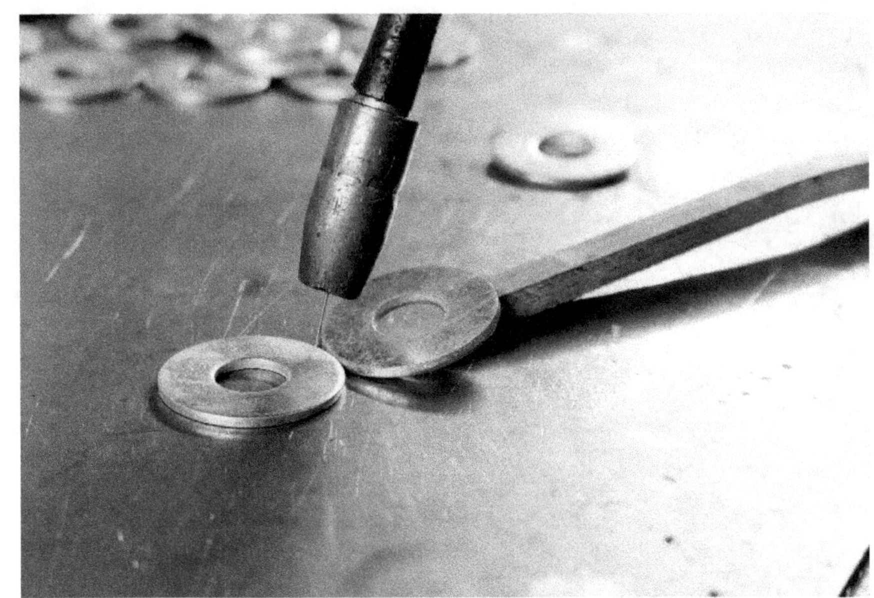

Choose one washer to be the center washer and using a prop (something approximately 1/2" tall) tack weld a washer to it in two places.

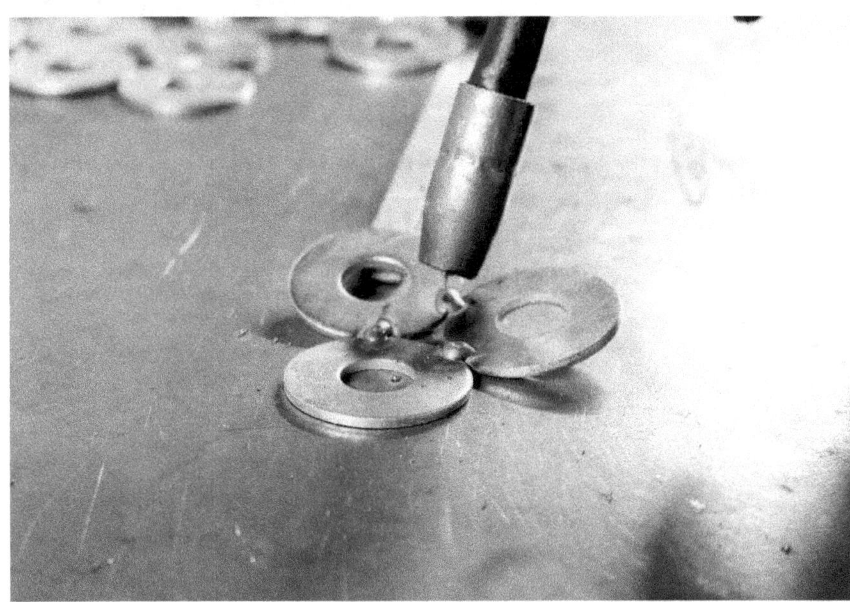

Using the same prop put a washer next to the first one and against the center washer and tack weld it to the first two.

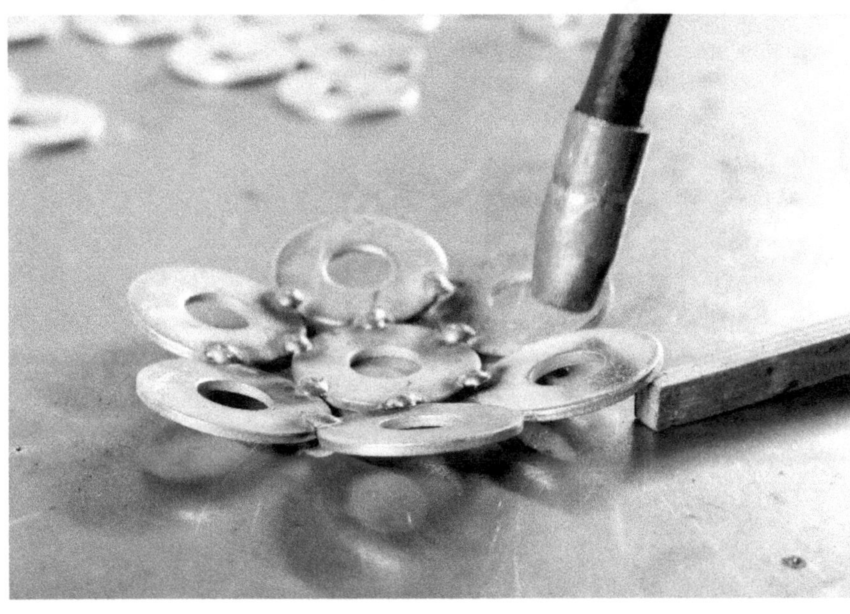

Continue propping and tack welding washers around the center washer until you have completed the circle.

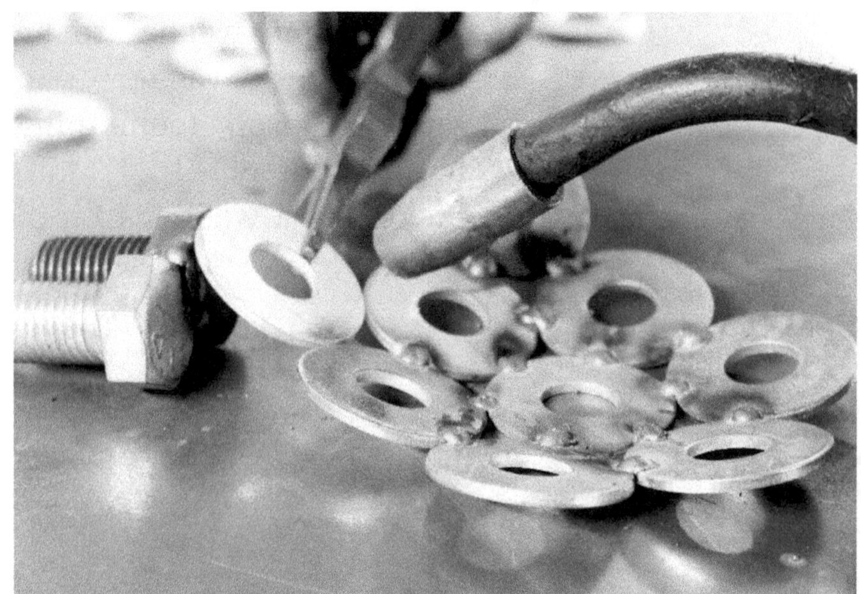

Choose a taller prop and work your way around the next layer.

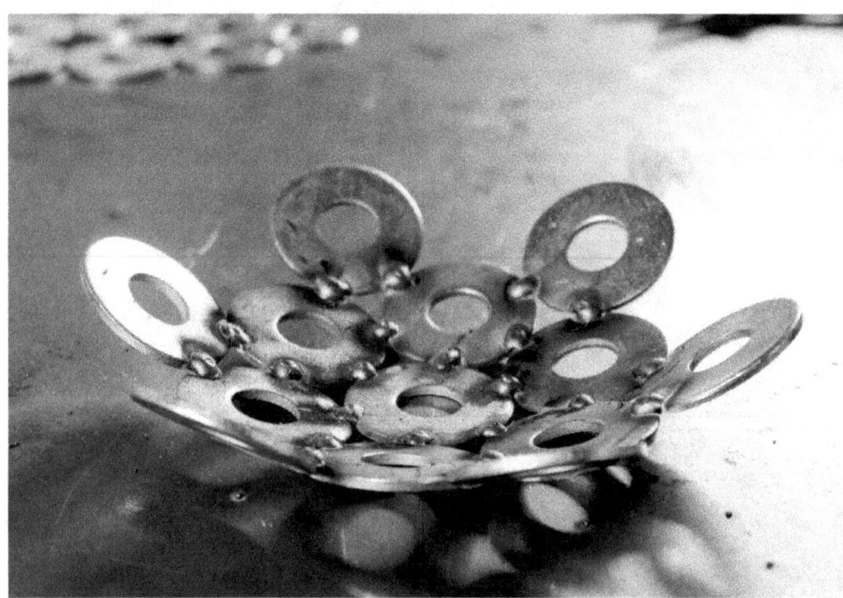

If you want a large bowl you can continue working around and around staying consistent with the angle that you are welding each row.

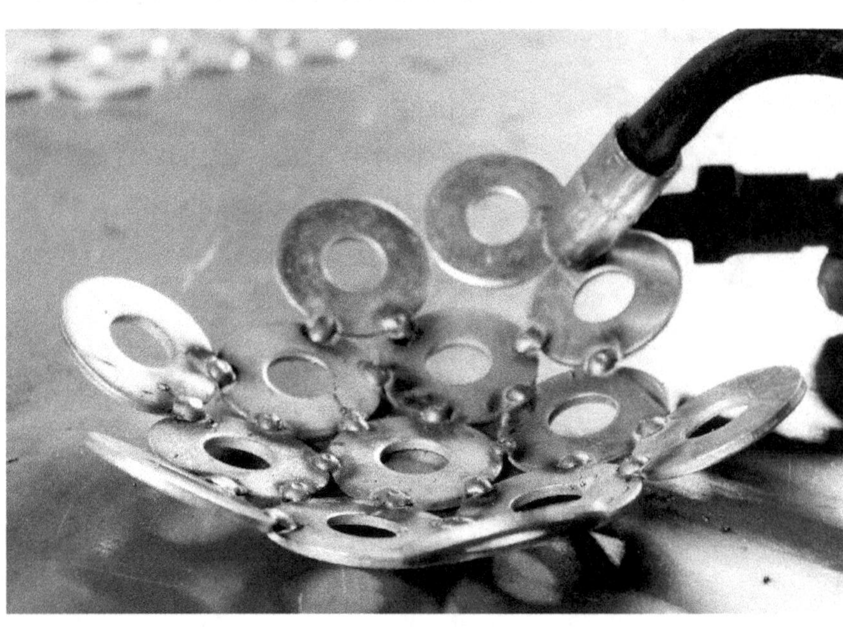

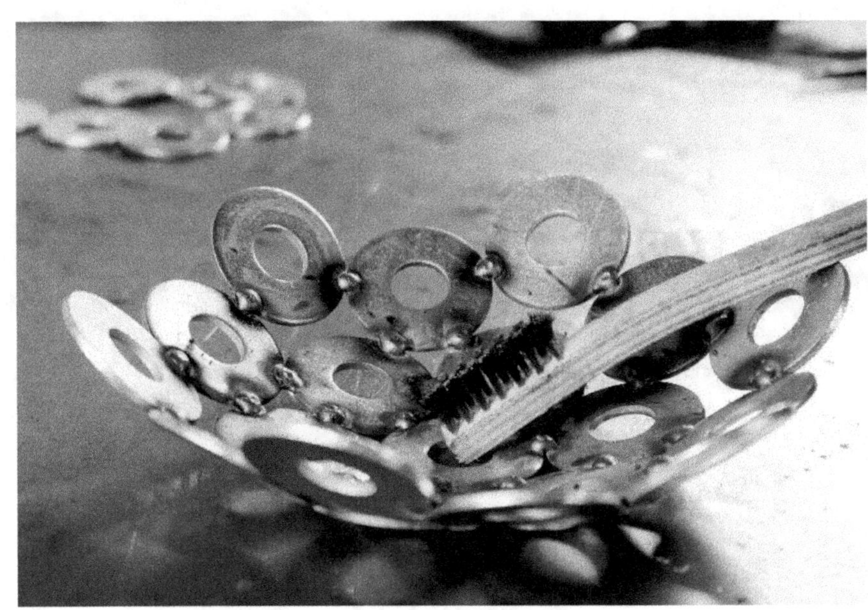

When you haveyourbowl the size you wantsimply clean any weld discoloration withawire brush and chipanyspatter with a hammerandchisel. Finish with clearcoator paint.

Coat Rack

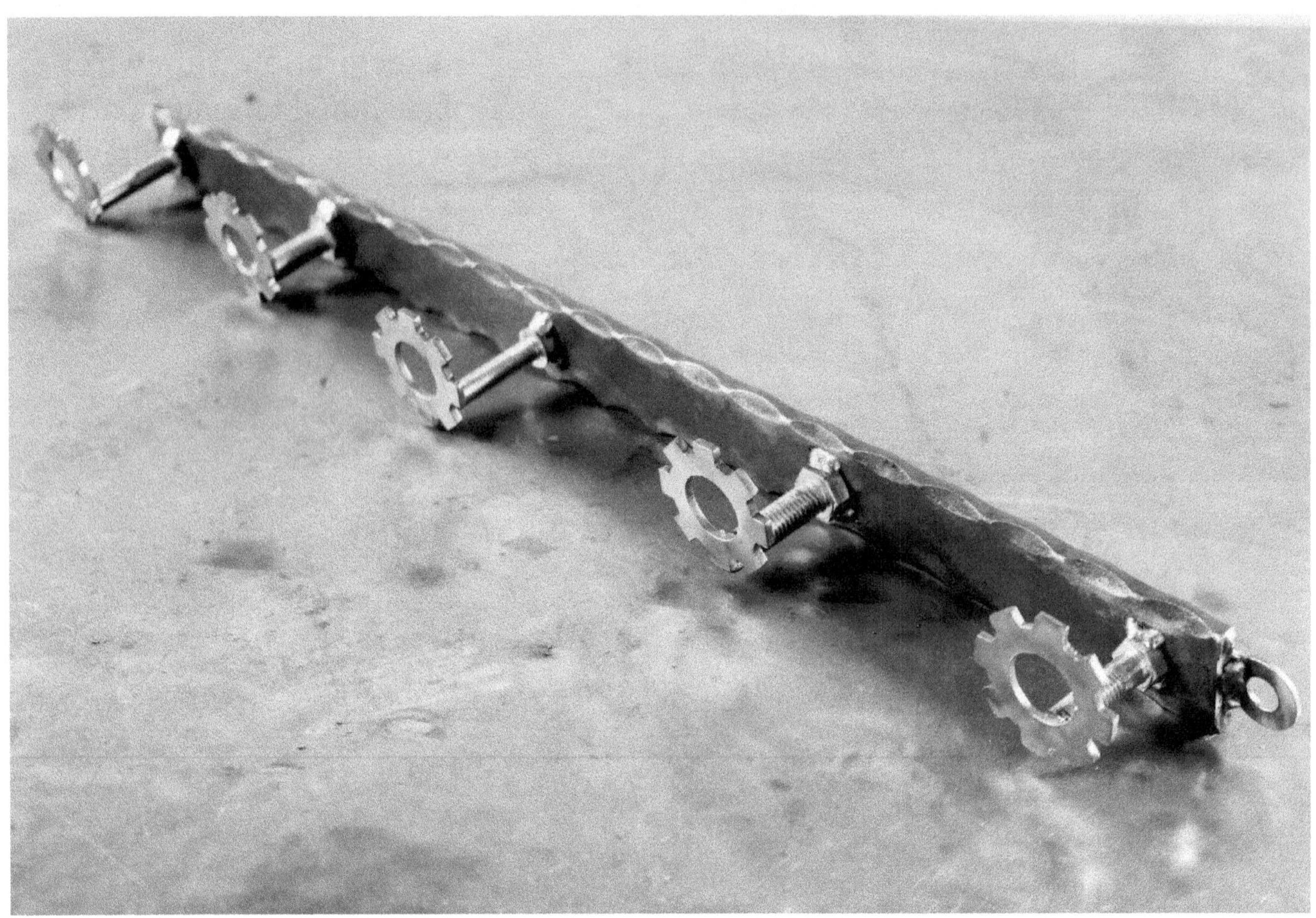

Difficulty

Materials

Bar stocksteel (I used a short piece of ornamental steel I had left over from another sculpture I made.)

Gears areoptional, you can use wrench heads, sockets, or any number of cool things youfind laying around!

Bolts

Two heavyduty washers

Tools

Hammer and chisel

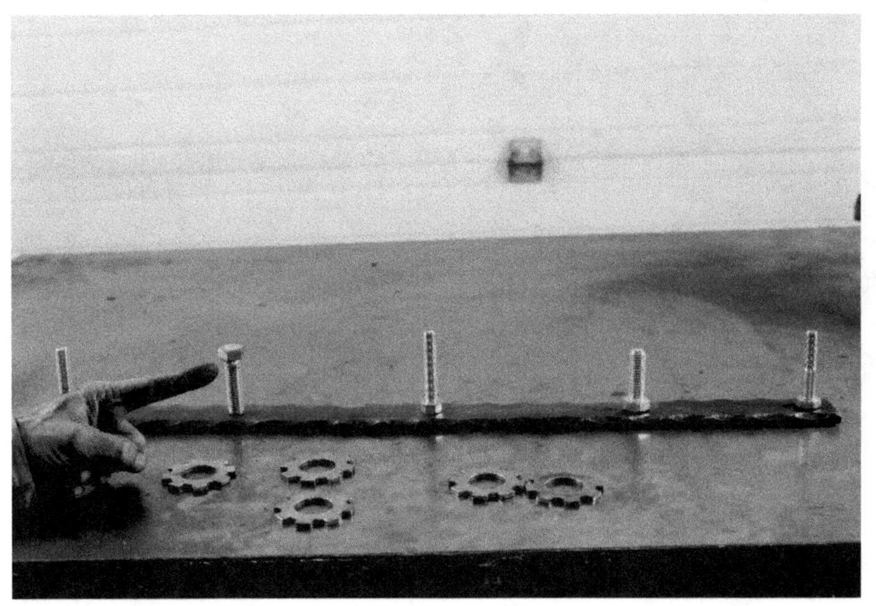

Lay the bolts out evenly separated on the bar stock. If you don't have anything to weld to the ends of the bolts place them head side out like the one I'm pointing to. If you have something to weld to the ends you can weld the heads down. Artists choice!

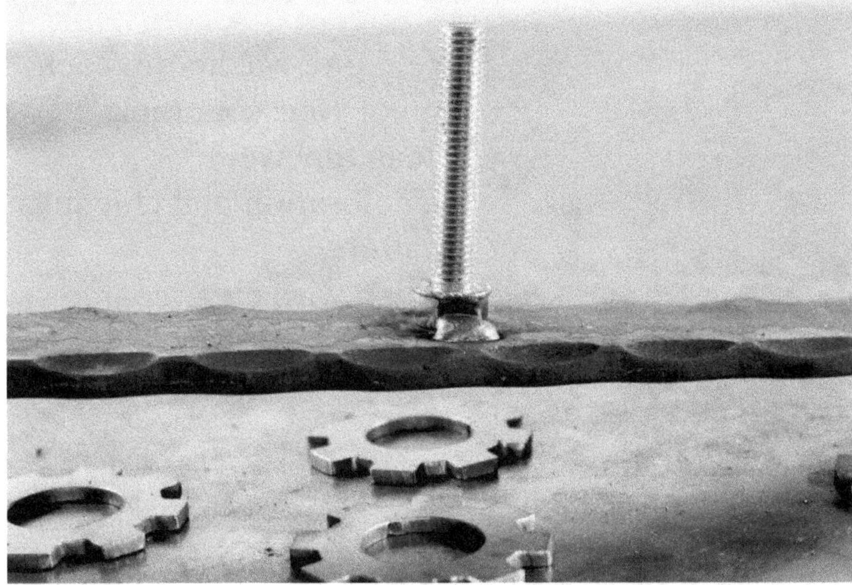

Weld each bolt to the bar stock.

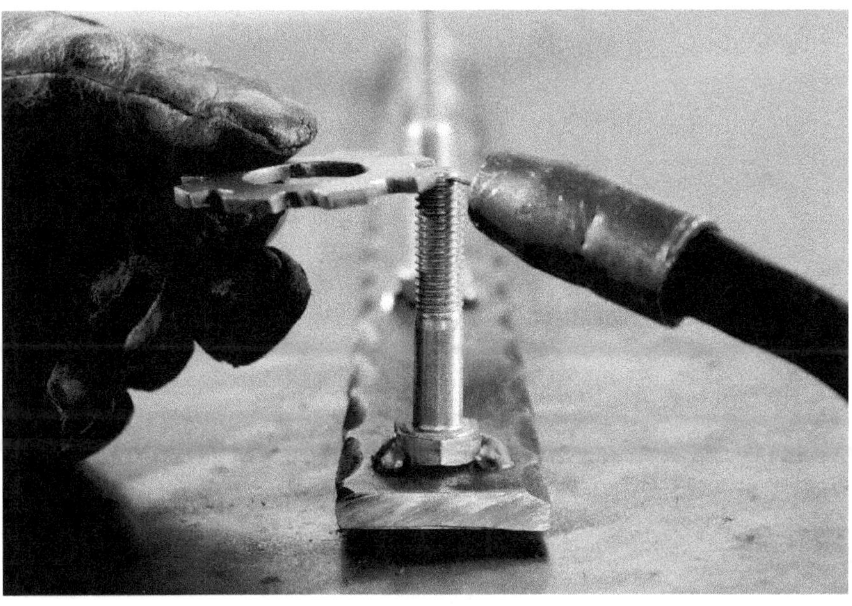

If you choose, weld something decorativeto the bolt at a 90 degree angle.

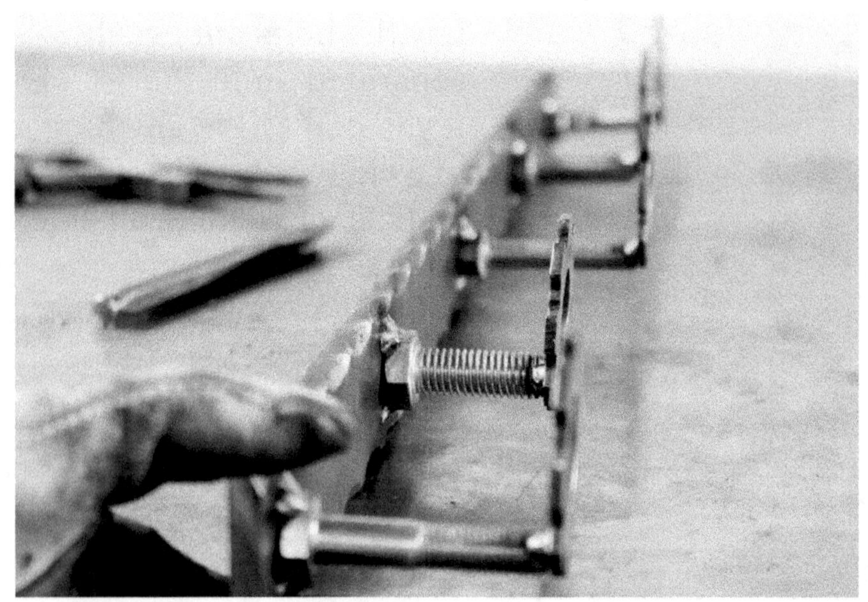

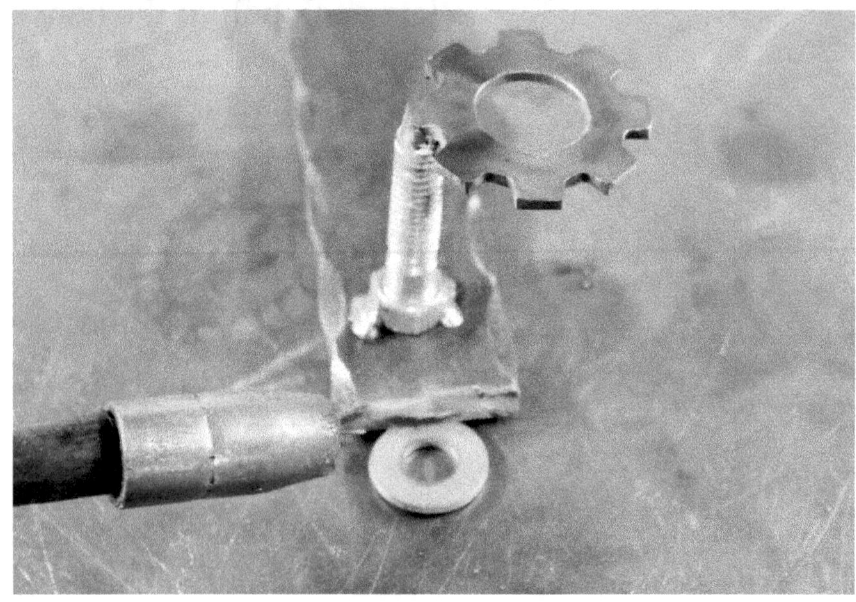

Weld one washer on each end of your coat rack. Clean any weld discoloration and chipany spatter. Finish with clear coator paint.

Dog

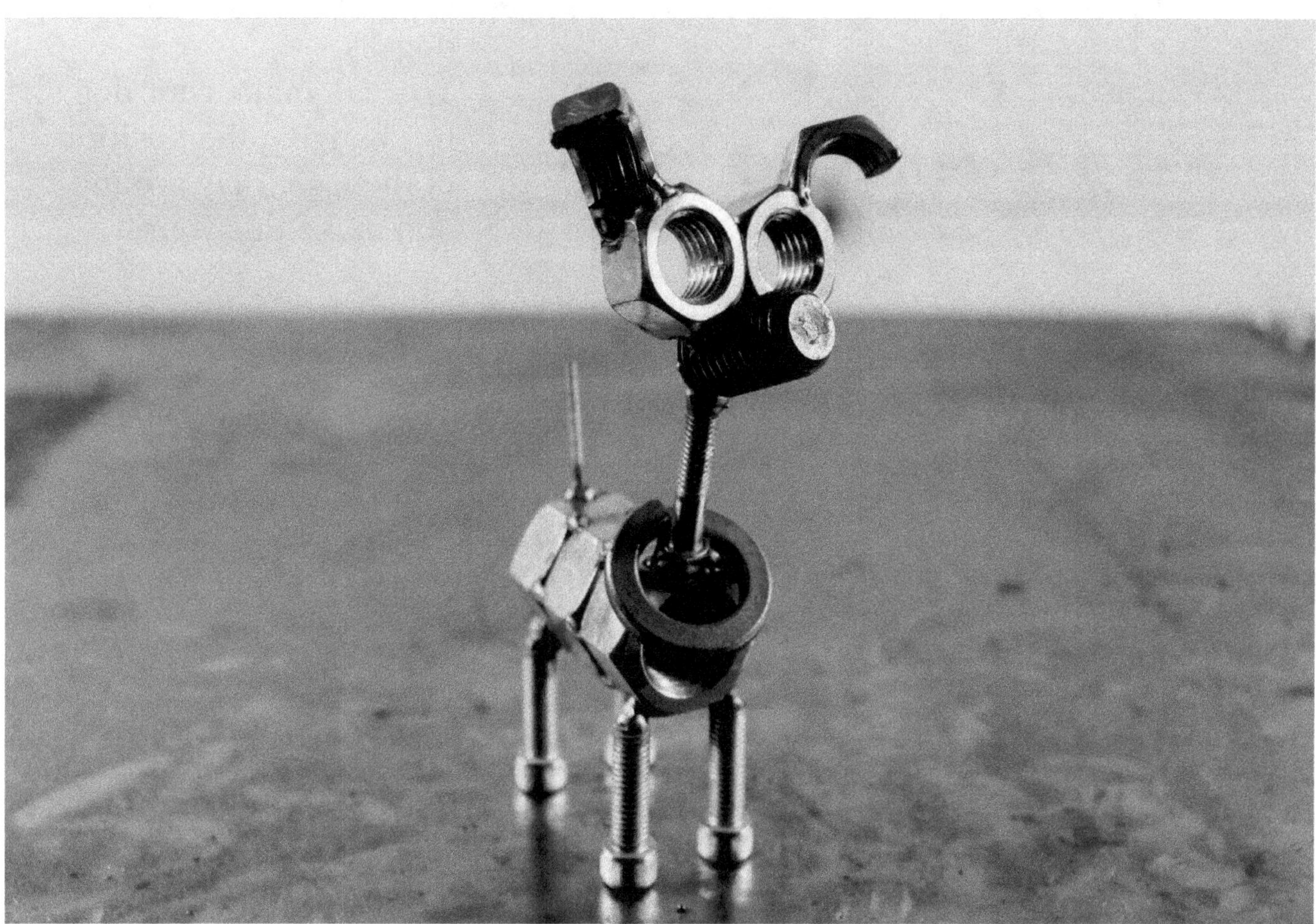

Difficulty

Materials
3 Nuts for the body
3 Nuts for the eyes and ears
4 Bolts for legs
1 Bolt for the nose
1 Bolt for the neck
1 Bolt for the tail
1 Washer for a collar!

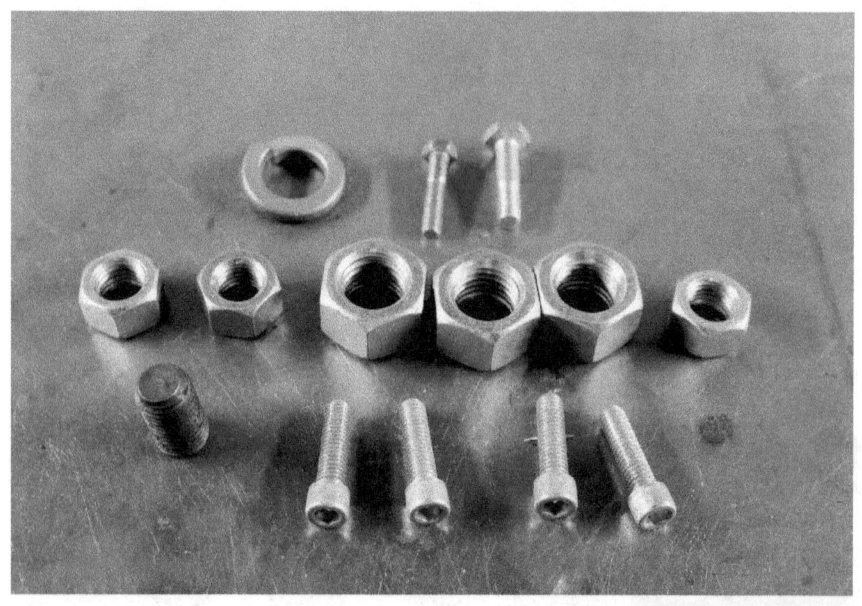

By changing the size of the nuts and bolts you can create different types of dogs!
You can make your dog sit by changing the position of the legs. Play around and make this yours!

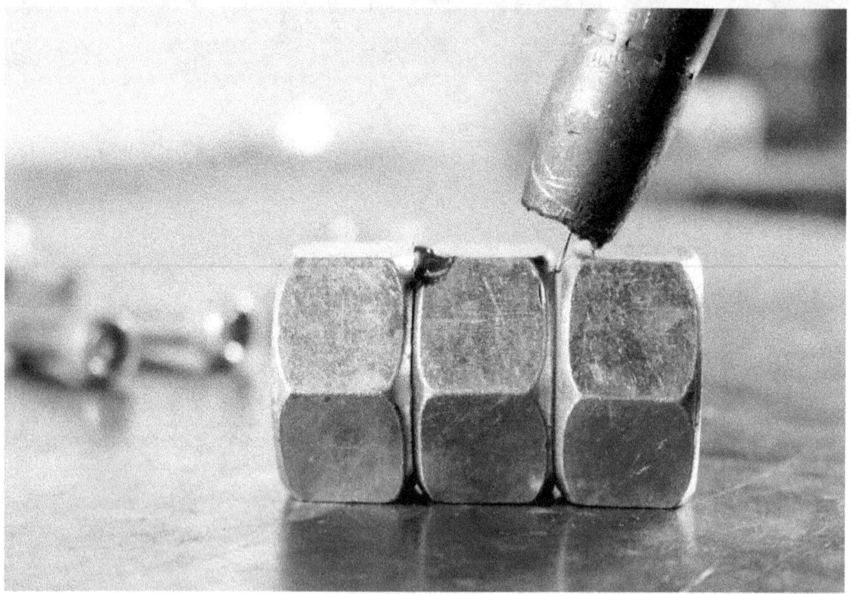

Weld the three large nuts together to make the body.

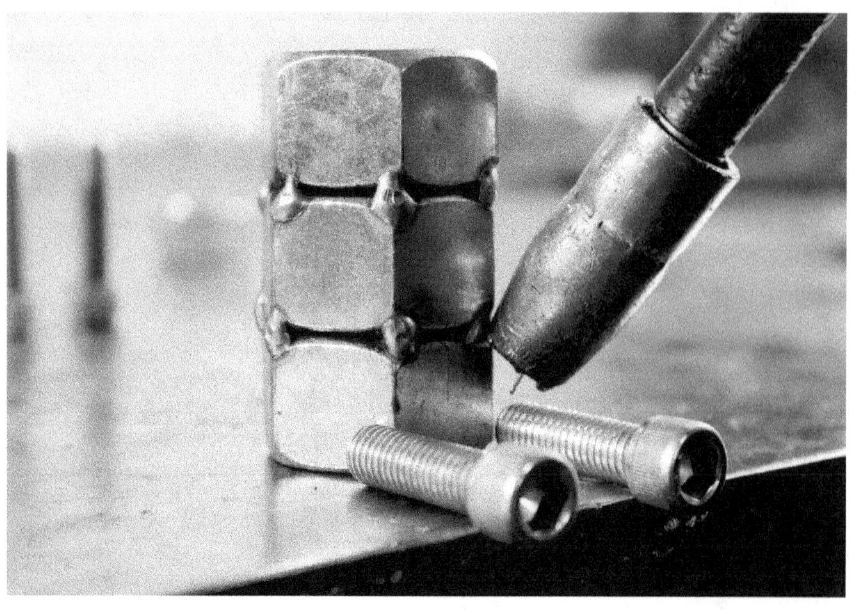

Stand the nuts up and lightly tack weld the two legs on. We lightly tack weld them so that if we need to make adjustments to make him stand level we are able to.

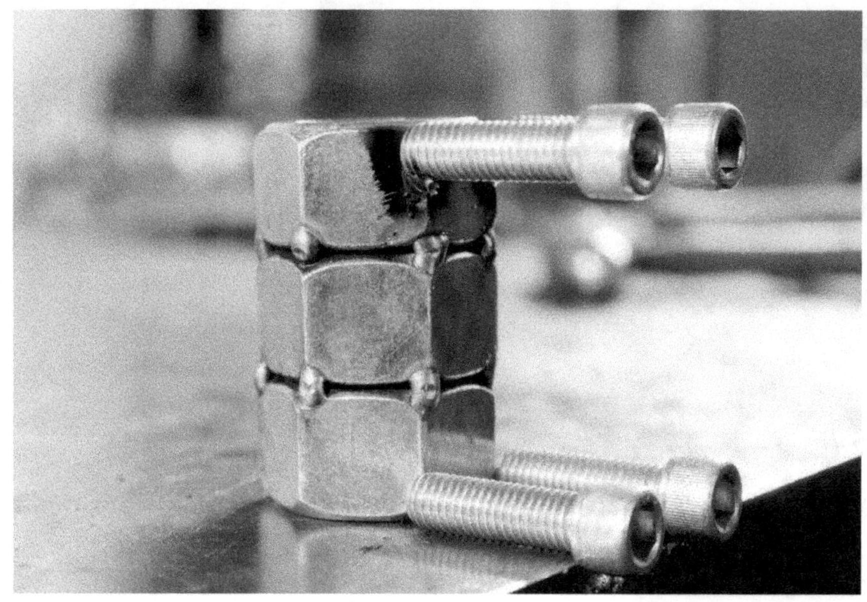

Flip him over and lightly tack weld the other two legs on.

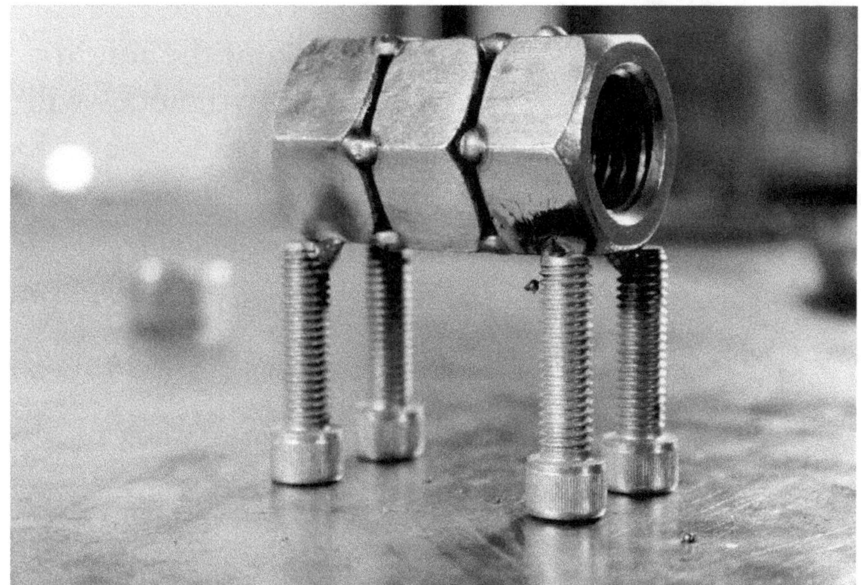

Stand him up and check to see if he is standing level. If you need to adjust the legs lightly tap them until he is level and then weld them in place.

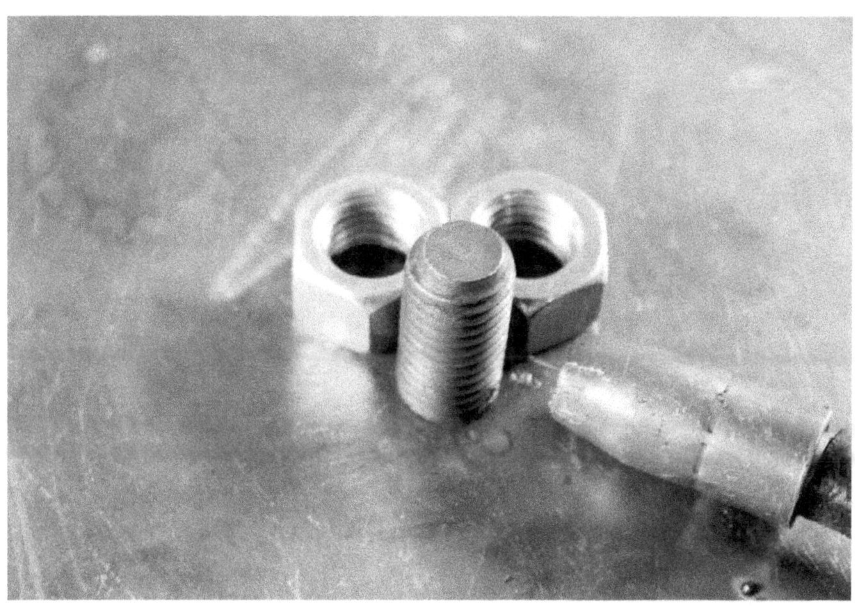

(The nose is a bolt I had cut the head off of for another project. If you haven't already cut the head off a bolt for thenose do so now.)
Tack weld the nose totwo nuts to make the face.

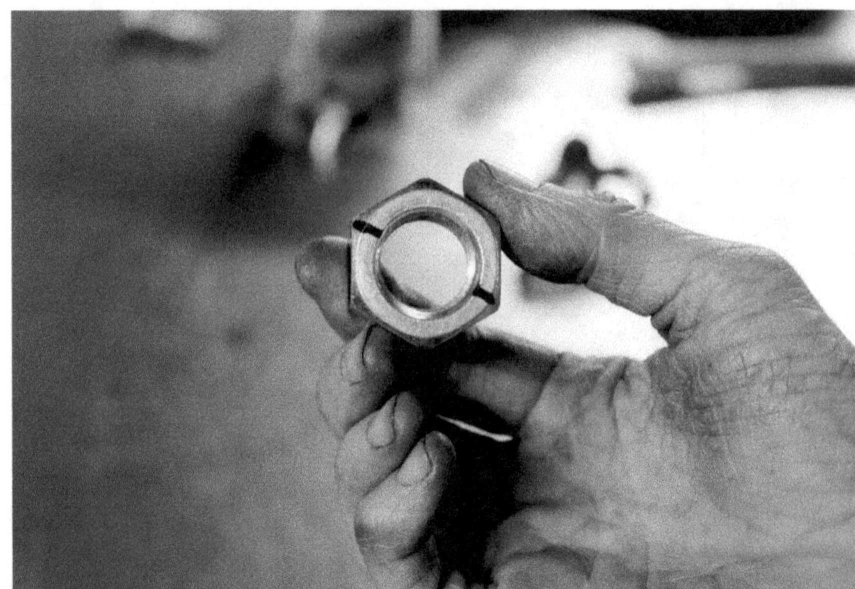

Mark the third nut like this.

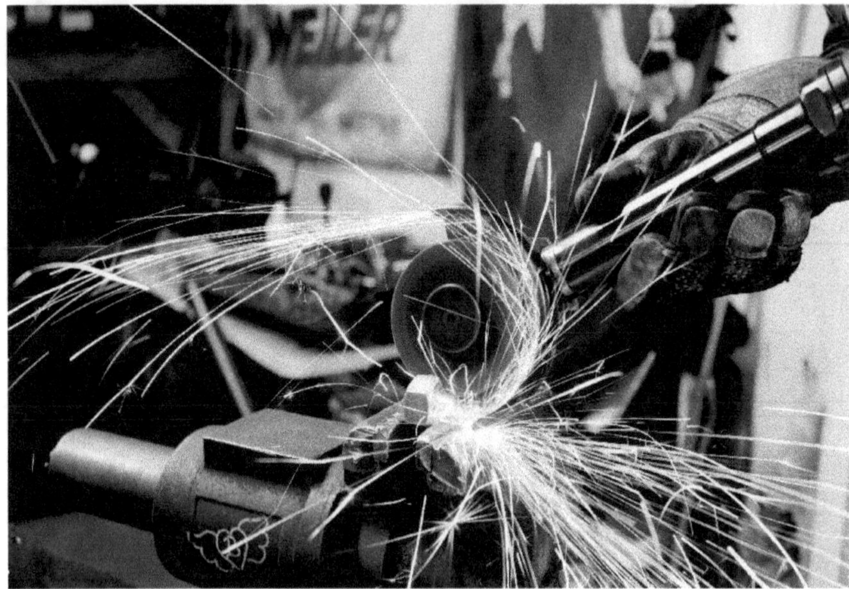

Clamp and cut the nut in half. These two pieces will make the ears.

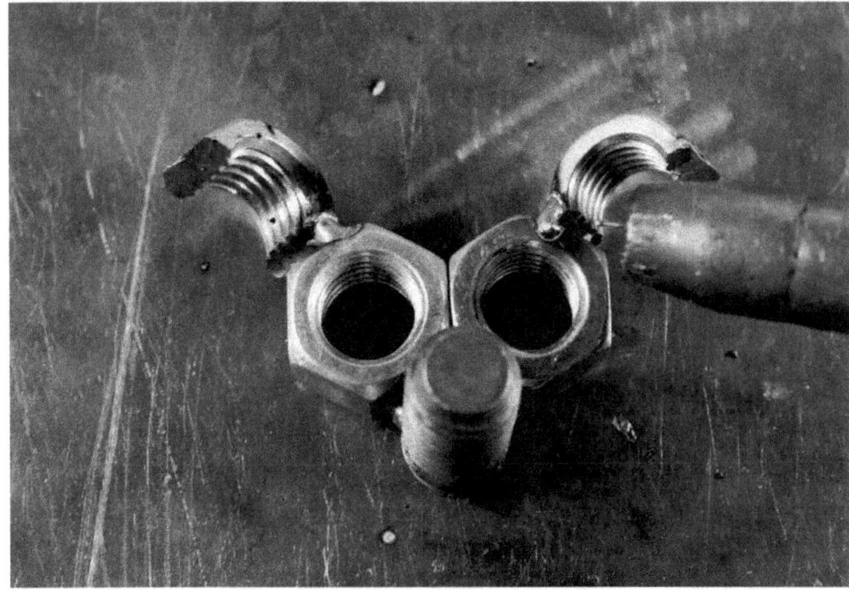

Tack weld the ears on the eyes.
Deburr any sharp edges.

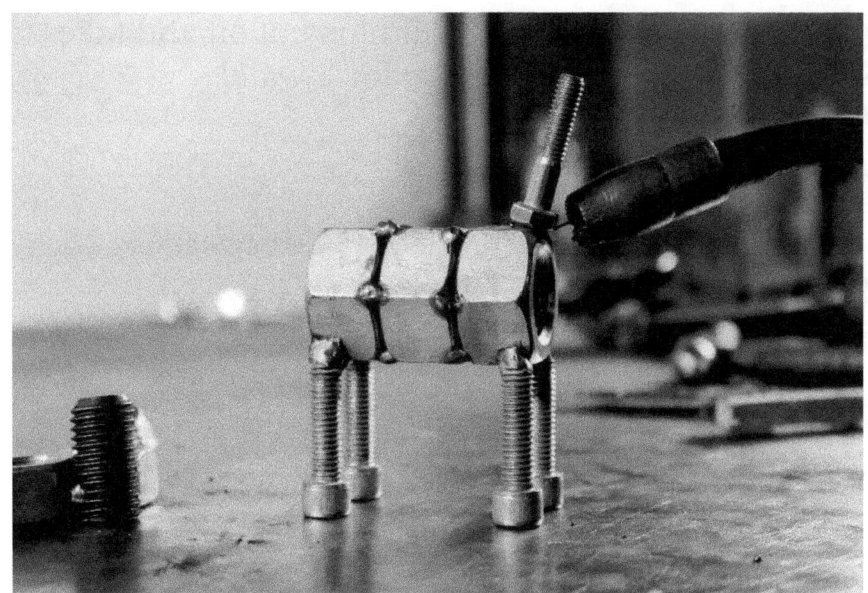

Tack weld the neck bolt (what are weld welding here Frankenstein?) onto the body.

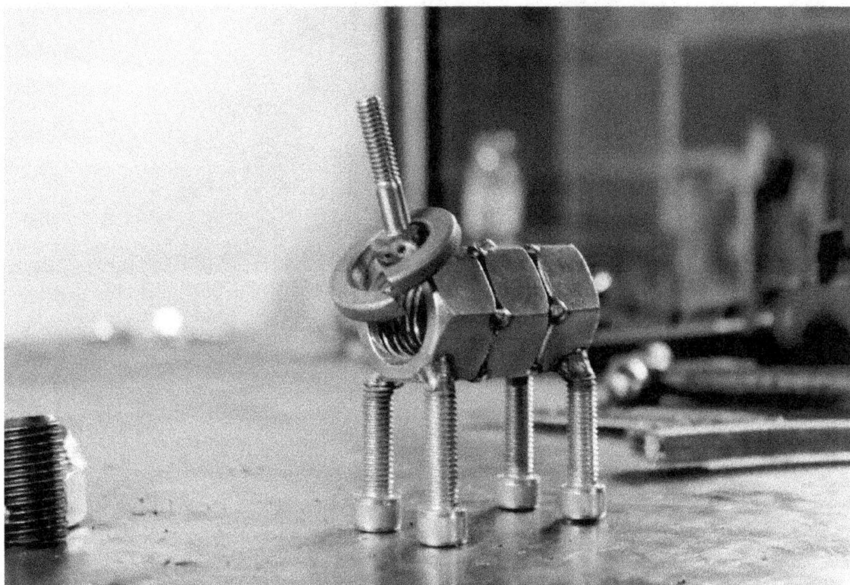

Place the collar on the neck.

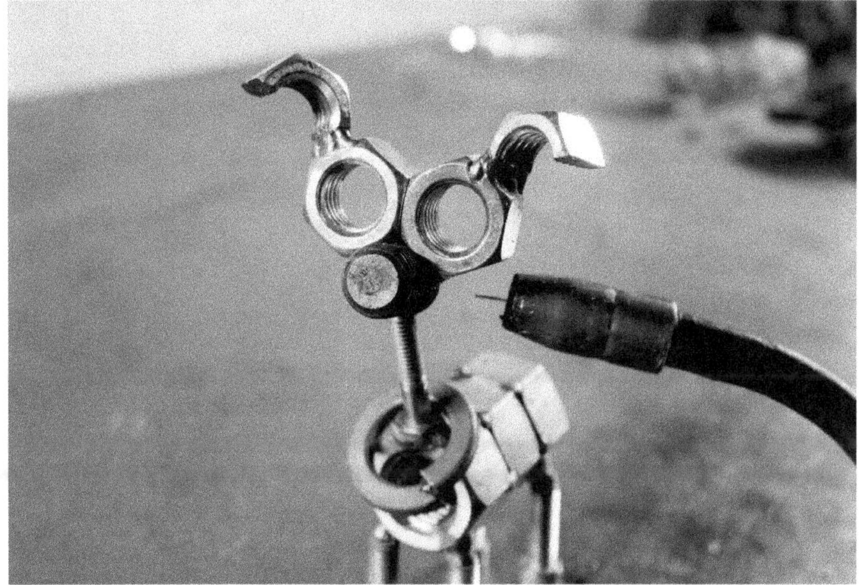

Weld the head on theneck.

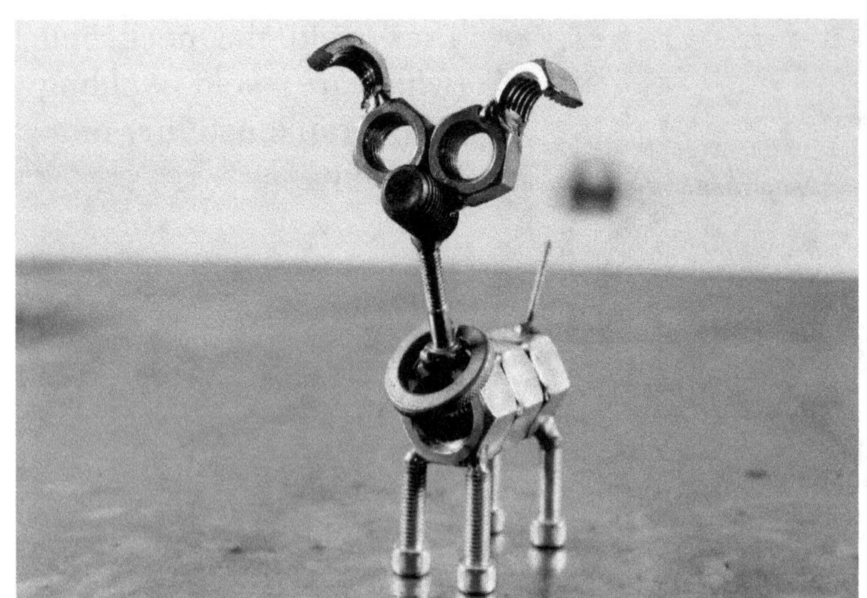

Weld his tail on and take him for a walk!

Bulldozer

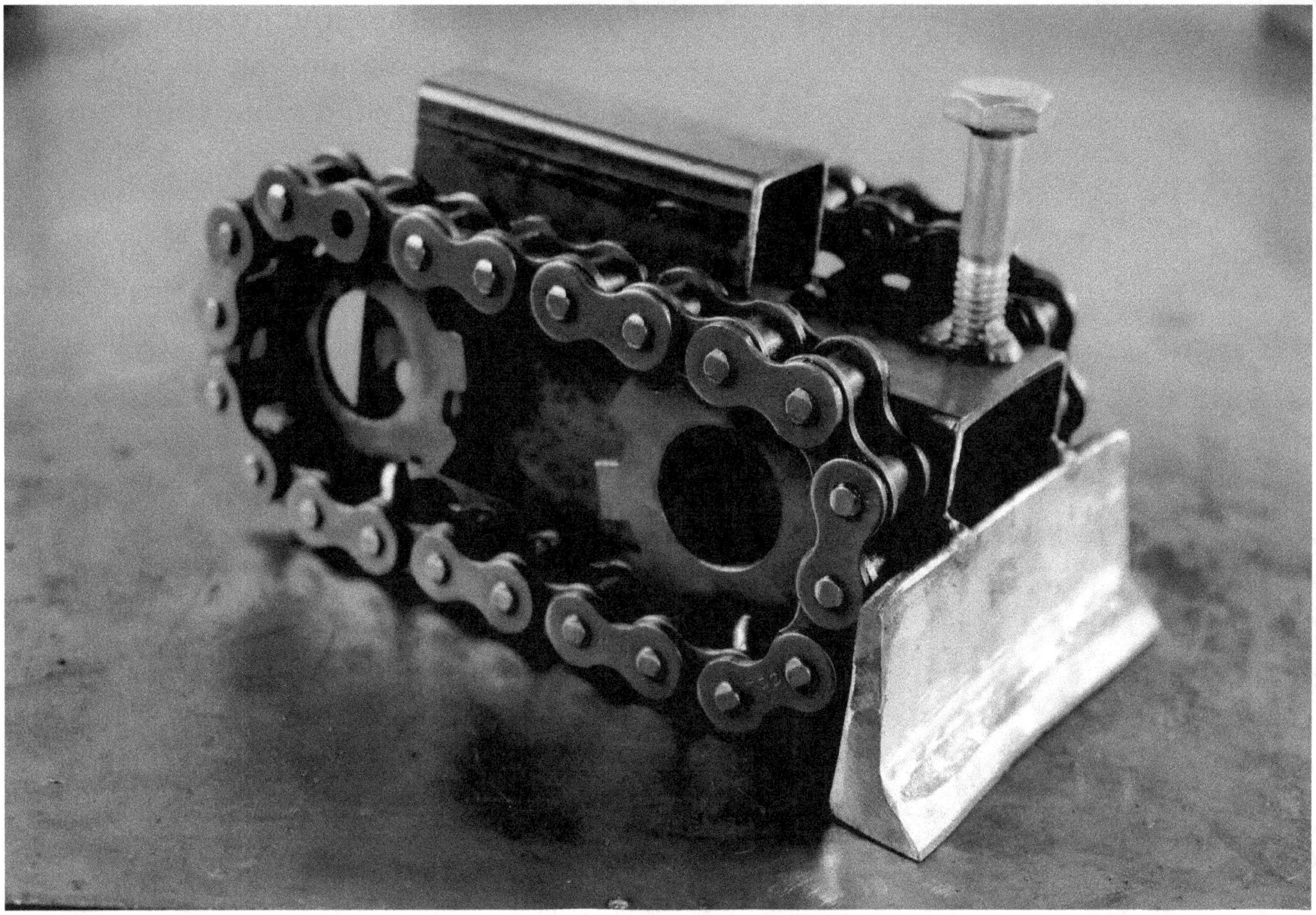

Difficulty

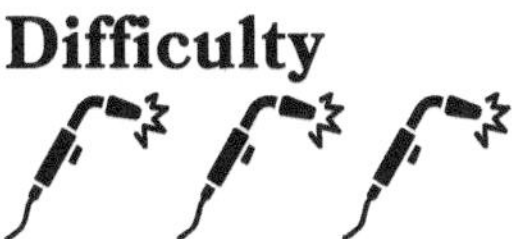

Materials

Square tube 1 large piece 5" long and 1 small piece 3" long
Angle iron 5"long
4 Washers, gears or nuts
2 pieces of medium chain for the track over the wheels
1 Bolt

Tools

Hammer and chisel
Wire brush
Grinder with cut off wheel and sanding disk

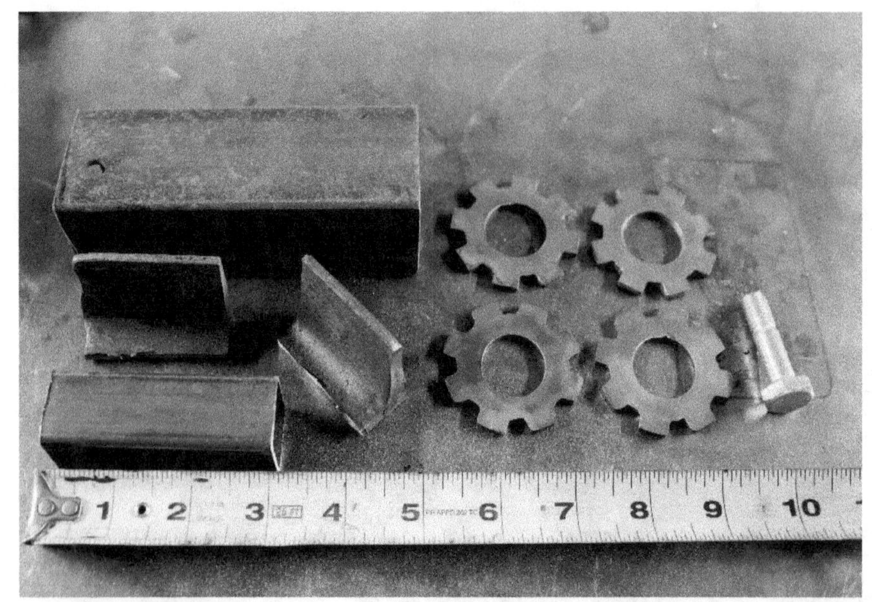

To make my bulldozers blade I welded two pieces together and ground it to look like one piece. You're an artist, if what you want is not available, make it yourself!
Clean any rust from your pieces with a wire brush.

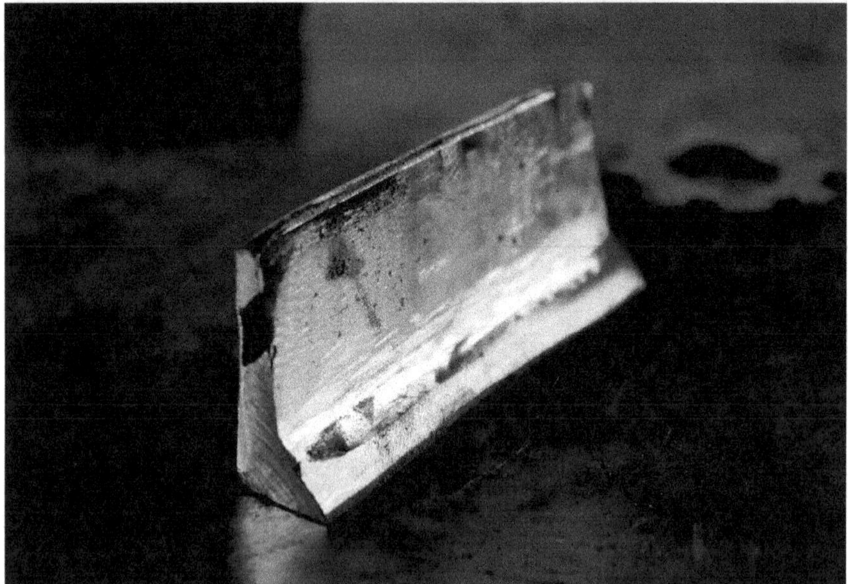

Cut one side of your angle iron down to 1/2" from the angle

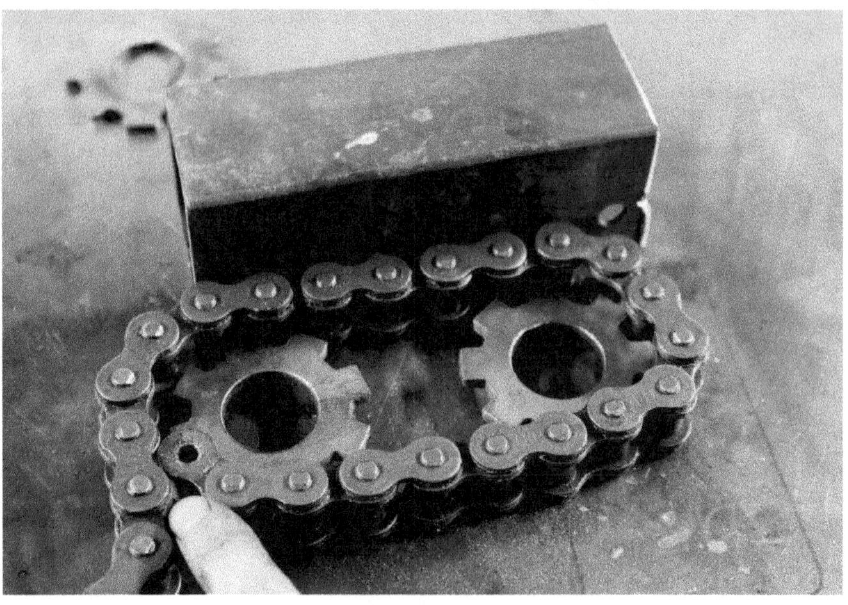

Measure how long the chain will need to beto wrap around both tires. Cut your chain witha chain break or grindthe pin down to the linkand hammer the pin outwitha punch.
Repeat for the otherside.

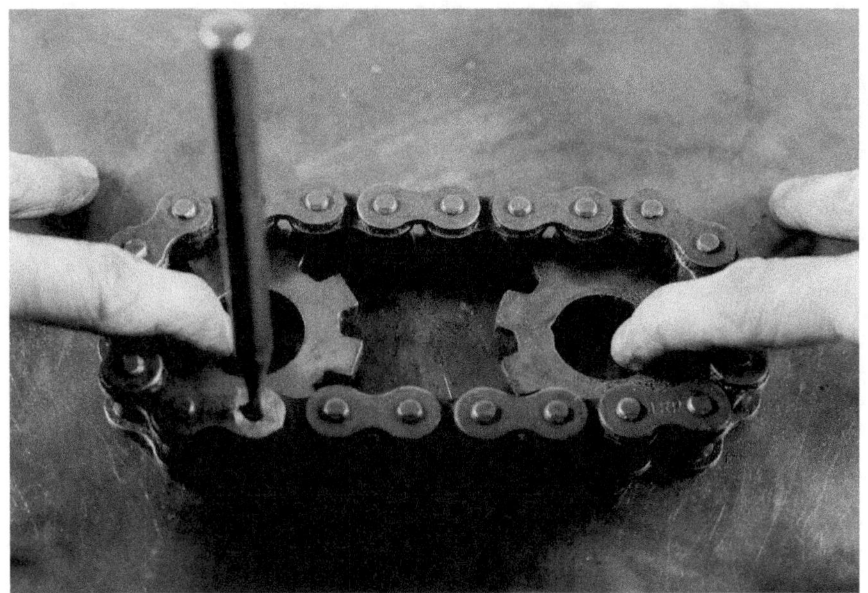

Place the two washers inside your chain, place a punch in the hole where the two chains meet and pull the chain outward to tighten it.

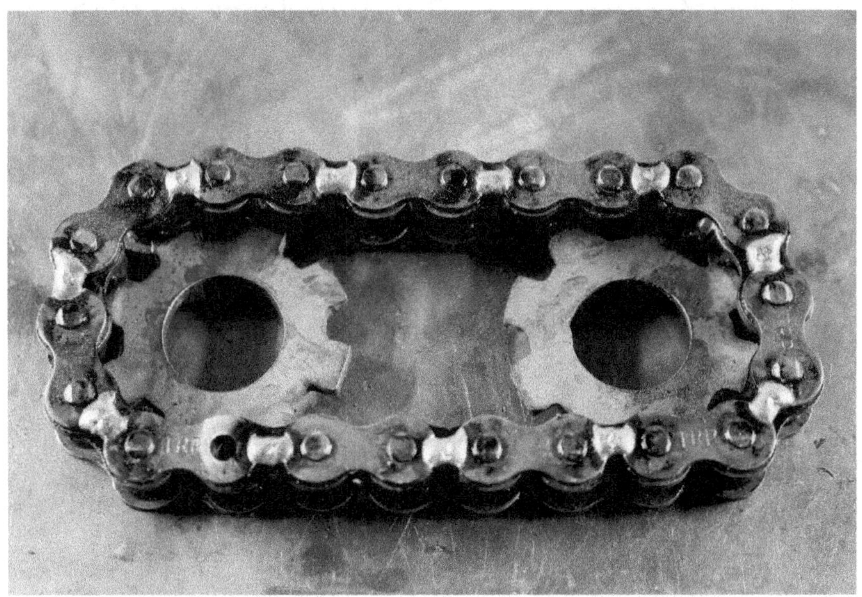

Weld each chain link to the link next to it.

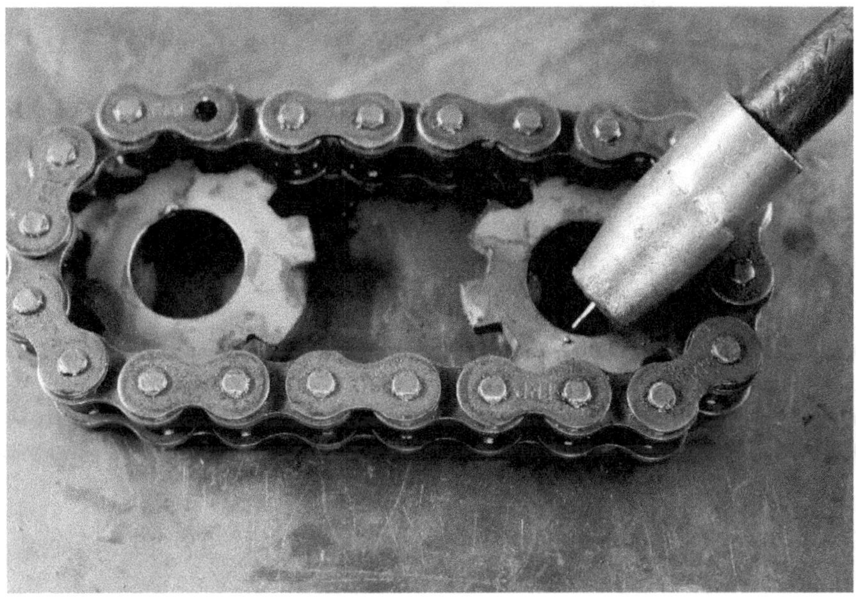

Flip your track over and weld the tires inside making sure they are as far out to each end as possible.

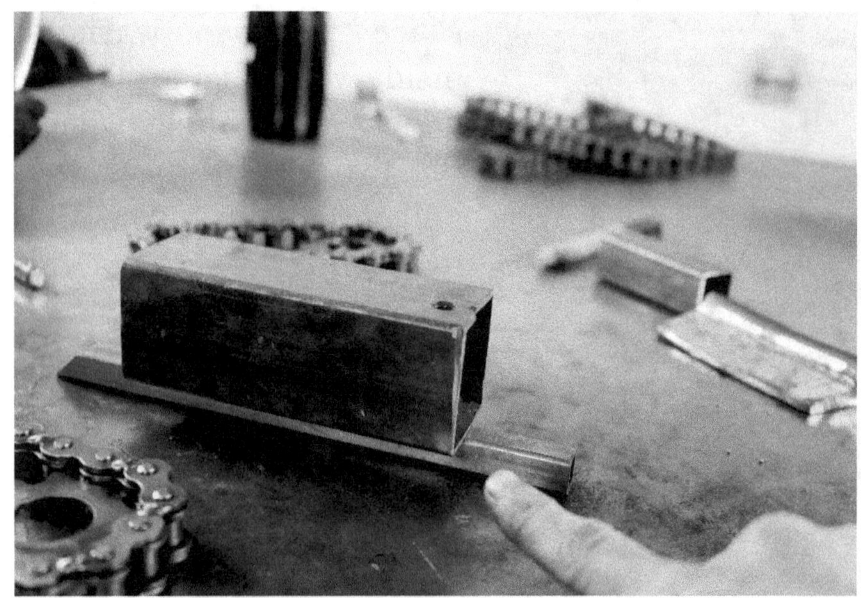

Place the large piece of square tube on something that is 1/2” tall

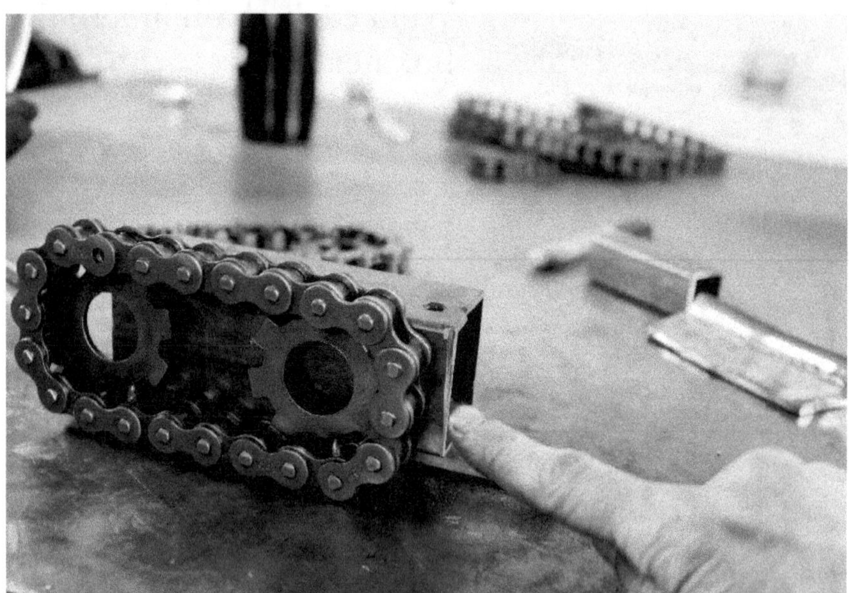

Stand the track up to the large piece of tube. Leave 1/2” at the front of the tube to make sure the track doesn’t interfere with the blade. Tack weld the track to the body top and bottom.

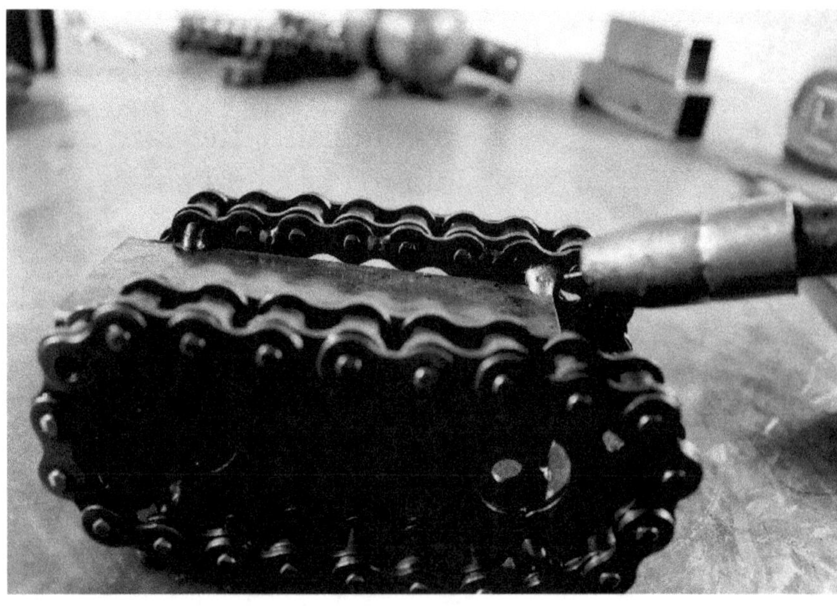

Repeat with the other side keeping the track 1/2” back from the front of the tube.

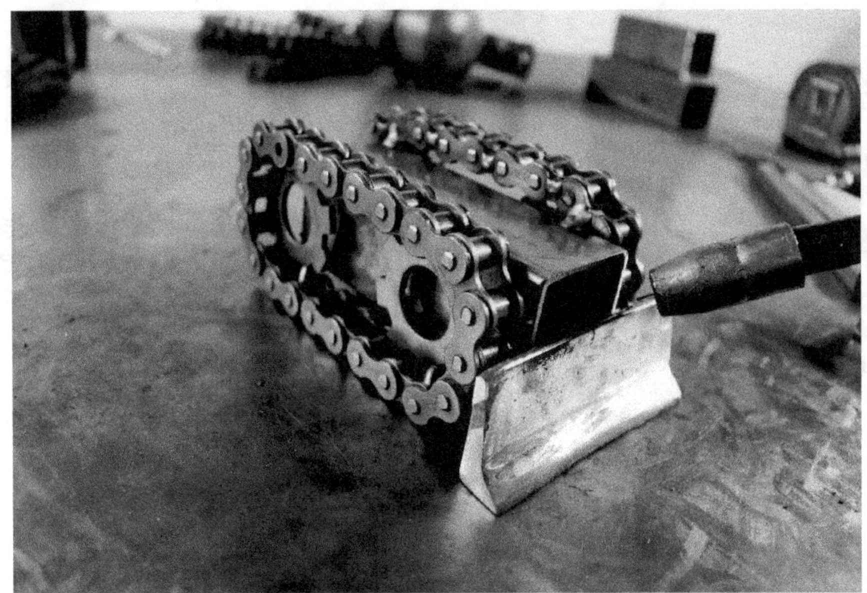

Center the blade on the front and weld it in place with one tack weld on each side top and bottom.

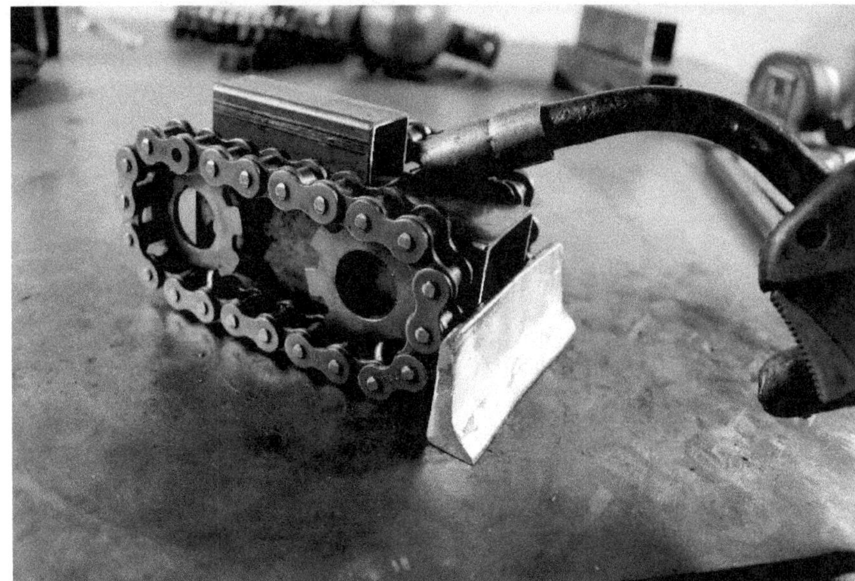

Center the cab at the back of the bulldozer and weld it in place with one tack weld at each corner of the square tube.

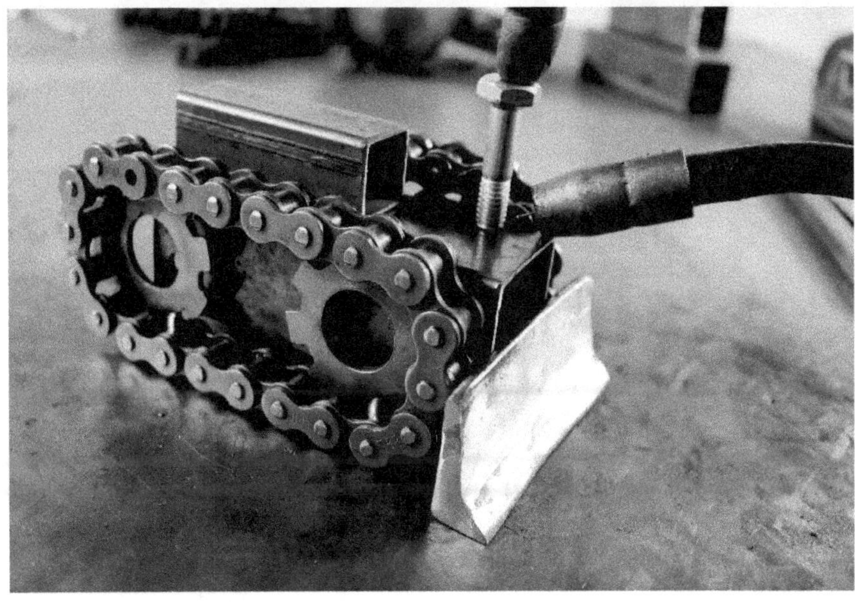

Hold the bolt in placeto the left or right of thecab and tack weld it in place.

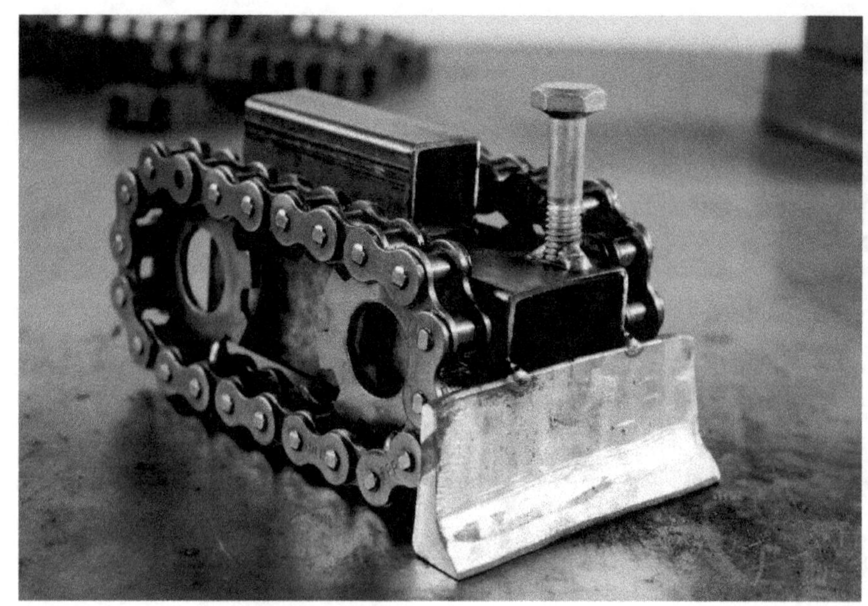

Clean your welds with a wire brush and chip any spatter with a hammer and chisel. Finish your dozer by painting or using a clear coat made for metal.

Candle Holders

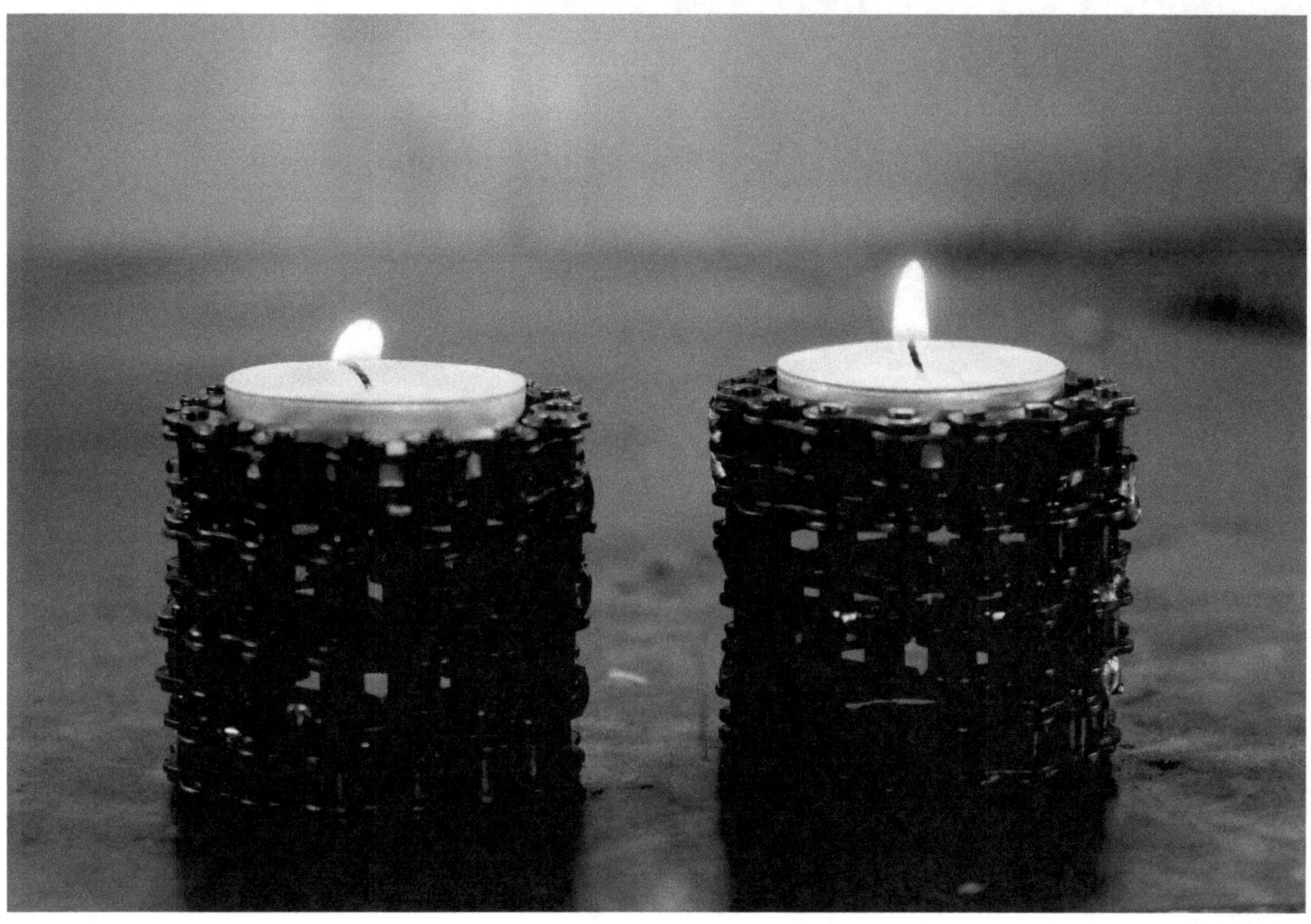

Difficulty

Materials

Chain small or large

Piece of steel for inside for the candle to sit on (I used a butter knife blade. You can coil up chain to weld inside or use any number of objects for this.

Tools

Hammer

Chisel

Punchorchain breakertool

Wire brush

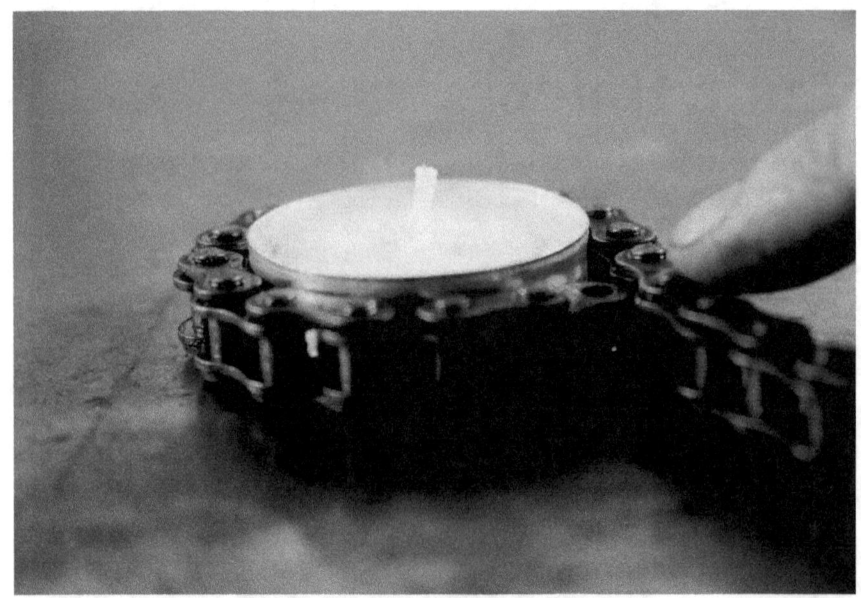

Wrap the chain around the candle to get the length and mark the link that will have to be broken.
I used tea candles, but you can do this with any size or shape candle.

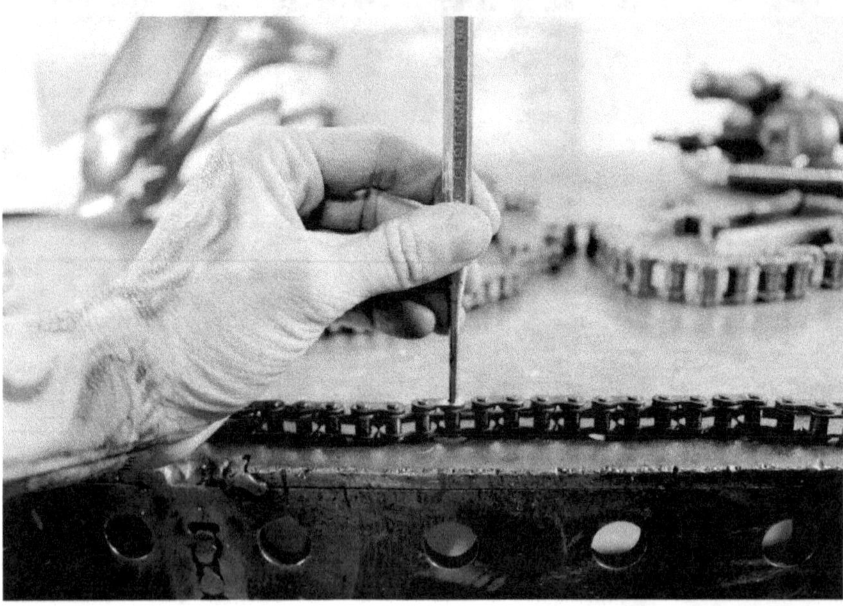

Break the chain with a chain breaker tool or grind the pin down to the link and then hammer the pin out with a punch.

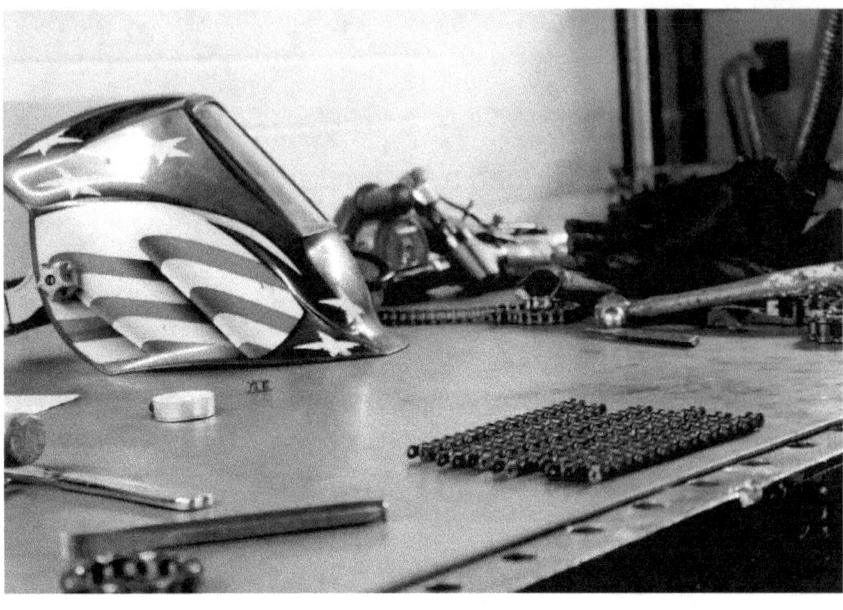

Choose how tall you would like your candle holders, I went with four chains high, and then break as many lengths of chain as you will need.

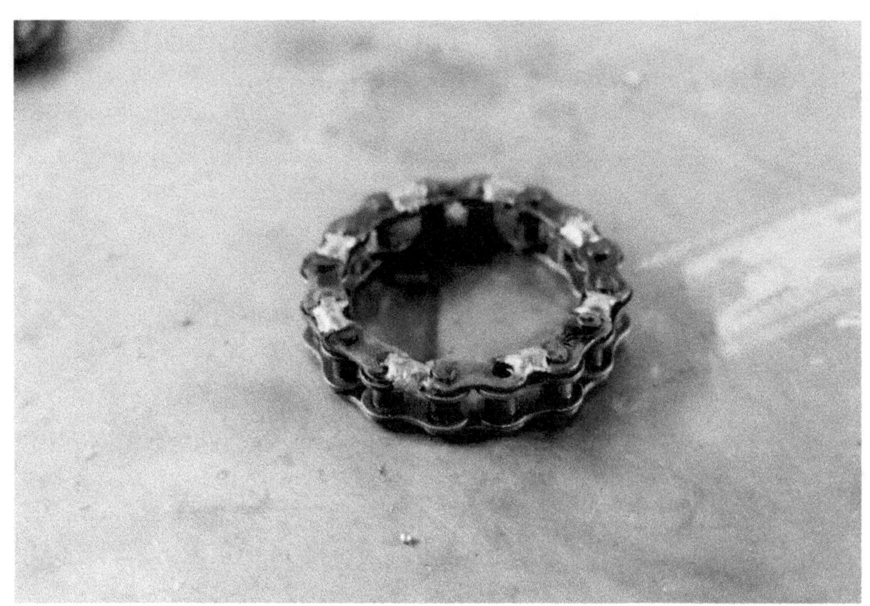

Weld all the chain pieces in the shape you are creating by tack welding each link to the link next to it.

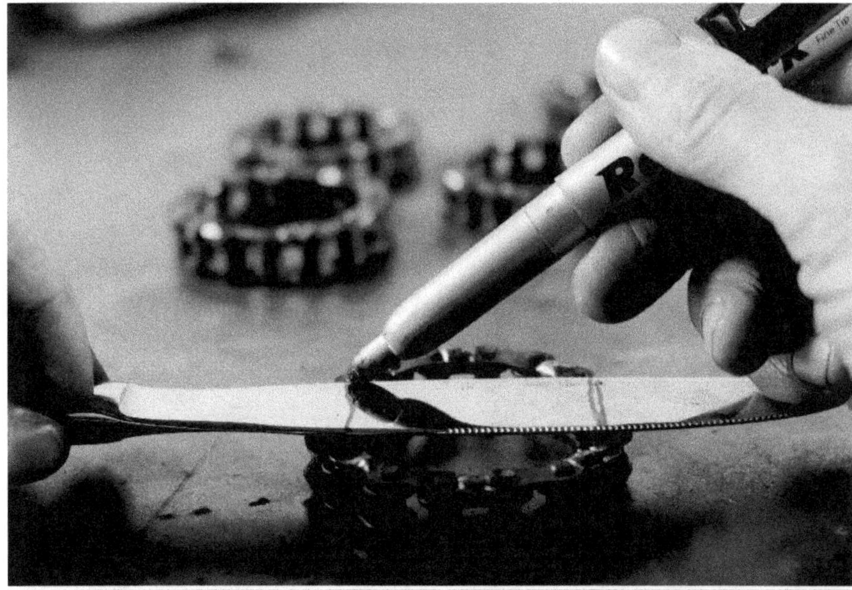

Mark and cut the piece of metal you will use for the inside of the holder for the candle to sit on.

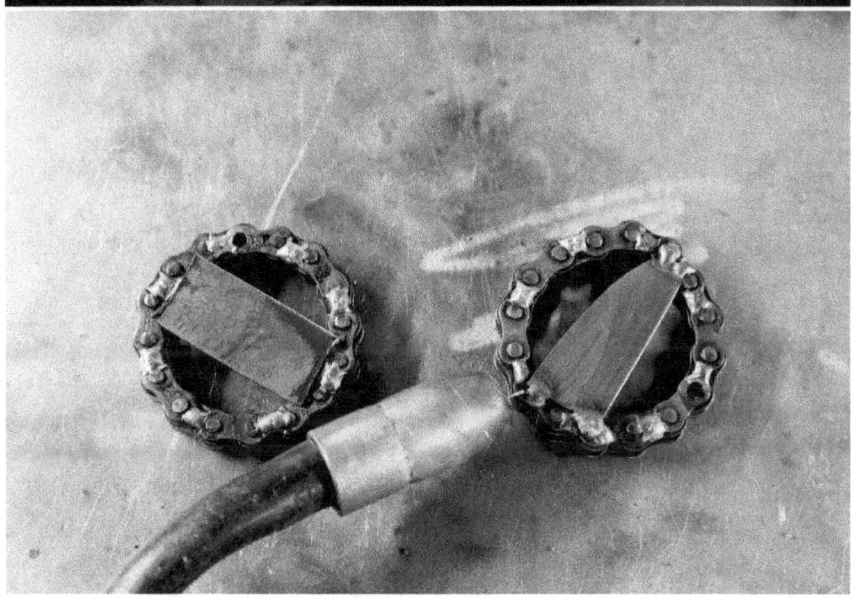

Tack weld them on.

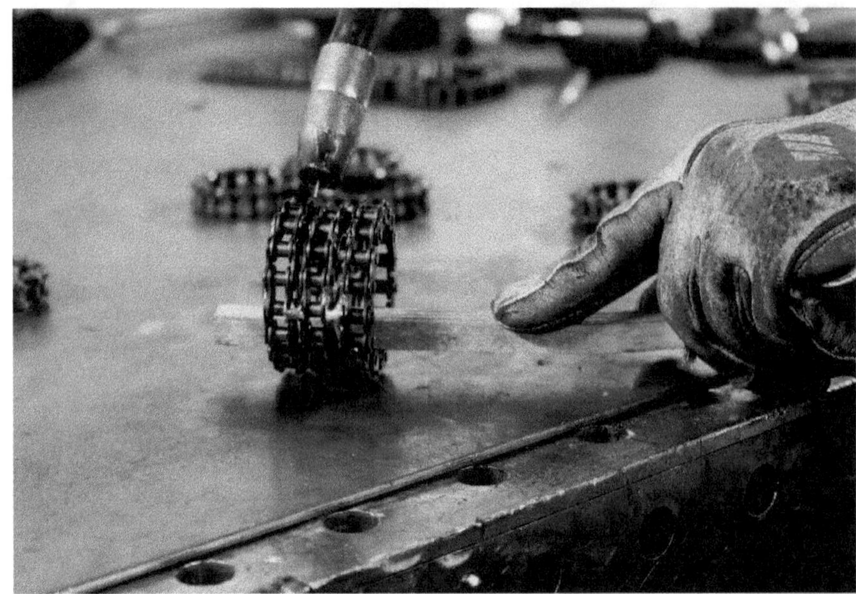

Tack weld your bottom layers together.

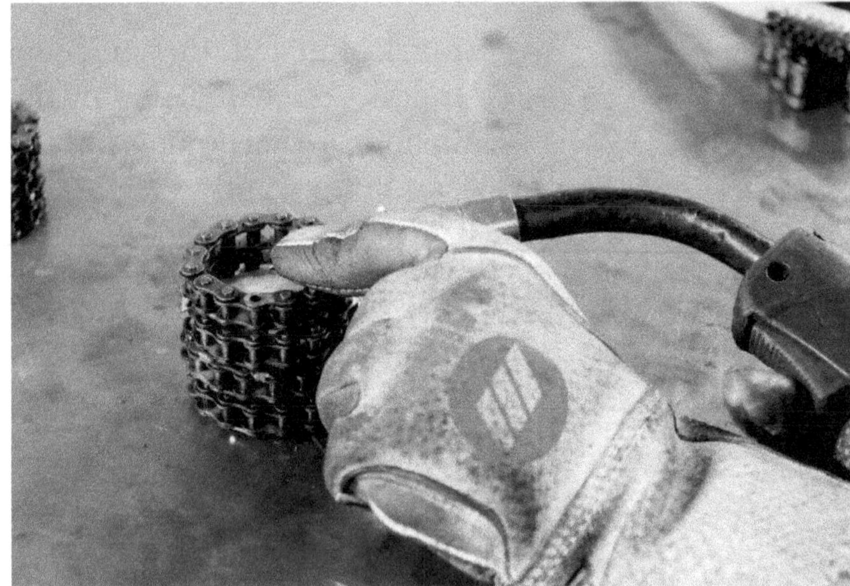

Tack weld your top layer on.

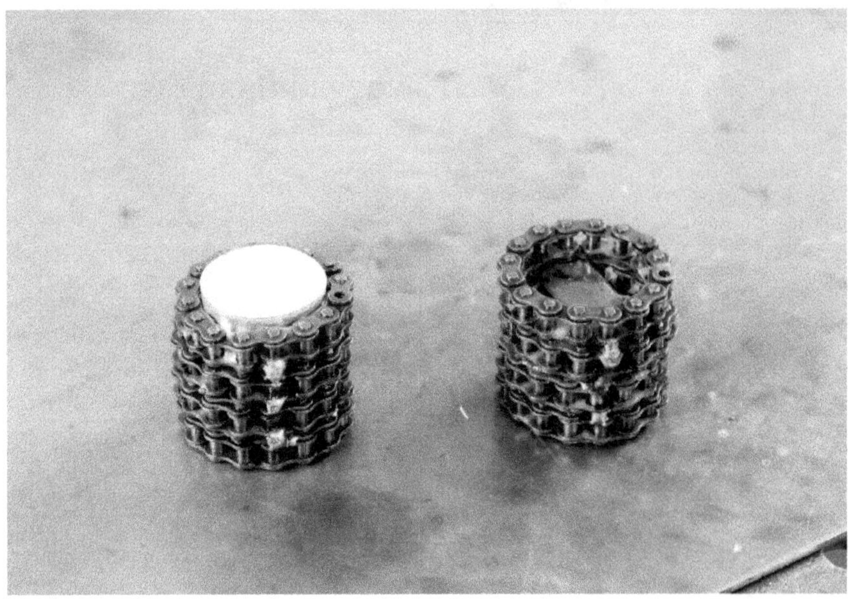

Clean with a wire brush and chip any spatterwith a hammer and chisel. Finish with paint orclear coat to prevent rusting.

Steampunk Bookends

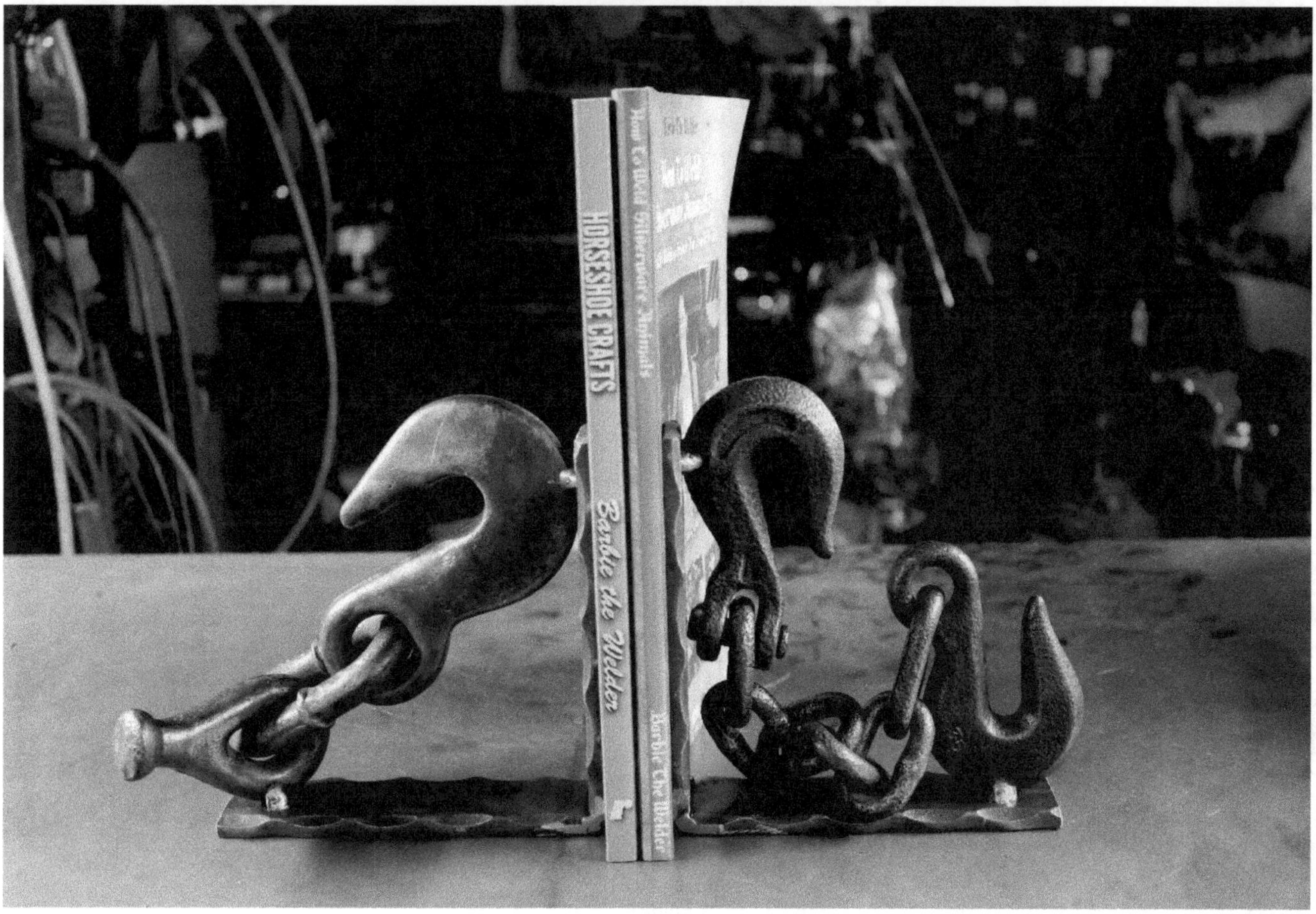

Difficulty

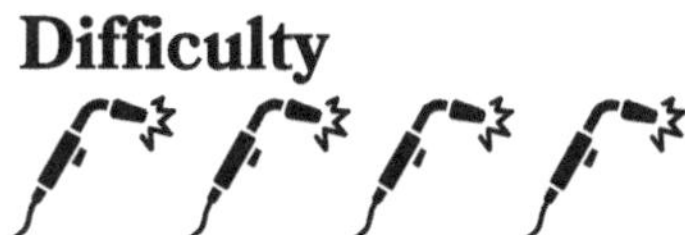

Materials

24” of flat stock 2” wide (I used left over ornamental, you can use plain flat stock and decorate it if you choose or you can take scrap angle iron and cut it into flat stock.)

Vintage tools, chain, gears, anything old and rusty you love the look of, keeping in mind that you will need enough weight to hold up books.

Tools

Grinder with sanding disk and cutoff wheel
Wire wheel or brush
Tape measure
Square

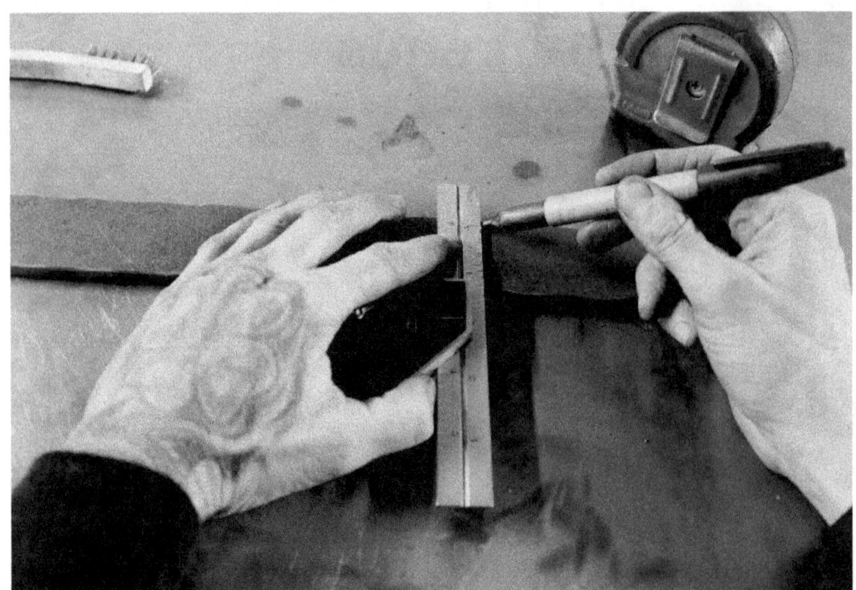

Use the tape measure and square and mark four pieces of flat stock 6” long. Clamp and cut the four pieces being careful to make your cuts straight.

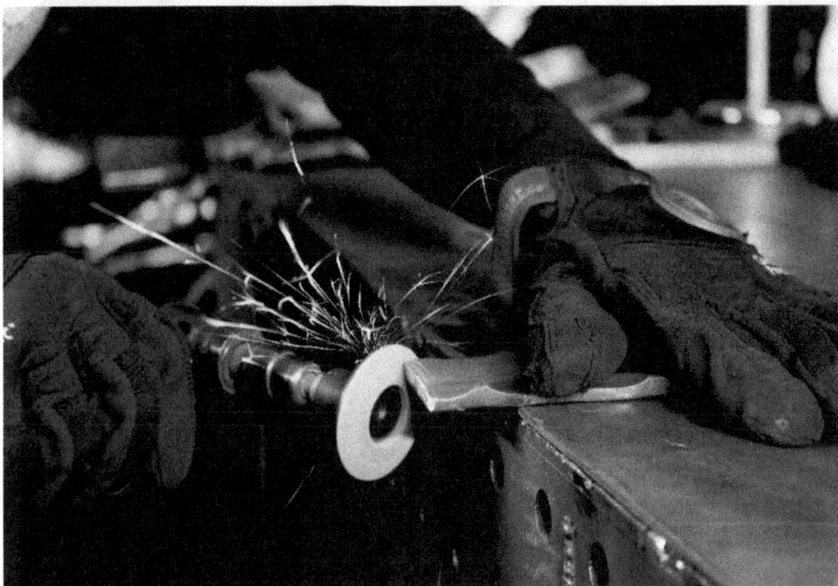

Smooth the cut edges.

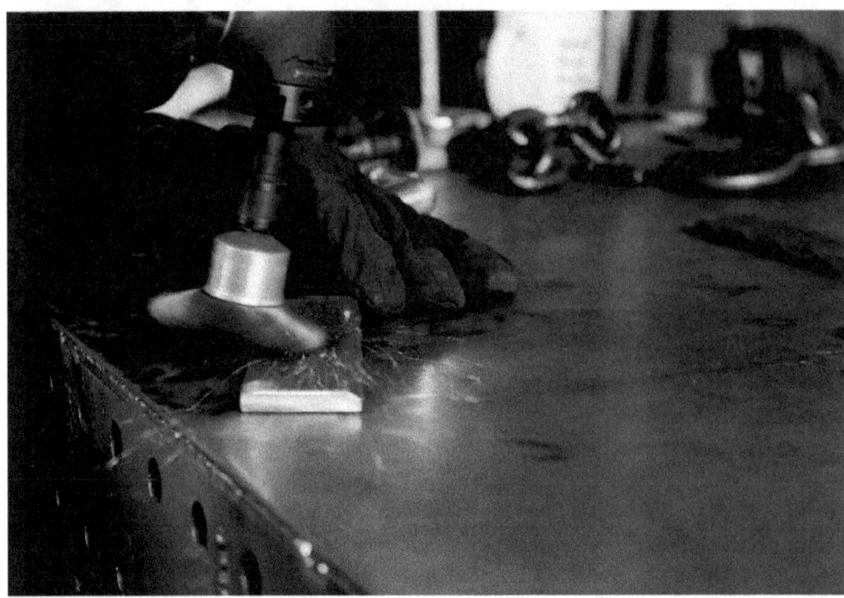

Clean your material with a wire wheel or cup brush.

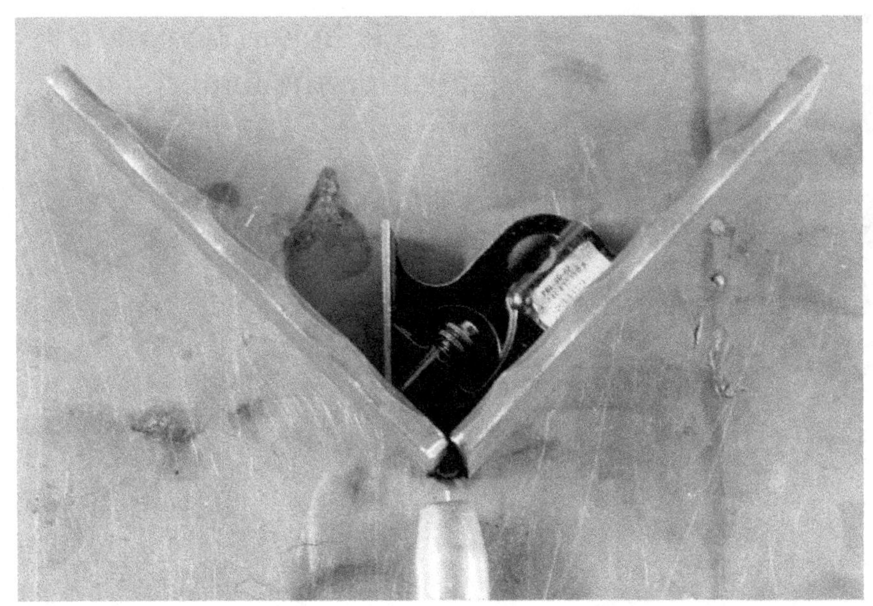

Using the square, hold two flat stock pieces corner to corner at 90 degrees and place one small tack weld at the top and bottom. Stand the piece up and make sure it is square to on the side and at the back. Adjust if necessary.

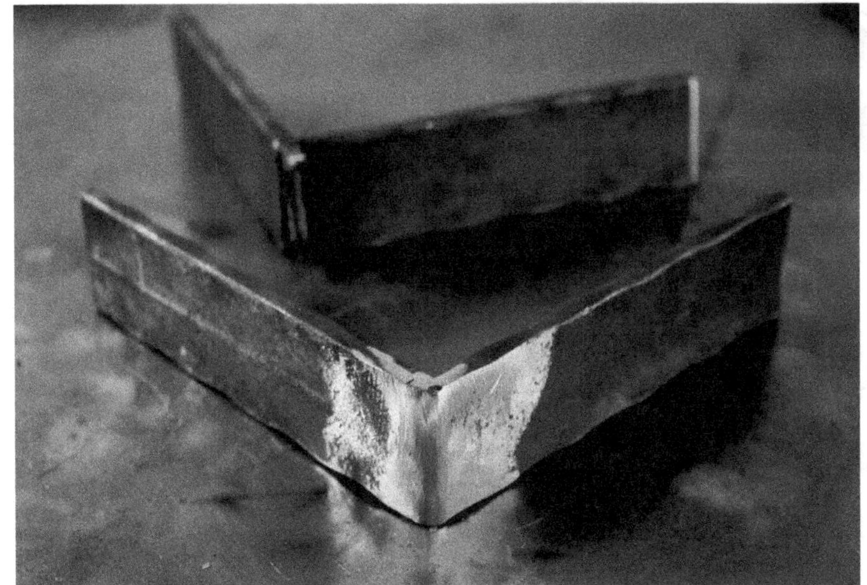

Weld the back and grind it smooth.

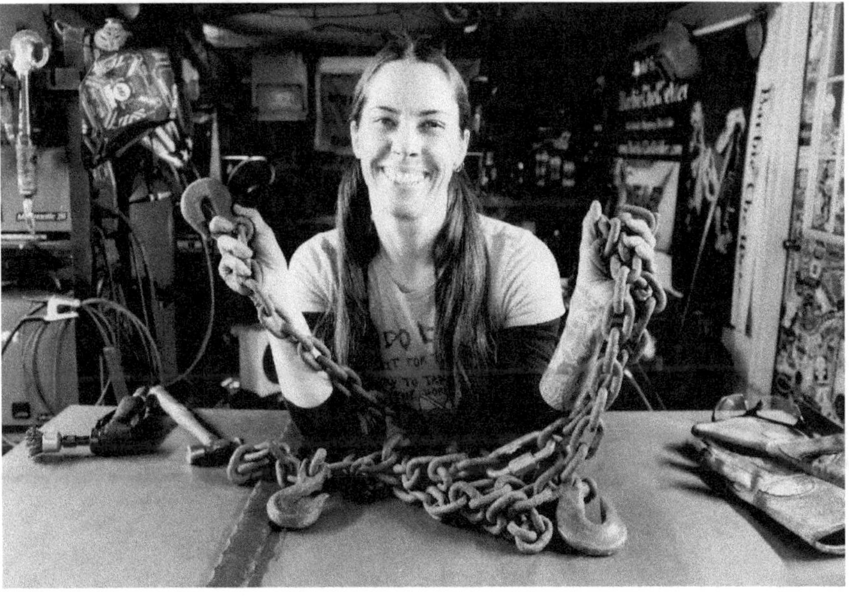

Prepare your material by cleaning any rust or paint with a wire wheel or cup brush.

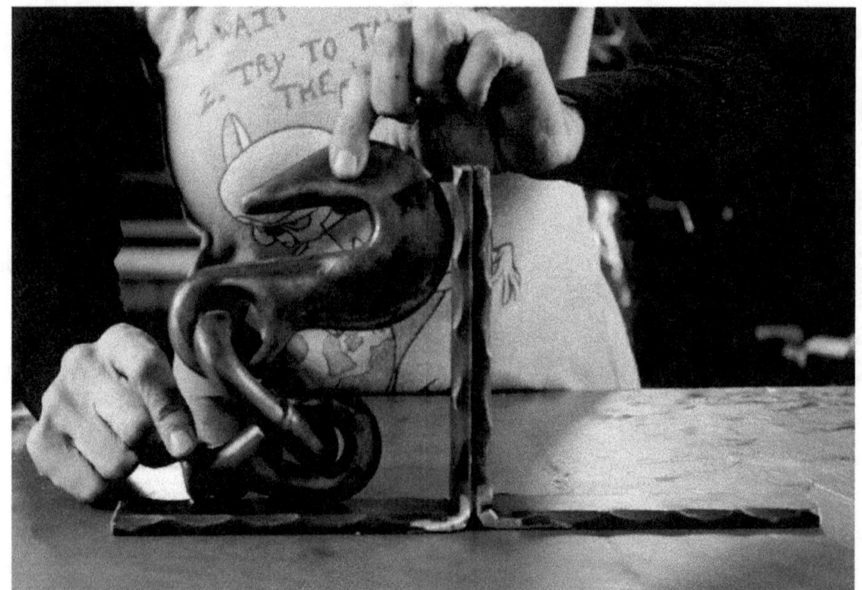

Decide how you want to position the material on the base.

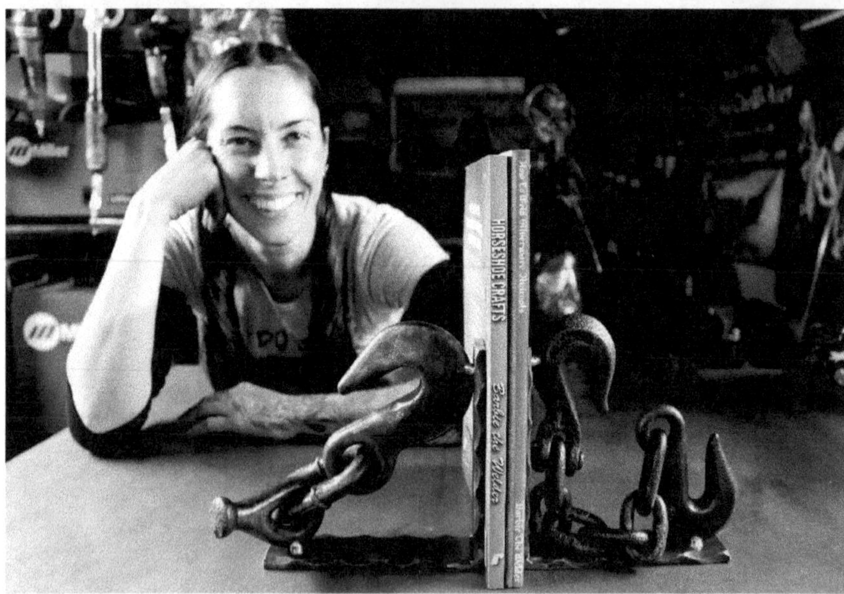

Tack weld the pieces securely to the base. Clean any weld discoloration and spatter. Finish with a clear coat spray to protect it from rusting.

Steampunk Whisky or Wine Rack

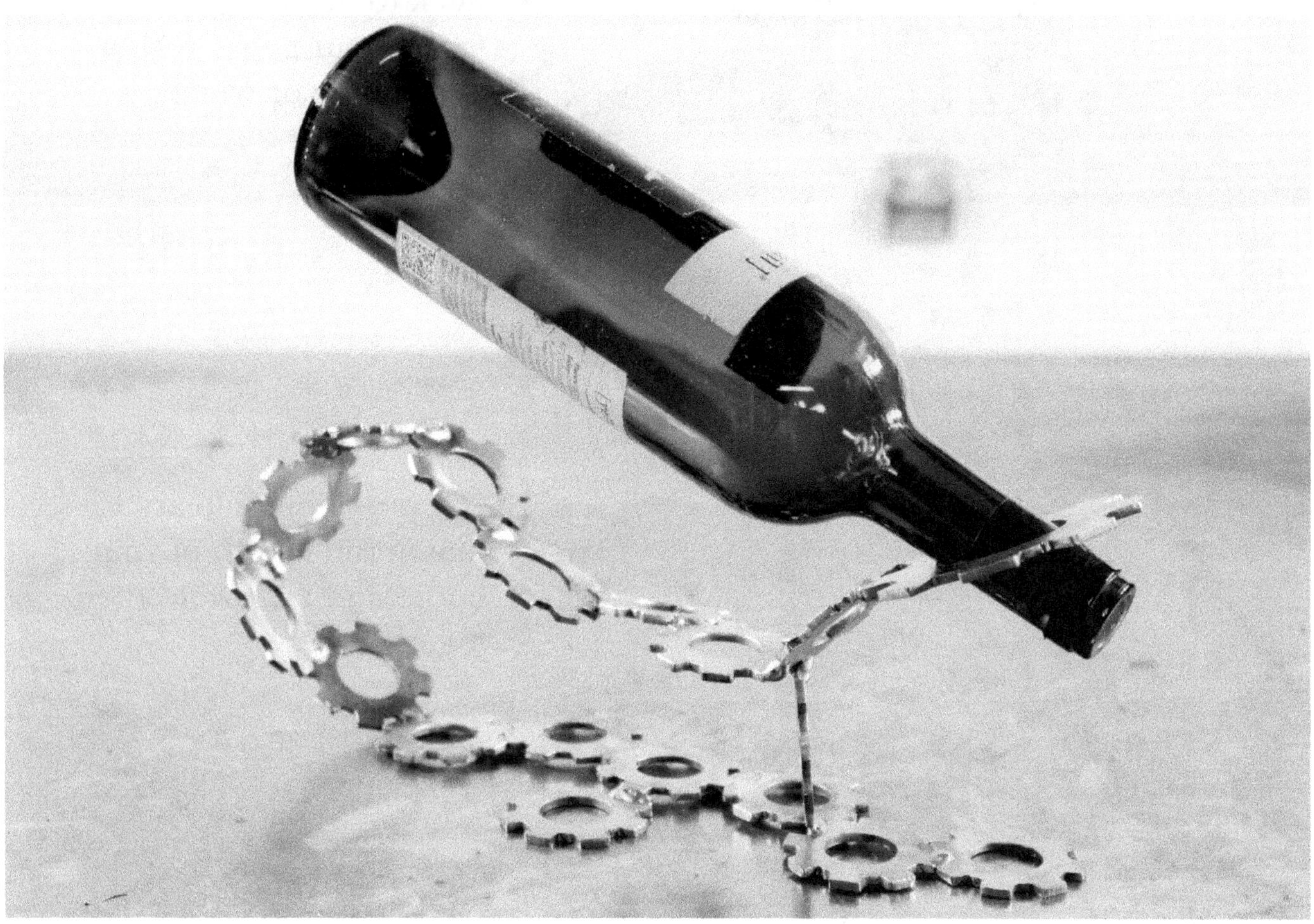

Difficulty

Materials
Gears with one being large enough for the bottle neck to fit through

Tools

Hammer and chisel
Bottle to check balance

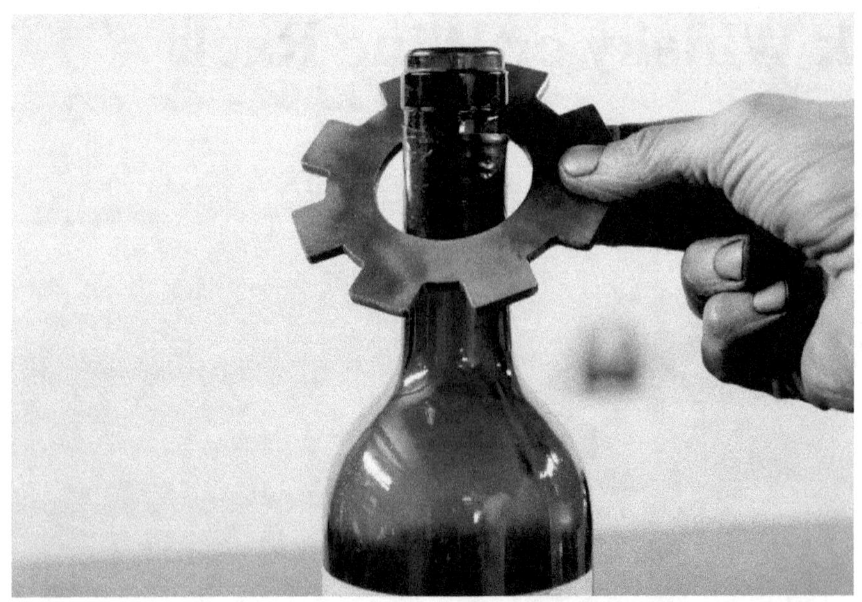

One gear must be large enough for the wine bottle neck to fit through. Clean your gears with a wire brush or wheel.

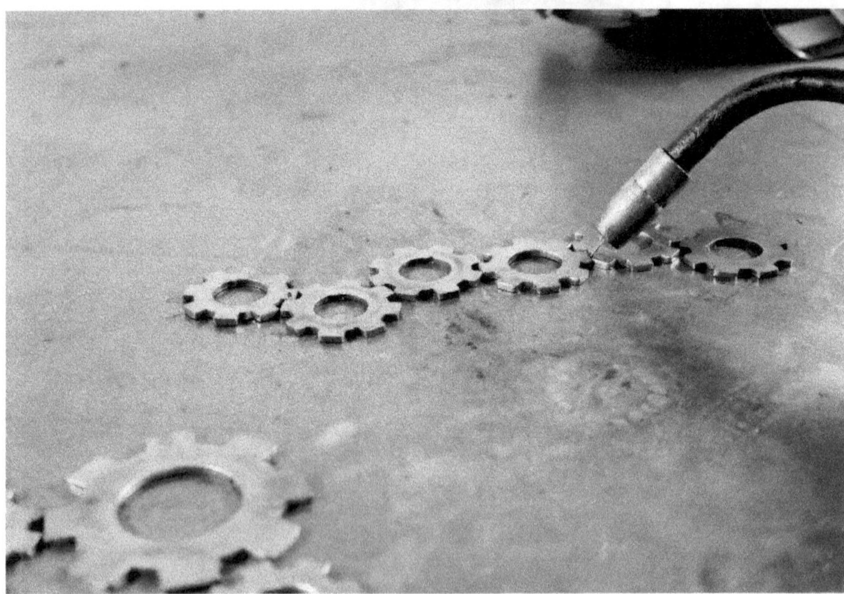

Lay out enough gears to match the length of your bottle and tack weld them together.

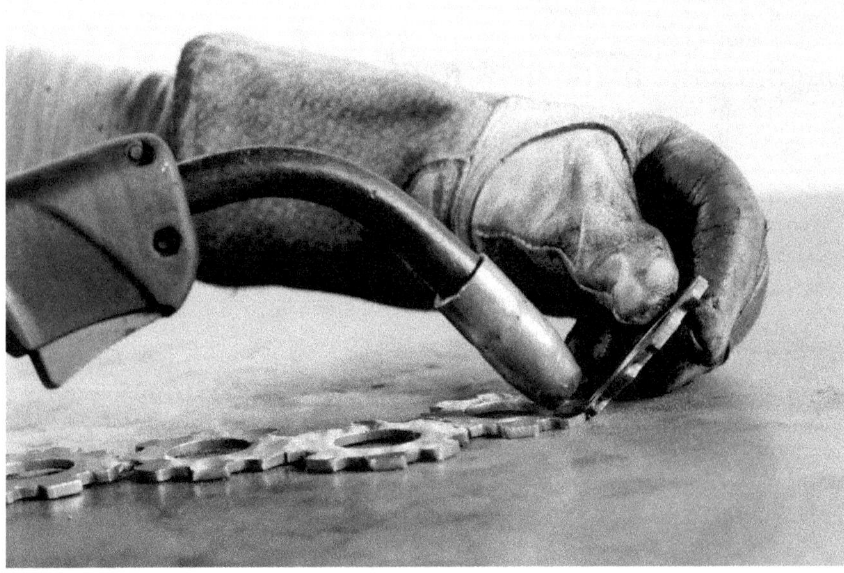

Hold a gear up at an angle and tack weld it

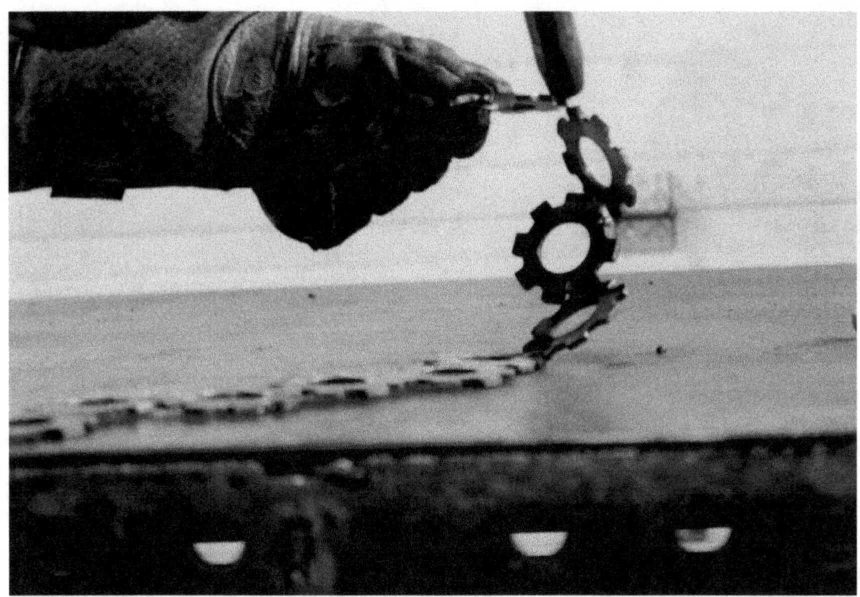

Continue welding gears up and around until you have them back over the base.

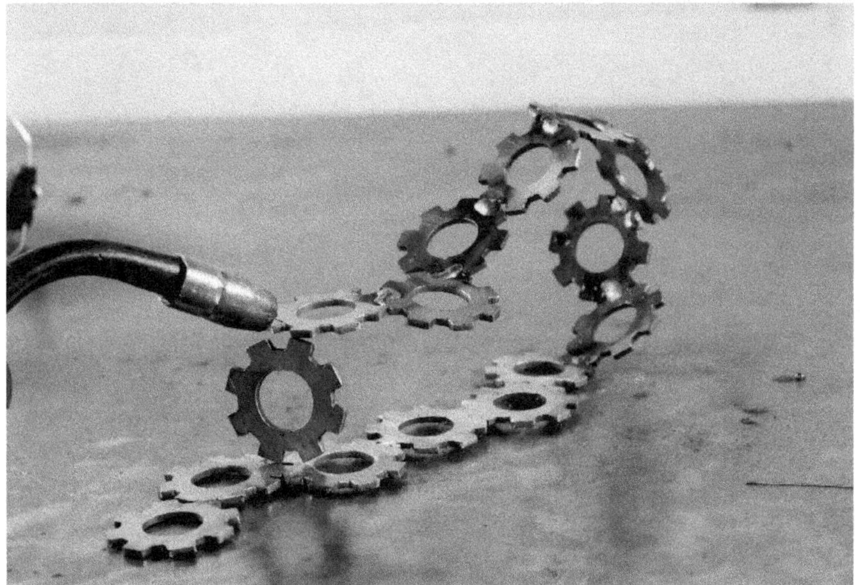

You may find it necessary to weld a gear from the top to the base to give it stability like I did.

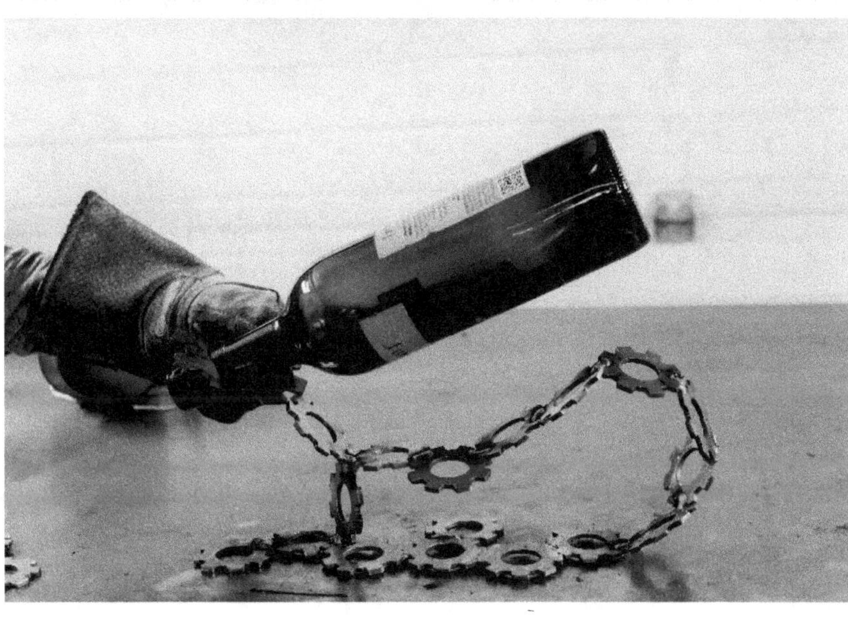

Check the angle the gear thatholdsthebottleneeds to be before you weld it. This prevents having to cut the gear back off because the bottle interfereswiththerack.(If my gearwasangleddown further the bottle would hit therack.)

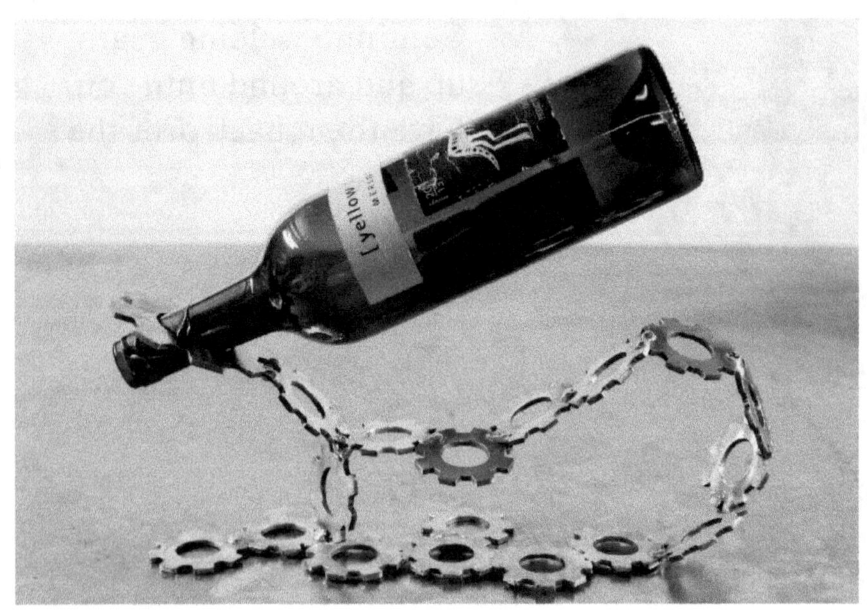

Clean any weld discoloration and ship any weld spatter.
Clear coat finish to prevent rust.

Pencil Holder

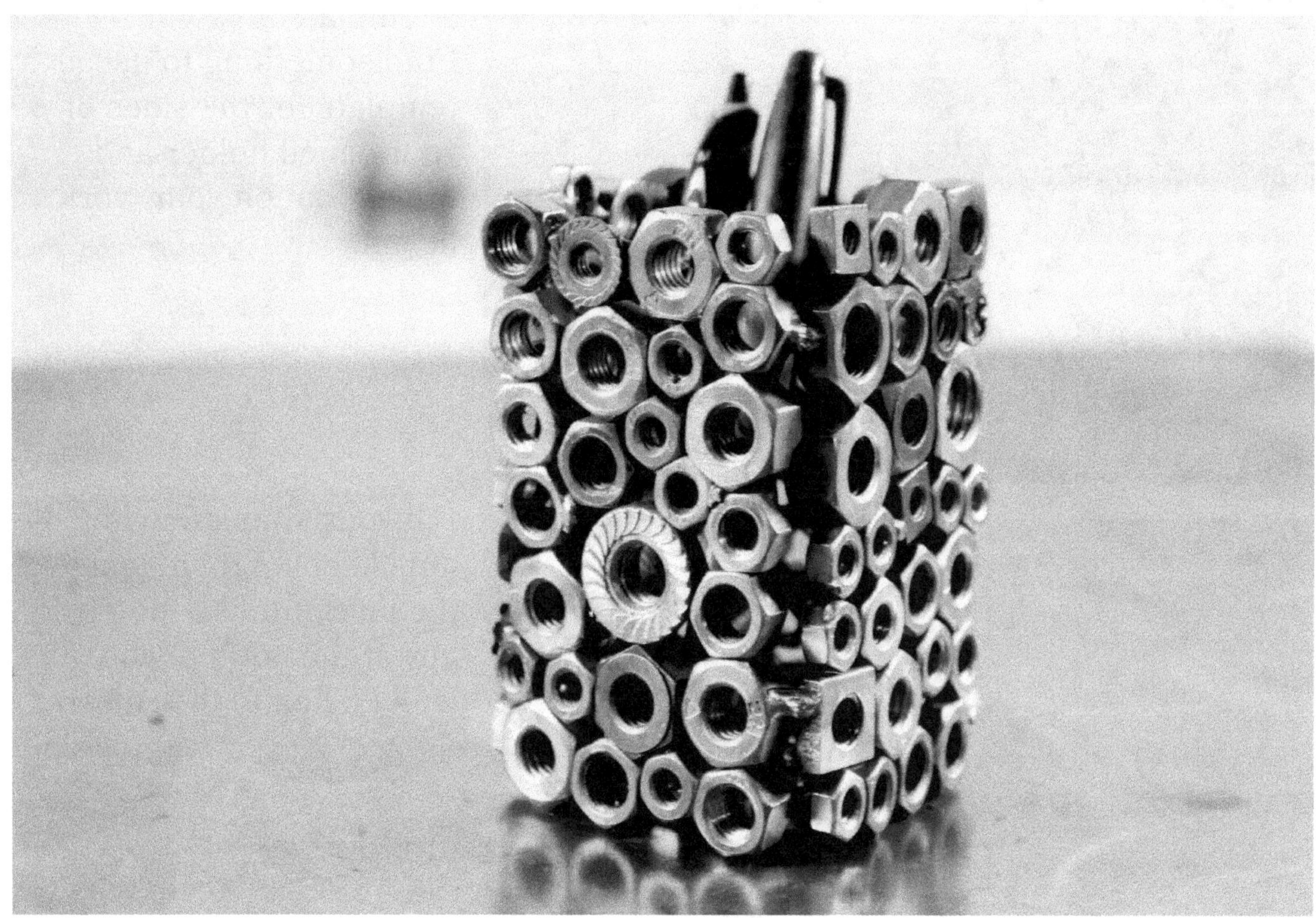

Difficulty

Materials

Nuts

Tools

Hammer and chisel
Wire brush
Something to use as atemplate for the sides

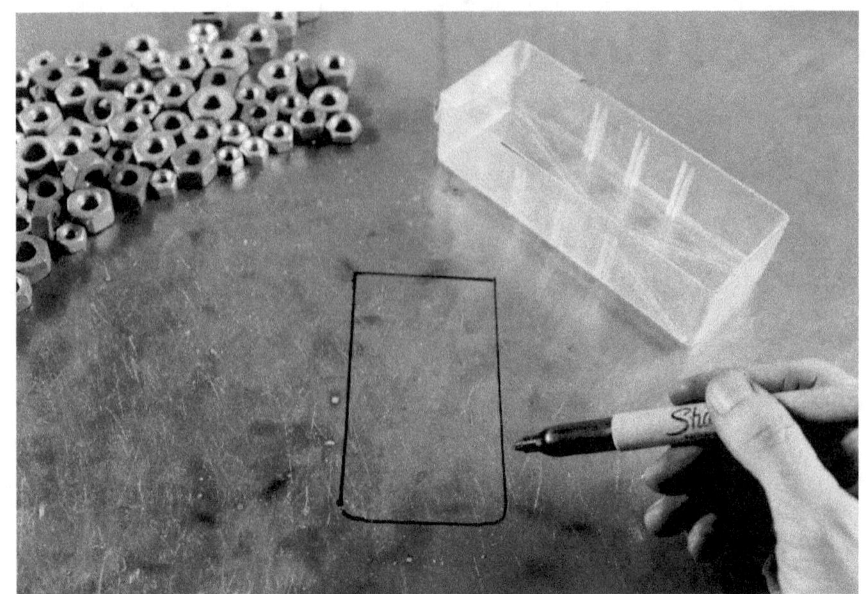

I used the little plastic bin the nuts were stored in as a template.
Find something to use as a template for the sides of your pencil holder and trace it out on your work bench.

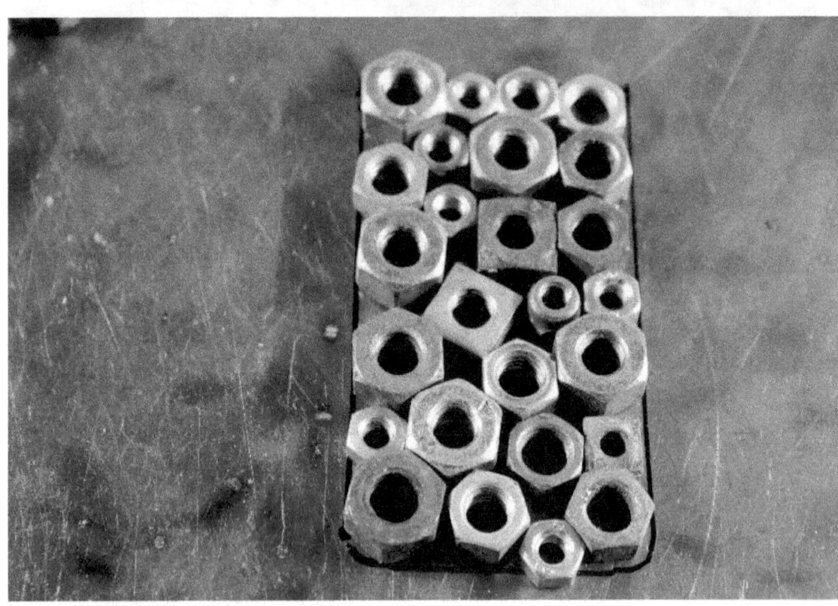

Fill your template with nuts keeping them inside the lines. (unlike that little guy at the bottom who won't listen to the rules!)

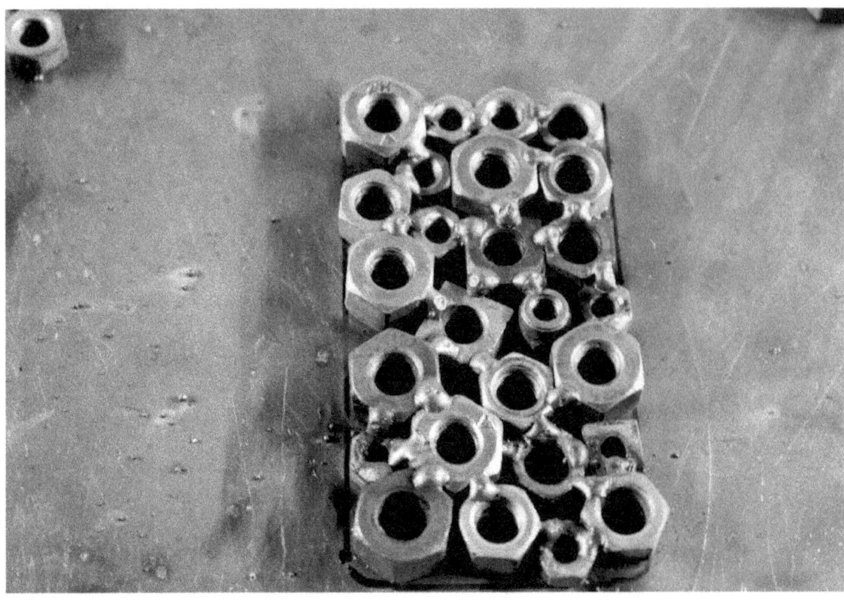

Tack weld everythingto everything.

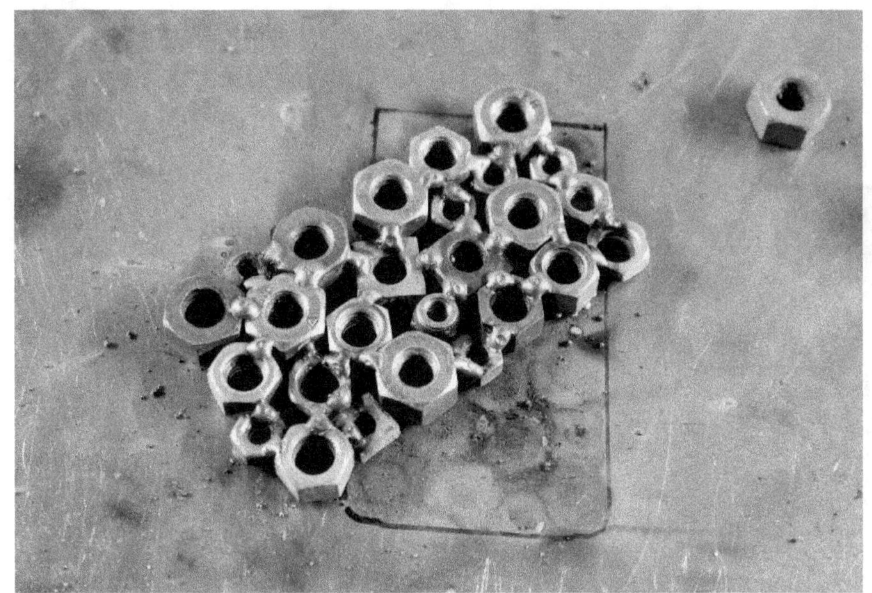

Repeat this step three more times until you have four sides.

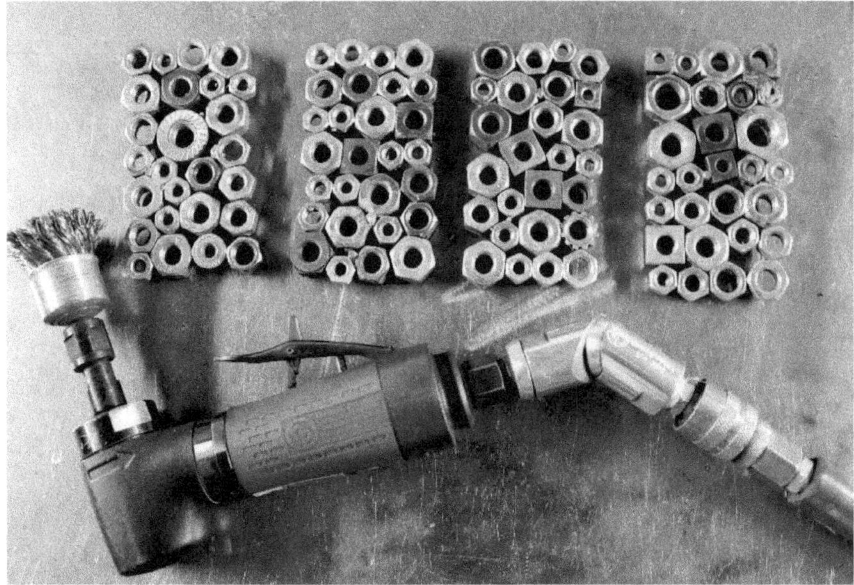

Clean the pieces with a wire brush and chip any weld spatter with a hammer and chisel.

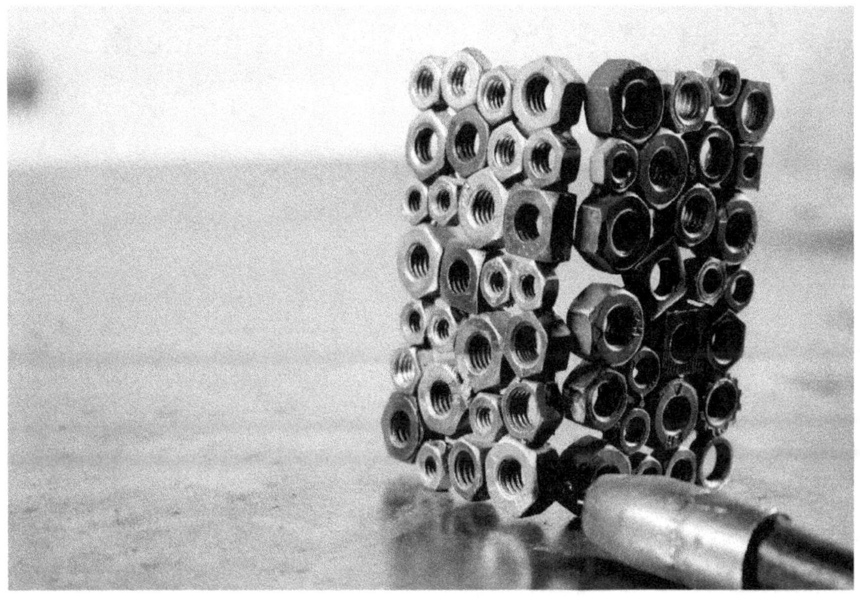

Stand two sides up at a 90 degree angle and tack weld them together corner to corner as shown.

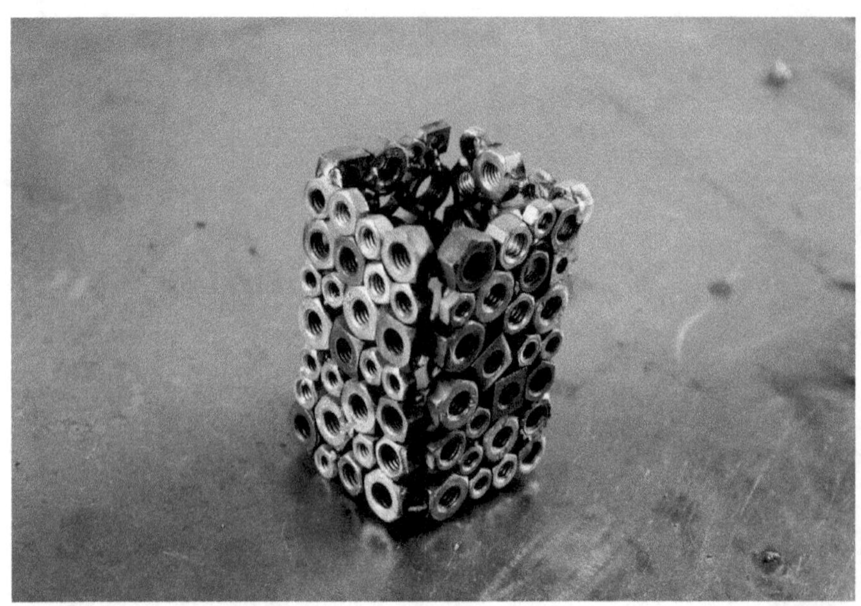

Tack weld the other sides on using light tack welds so that you can adjust the squareness of the box.

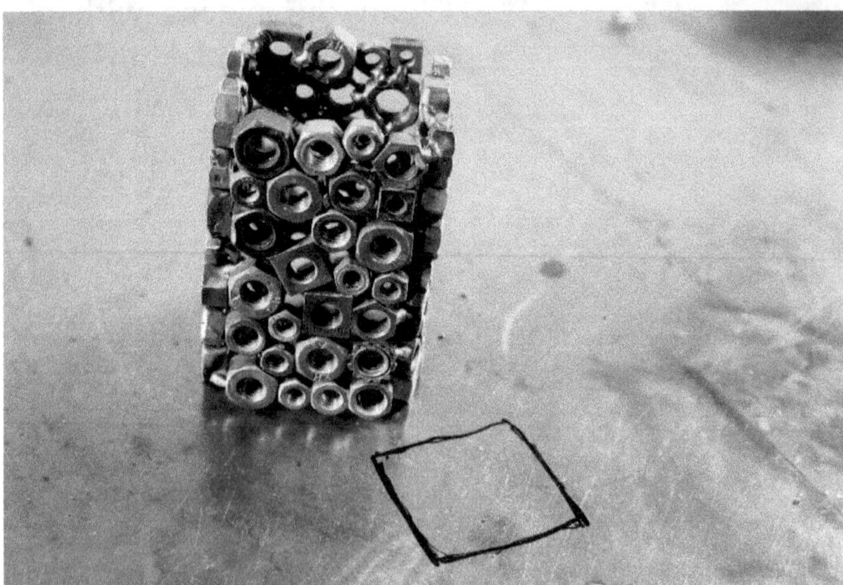

Check the squareness of the box and adjust if necessary.
Trace the inside of the box on your work bench.

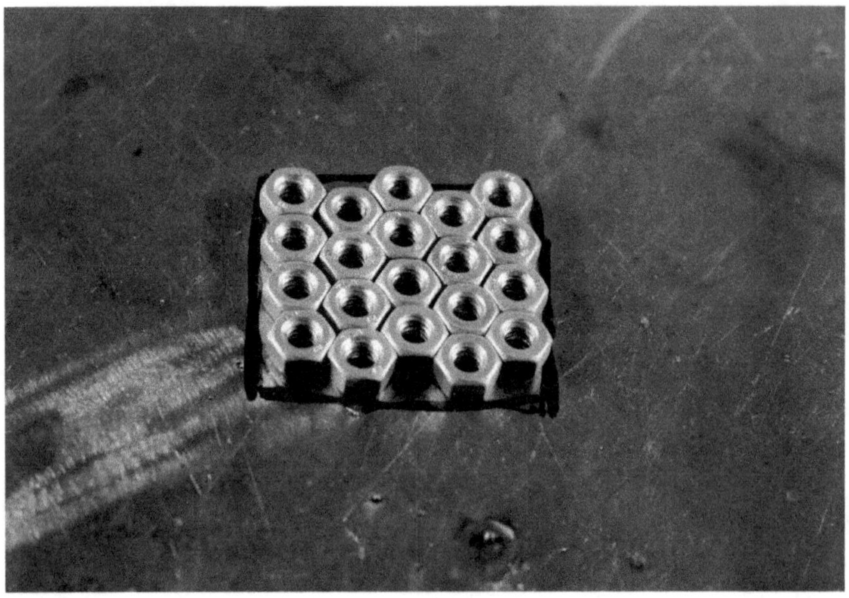

Lay out nuts inside the box.

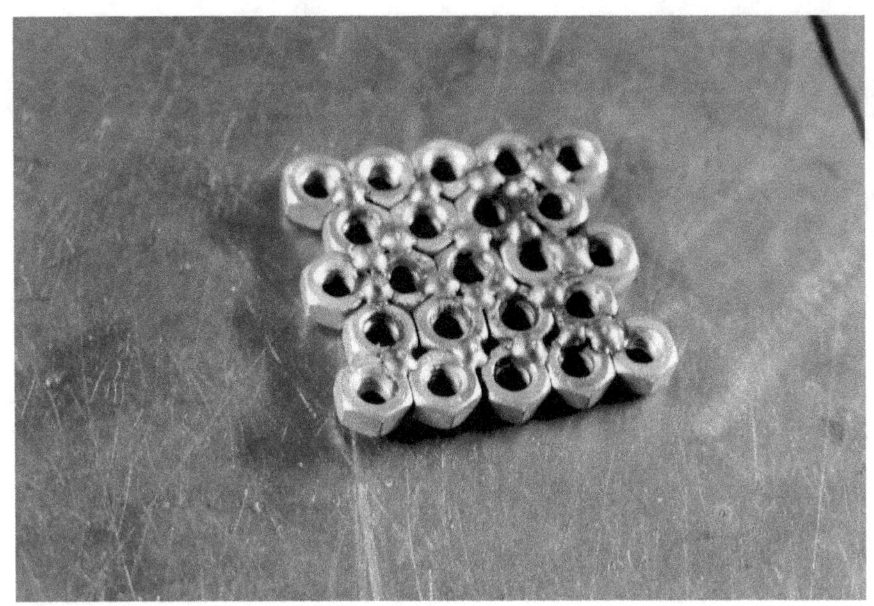

Weld everything to everything.

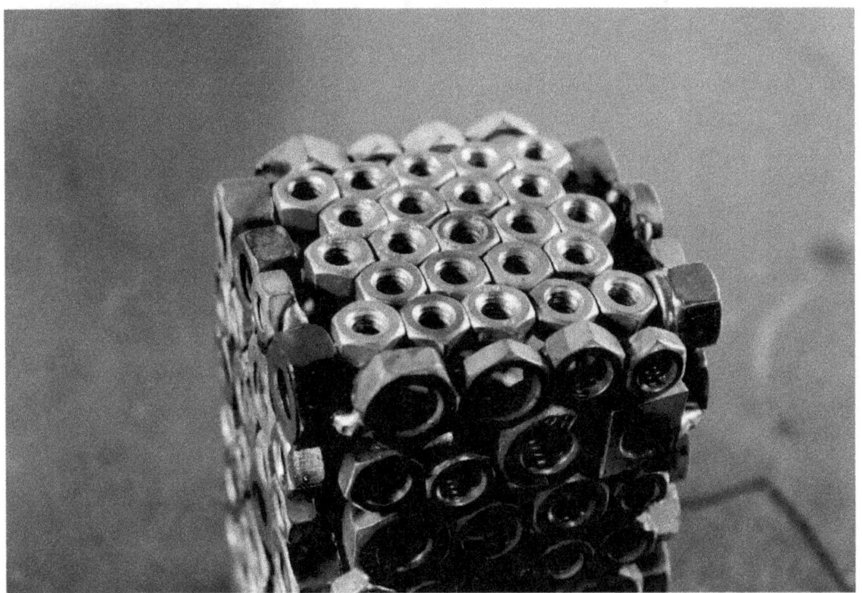

Fit the bottom into the box. If your fit is not exact use a grinder to make them fit using a really big hammer, just kidding, don't do that!

Tack weld them in place making sure the welds won't interfere with the box sitting flat.

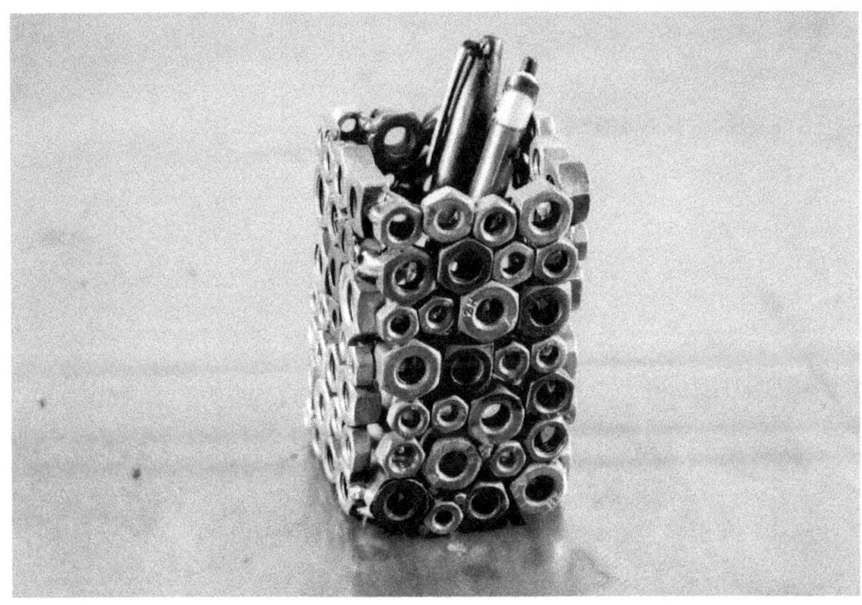

Clean with a wire brush and chip any weld spatter with a hammer and chisel. Clear coat it to prevent rust. Sit back and enjoythe fruits of your labor!

Jewelry Tree

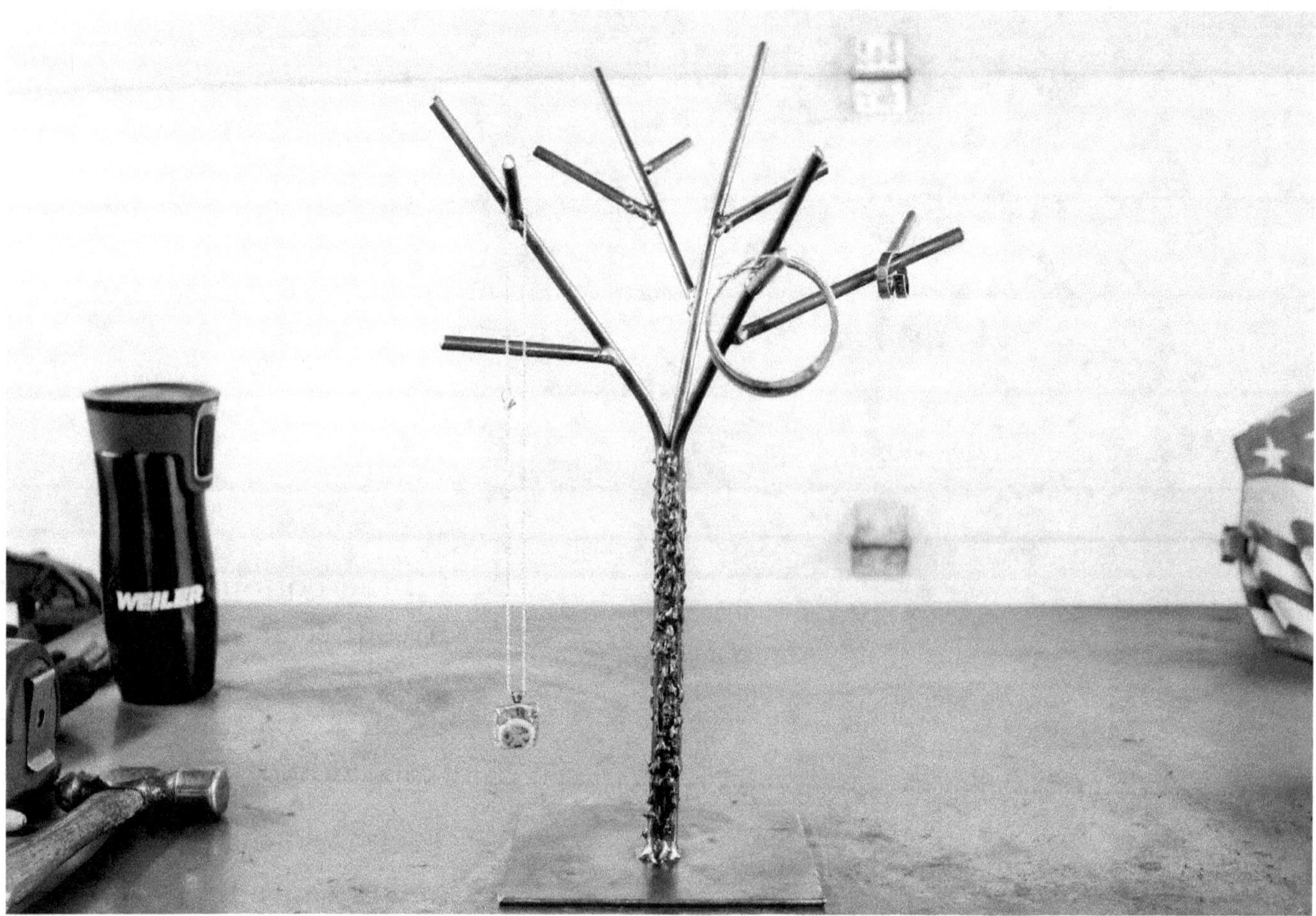

Difficulty

Materials
5' length of 1/4" round bar
5" by 5" steel plate or something to use as a base

Tools

Hammer
Chisel
Wire brush
Grinder with cut off wheel and sanding disk

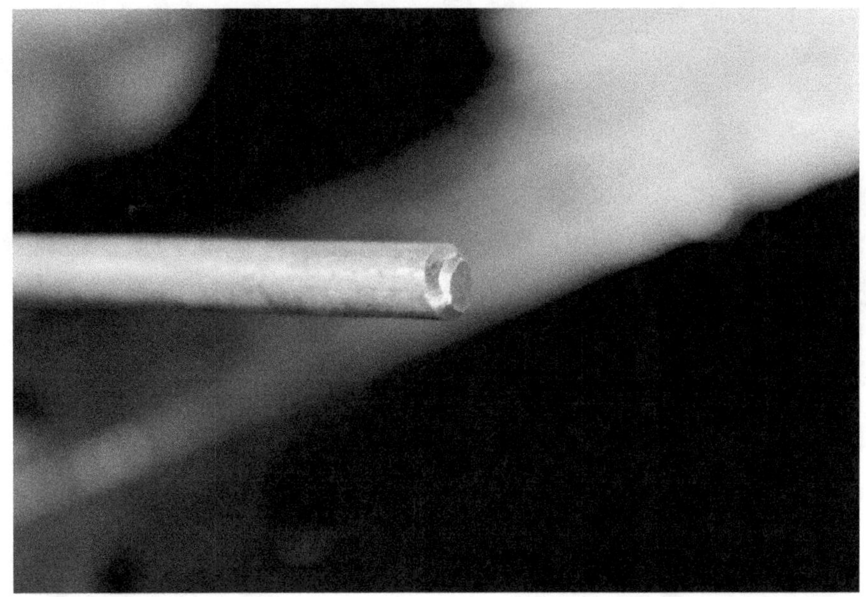

Cut three pieces of the round bar 15" long and cut the remaining material into pieces ranging from 1.5" to 5" long.
Deburr one end of each piece of material as shown.

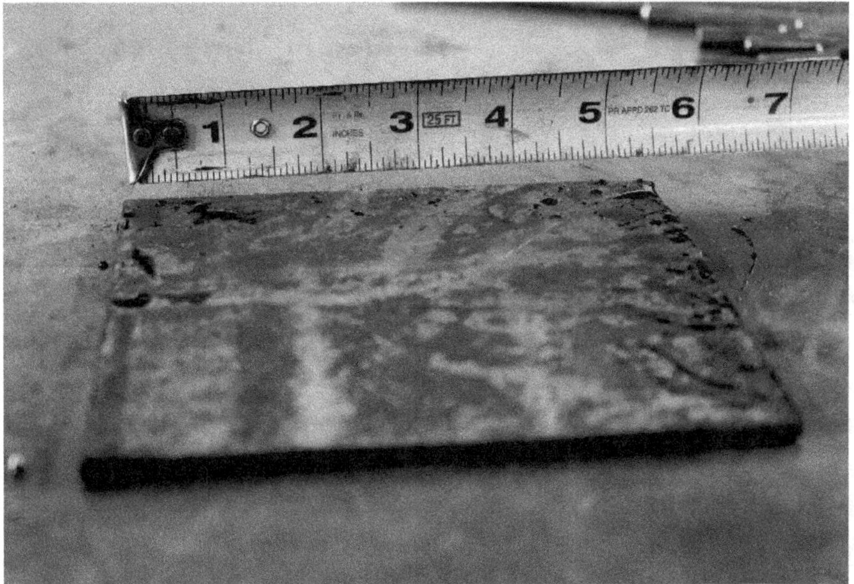

Cut and clean the base.
Deburr all edges.

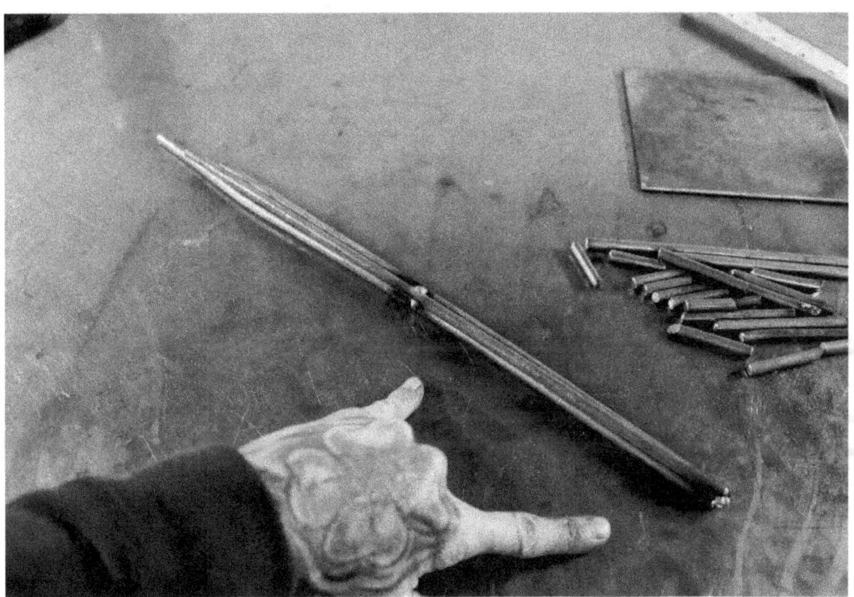

Tack weld the three pieces of 15" round bar together at the center and on one end.

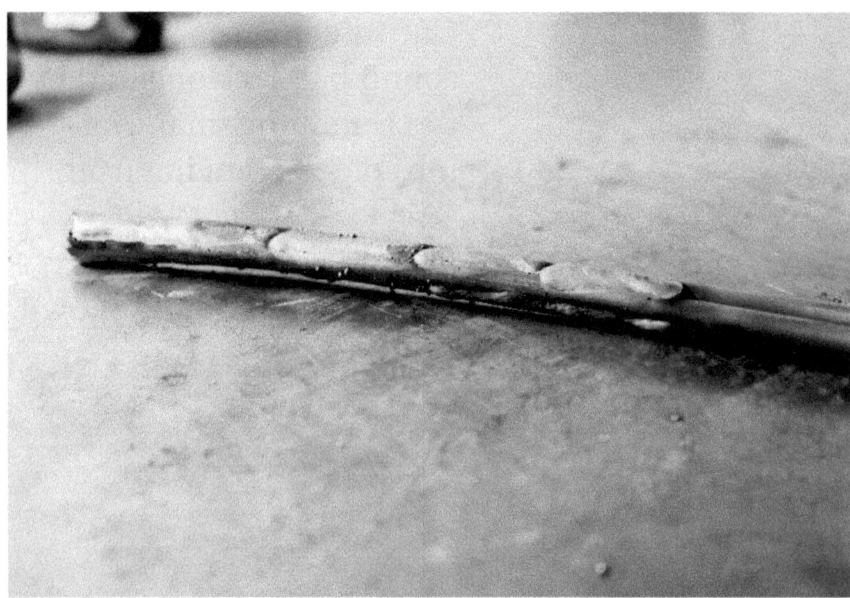

Weld the round bar from the center to the end all the way around.

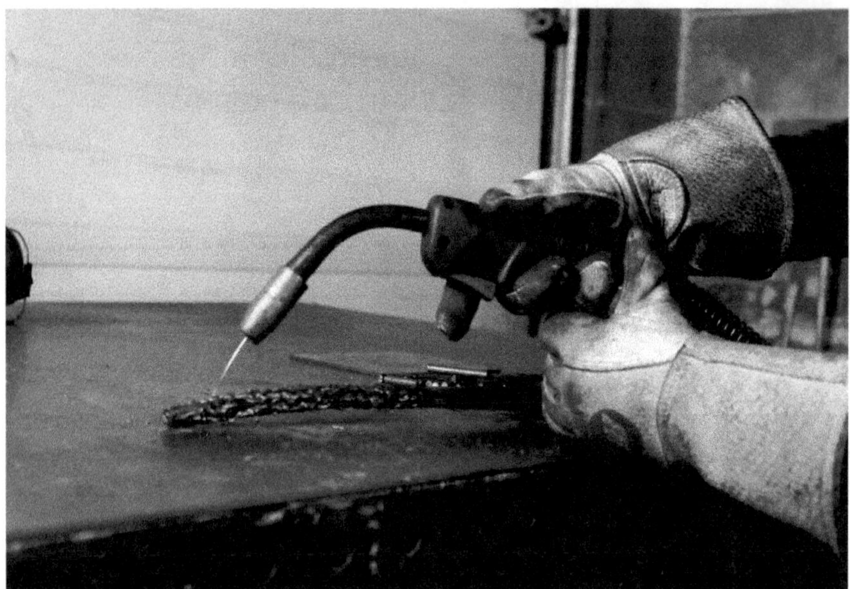

This is absolutely NOT proper welding technique, but it makes a really cool texture for the tree trunk. Hold your torch 3-4” away from your work piece and weld up and down the trunk of the tree.

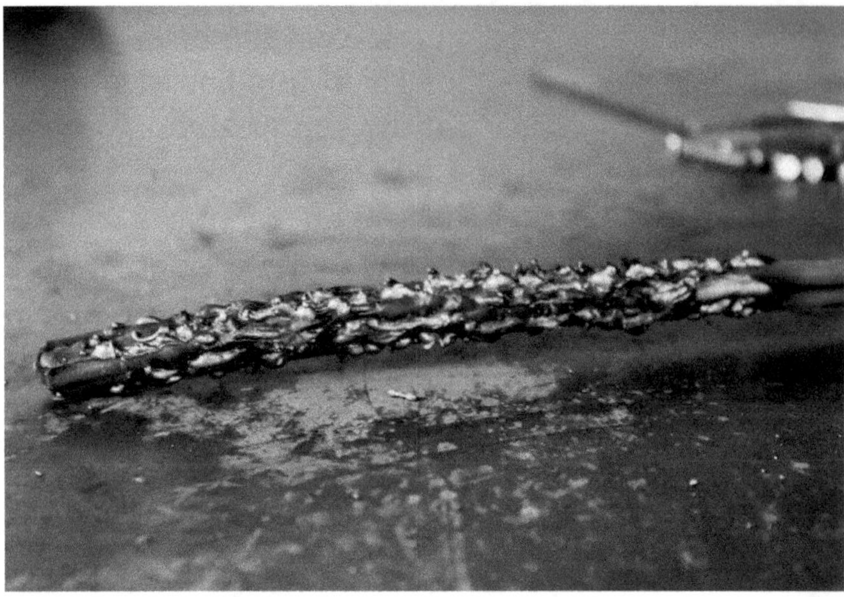

Textured tree trunk. Clean discoloration with a wire brush.

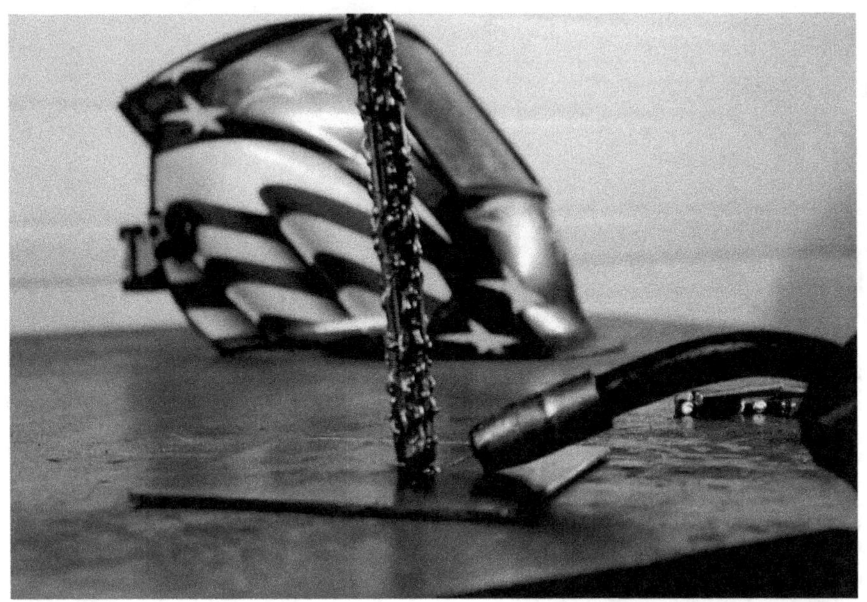

Hold tree trunk on the base plate and tack weld it. Check to make sure it is standing up how you want, adjust as necessary, and weld it in place.

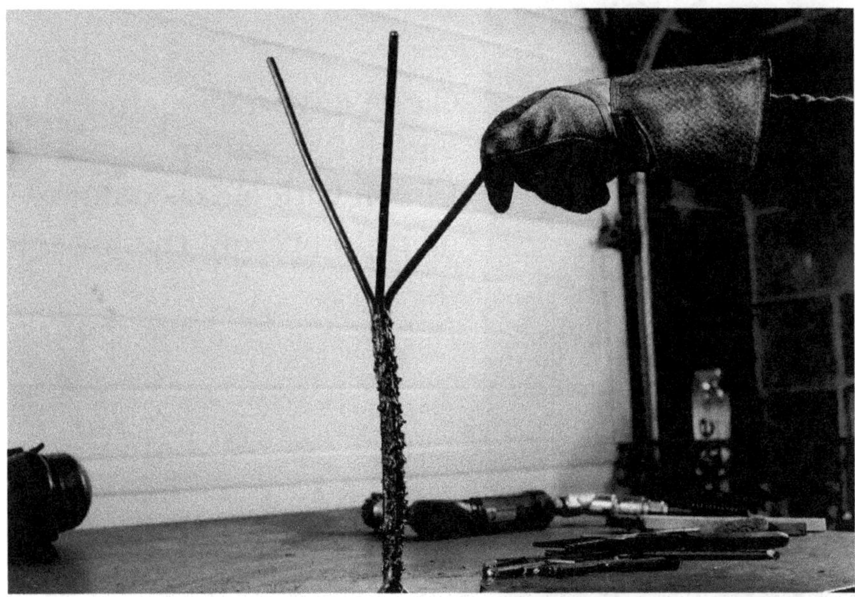

Pull the three unwelded pieces apart to a position that looks good and treelike to you!

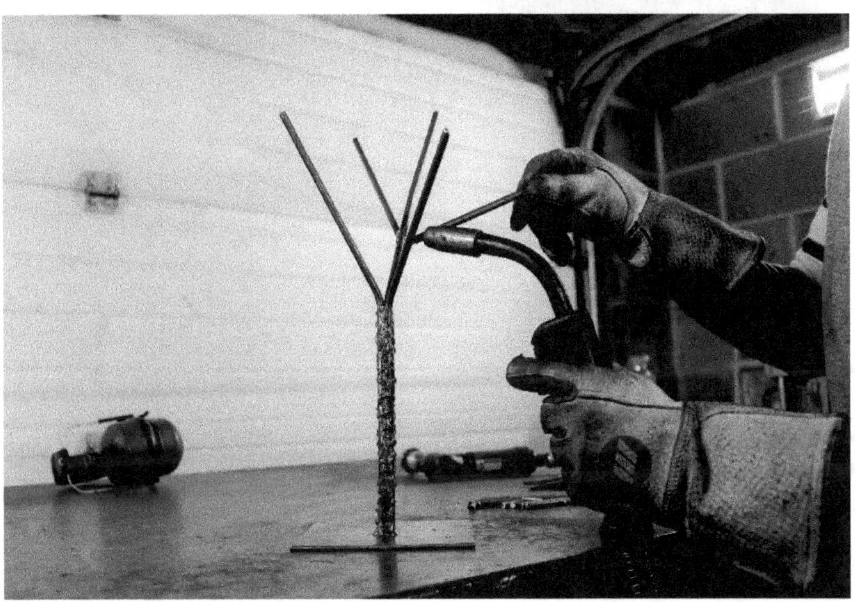

Hold and weld the small pieces on the branches at an upward angle.

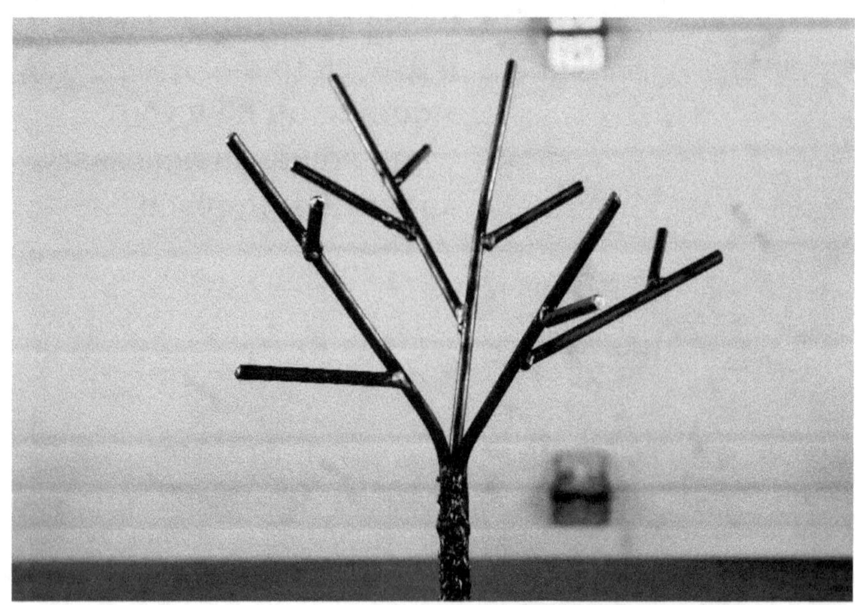

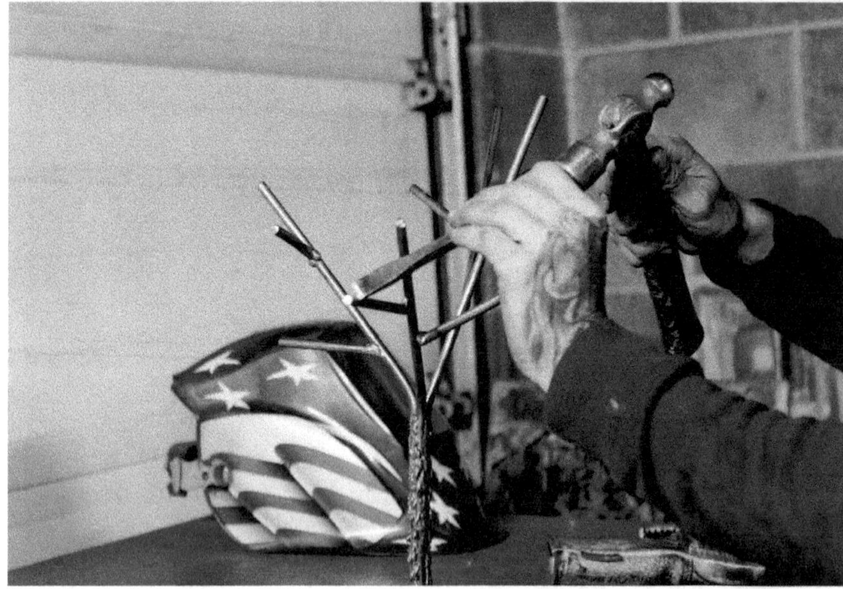

Clean any weld spatter and discoloration. Finish with clear coator paint to prevent rusting.

Scorpion

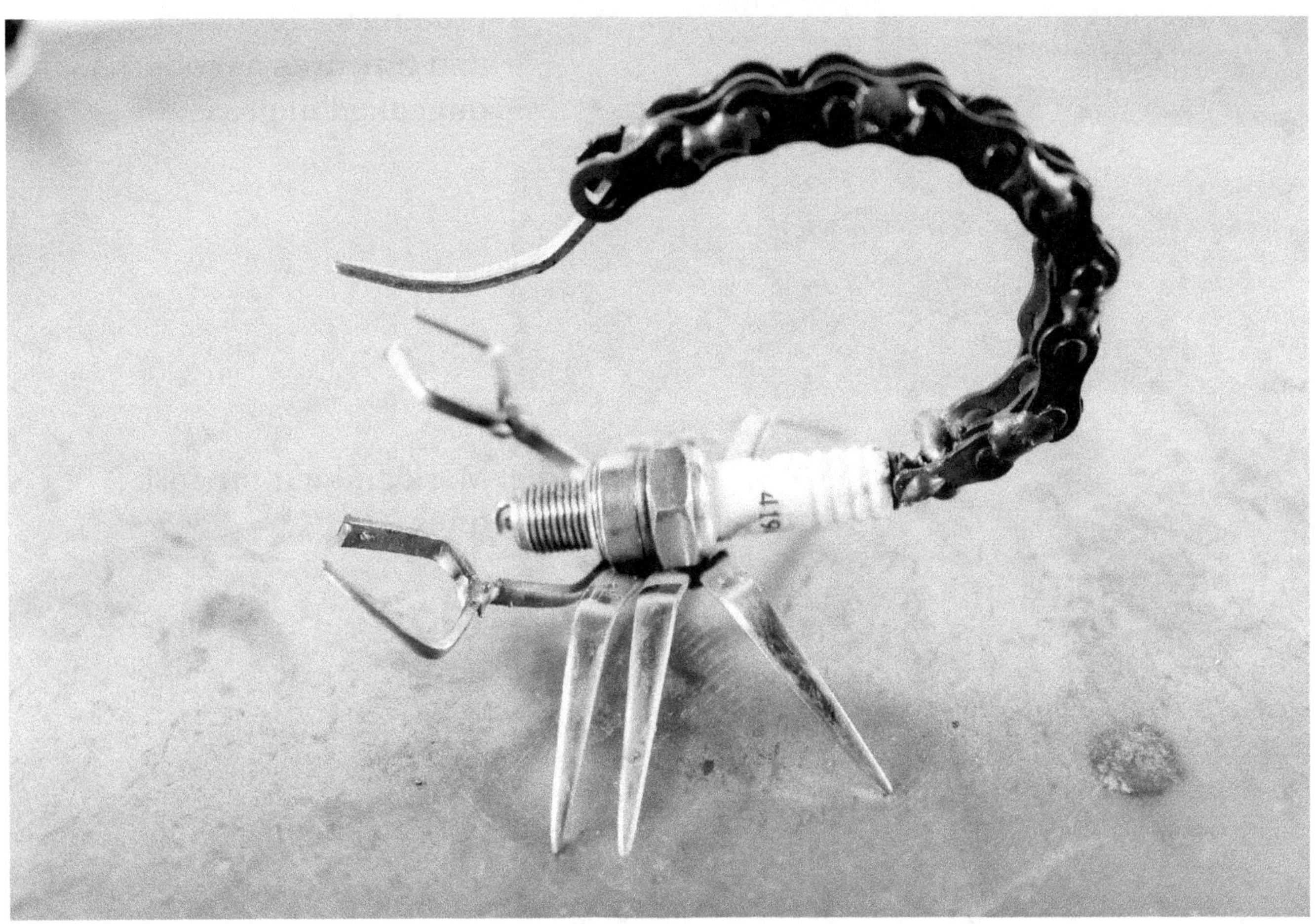

Difficulty

Materials

3Forks
6"length of small chain
Spark Plug

Tools

Hammer and chisel
Wire brush
Grinder with cut off wheel and sanding disk

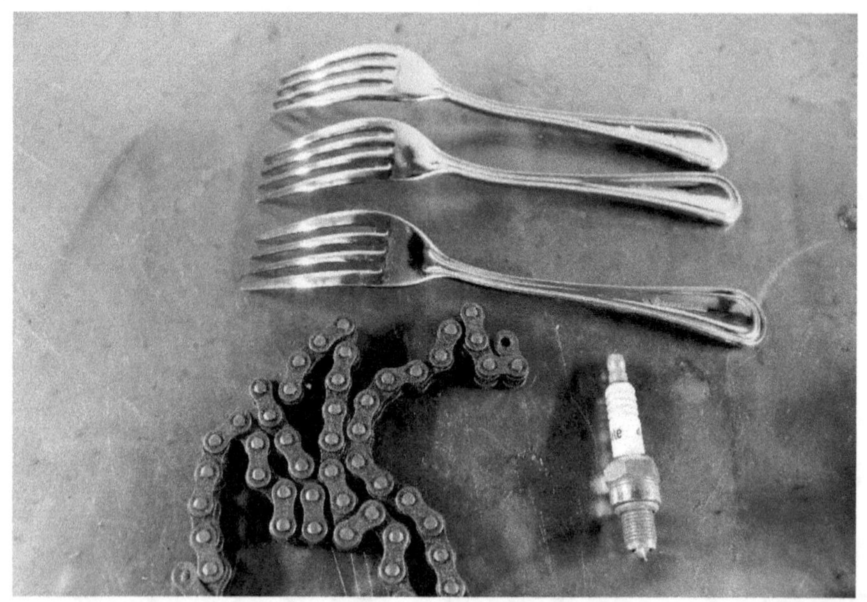

Clean chain with a shop cloth to remove as much grease as possible. Welding chain always produces a lot of smoke and tiny fires as it burns out caked in grease.

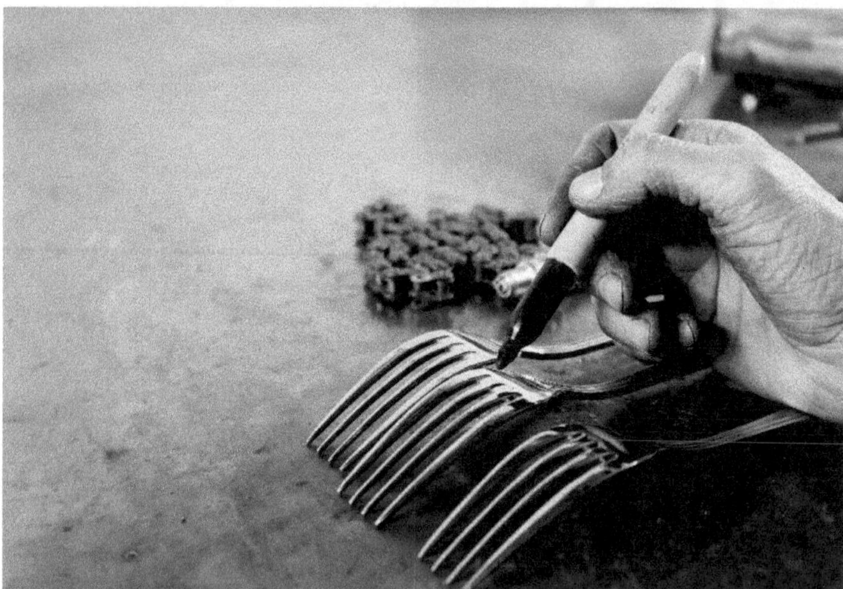

Mark and cut the fork tines.

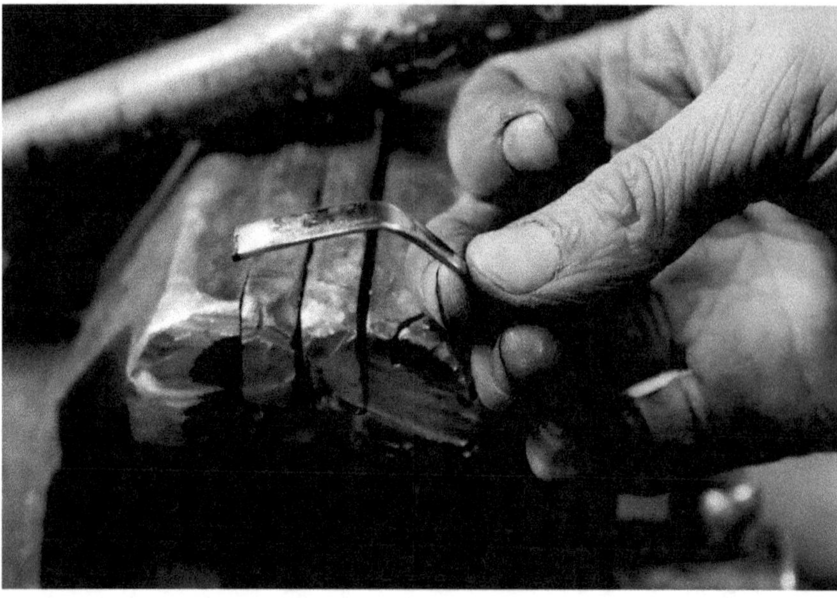

Clamp and bend the six larger outside tines toa45 degree angle.

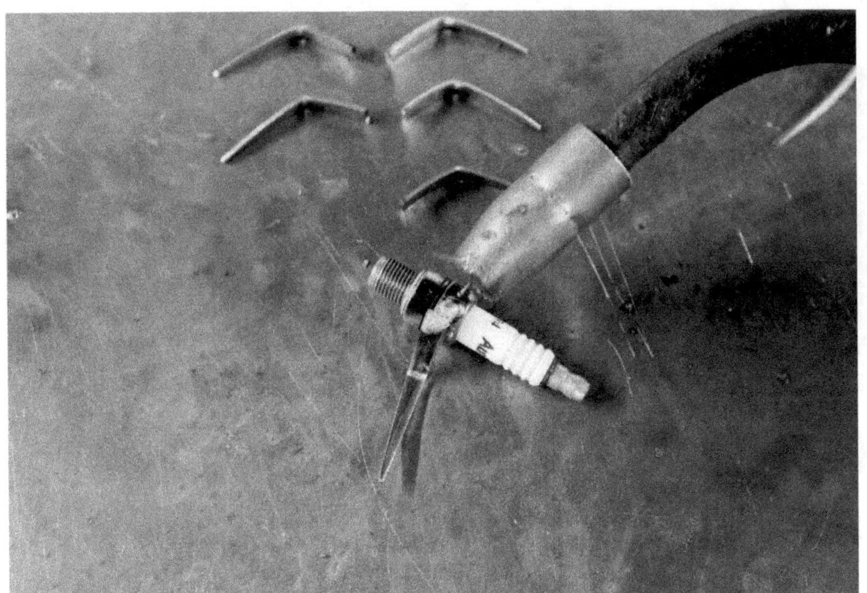

Hold and tack weld a tine to the underside of the sparkplug.

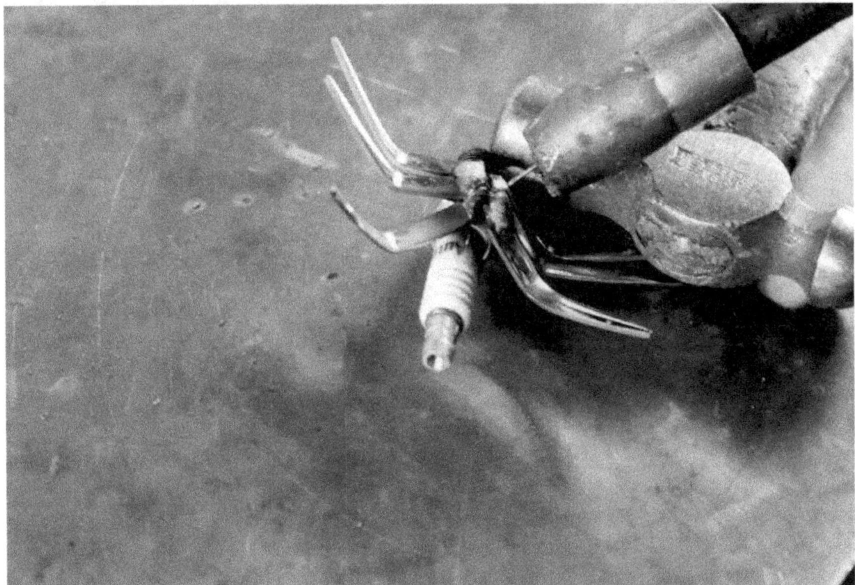

Continue welding the tines under the sparkplug until you have six welded on.

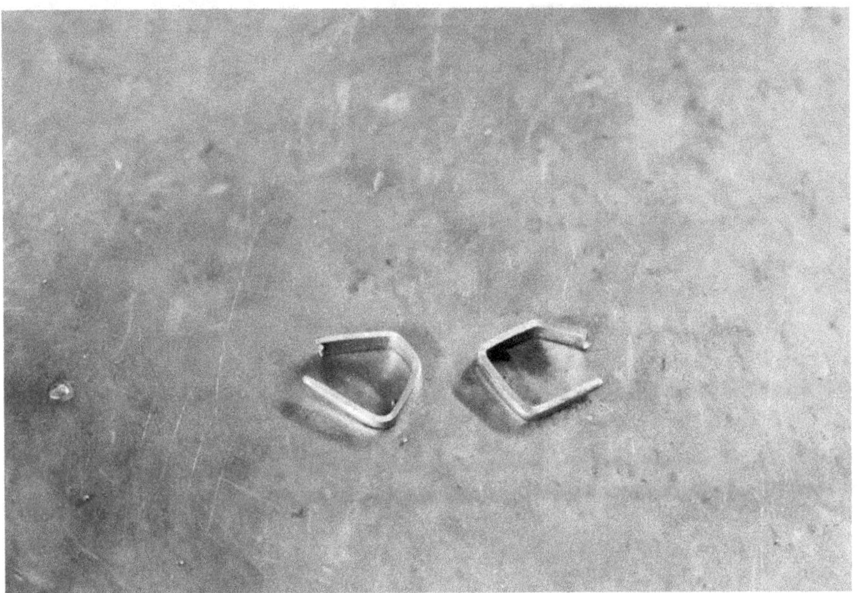

Bend two tines like this.

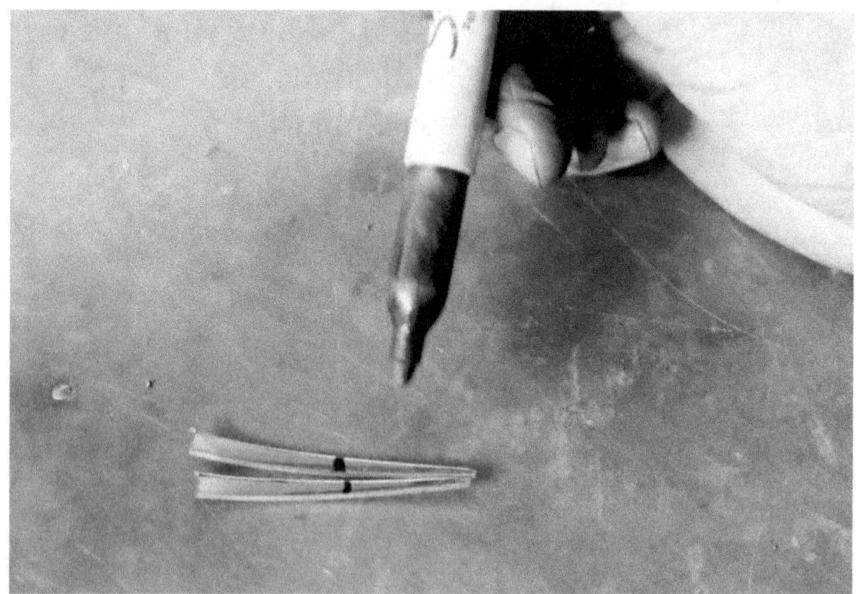

Mark, clamp, and cut two tines at the center keeping the thicker halves.

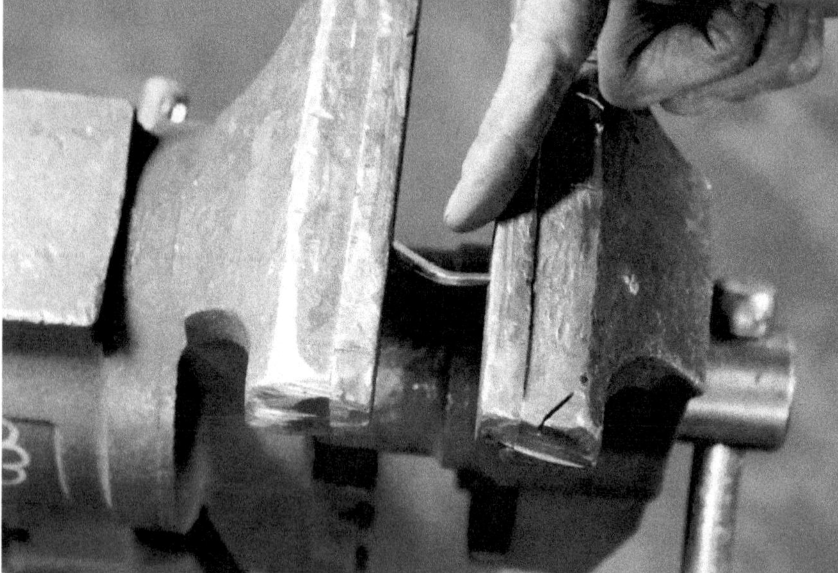

Gently curve the two half tines.

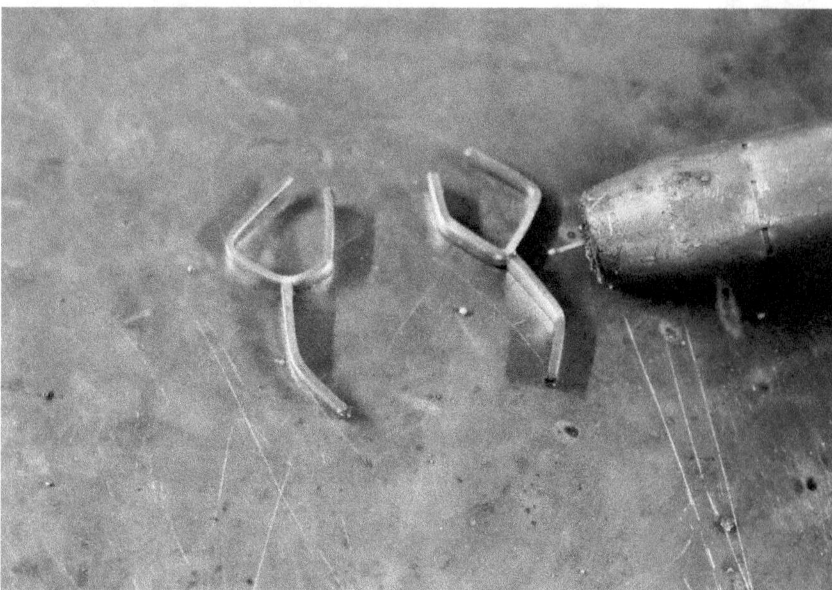

Very carefully tack weld the curved half tines tothe bent tines.

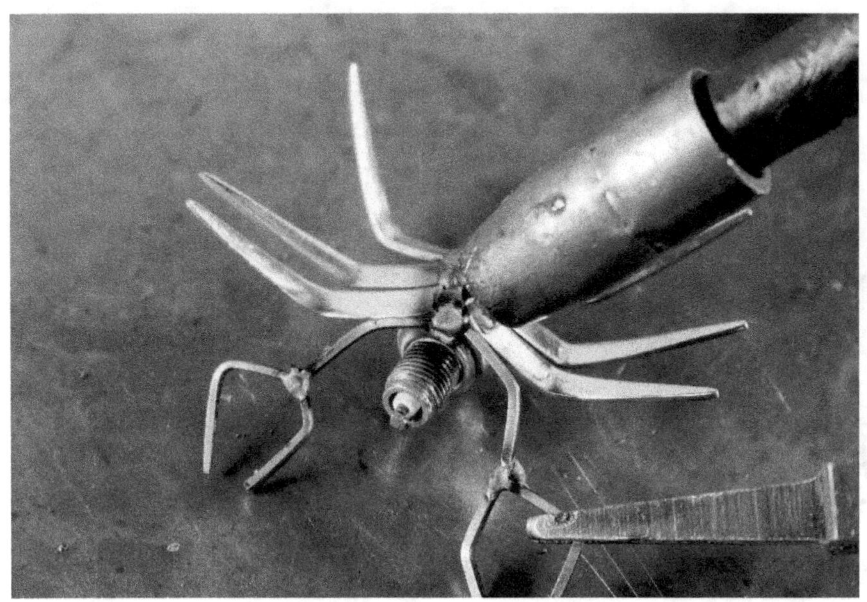

Hold and weld the claws to the underside front of the sparkplug.

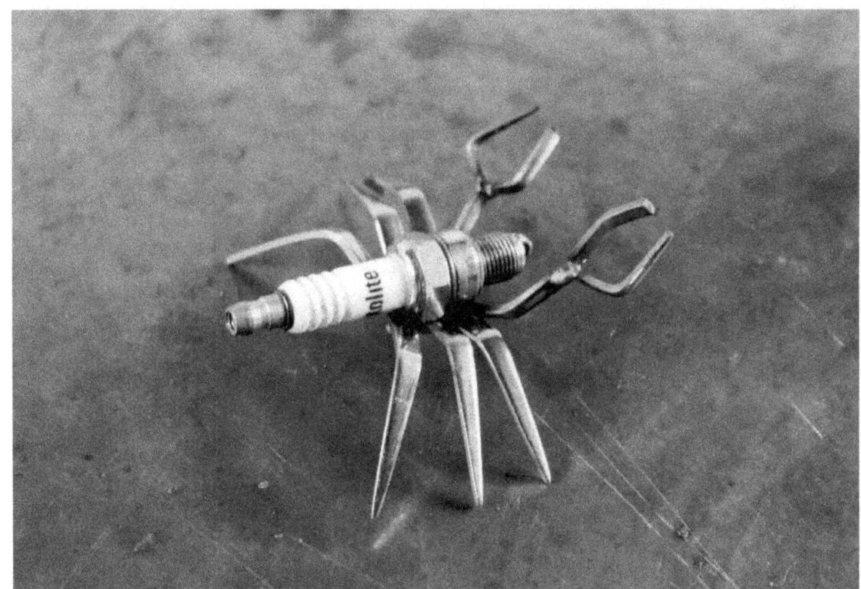

Flip him over and he's starting to look official! Clean any weld spatter and discoloration.

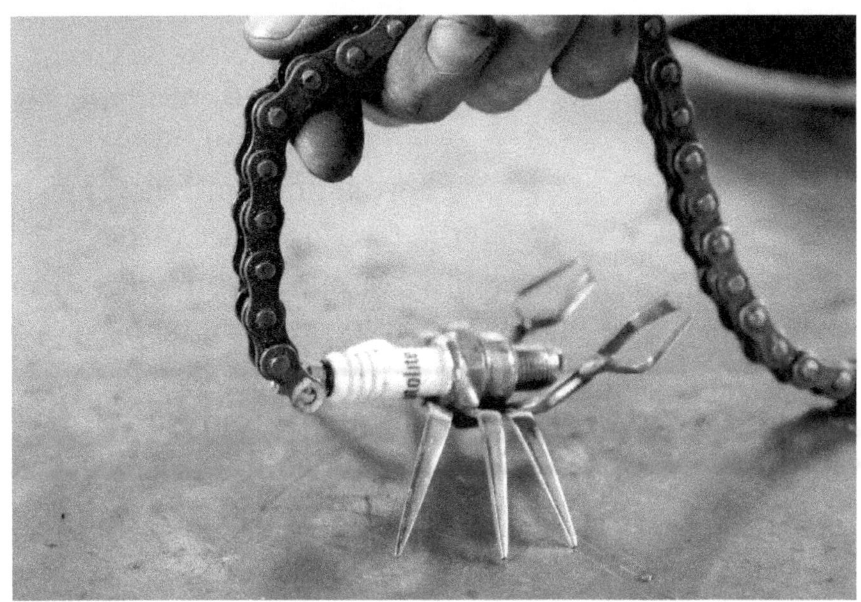

Hold the chain up to his buns and decide how long you want the tail to be. (Do scorpions even have buns? I'm going to have to Google that later!)

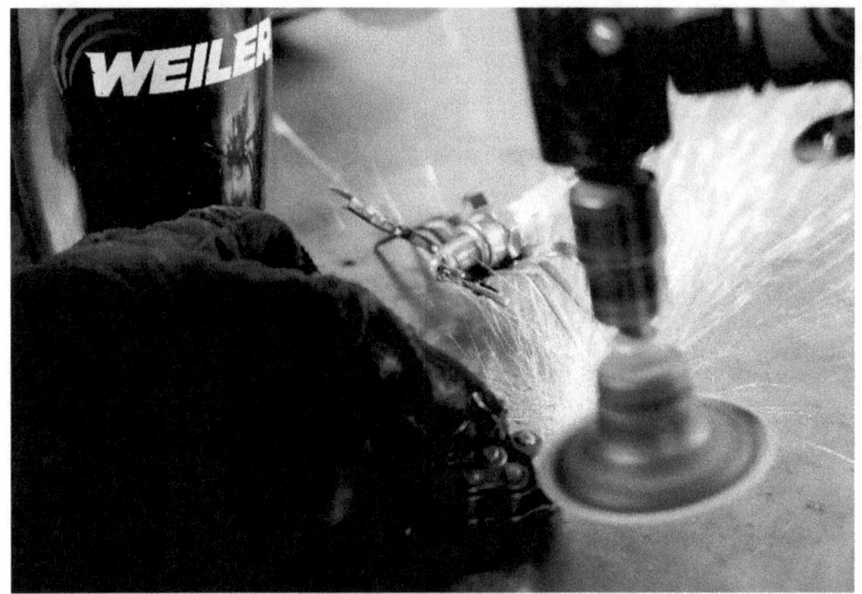

To separate the chain grind the pin down to the link and then hammer it out with a punch, or if you're fancy use a chain break!

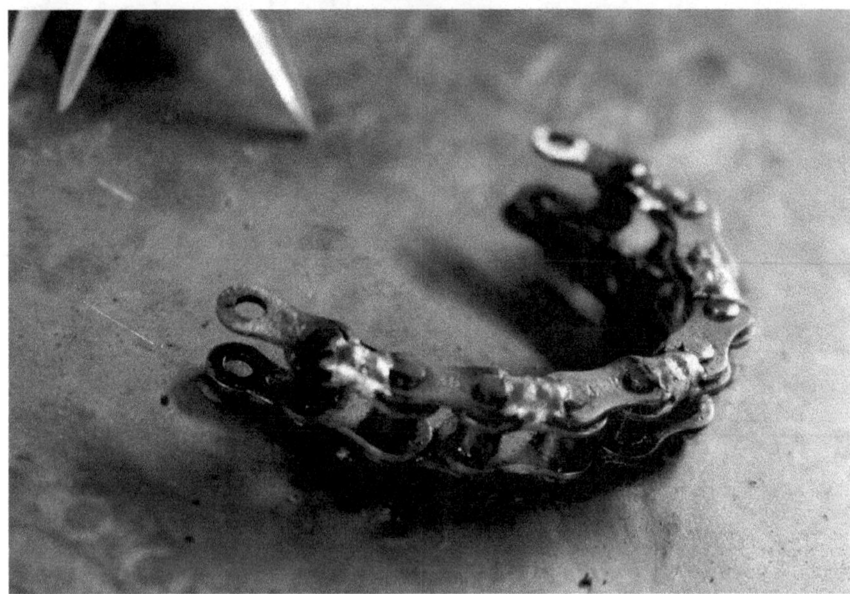

Curve the chain into the shape you want for the tail and weld each link together.

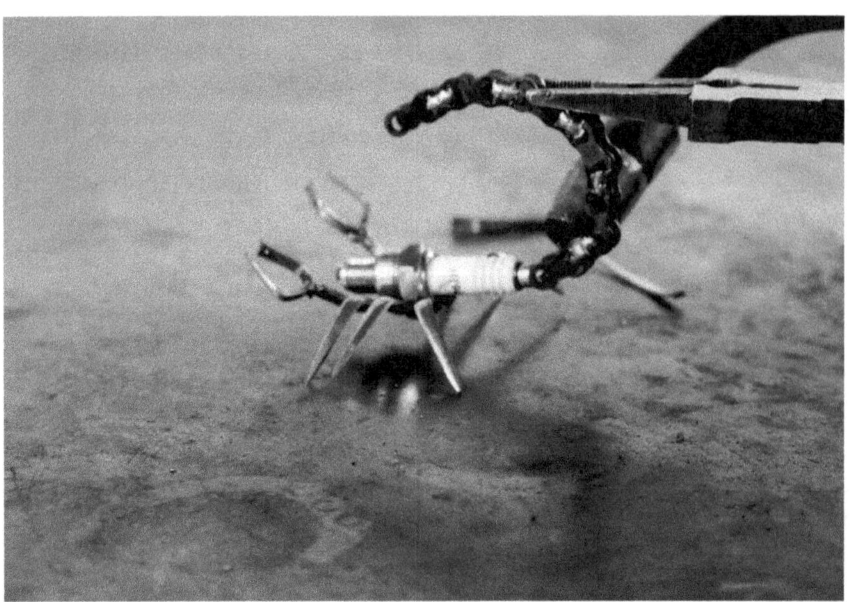

Weld thetailtothe scorpion's butt, really, I need toGooglethis! There isnometalbetween the frontandbackofthe sparkplug so you will need to put a piece of metal from the bench to the tailtogrounditin order to weld it.

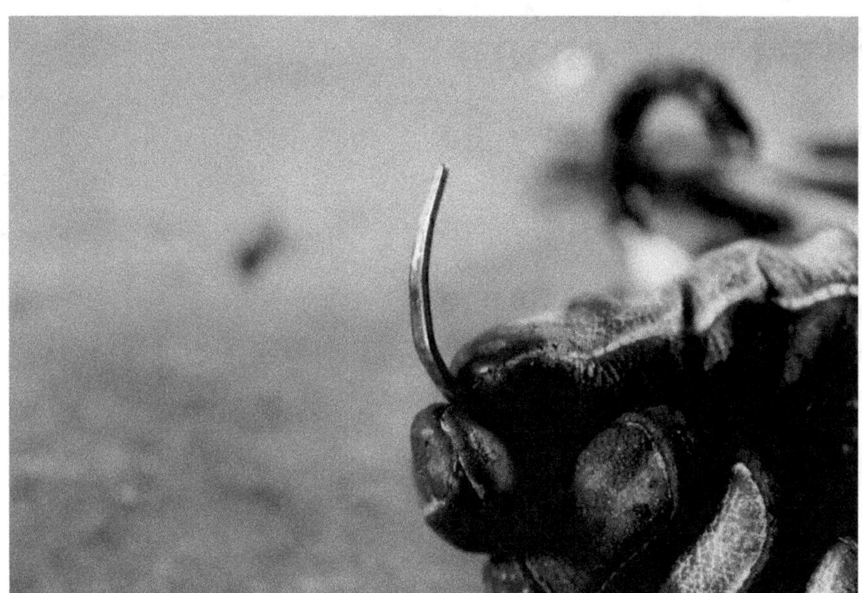

Gently curve a fork tine.

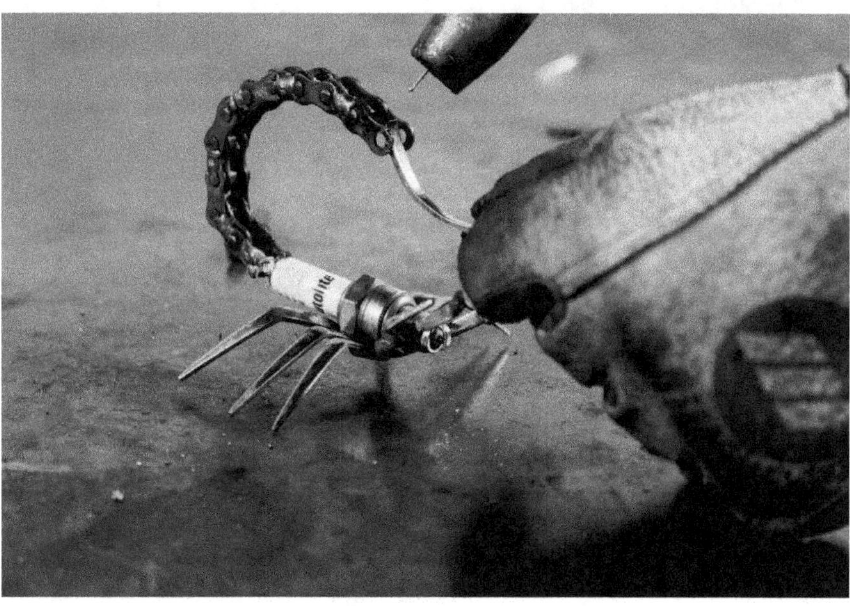

Hold it up to the tail and tack weld it on.

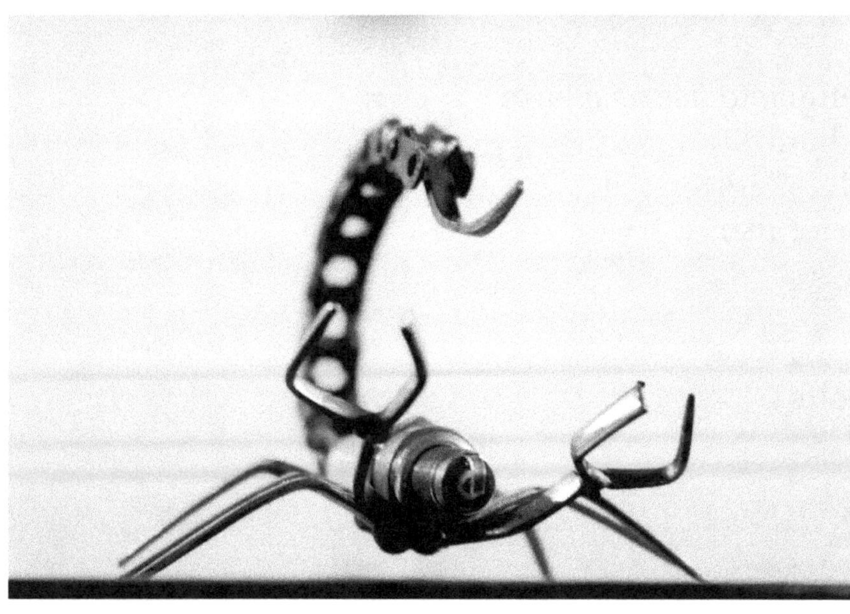

Clean the scorpion with a wire brush and chip any weld spatter. Finish with a clear coat to prevent rust and don't get stung!

Fly Fisherman

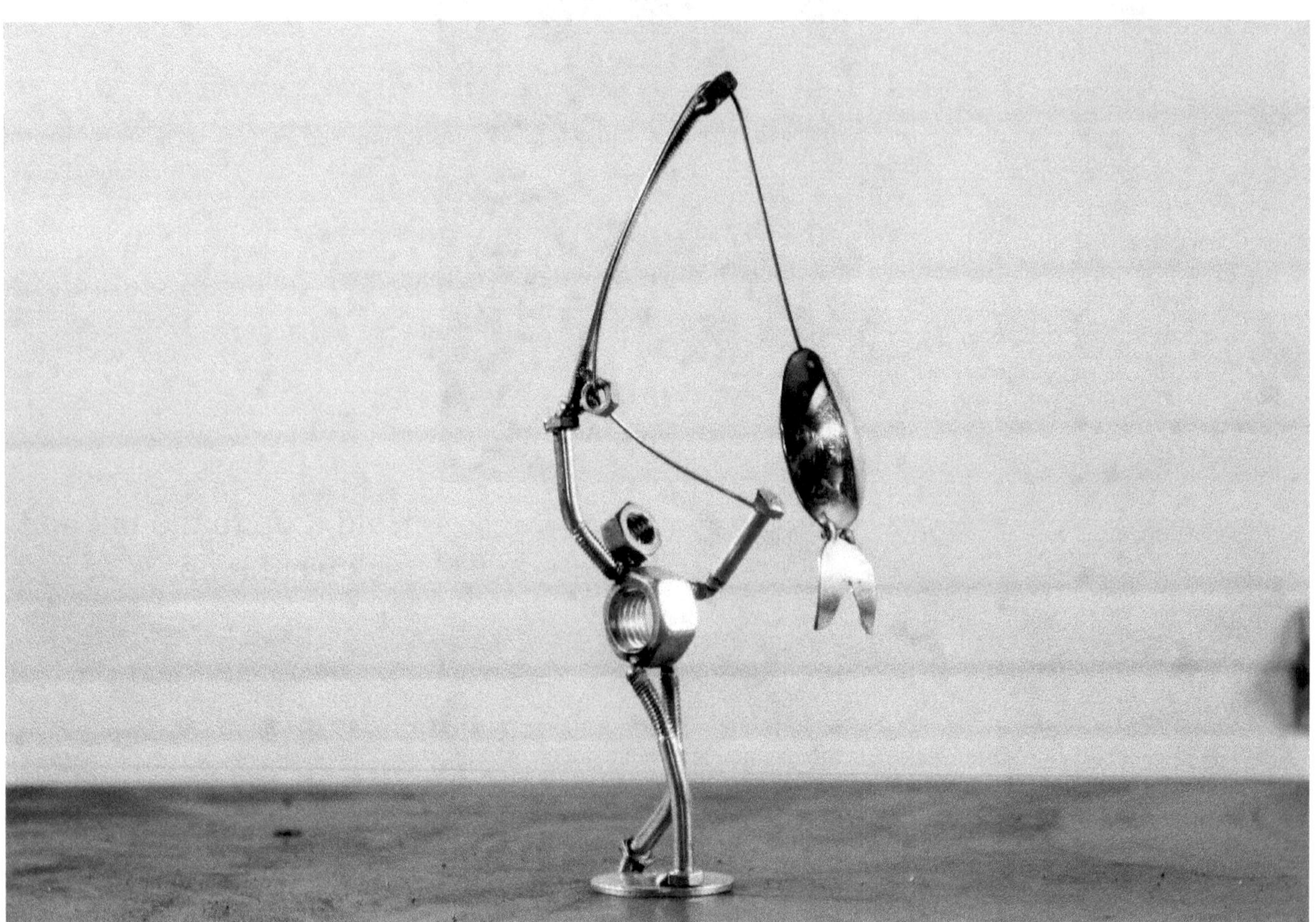

Difficulty

Materials

Large washer or piece of something to use as a base
Bolts 1 very long, 2 long, 2 medium
Nuts 1large, 1medium, 2 small
Spoon and fork and small wire for fish

Tools

Hammer
Viseorwaytoclampand bend bolts
Pliers or whelpers

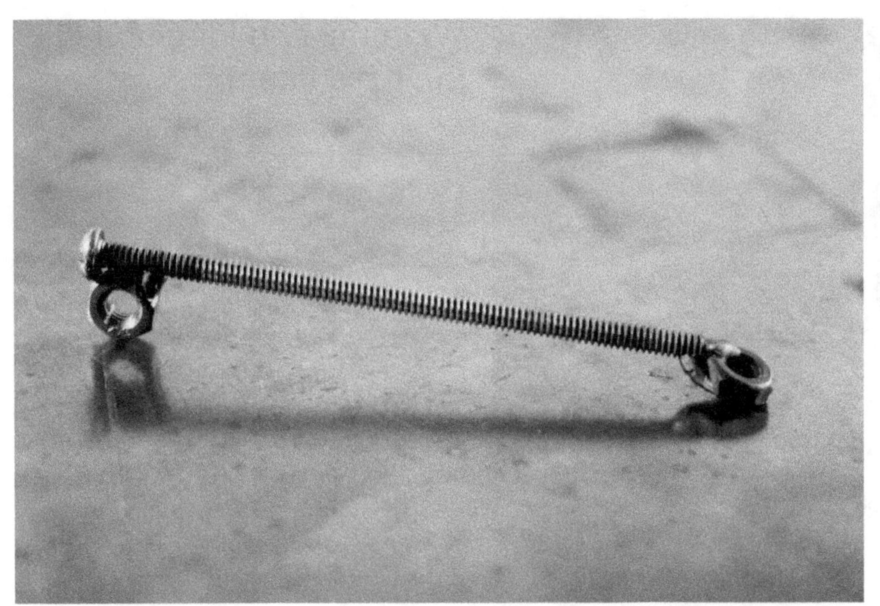

Weld the two small nuts to the end of the very long bolt as shown.

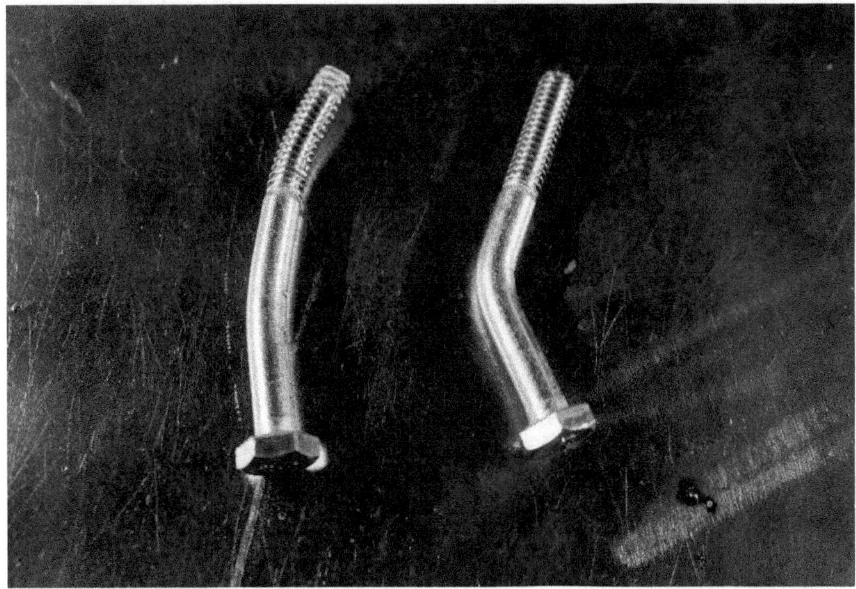

Clamp and hammer the two long bolts like this.

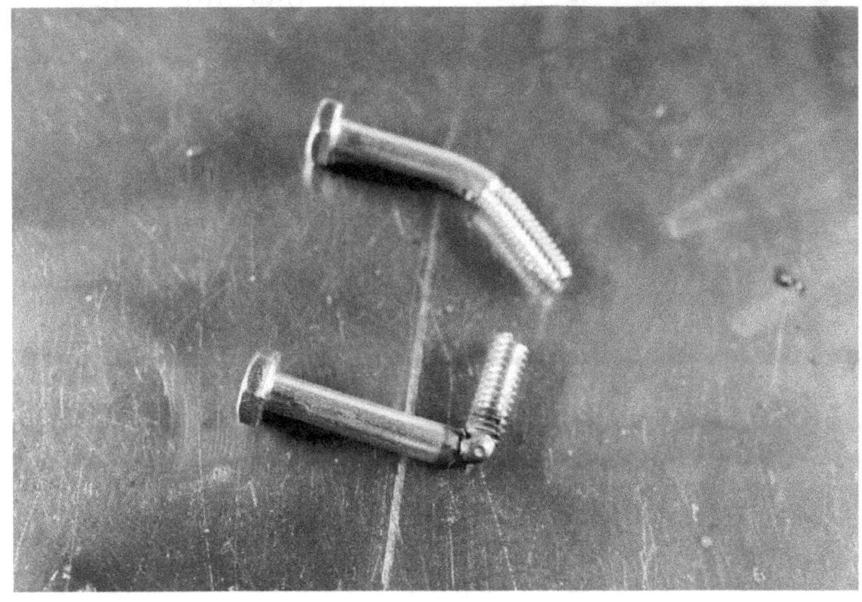

Clamp and hammer the two medium bolts like this. Mine broke so I welded it back together.

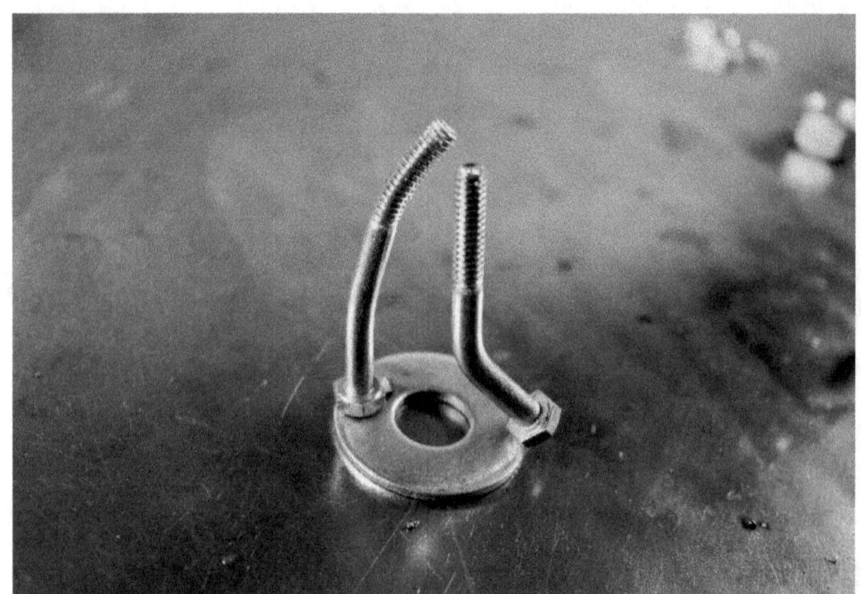

Weld the two long bolts to the base like this.

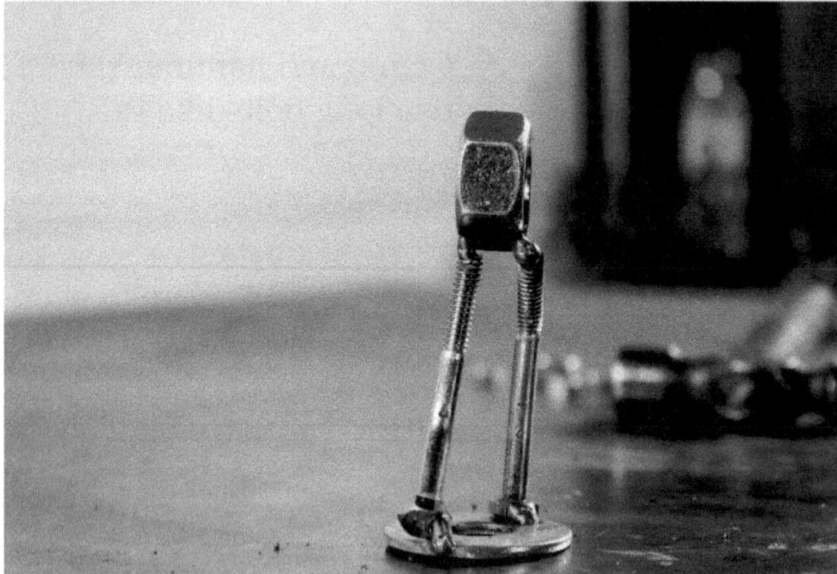

Weld the large bolt to the legs like this.

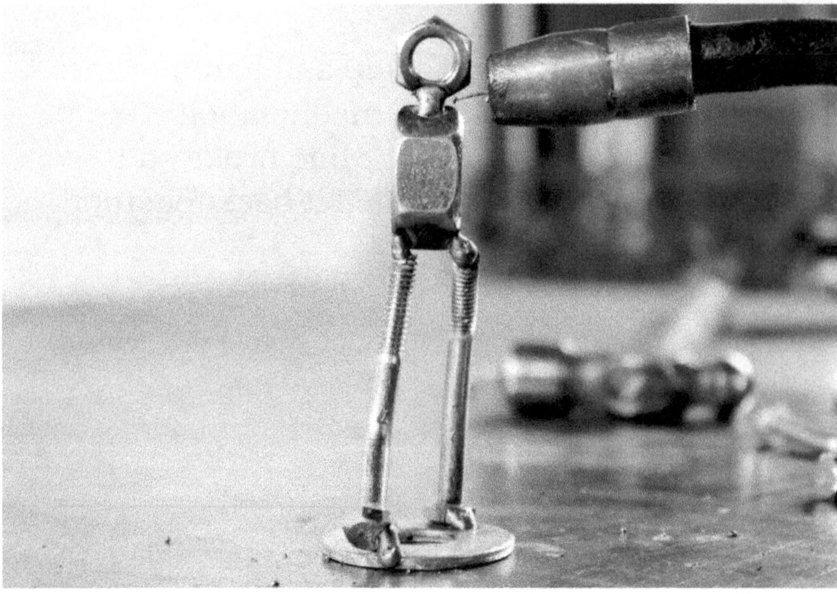

Weld the medium boltto the body like this.

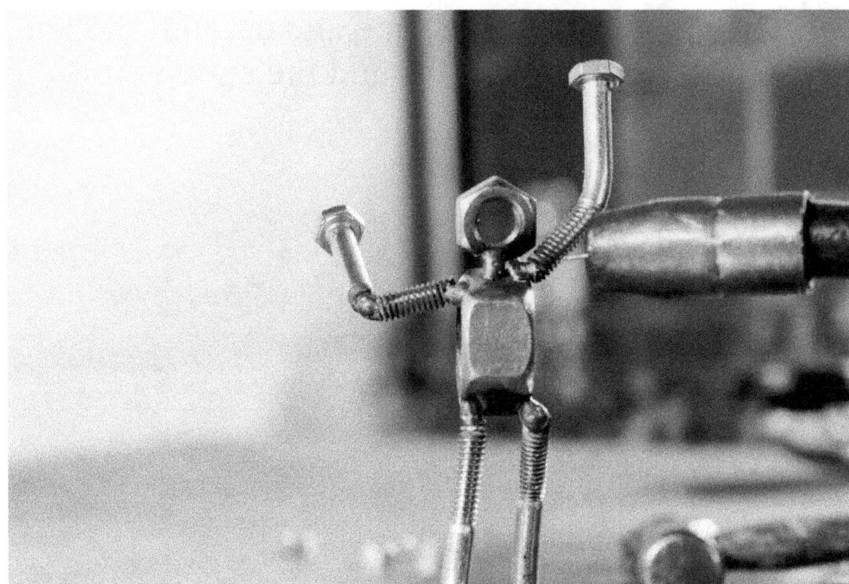

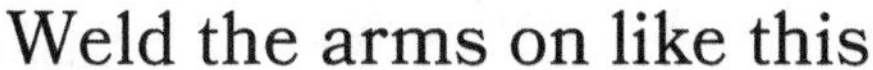

Weld the arms on like this.

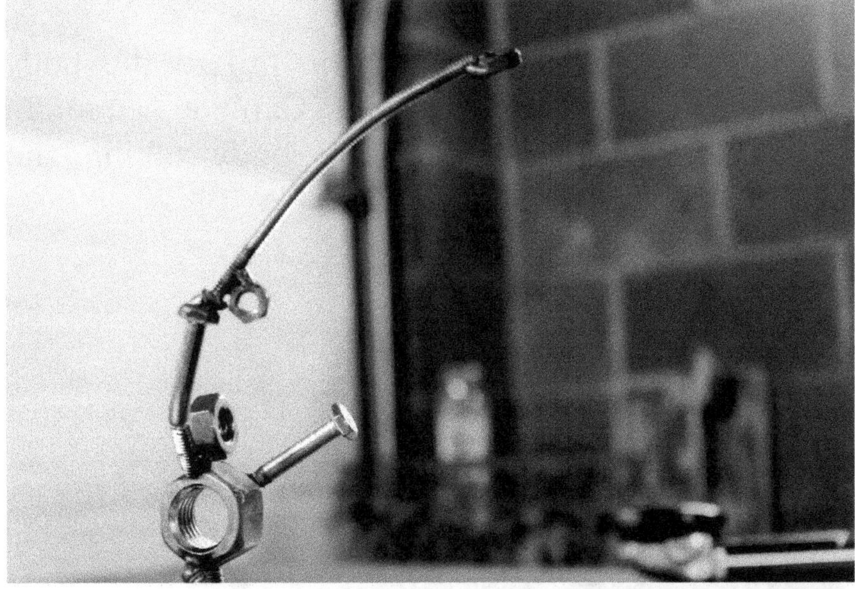

Weld the fishing pole to the hand like this.

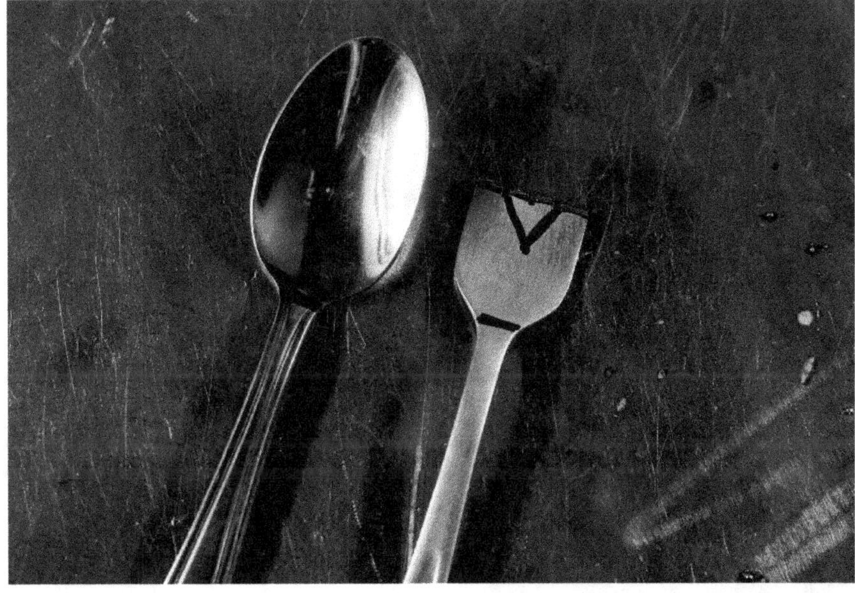

Cut the tines off the fork and then mark and cutthe fork and spoon like this.

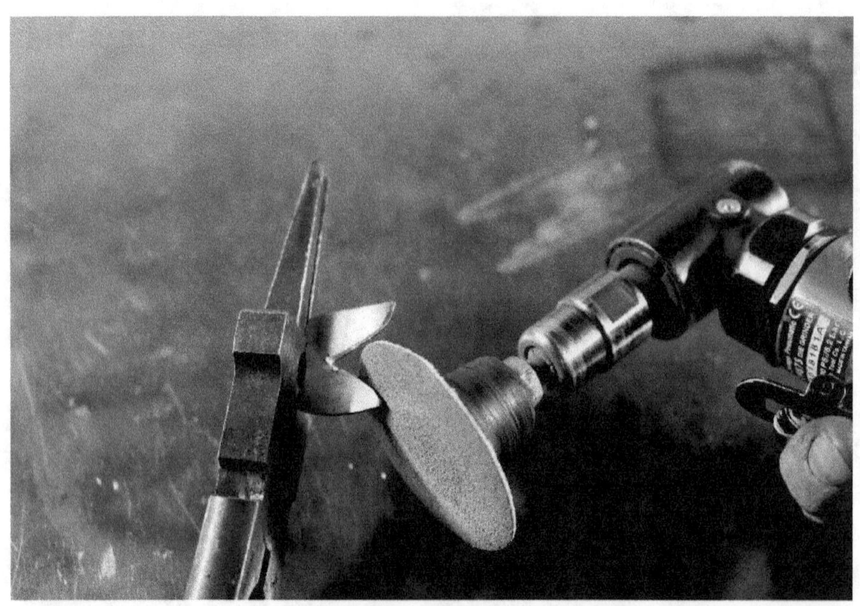

Shape and smooth the tail fins and the spoon bowl.

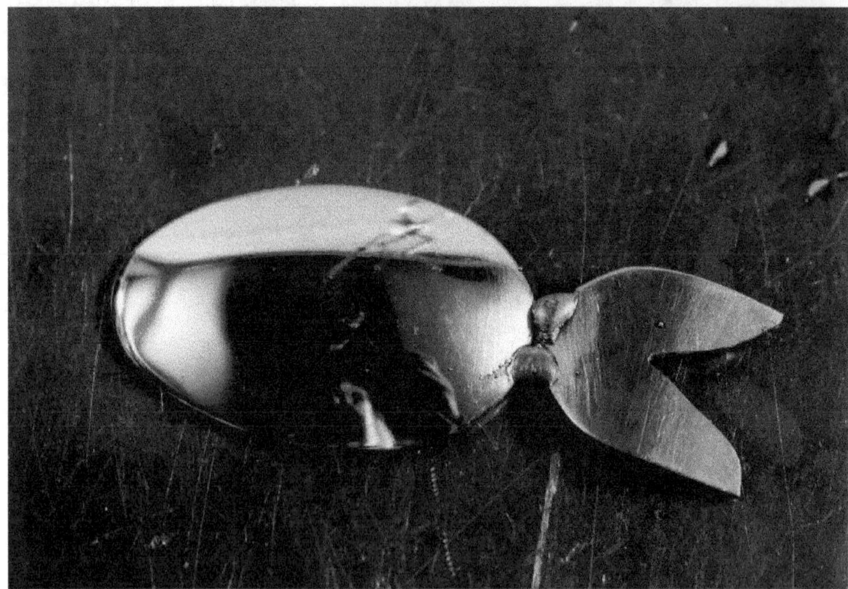

Weld the tail to the body like this. Can you see me in the fish body taking the picture?

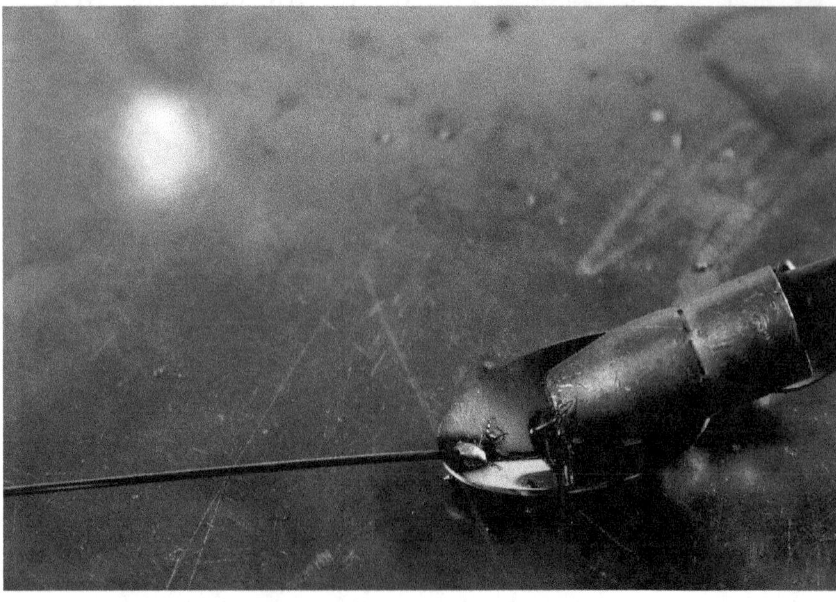

Carefully tack weld a length of wire (filler wire or coat hanger) to the inside of the fish body.

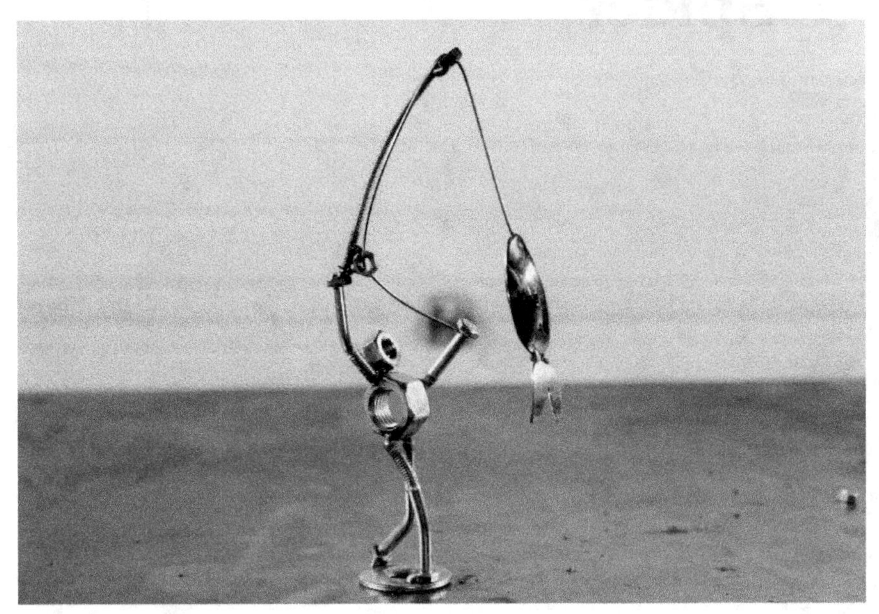

String the line through the fishing pole and over to the fisherman's other hand. You may or may not have to tack weld the line to his hand. I did not and was able to bend it so the bolt head (hand) holds it. Clean and finish with clear coat.

Spider

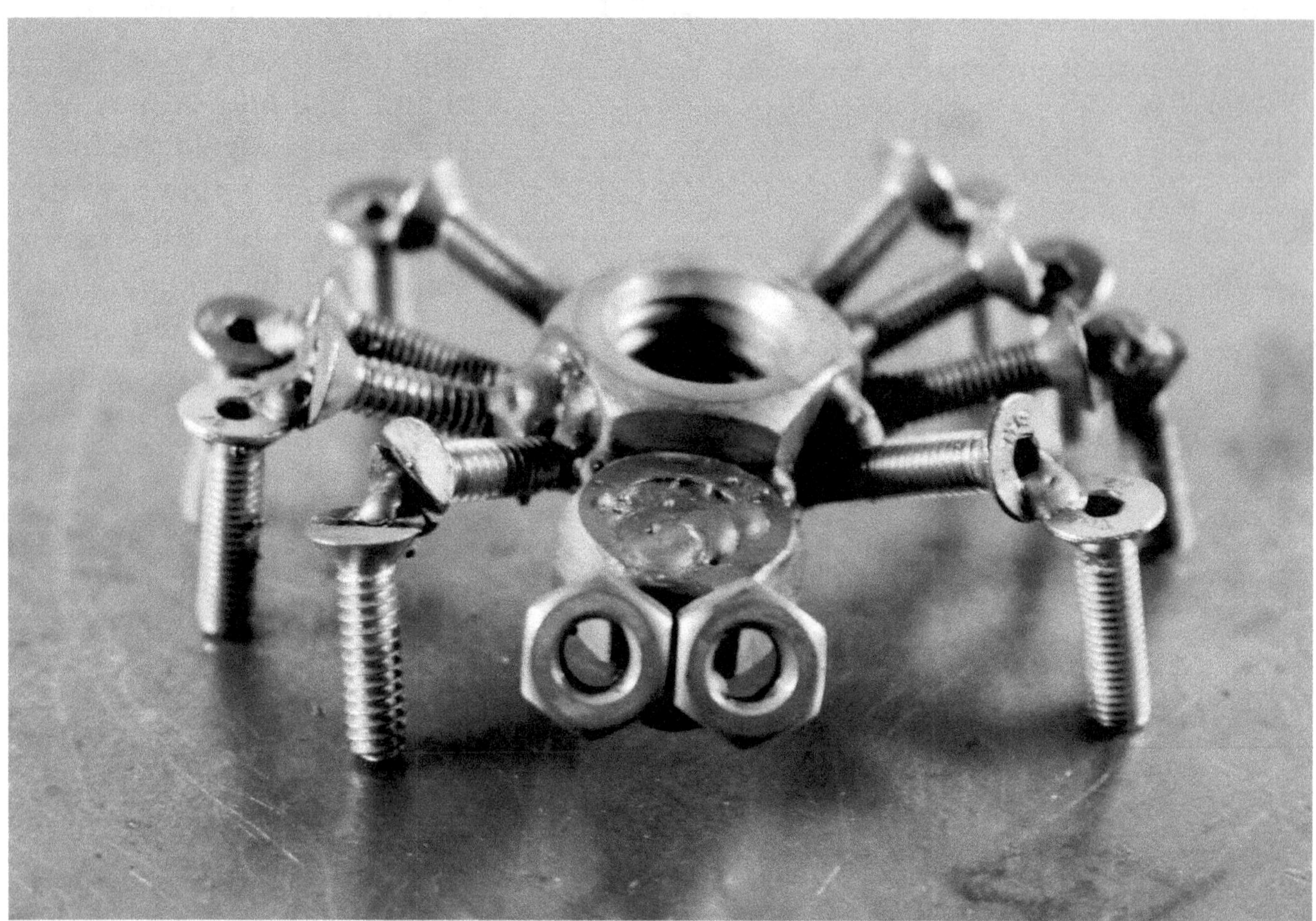

Difficulty

Materials

1 large nut
1 medium nut
2 small nuts
16 small bolts or round bar to use as legs

Tools

Hammer and chisel
Wire brush
Pliers or whelpers

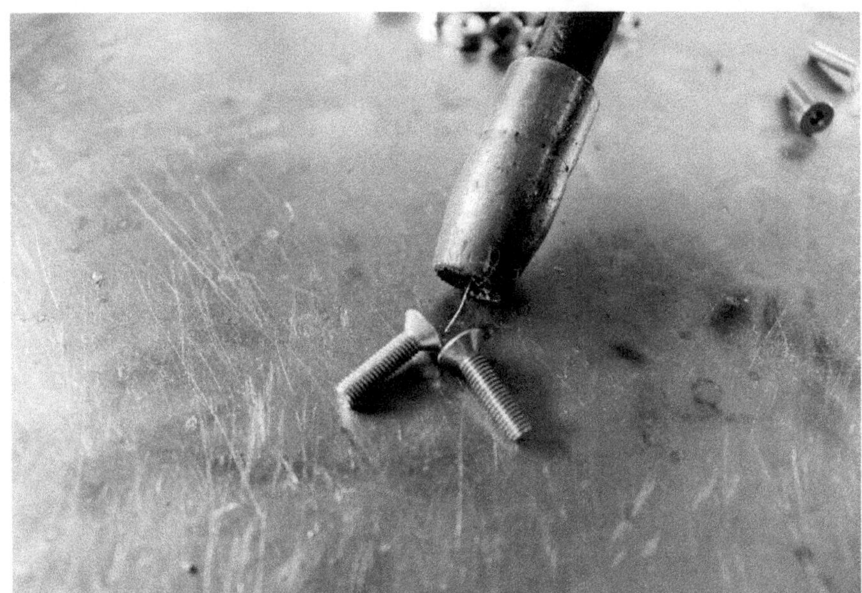

Weld two bolts together like this.
Repeat with all the other bolts to make eight crazy spider legs.

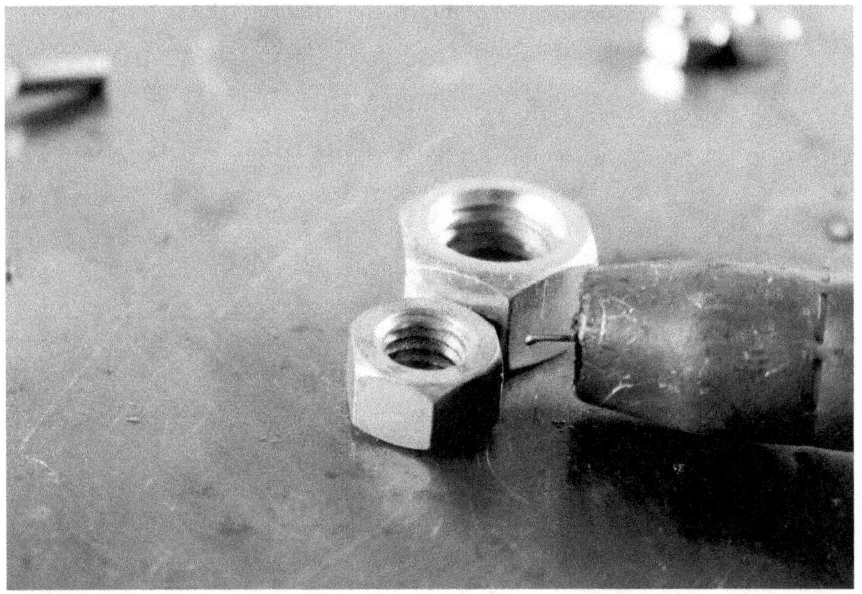

Weld the medium bolt to the large bolt by placing a small tack weld on each side.

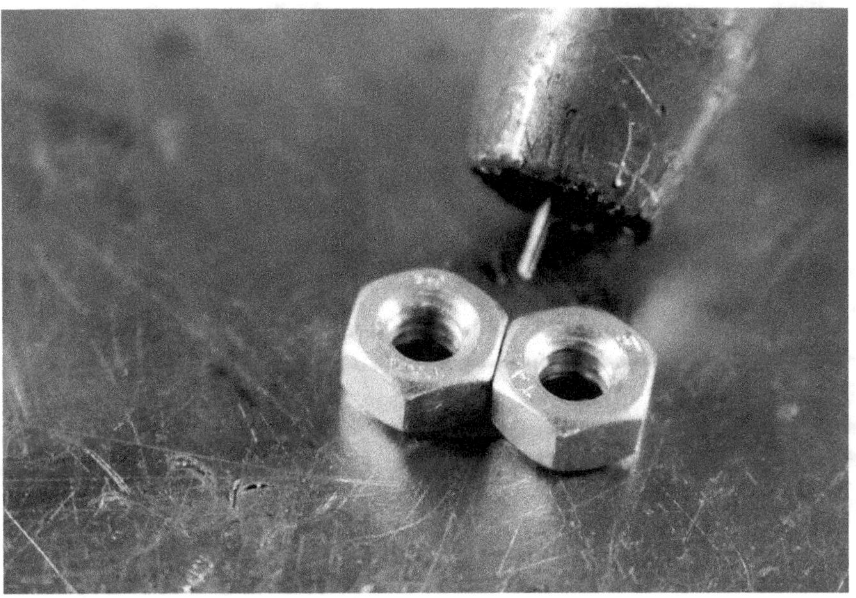

Weld the two small nuts together by placing asmall tack weld on either side.

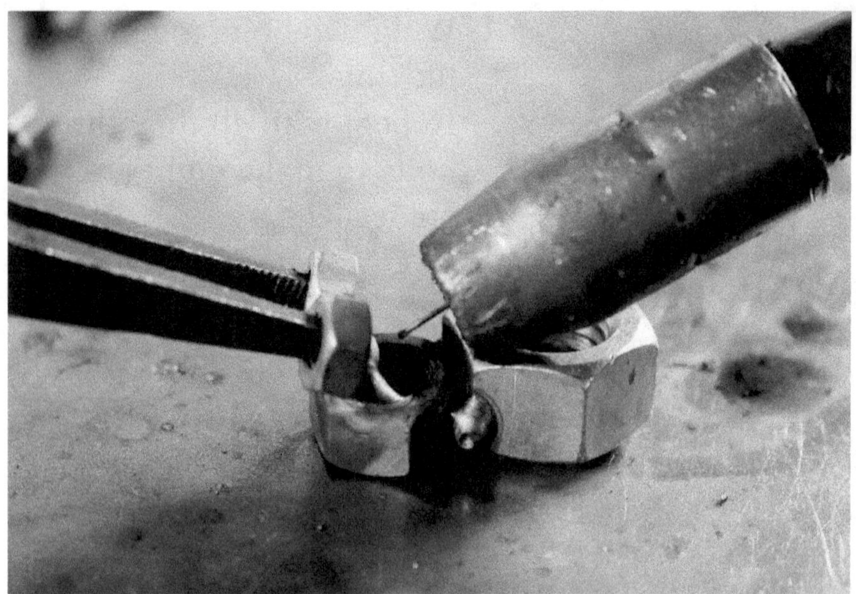

Hold the two small nuts, eyes, up to the front of the medium nut and tack weld them in place.

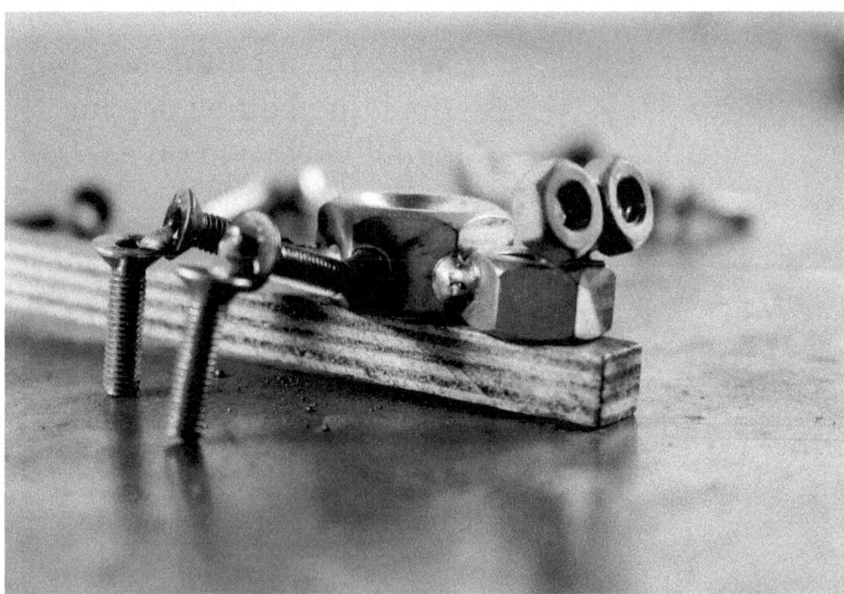

Use something to prop the body of the spider up approximately 1/2" and hold and tack weld the legs on.

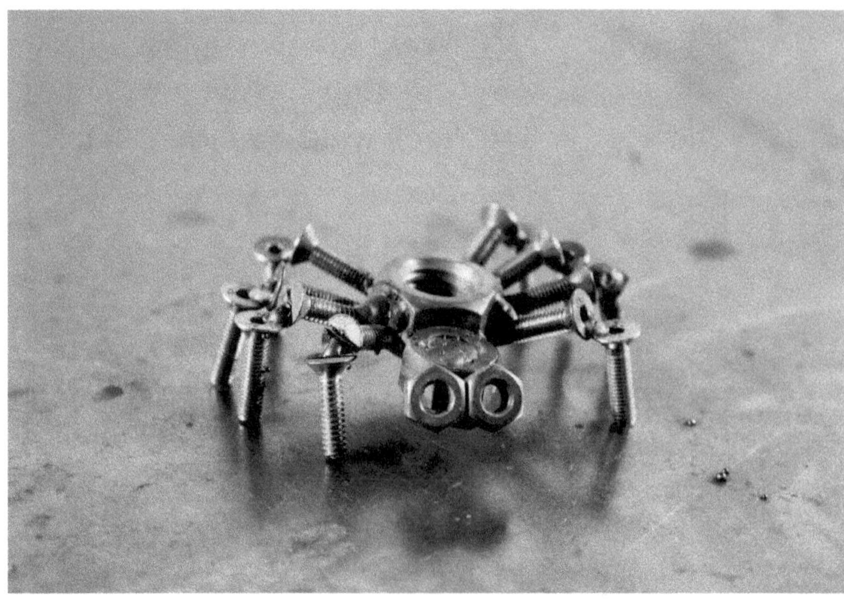

Clean any weld spatter and discoloration and finish with clear coat or paint to prevent rust.

Airplane

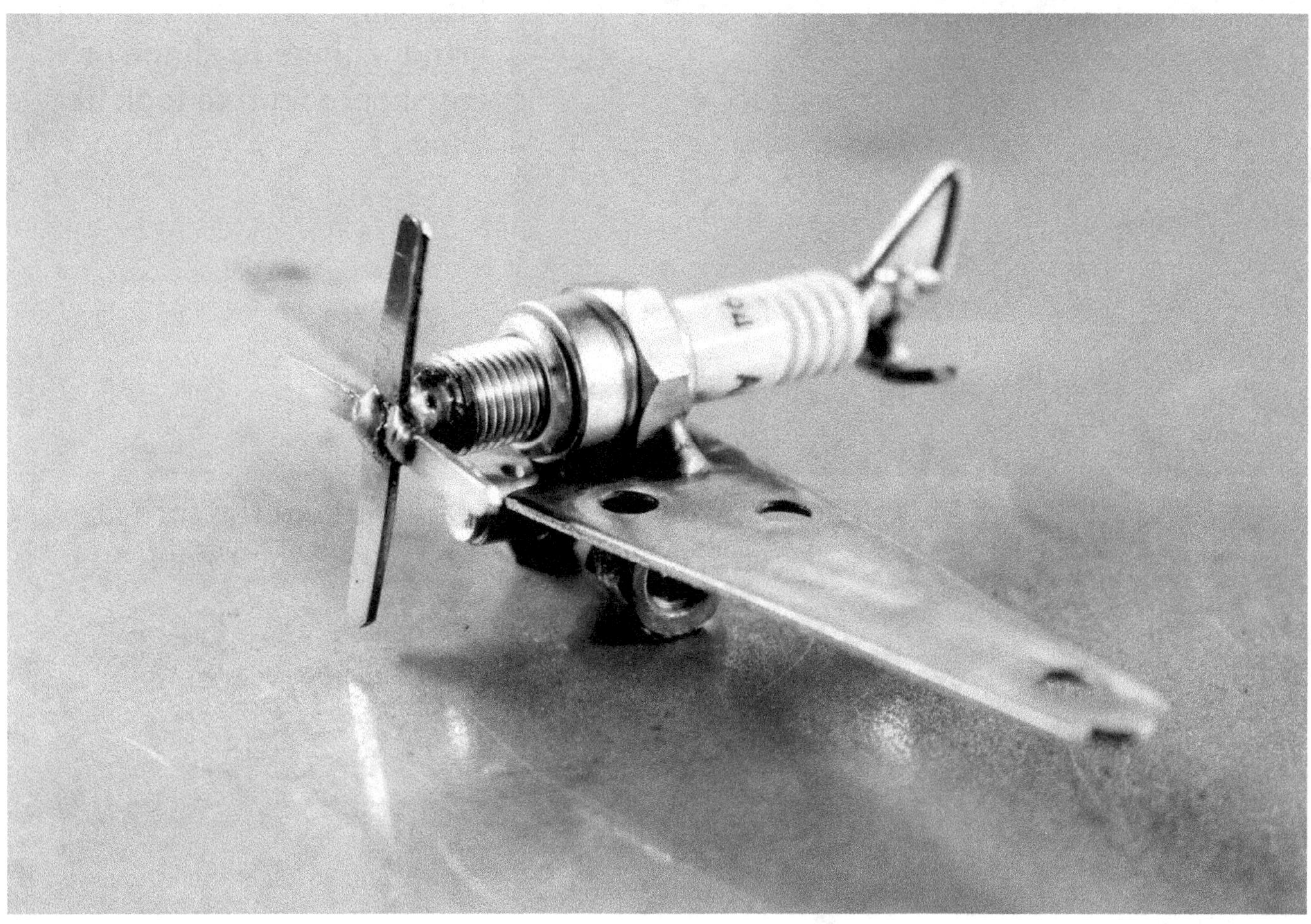

Difficulty

Materials
Spark plug
Narrow hinge (or cut a normal hinge into a wing shape)
Fork
2 Nuts

Tools

Pliers or whelpers
Grinder with cutoff wheel and sanding disk

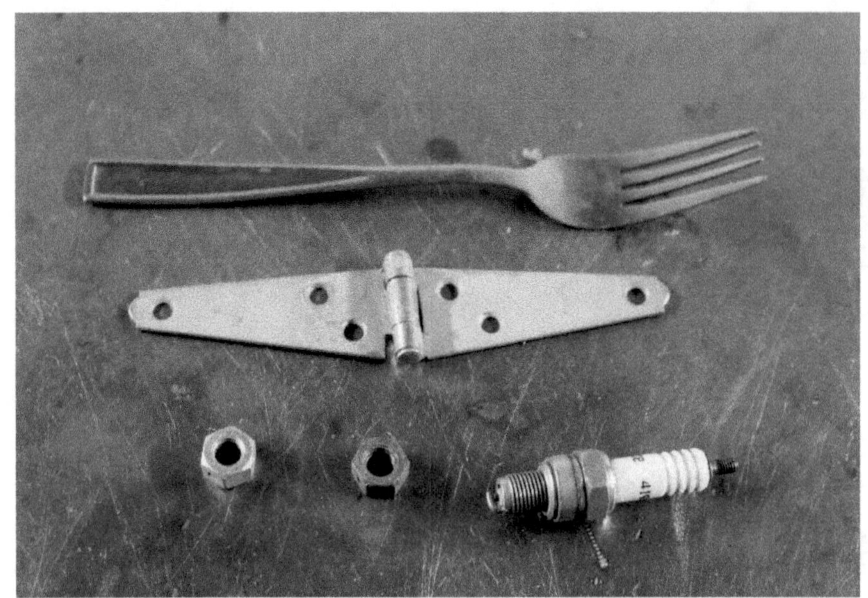

Can you see it yet?
If you don't have a hinge this shape you can cut and grind a hinge to shape or cut sheet metal to look like wings.

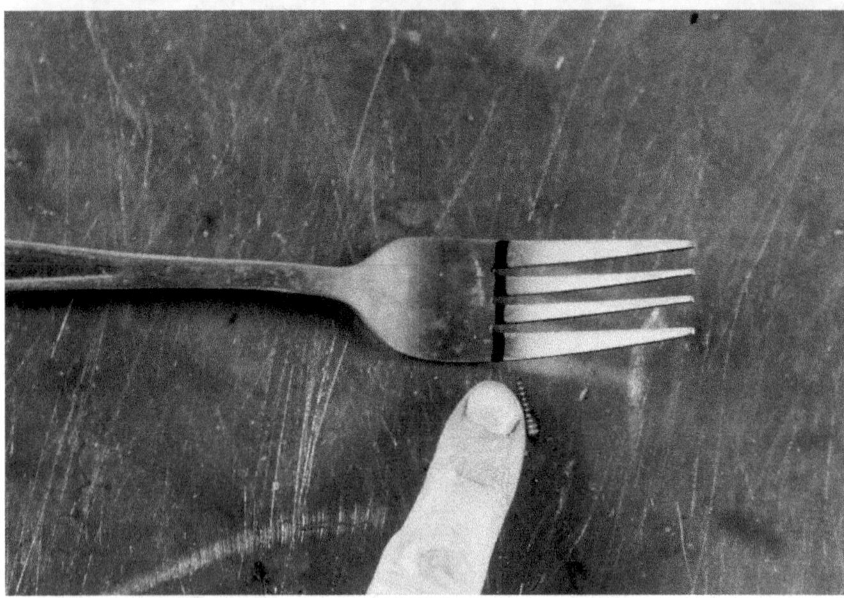

Mark and cut the fork at the base of the tines.

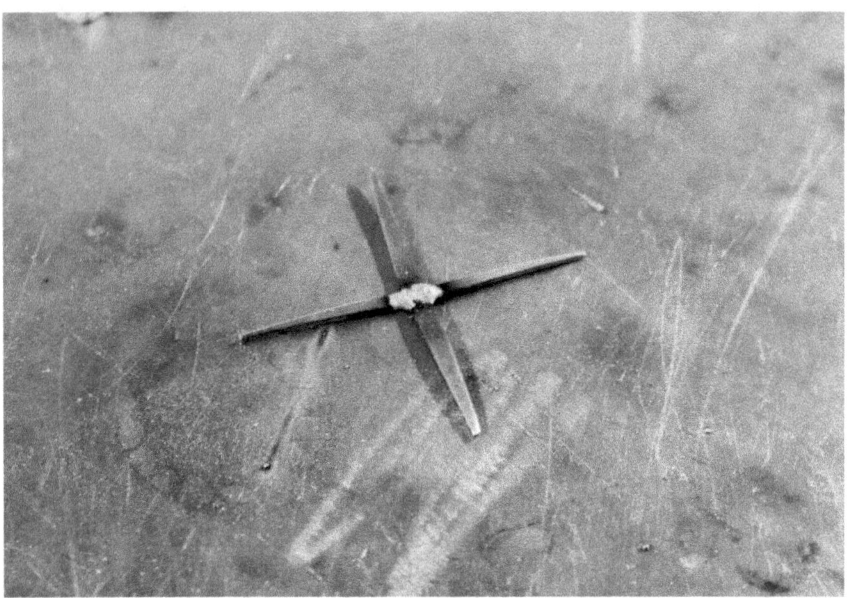

Carefully weldthetines together in theshapeofa propeller.
You may needtomake this smaller bygrinding down each propequally, this will dependonhow tall your airplaneis.

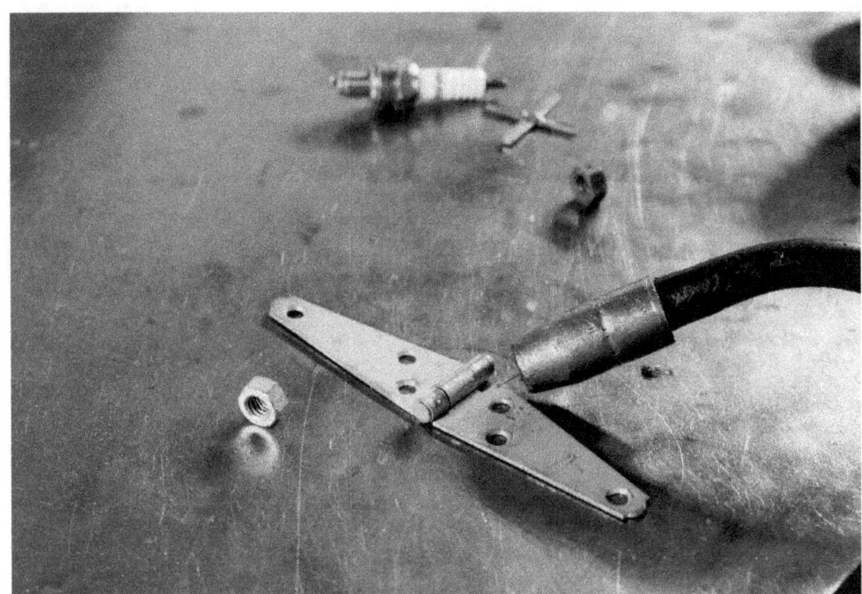

Lay your hinge flat and place a small weld on either side to prevent it from folding closed.

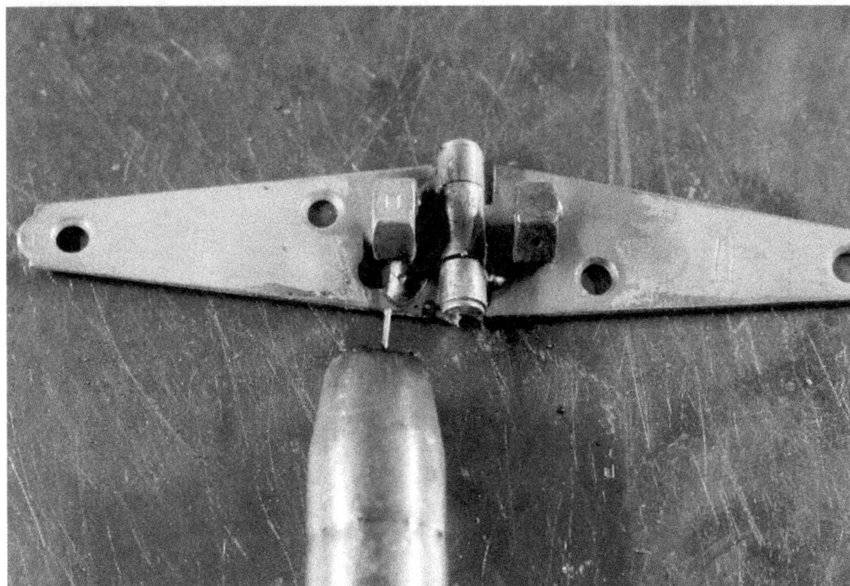

Weld the two nuts to the hinge by placing one tack weld on each side.

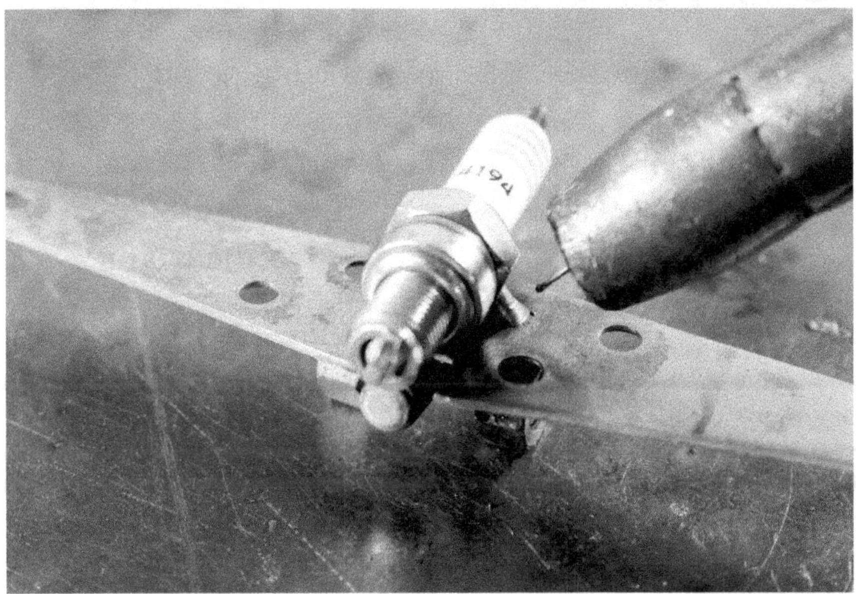

Flip the plane right side up and weld the spark plug on.

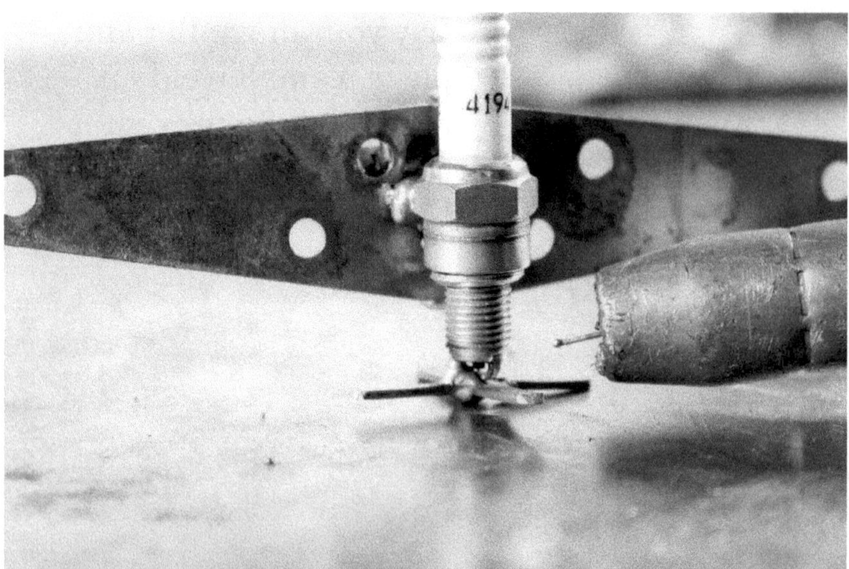

Gently weld the prop on.

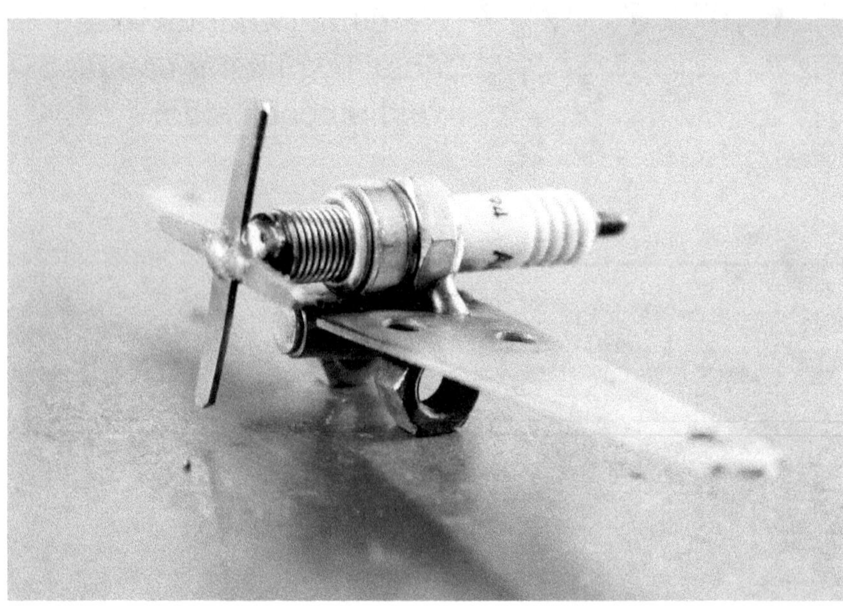

Iground my prop down to make it fit.

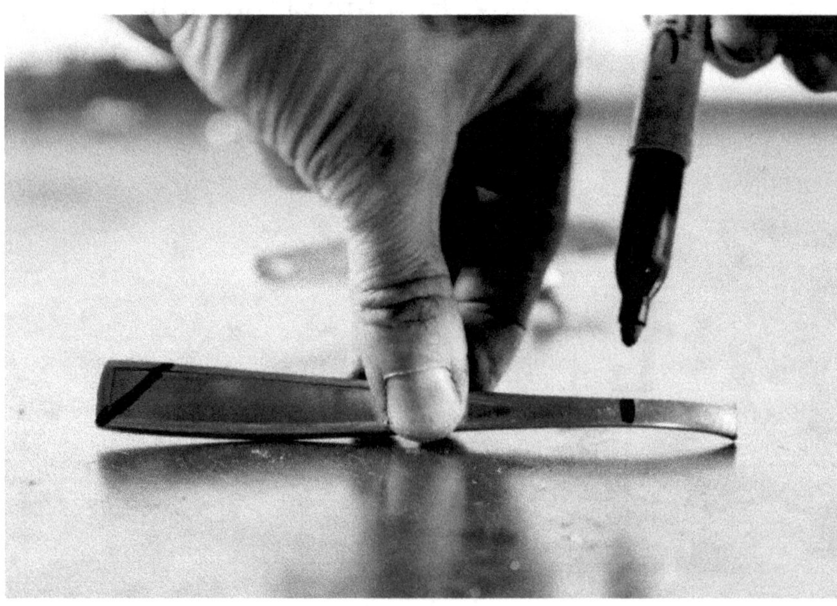

Mark a triangle on the handle of the fork.
Mark and cut a 1" piece from the narrow end of the handle. Cut the triangle and deburr.
Save the 1" piece for the next step.

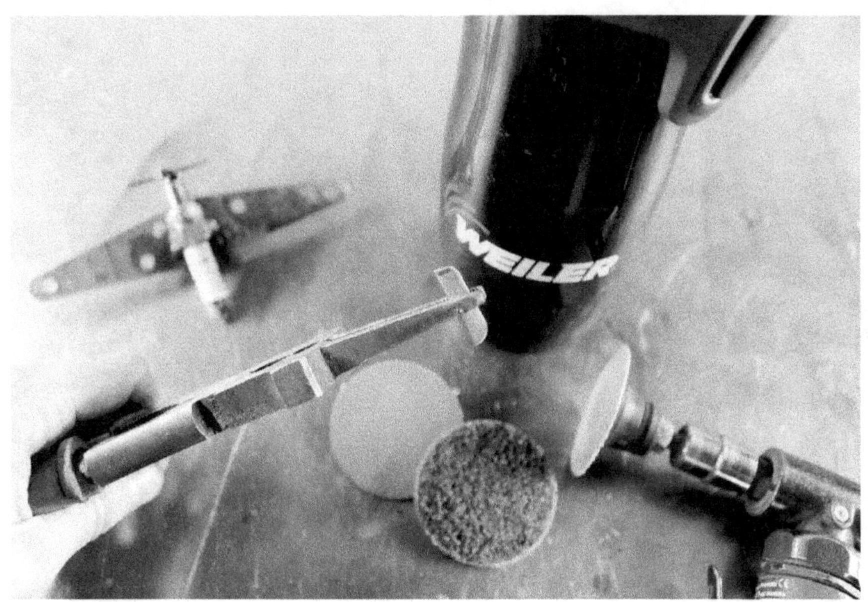

Shape the 1” piece like this.

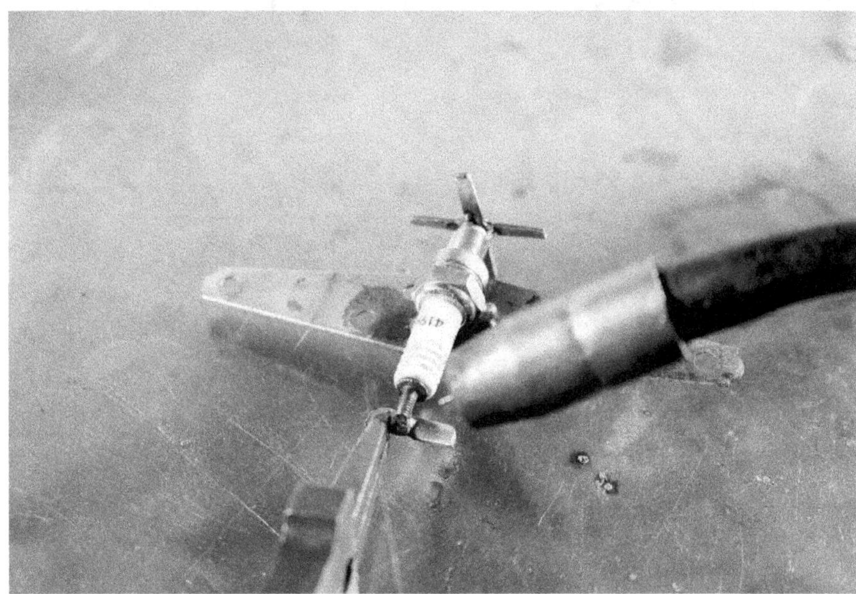

Hold the small wing up to the back of the spark plug and gently tack weld it on. Because there is no metal connection to the metal piece on the back of the spark plug you will need to have it touch your table or use a small piece of metal to act as a ground.

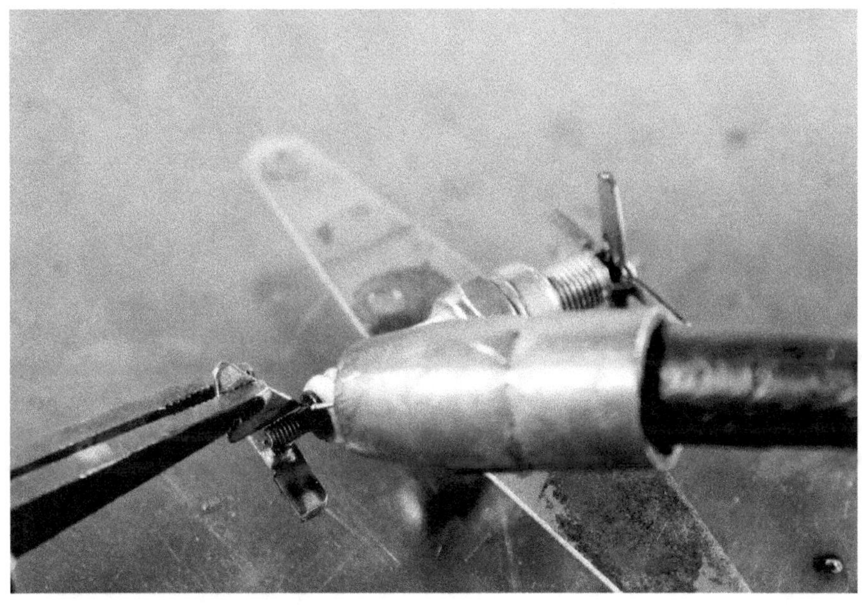

Hold the tail fin to the back and lightly tack weld it in place.
Clean any weld discoloration and spatter.
Clear coat finish.

Rose

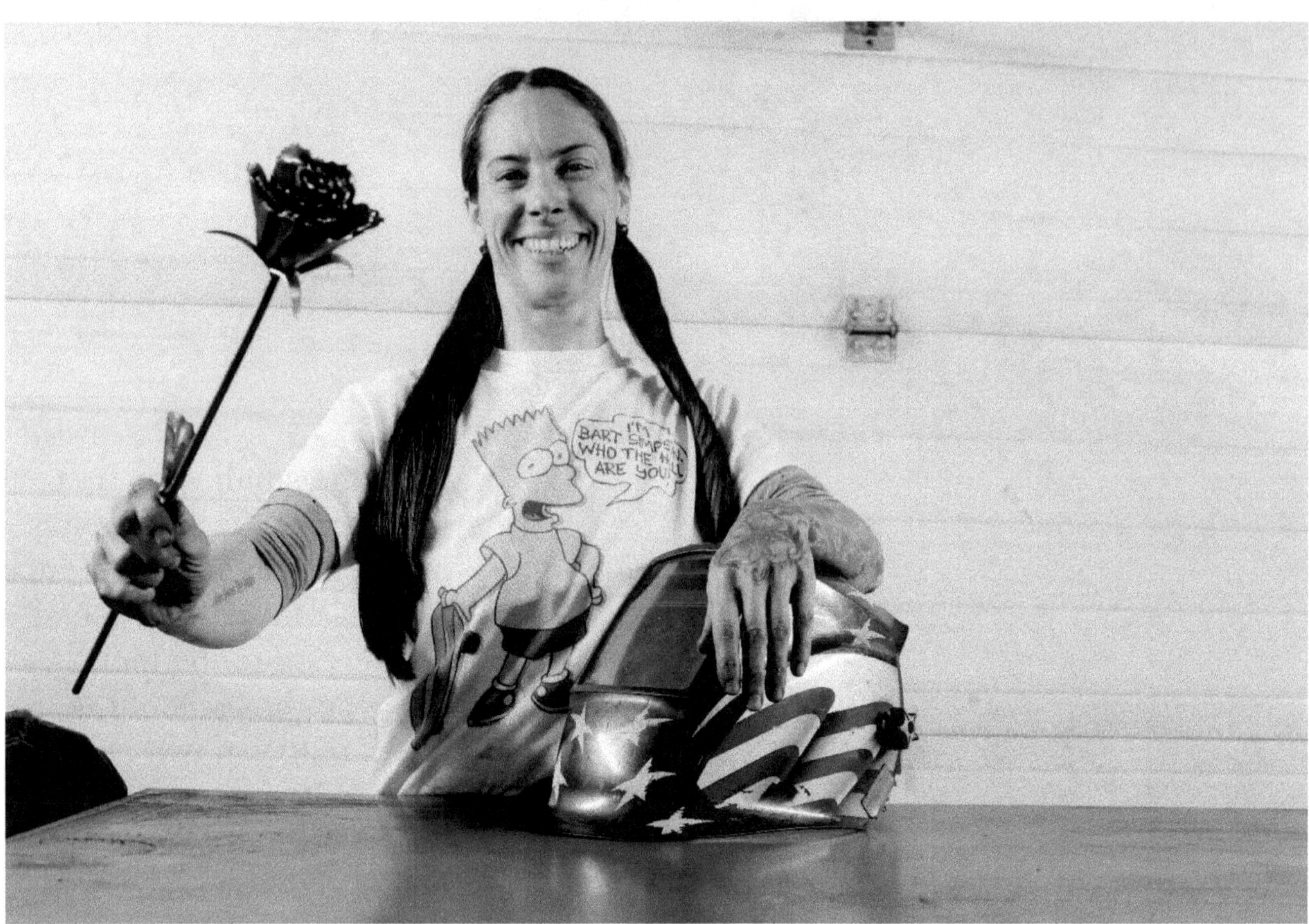

Difficulty

Materials

15" piece of 1/4" round bar or rebar
18 gauge steel sheet

Tools

Hammer and chisel
Wire brush
Tin snips or a plasmacutter
Grinder with cut offwheel and sanding disk

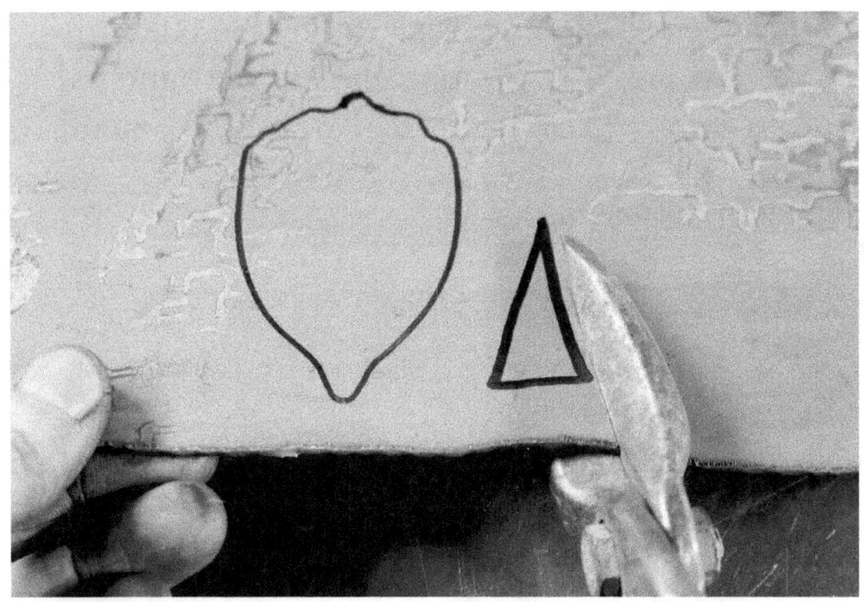

Mark and cut 18 pedals and 4 triangles.
I googled rose pedal outline to come up with this gem!

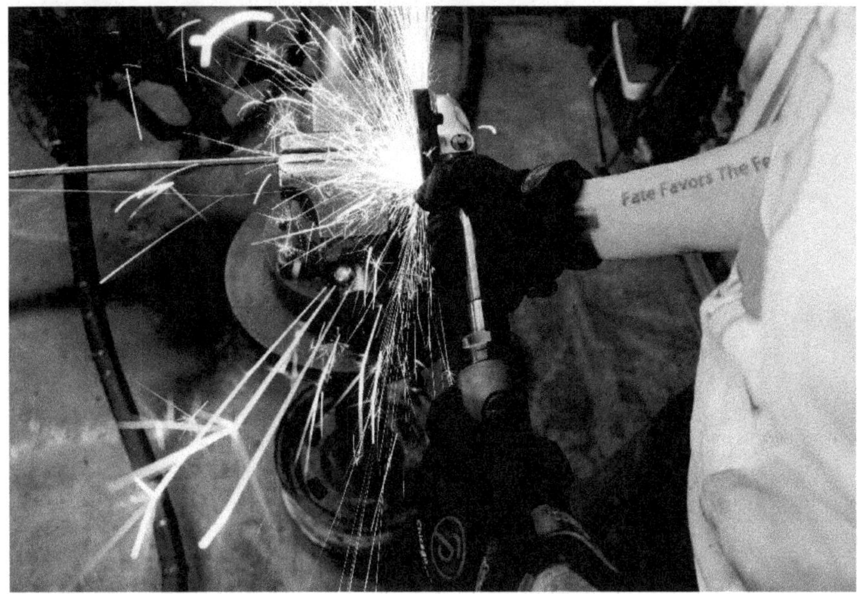

Clamp and cut a 15” piece of 1/4” round bar.

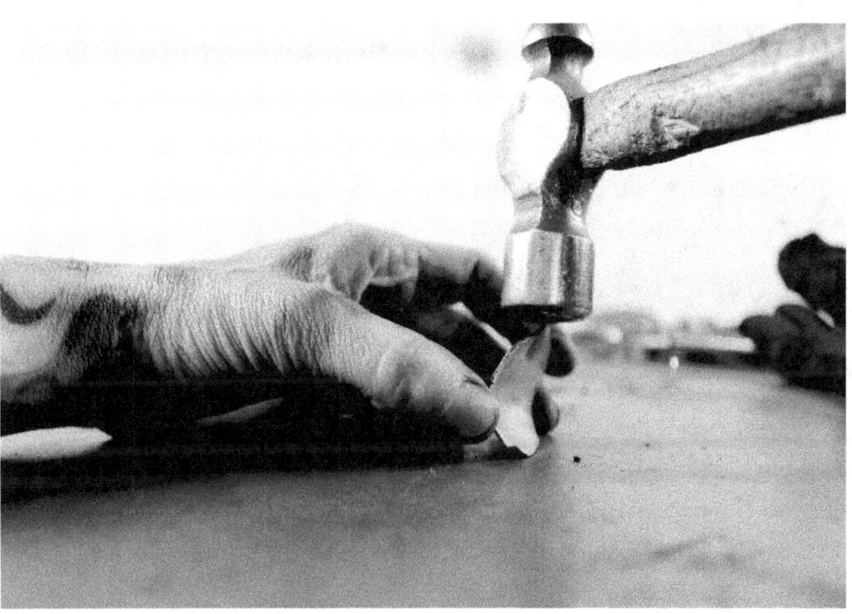

Carefully hold the pedals on their side and hammer them into a gentle curve.

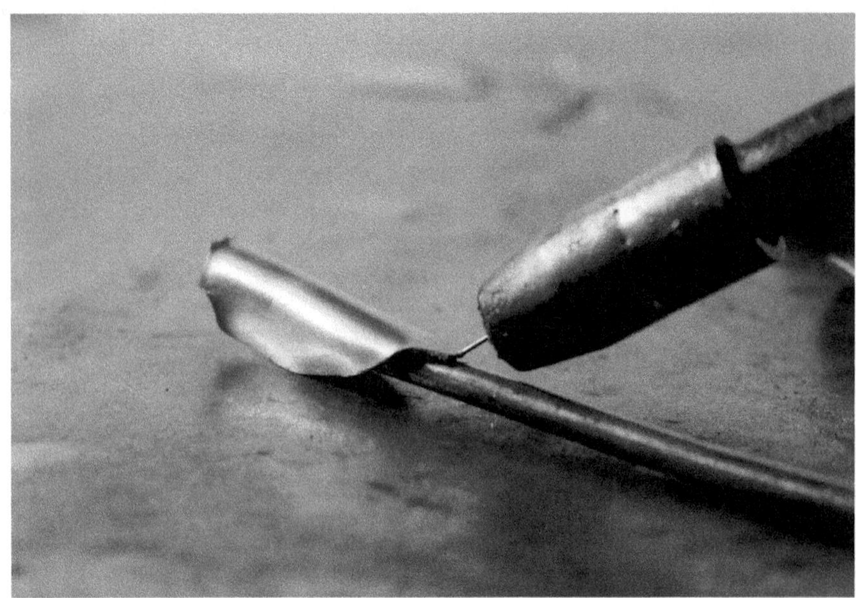

Tack weld a pedal onto one end of the round bar using two or three small tack welds.

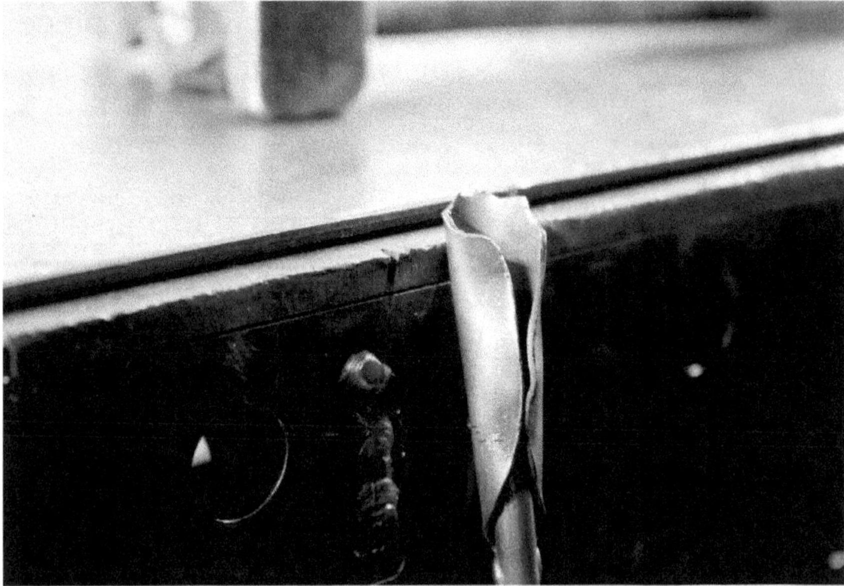

Hammer the pedal around the round bar.

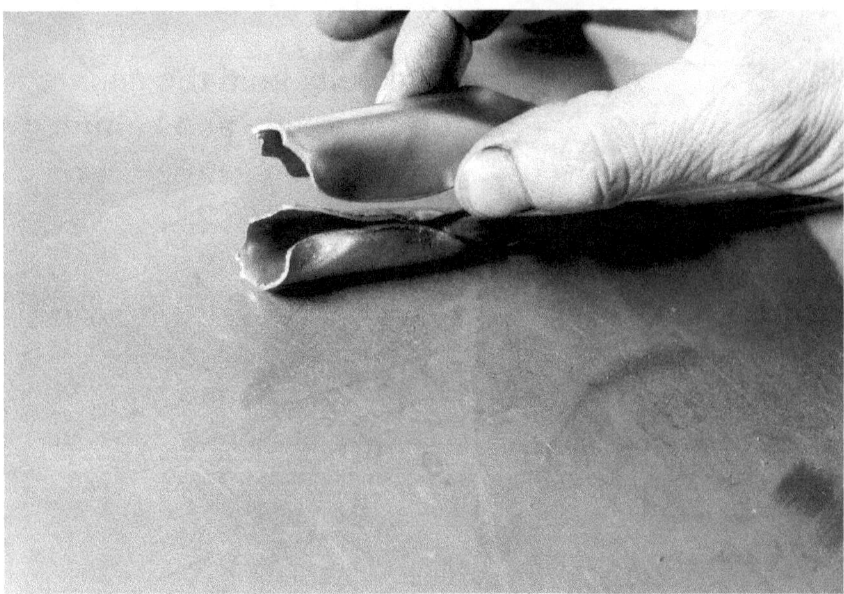

Place another pedal over the first one and tack weld the bottom to the round bar.

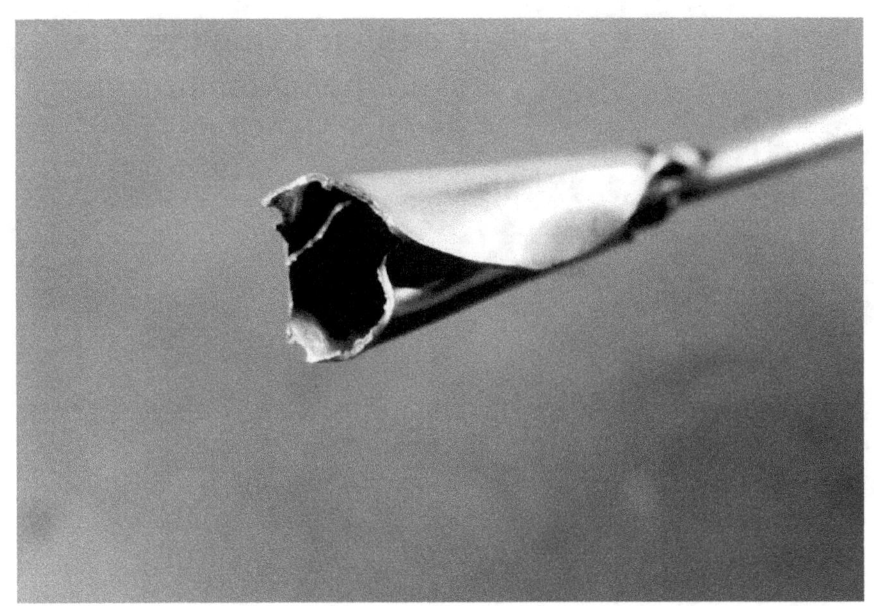

Hammer that pedal around the first pedal.

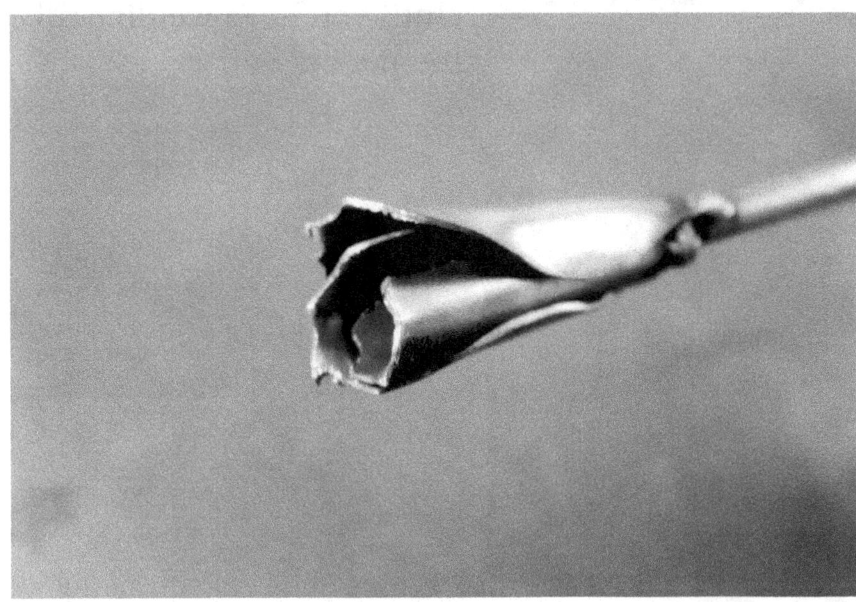

Weld a third pedal over one side of the second pedal and hammer it around.

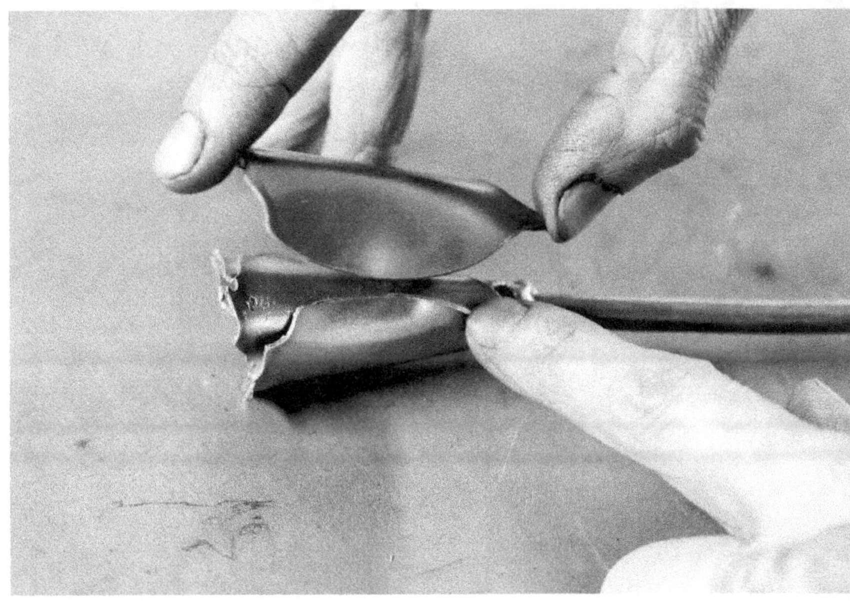

Add the fourth pedal overlapping the edge of the previous pedal and hammering it around.

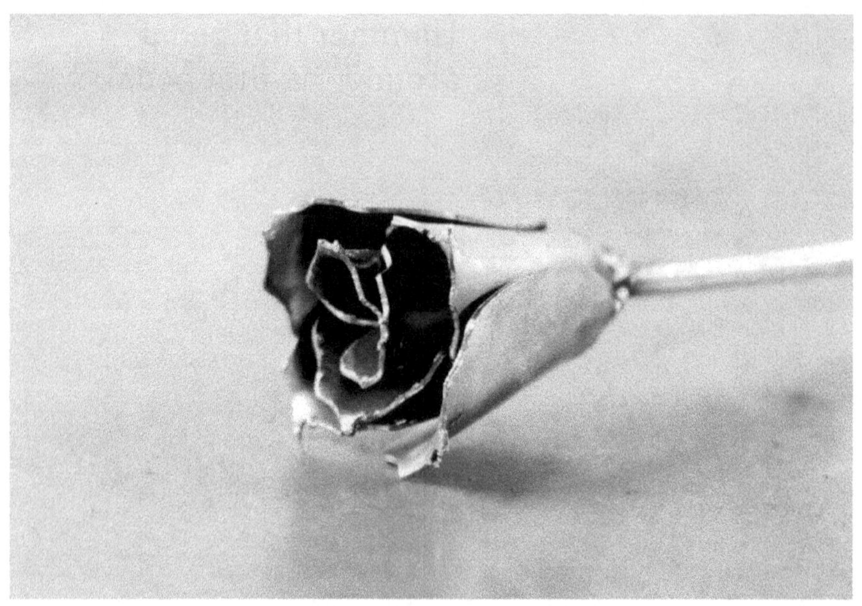

Continue adding pedals overlapping the previous pedal.

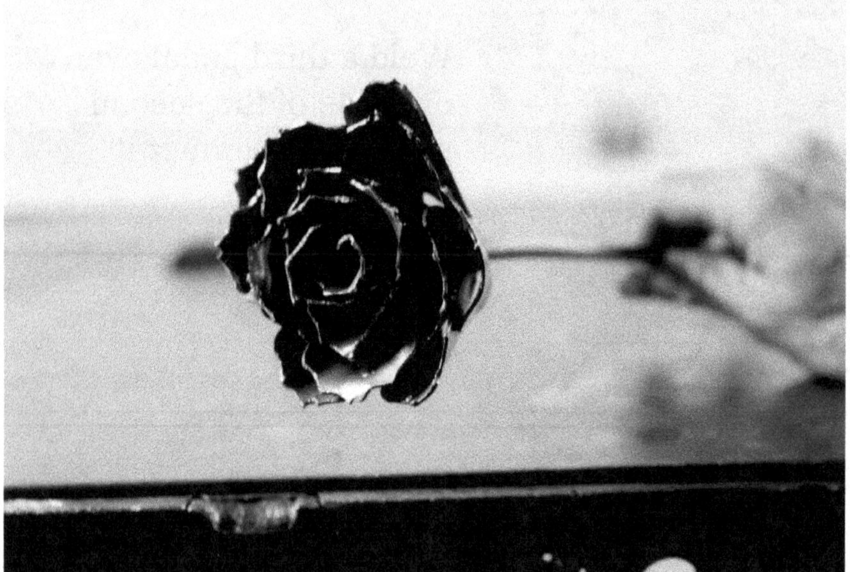

Until you have welding all the pedals on.

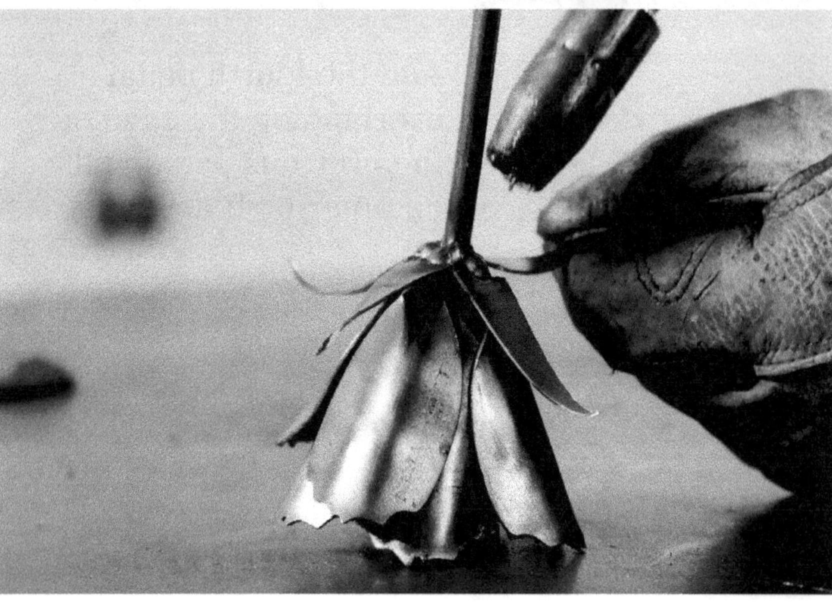

Hold the triangles under the flower and tack weld them on.

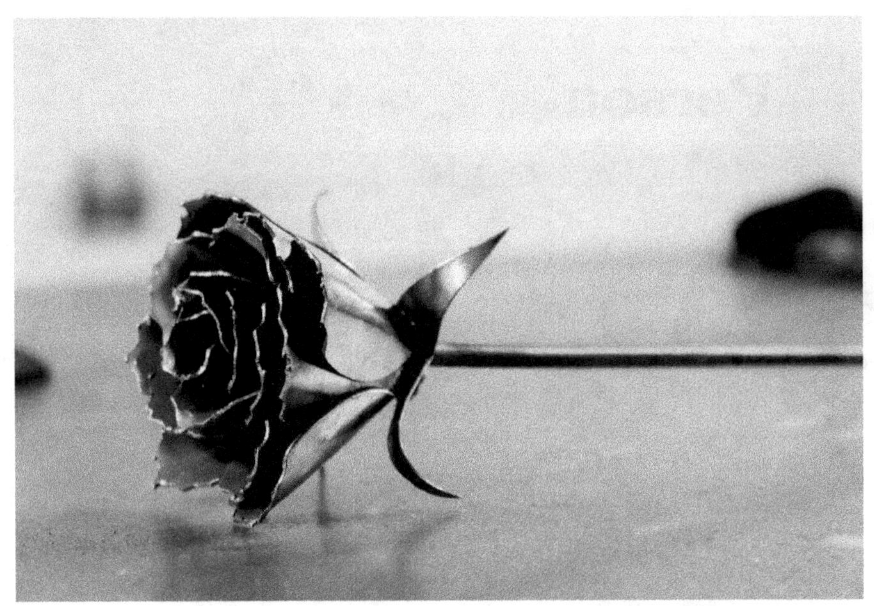

Curve the triangles down.
You can add a thorn if you choose by cutting a 1" piece of screw and welding it to the stem.
You can add a leaf by cutting a leaf shape from your sheet metal and welding it to the stem.

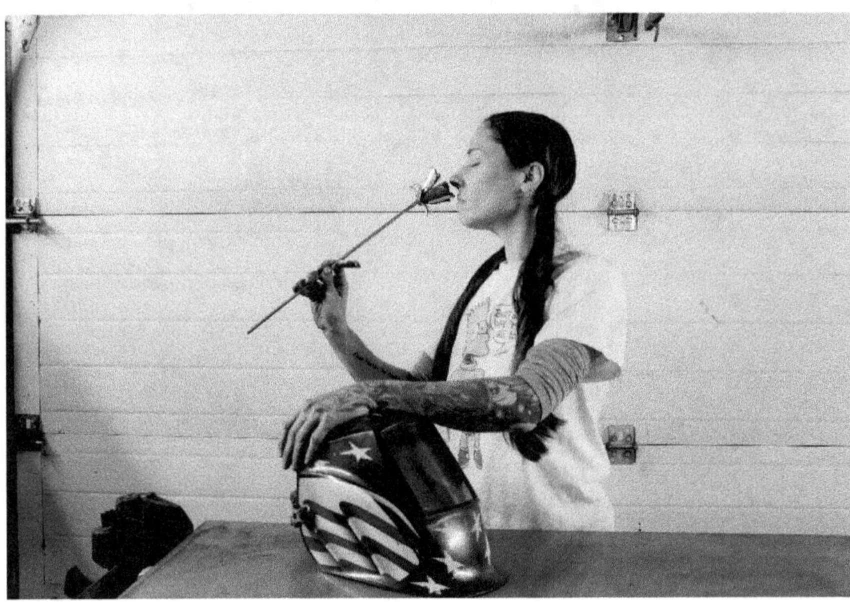

Clean any weld discoloration and chip any spatter.
Use heat from a torch to color the rose. Play around with the technique until you can get gold, purple, and blue roses!
Always stop and take time to smell the roses, even if they are steel!

Person

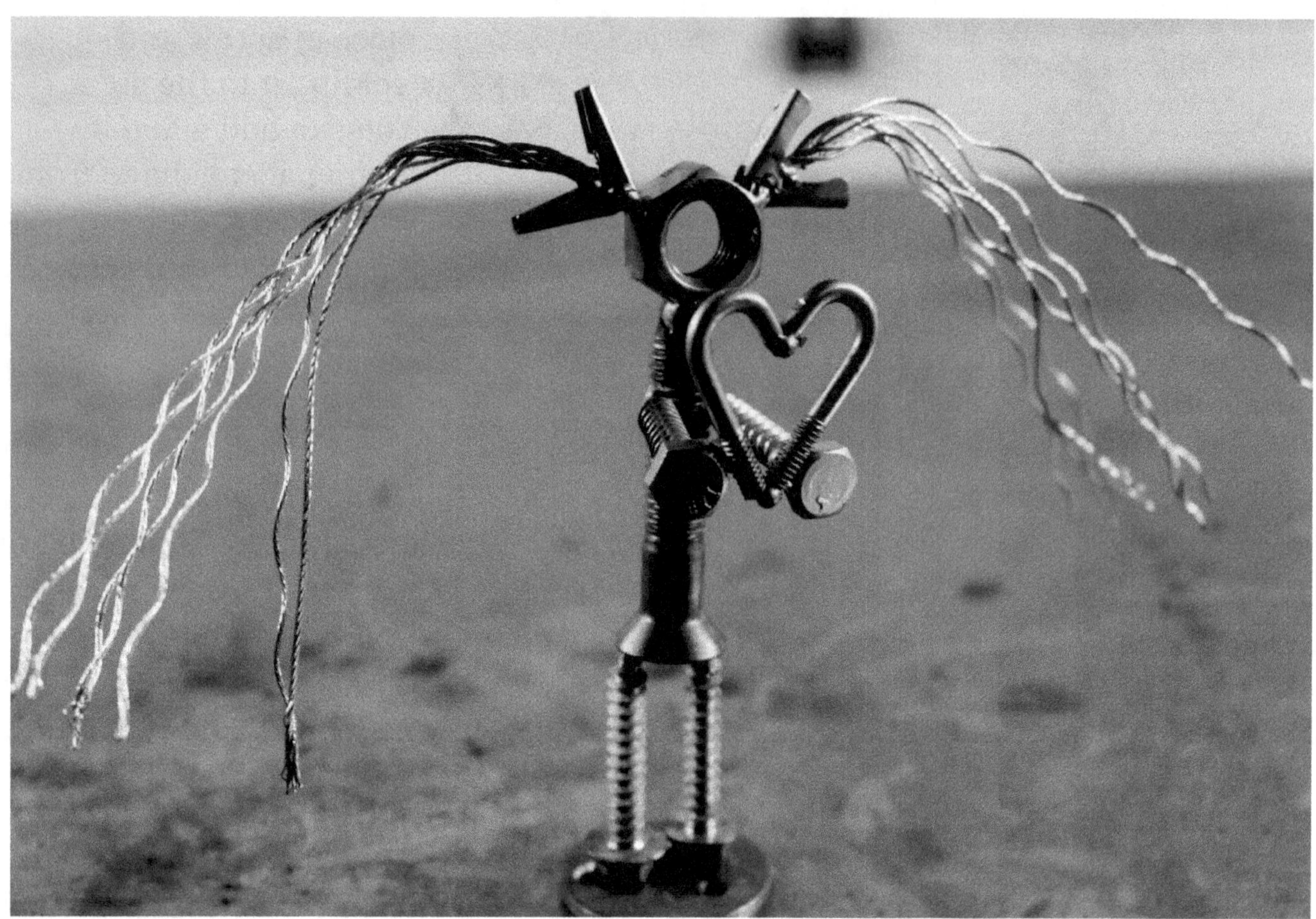

Difficulty

Materials (Materialswill vary depending on the person you want to make)
12" braded wire orwelding wire for hair
1 Large nut, 2 wingnuts
1 Large bolt, 4 medium bolts (I also used 2 cane shaped bolts to create the heart)
1 large washer or something for a base

Tools

Hammer and chisel
Wire brush

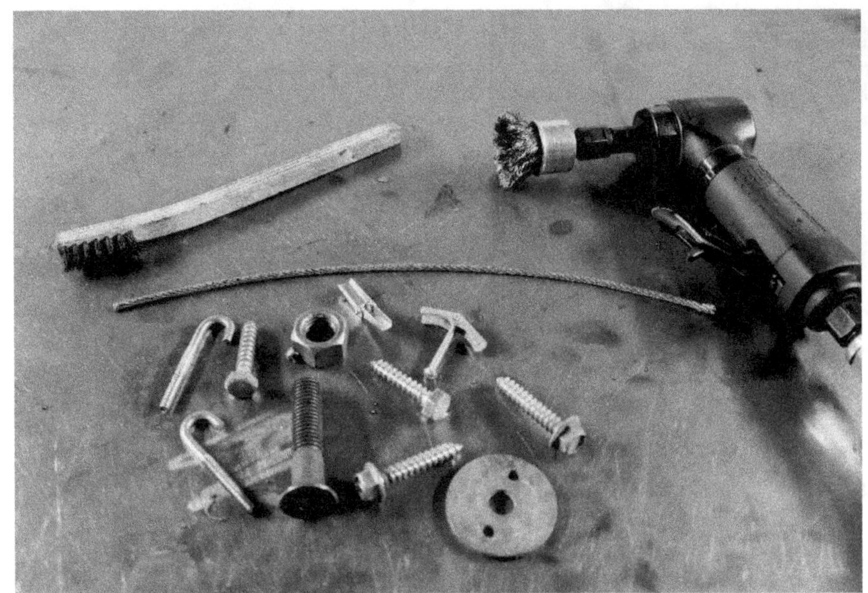

Clean any rusty materials with a wire brush or wheel.

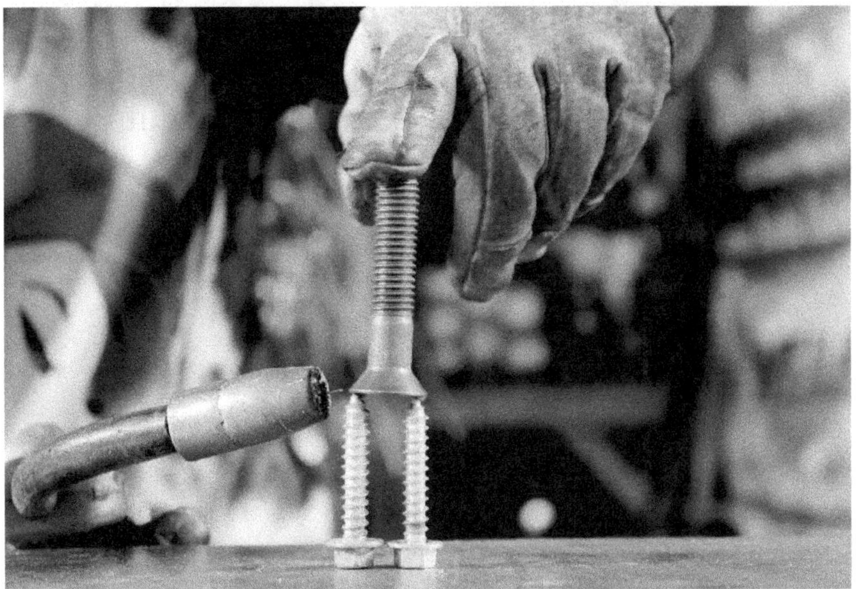

Stand two medium bolts up and tack weld the large bolt to it.
Tack weld the legs onto the base.

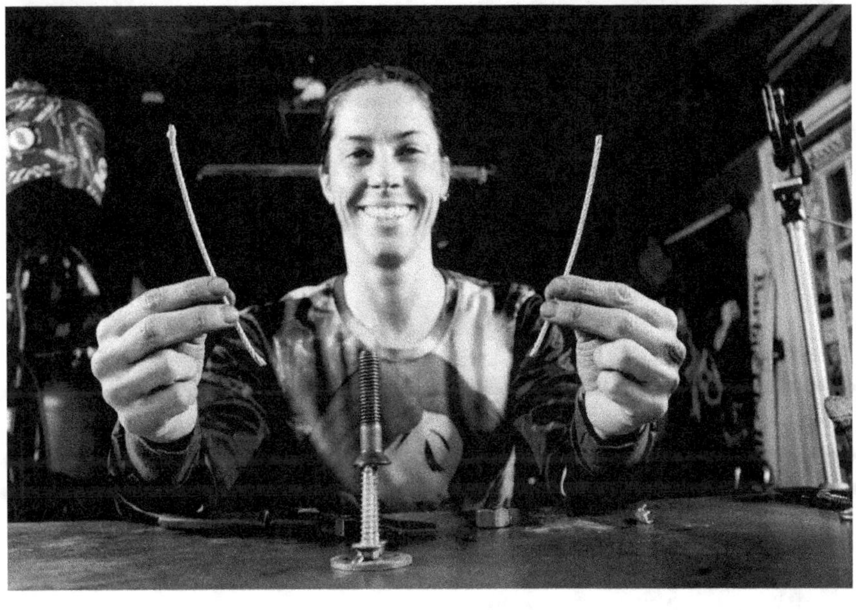

For hair cut the braded wire in half and placea small tack weld on one end of each.

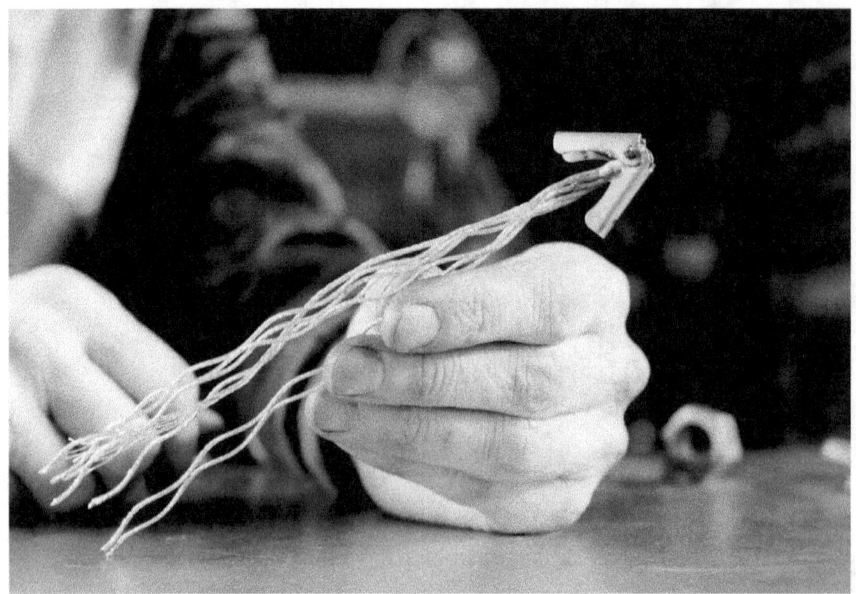

Weld the tack welded end of the braided wire ont the wing nut and unbraid the wire.

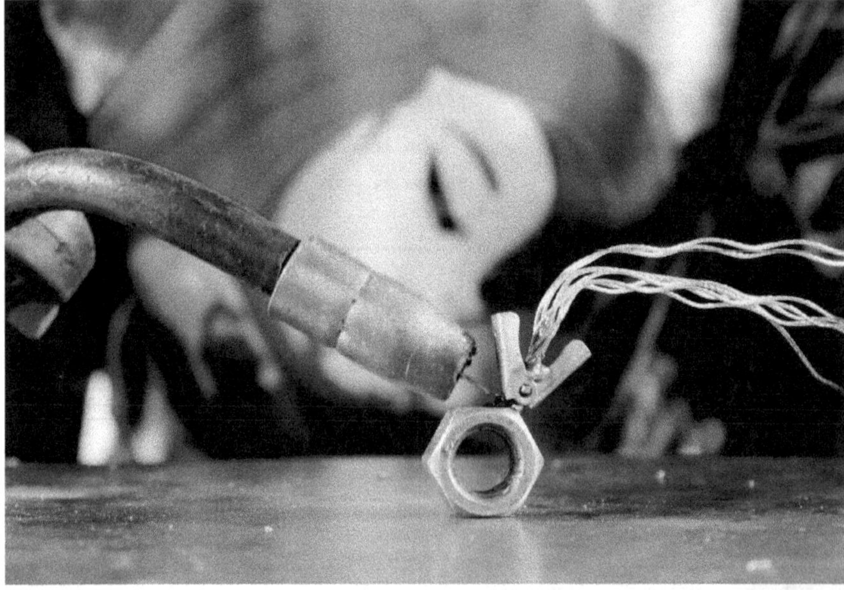

Weld the hair onto one side of the large nut.

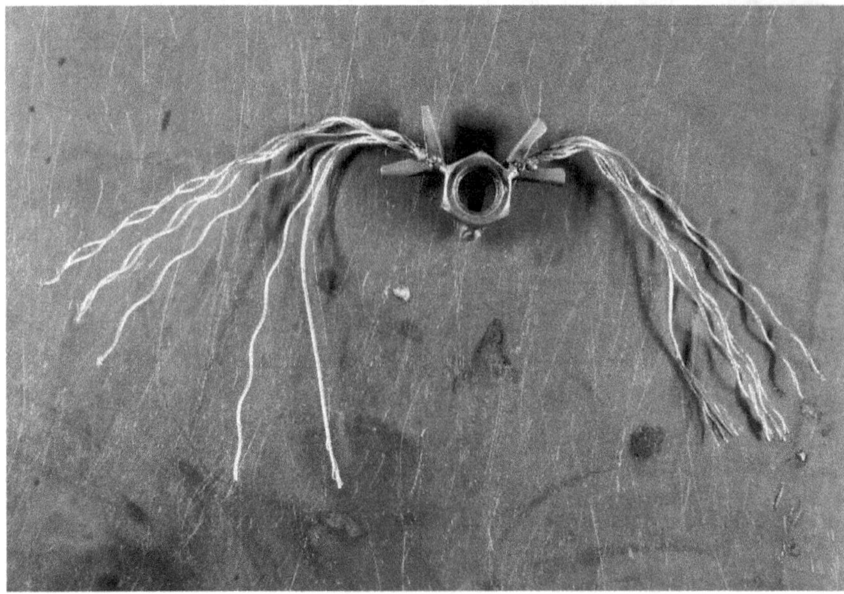

Weld the other side on and clean the welds with a wire brush.

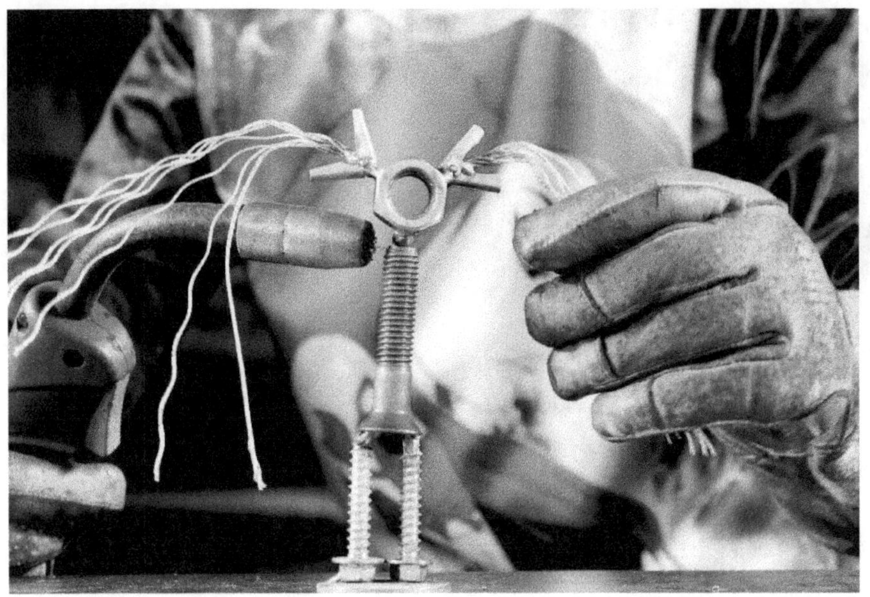

Hold the head up to the body and tack weld it in place.

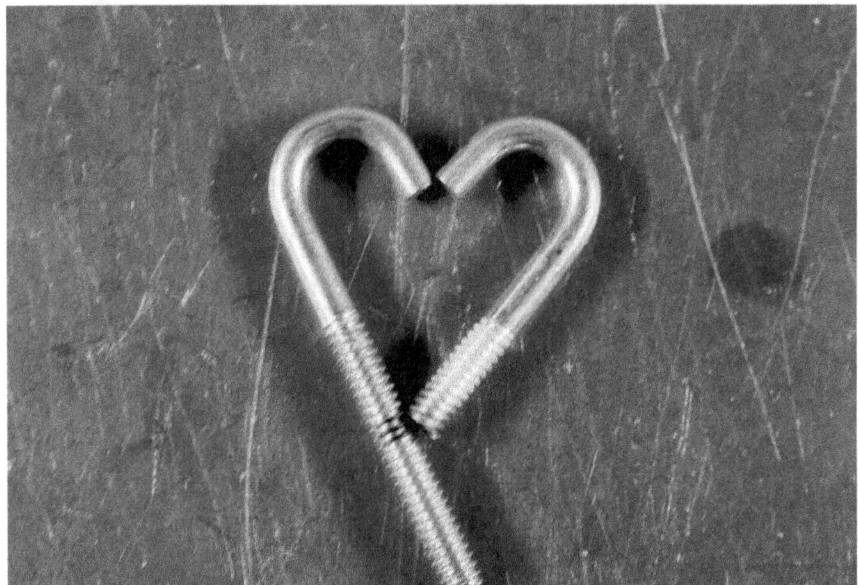

If you want a heart and can't find these gems, simply bend 1/8" round bar into heart shapes.

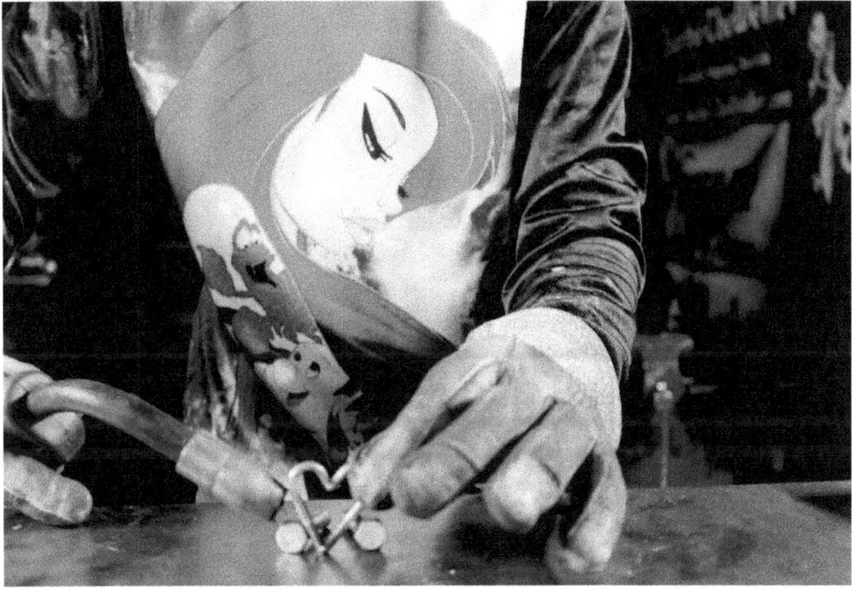

Weld the heart into the hands/arms using small tack welds.

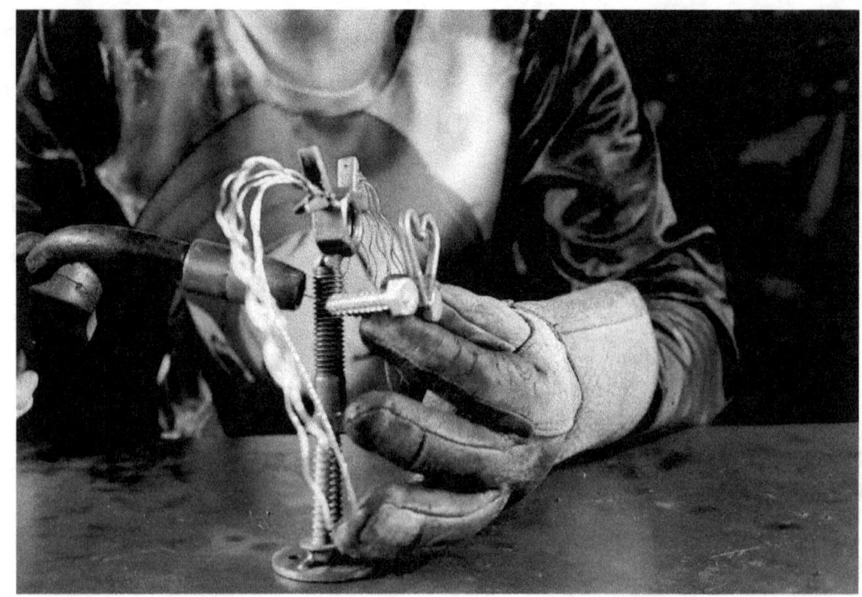

Weld the arms onto the body.

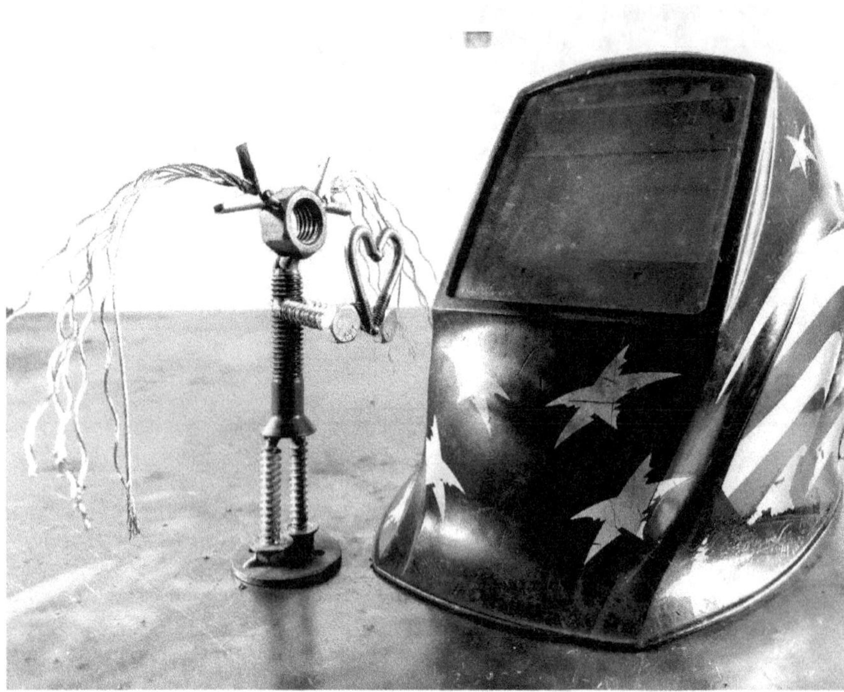

This is totally a self-portrait! I love welding! Clean any weld spatter and discoloration and finish by painting orusea clear coat to preventrust.

Medieval Battle Axe

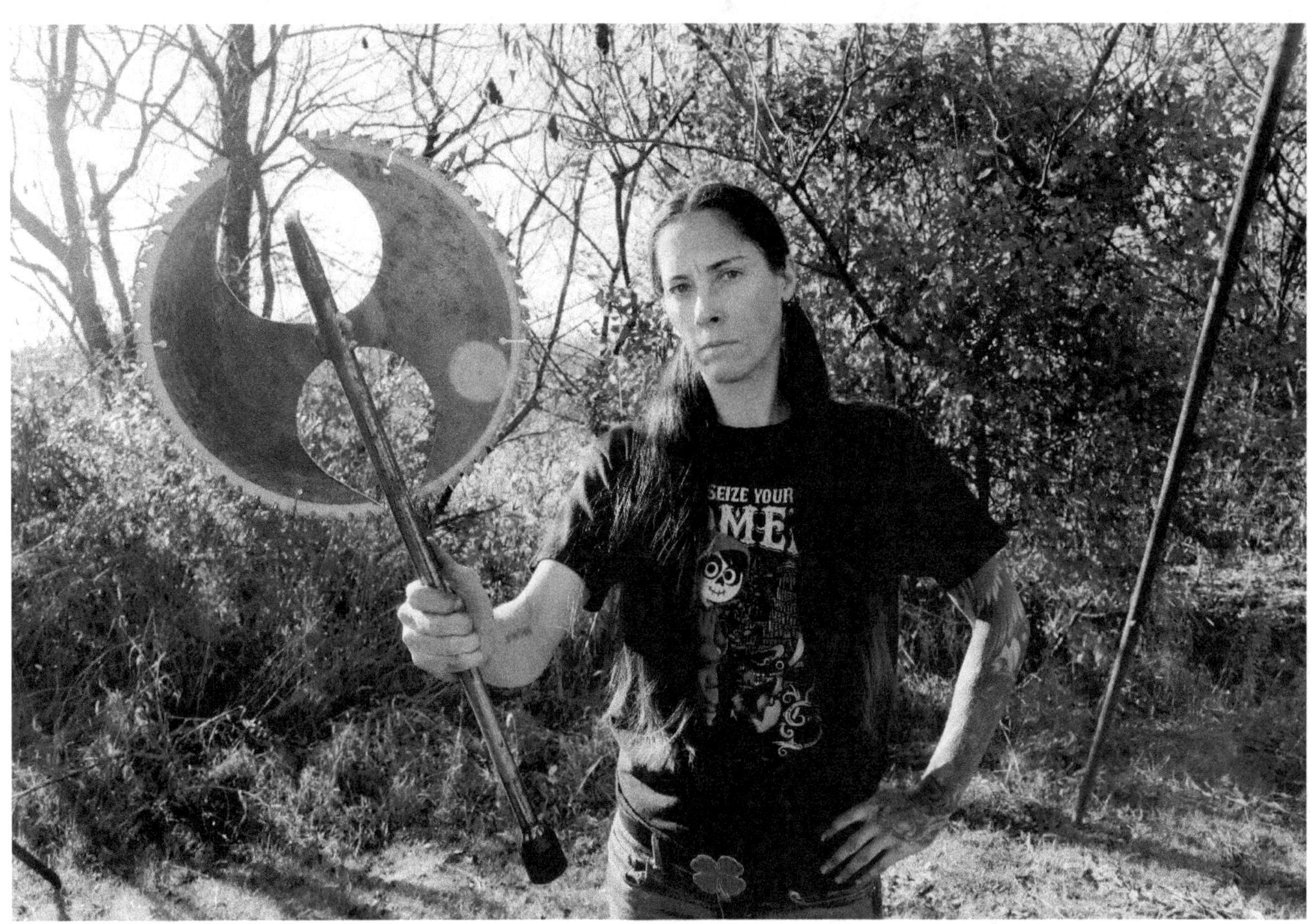

Difficulty

Materials

Saw blade
Breaker bar or round steel bar

Tools

Grinder with sanding disk and cutoff wheel
Straight edge
Something round approximately 4-6" in diameter
Marker

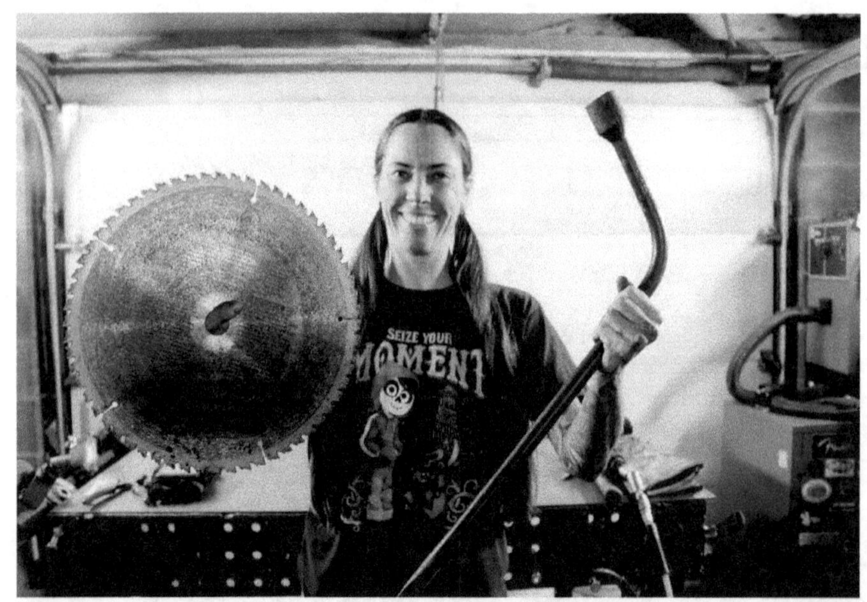

For my round bar I used this breaker bar and cut it in two spots to take out the curve and then welded the two pieces back together and ground it smooth.

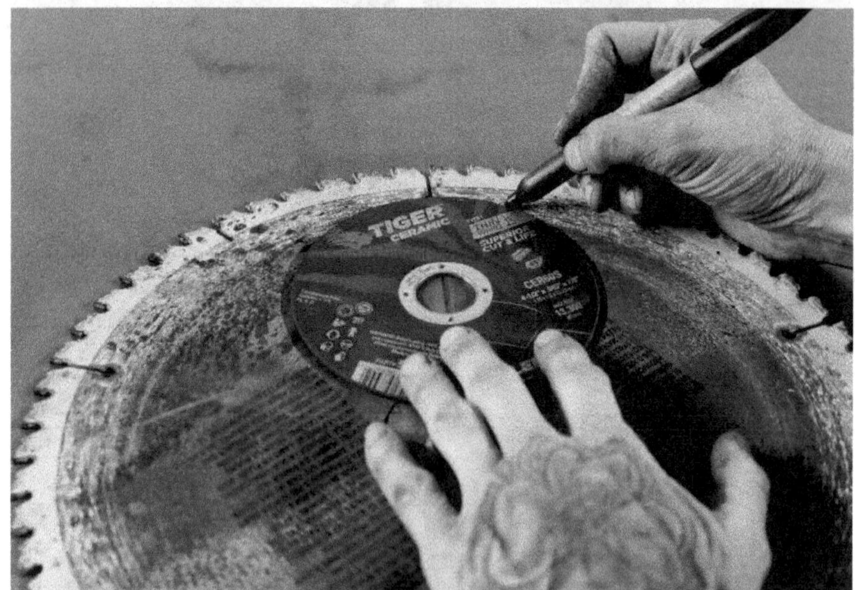

Mark a line down the center of your saw blade. Using something round, a small coffee can, the lid of a jar, or a cut off wheel, mark one circle on the top and one circle on the bottom making sure they are centered on the line.

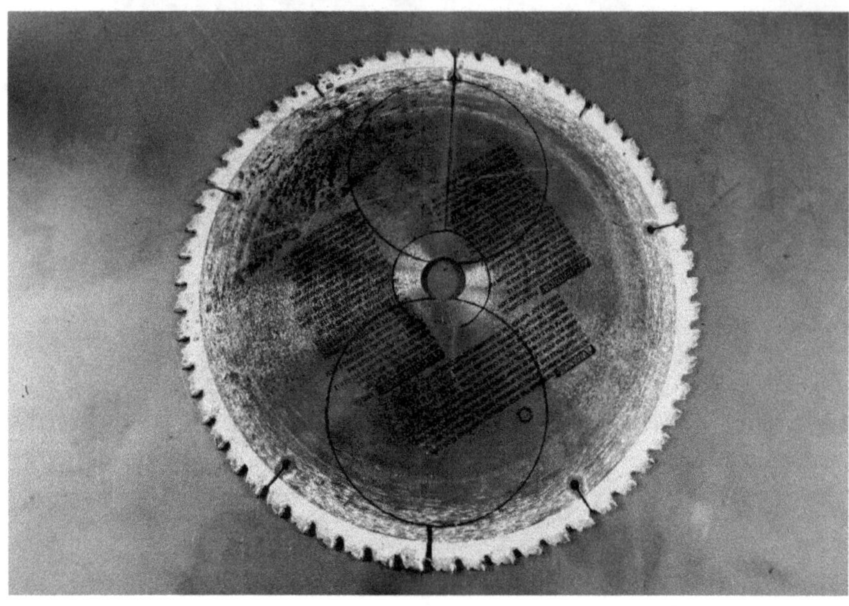

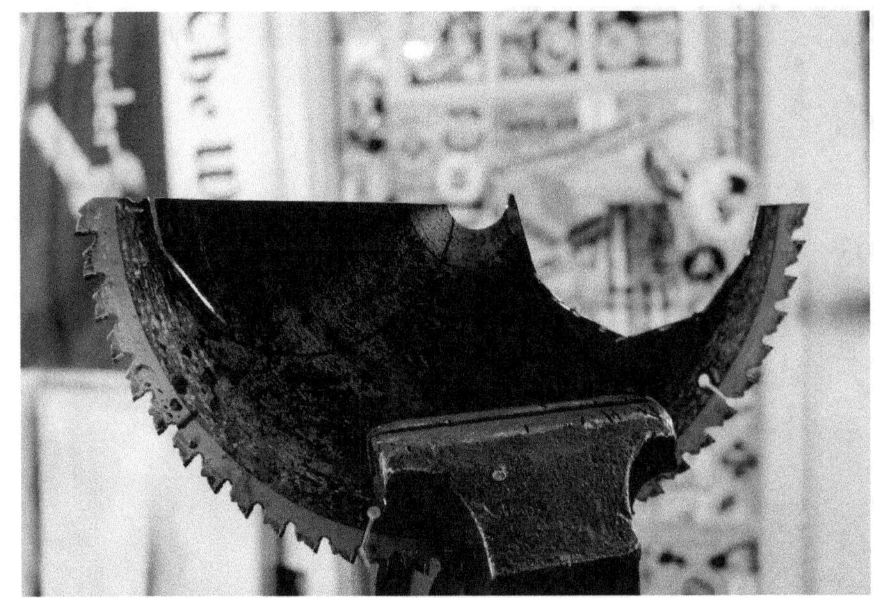

Clamp and very carefully cut the saw on all the lines you made using a cutoff wheel. (If you have a plasma cutter use that instead!)
Cut inside the half circles to leave room for grinding and shaping.

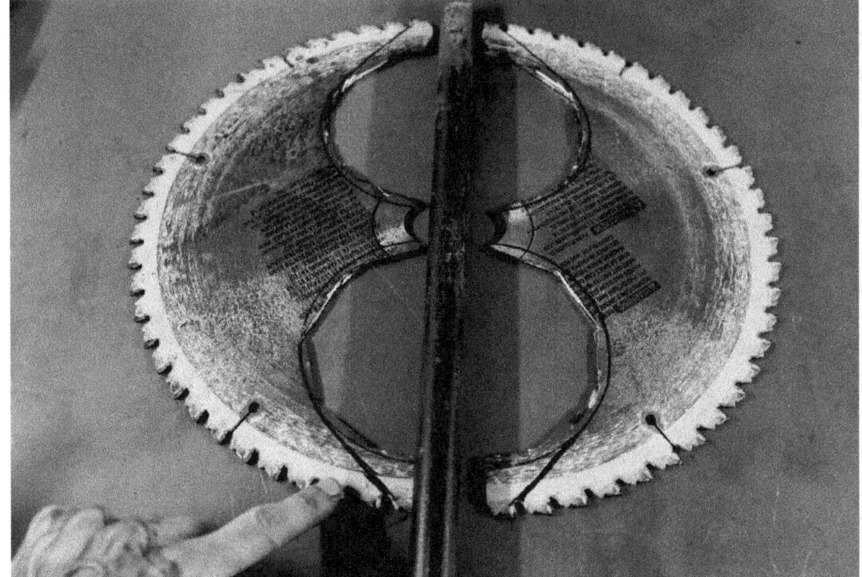

Mark lines as shown and cut.

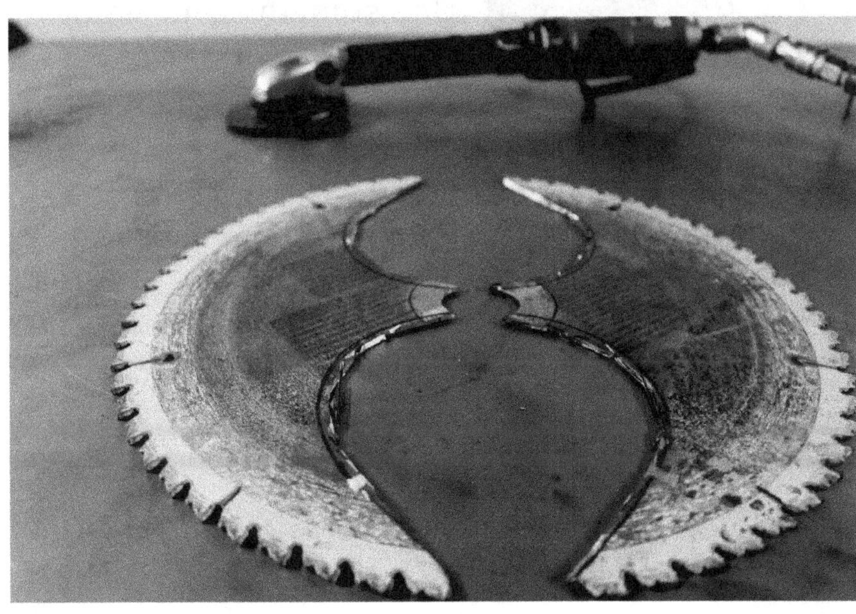

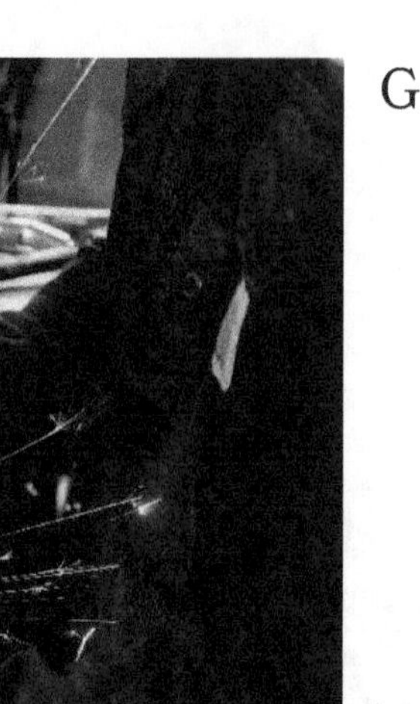

Grind all cuts smooth.

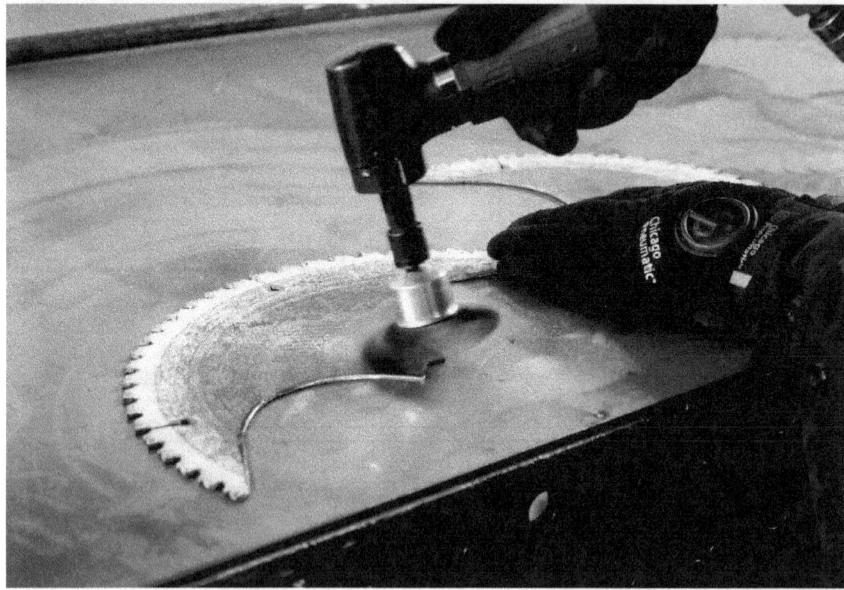

Clean any rust from saw blade and the round bar using a wire wheel or brush.

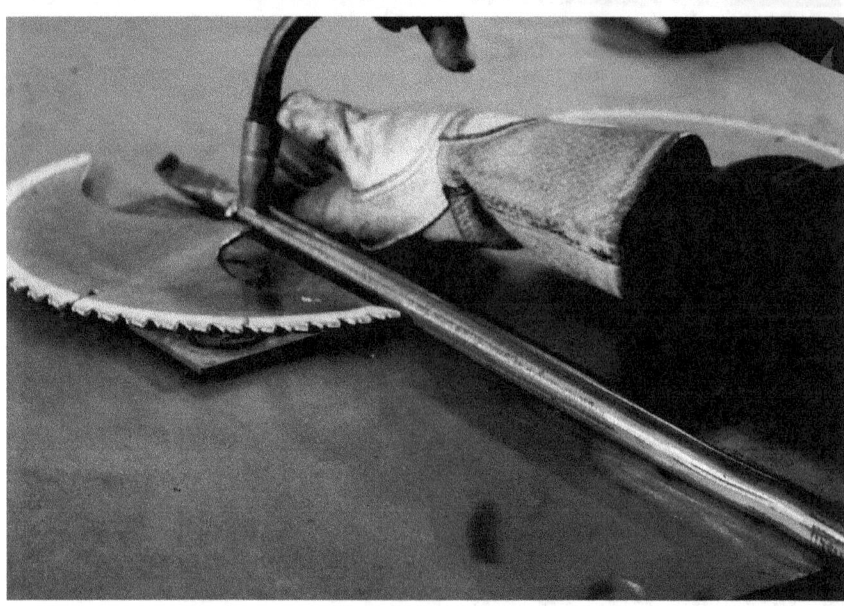

Use something to hold the saw blade up to the center of the round bar and tack weld it in place. Carefully flip it over and tack weld the back side.

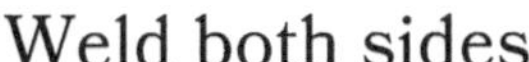

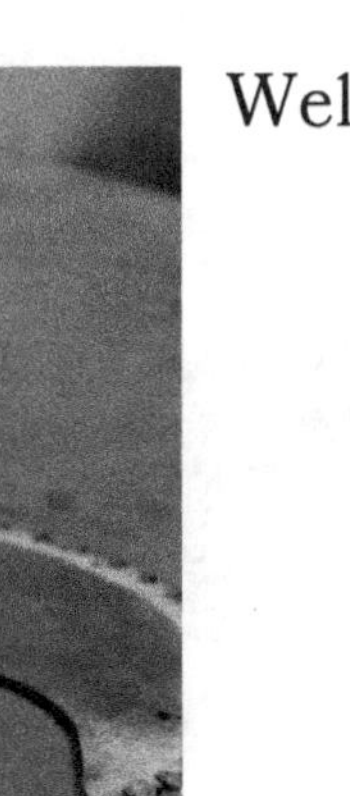

Weld both sides.

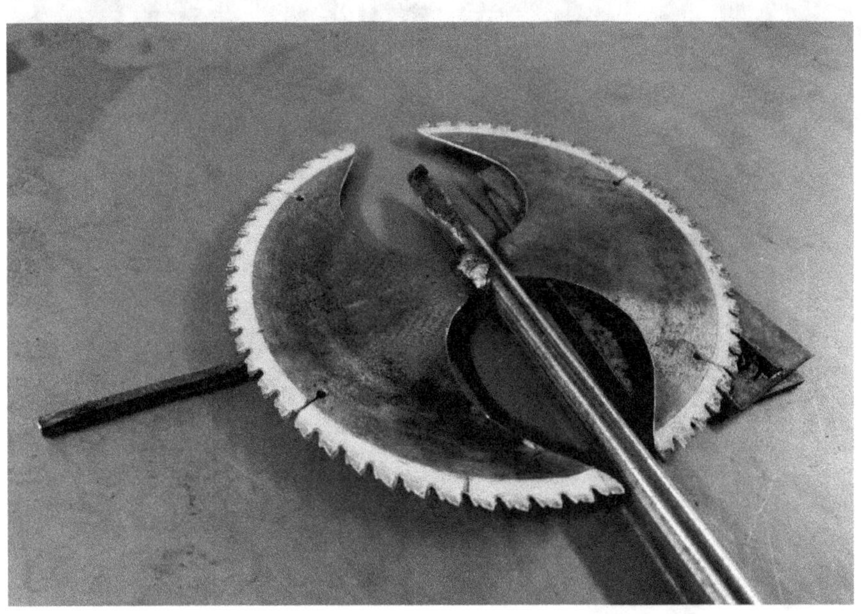

Prop the second side up keeping the first side level.
Tack weld both sides and then weld.
Clean any weld discoloration and spatter.
Finish with clear coat.

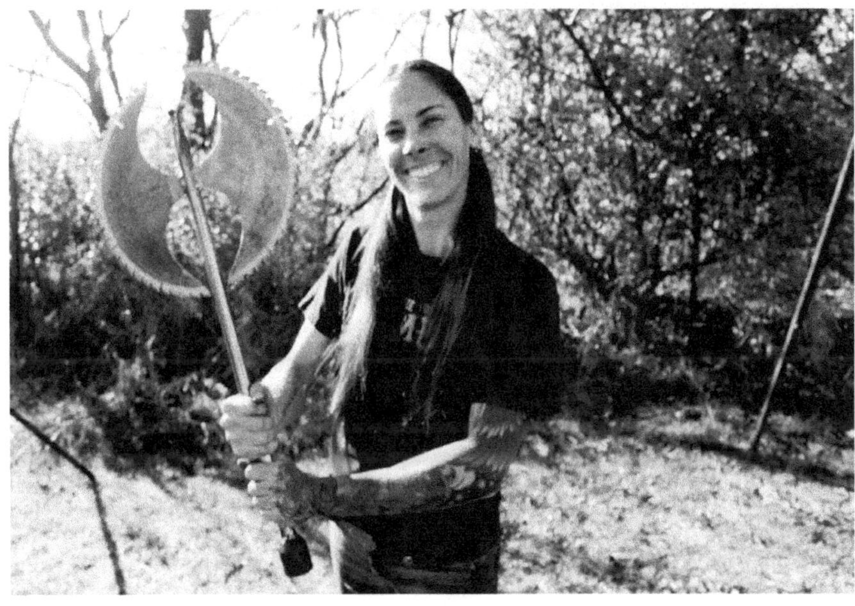

Get medieval!

Fisherman

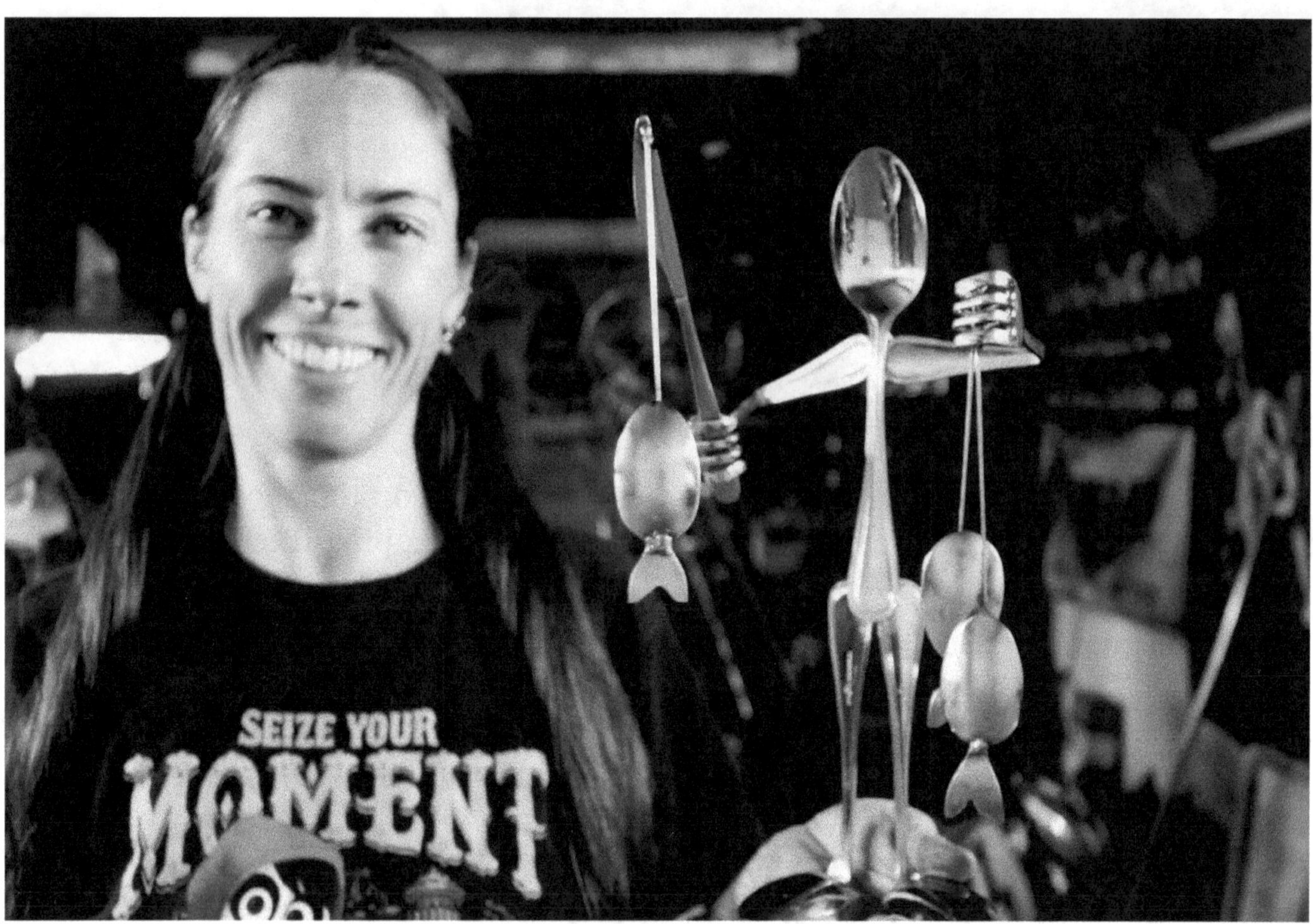

Difficulty

Materials 6Spoons (2 large spoons for the legs and head, and 3 small spoons for fish) 5Forks 1Knife Filler wire or thin wire

Tools

Needle nose pliers
Vise or clamp
Grinder with cut off wheel and sanding disk

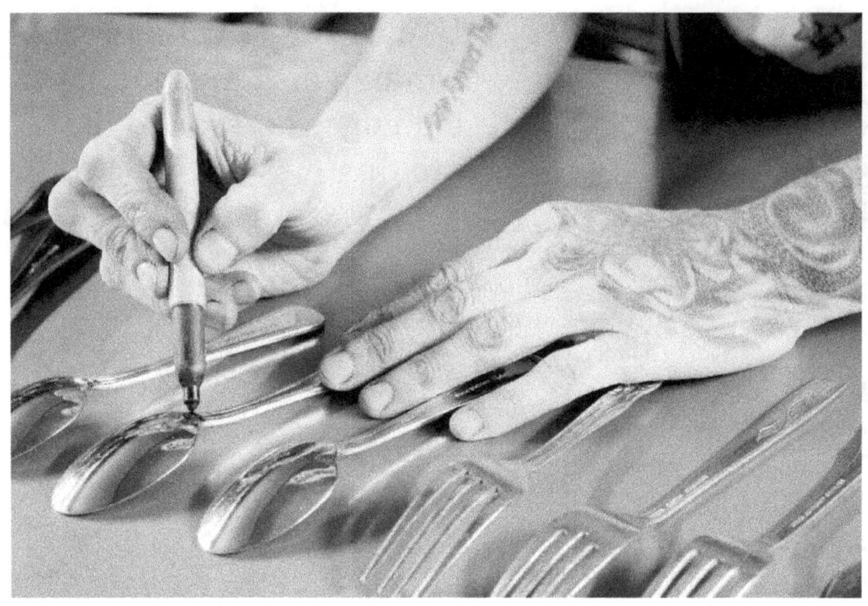

Mark the three small spoons at the handle base.

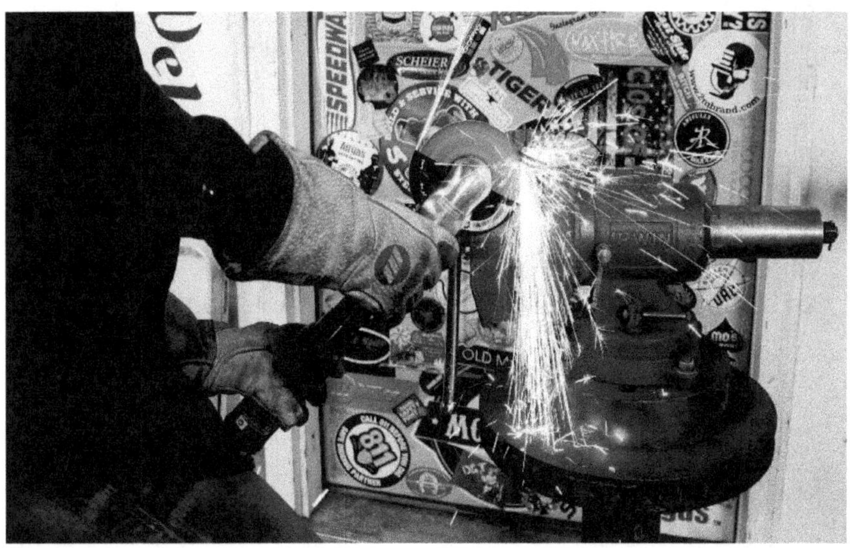

Clamp and cut the three spoons, saving the spoon bowls. These are the bodies of the fish.

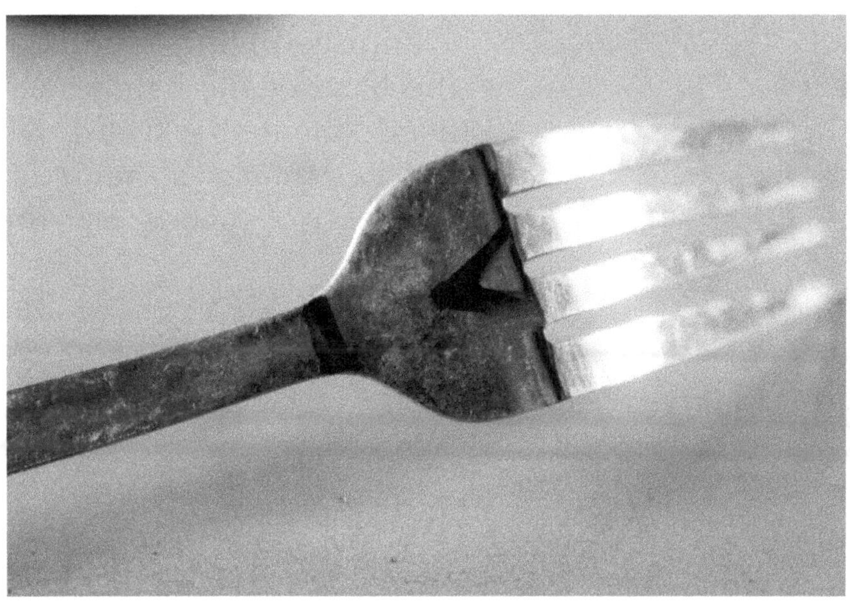

Mark and cut three forks as shown. These pieces are the tails of your fish. You can also choose to keep the two outer tines to give your fish some flair.

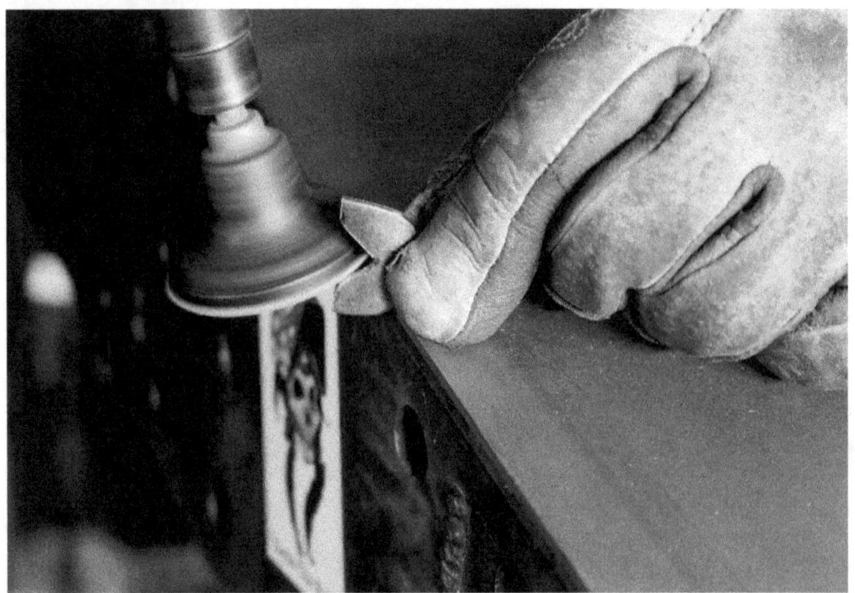

Use a grinder with a sanding disk to smooth the cut edges and round the tail fin.

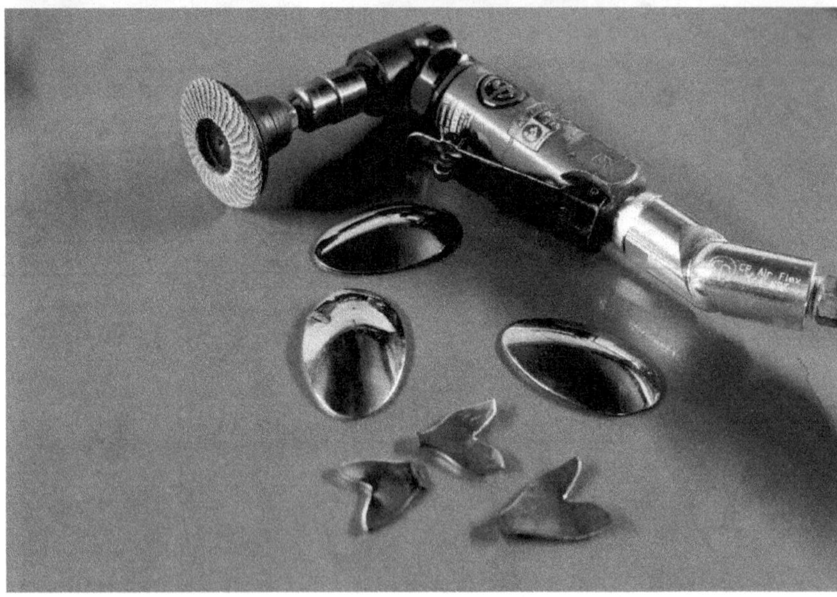

Fish bodies and tails smoothed and shaped.

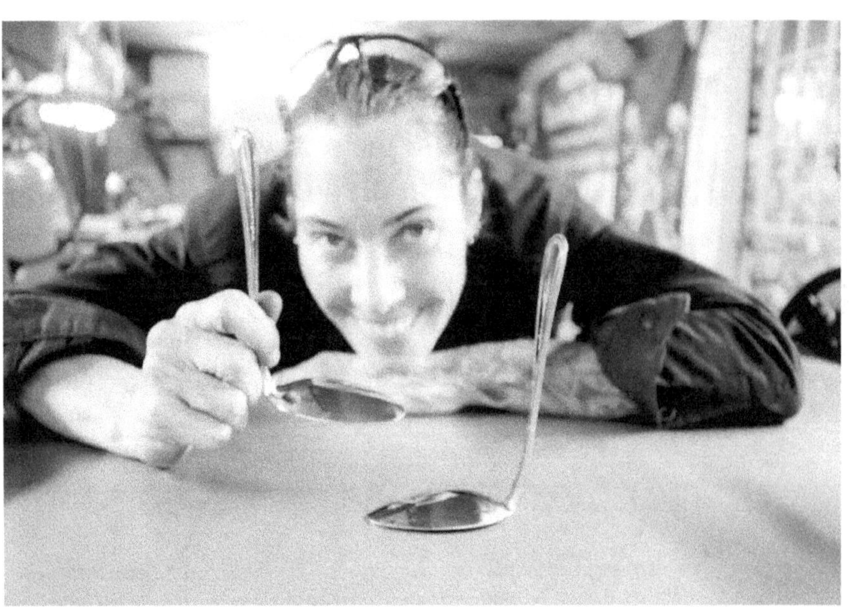

Clamp two large spoons at the base of the handle and bend them backward 90 degrees using a hammer. These two spoons are the legs.

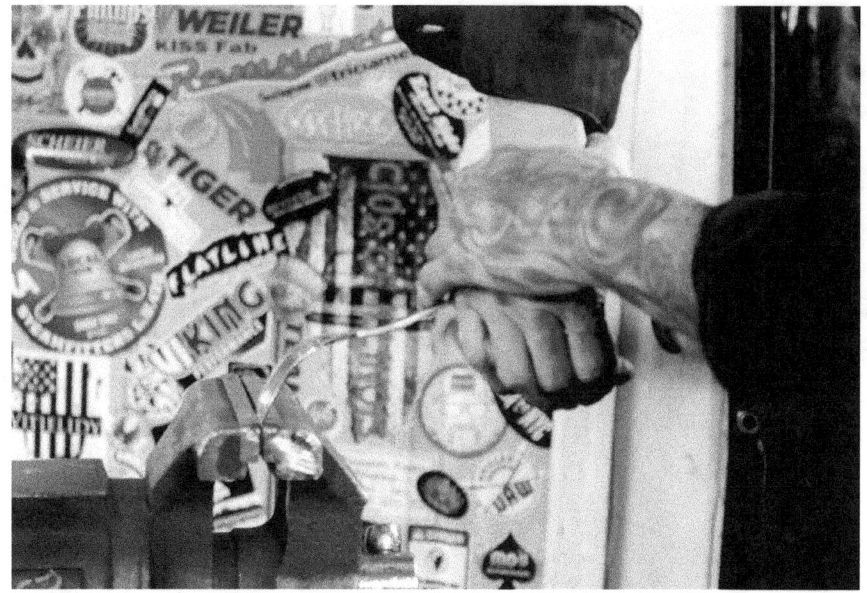

The two remaining forks are the hands and arms. Clamp the fork tines 1" from the end and bend them down 90 degrees.

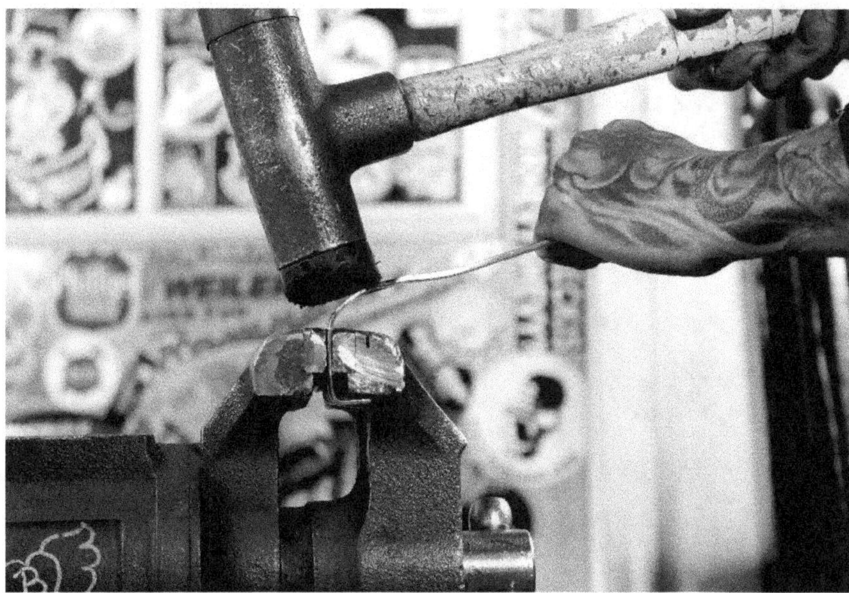

Clamp the tines 1.5" from the first bend and hammer the fork down another 90 degrees.

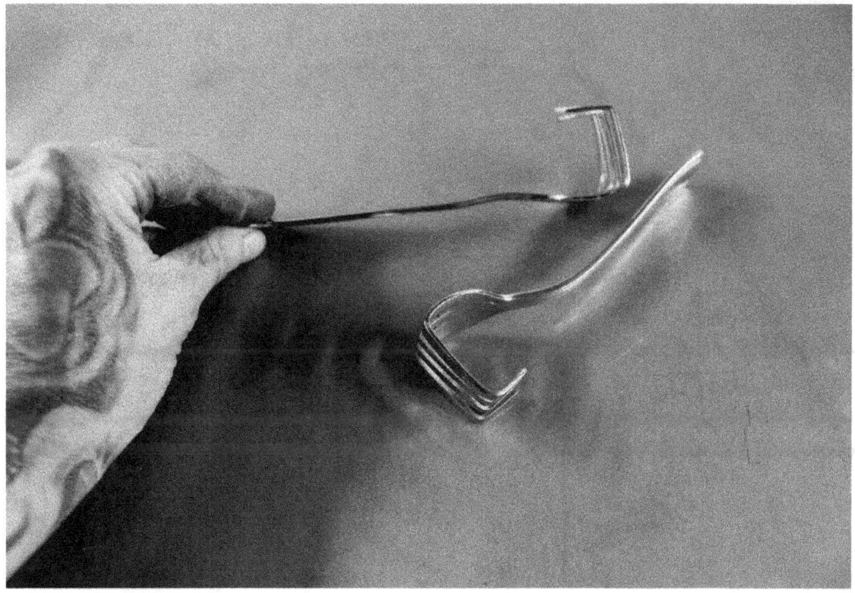

Repeat with the second fork.

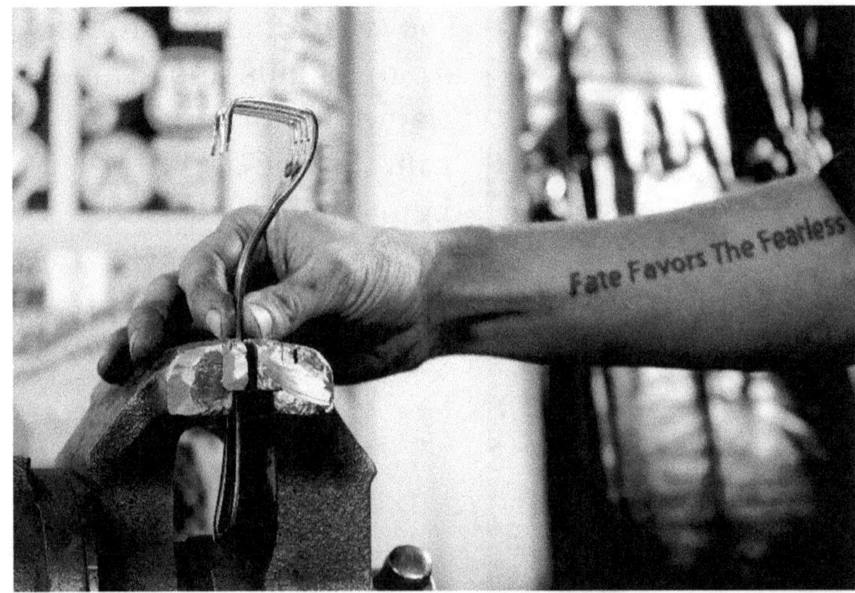

Clamp both forks halfway down the handle and bend them forward 90 degrees.

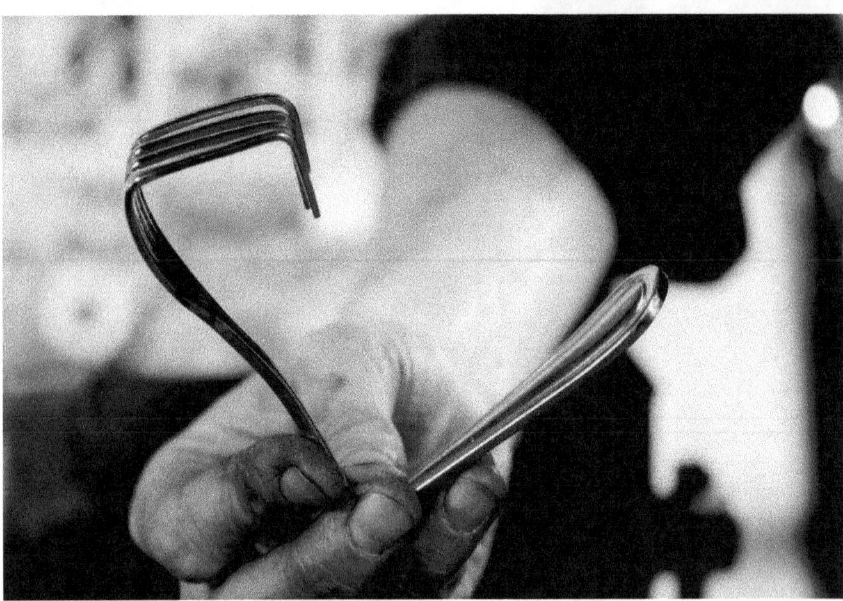

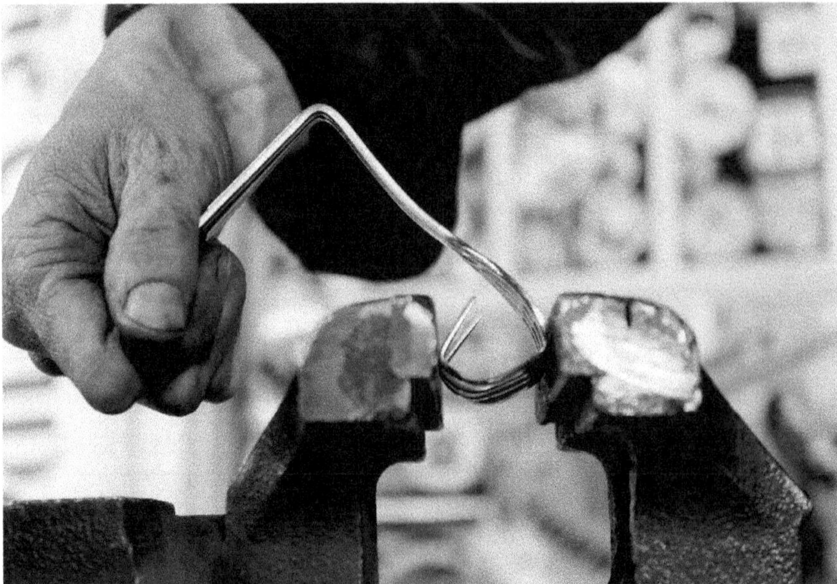

Squeeze the hands closed.

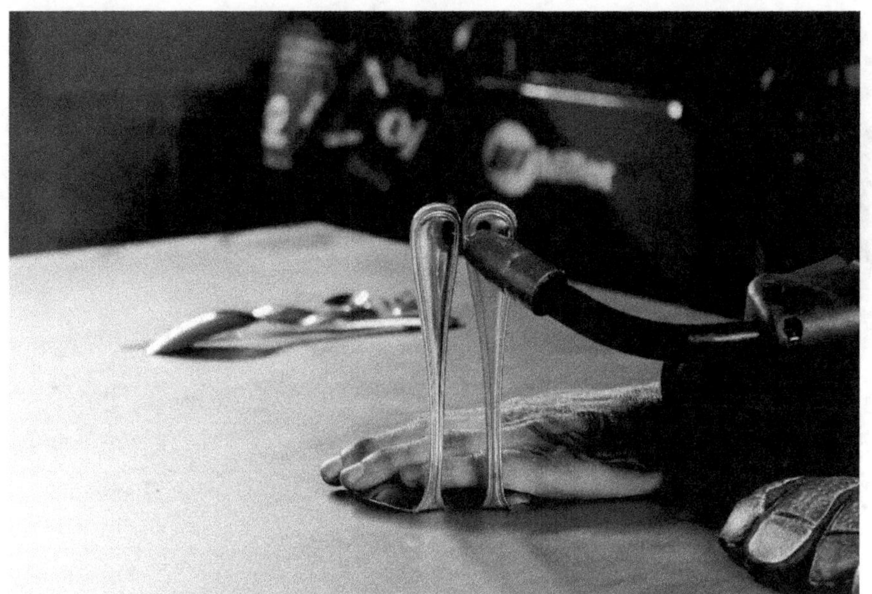

Hold the two legs with the tops touching and weld them together with two small tack welds.

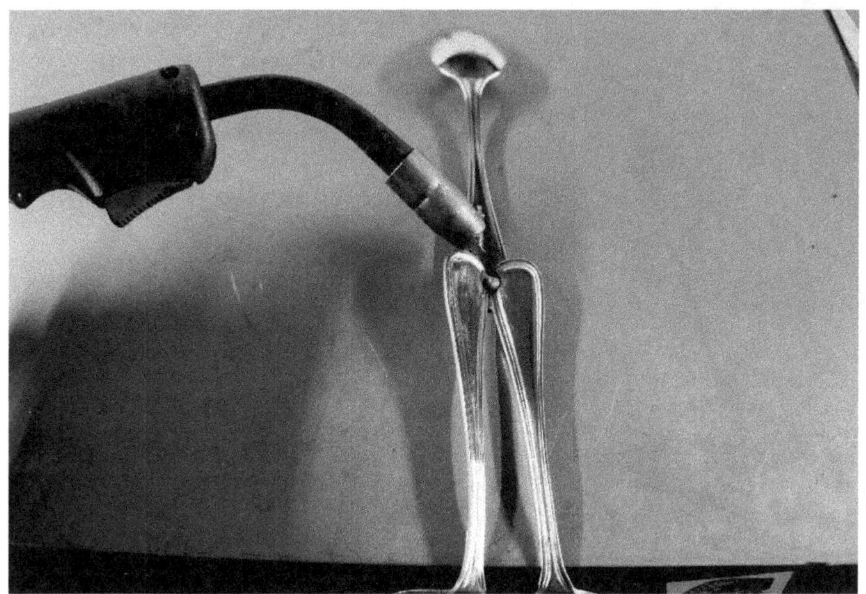

Lay the spoon face down and place the legs on top overlapping 1". (Hang the feet off the bench so that the body and legs aren't bent.) Weld the two pieces together using small tack welds.

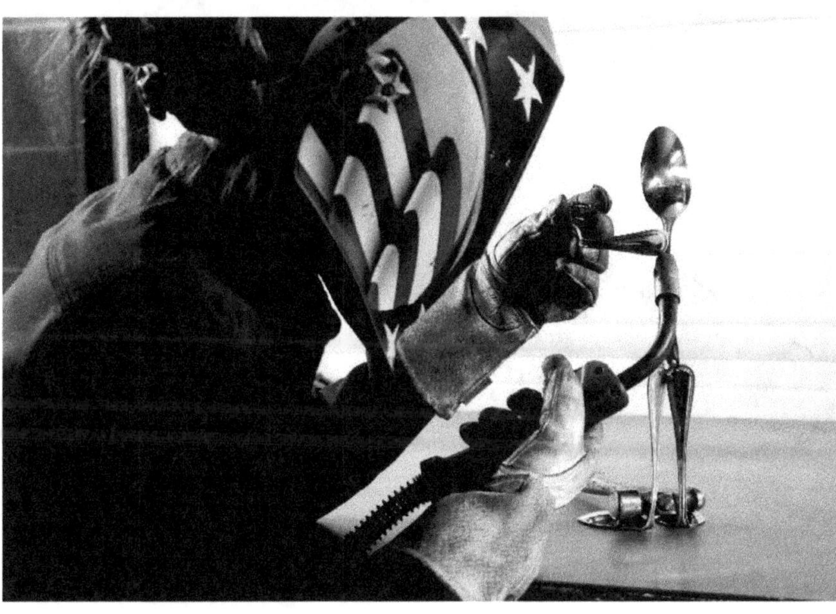

Hold one arm up to the back of the body and weld it using small tack welds. (I place my hammer on the feet to hold him in place.)

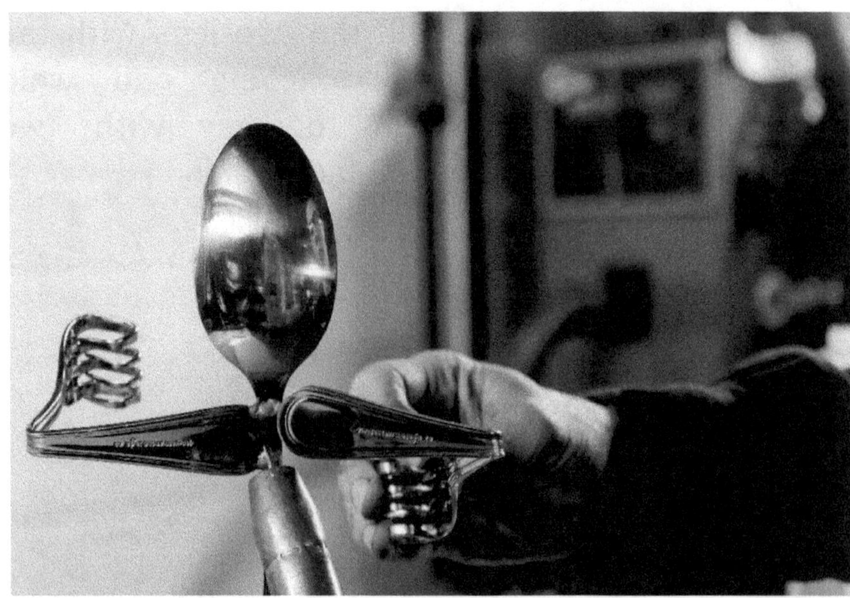

Hold and weld the second arm on.
Clean any weld spatter and discoloration with a wire brush and a hammer and chisel.

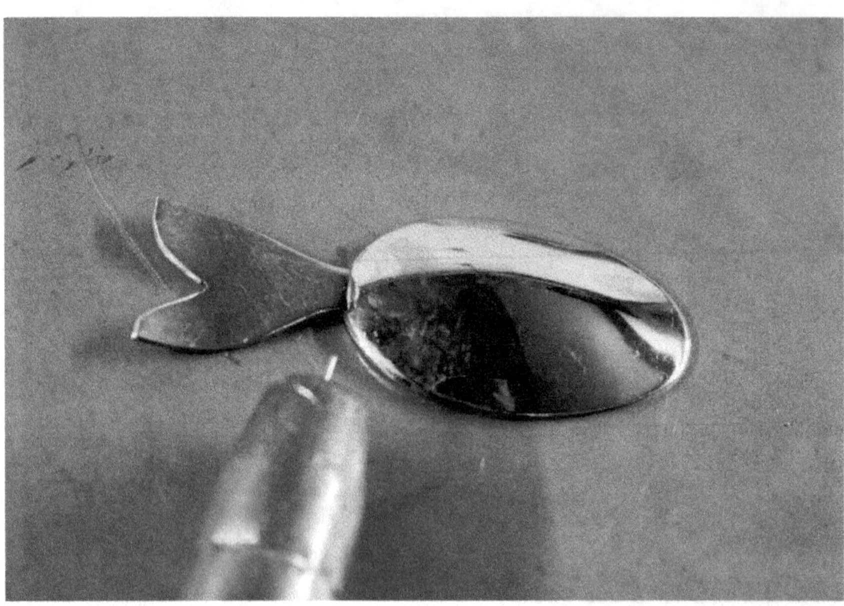

Weld the fish using small tack welds on the front and back of the body.
Clean weld discoloration and chip any weld spatter.

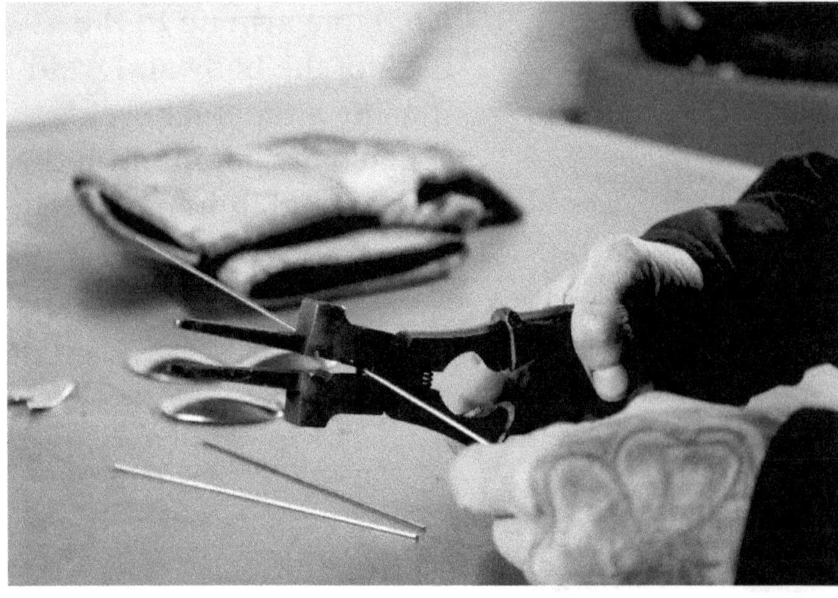

Cut three pieces of wire 6" long.

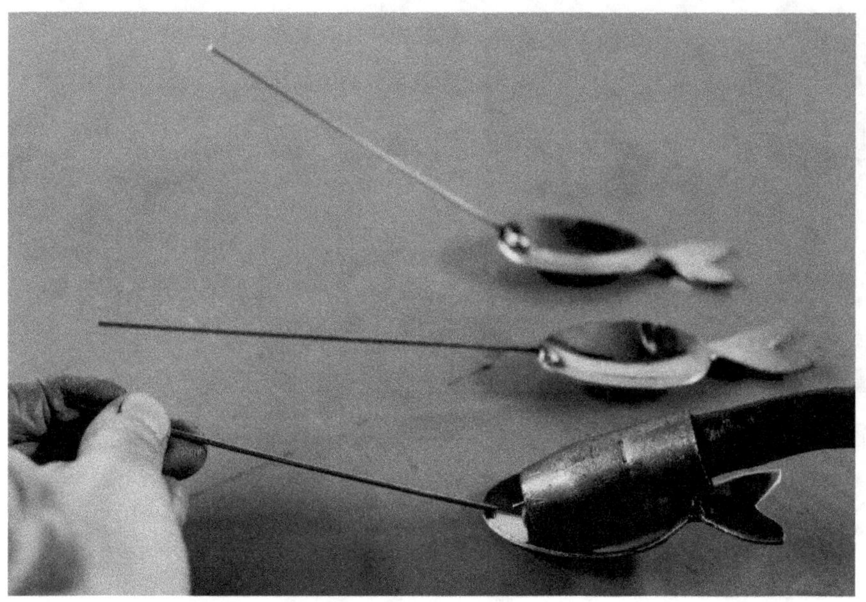

Hold the wire on the inside front of each fish and carefully tack weld in place.

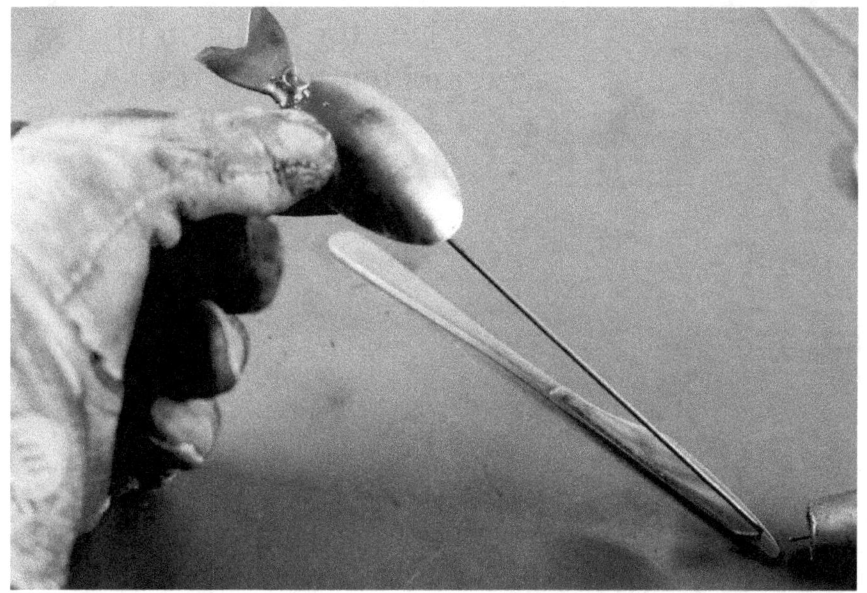

Hold the wire to the top of the knife with the fish at a 45 degree angle to the knife and tack weld it in place.

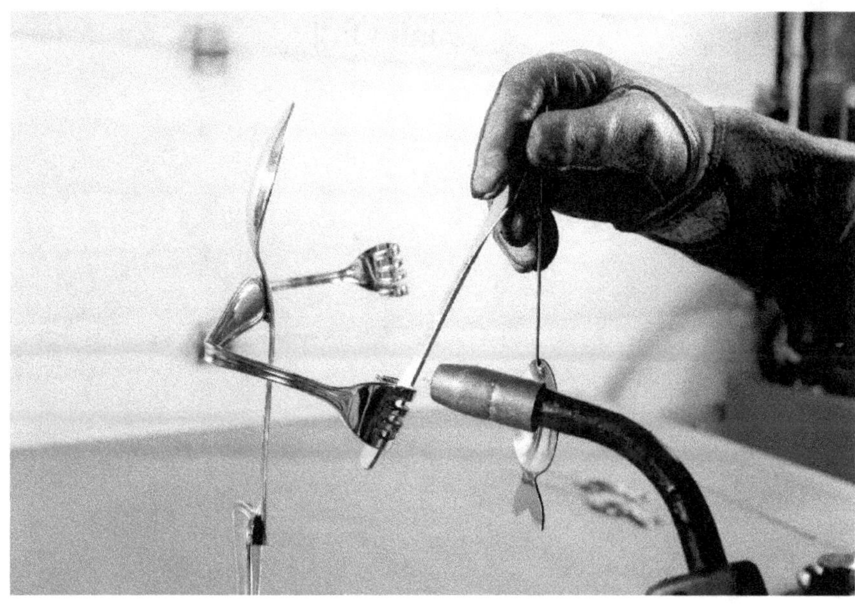

Hold the fishing pole in the fisherman's hand and tack weld it in place. Let the hand cool between each tack weld to prevent melting the tines off.

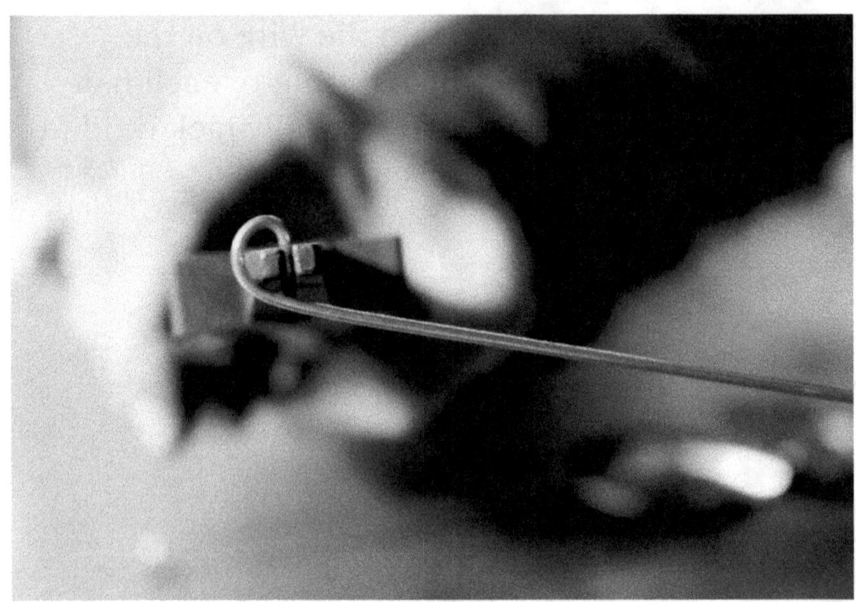

Curl the top of the two wires welded to the fish.

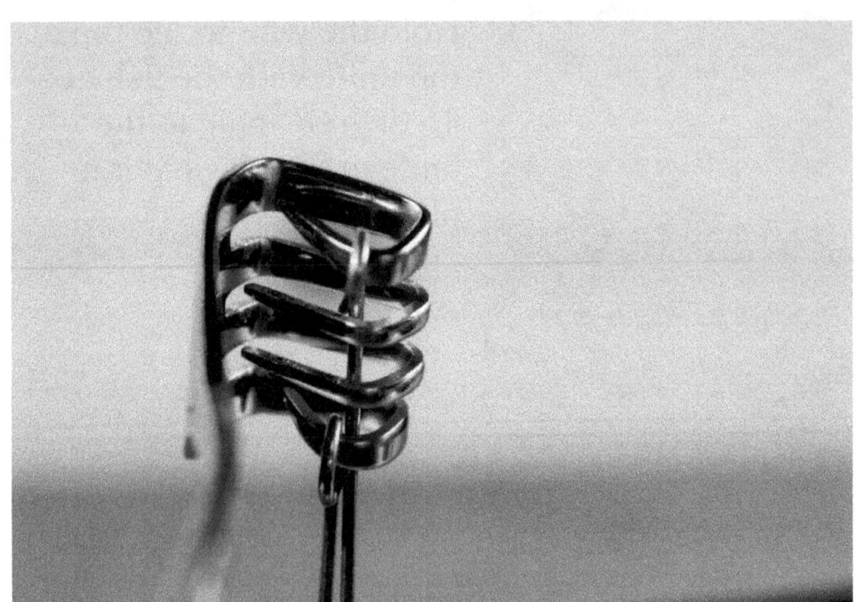

Place the loops on the top and bottom fingers and use pliers to pinch the tines closed.

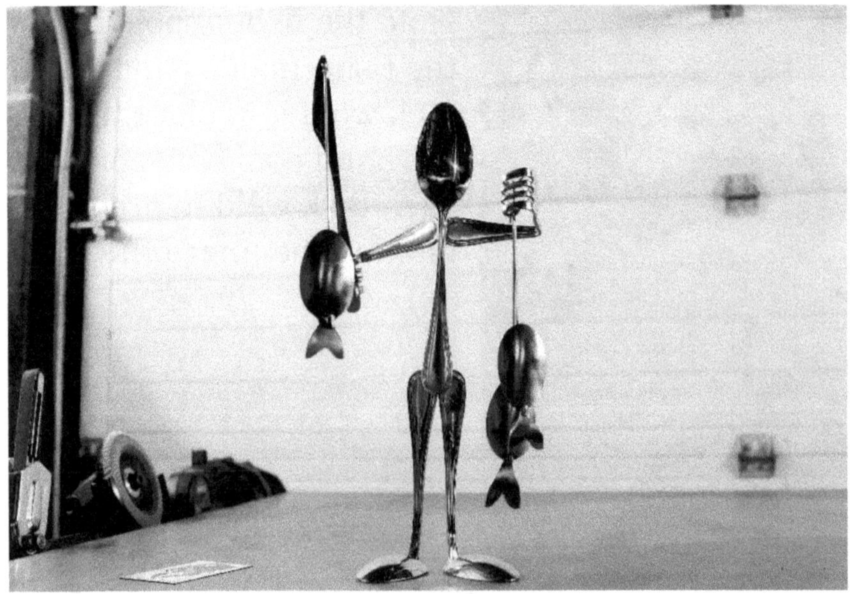

Fish On!!

Skeleton Hand

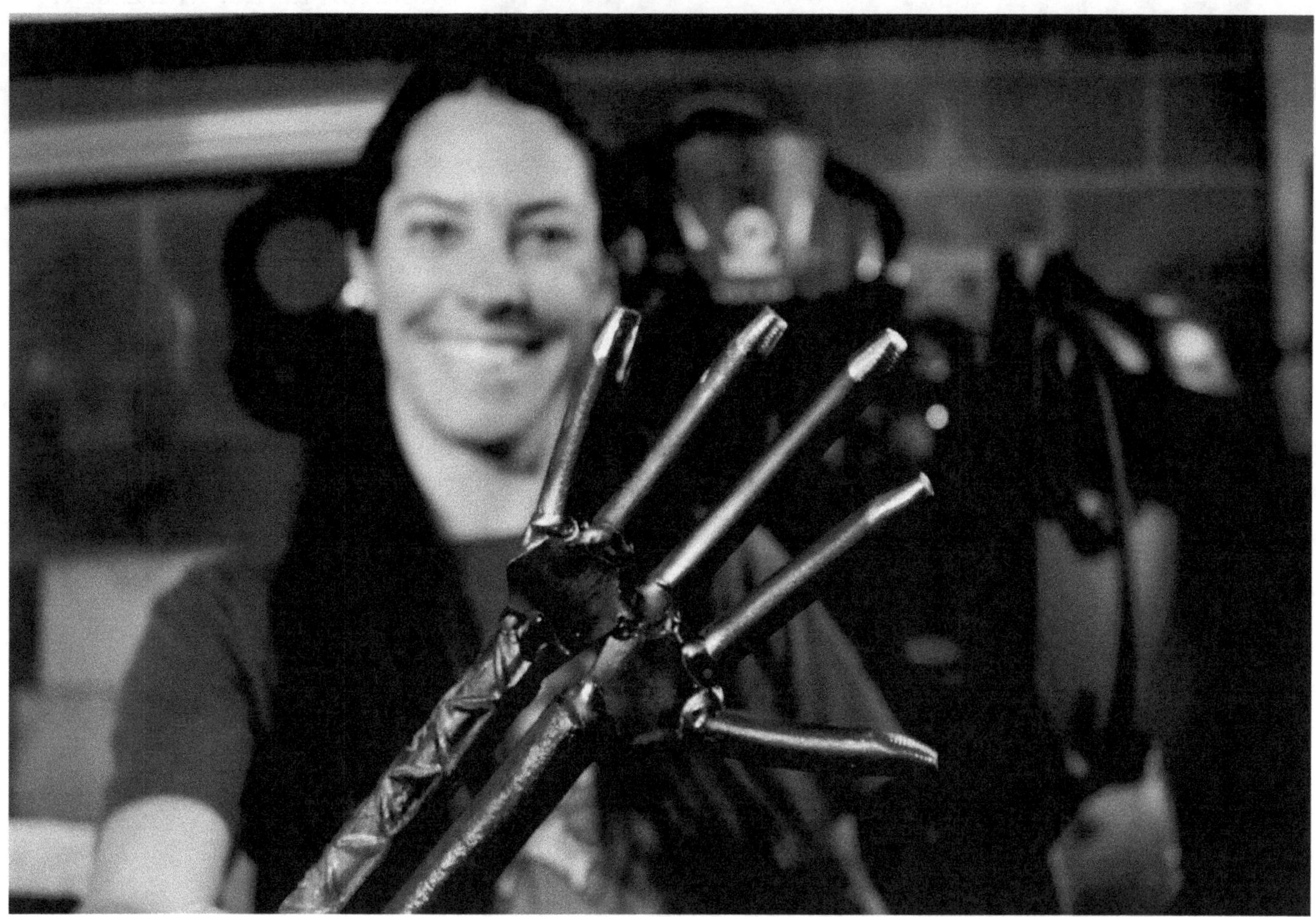

Difficulty

Materials

15"-20" of 1/2" round bar and 24"-30" of 1" Round steel bar
2 large bolts

Tools

Grinder with sanding disk and cutoff wheel

Extra

I created this hand in an easy style but if you want to get more details check out the steps I included after the basic steps.

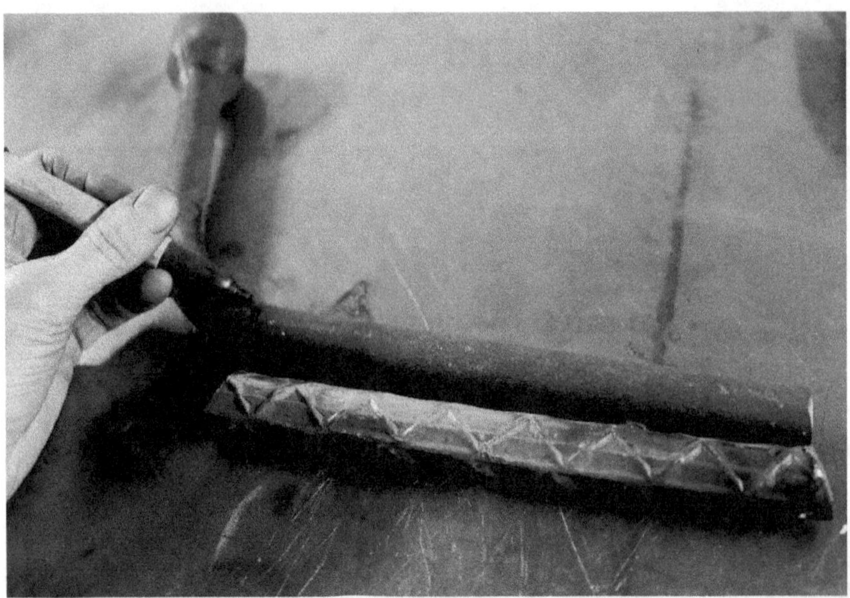

I use my arm and hand as a reference when making skeleton arms. Mark and cut the 1" round bar into two pieces the length of your forearm.

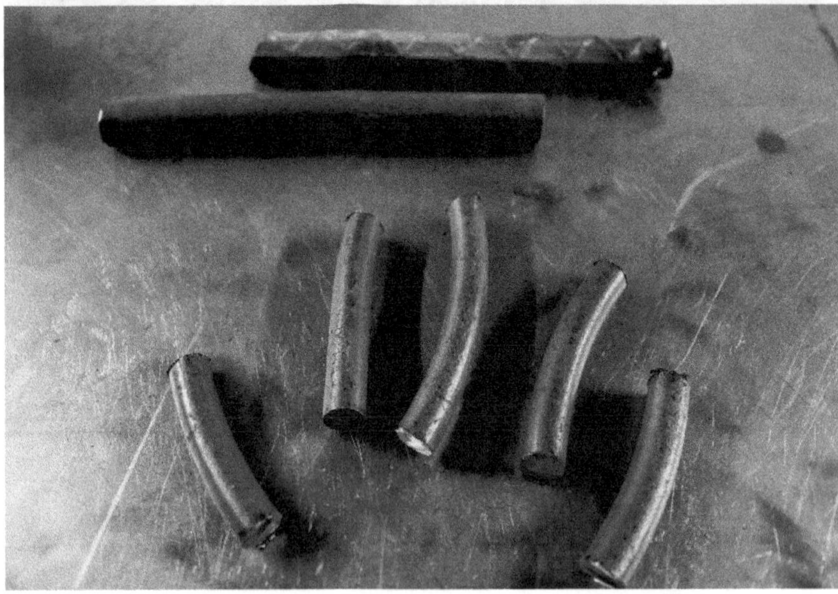

Mark and cut the 1/2" round bar the length of each one of your fingers.

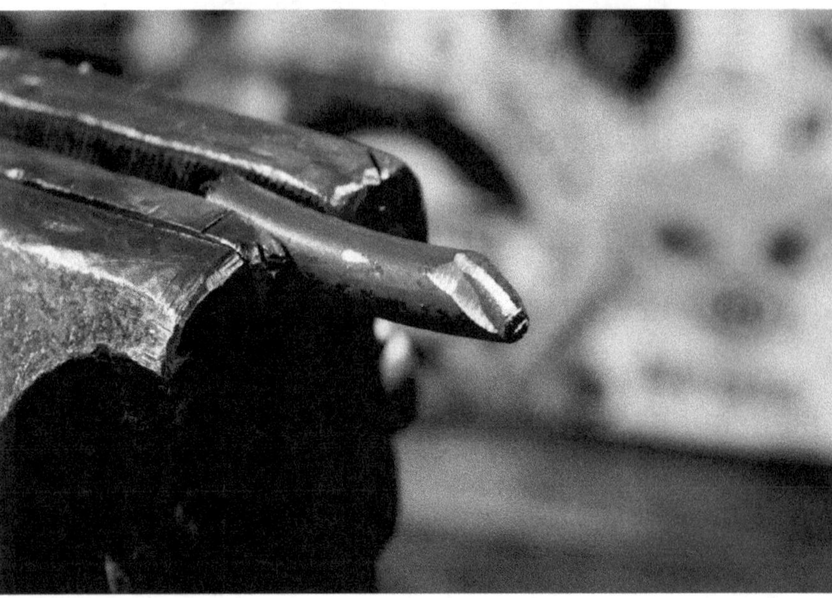

Grind fingertips on the ends of the five pieces of 1/2" round bar.

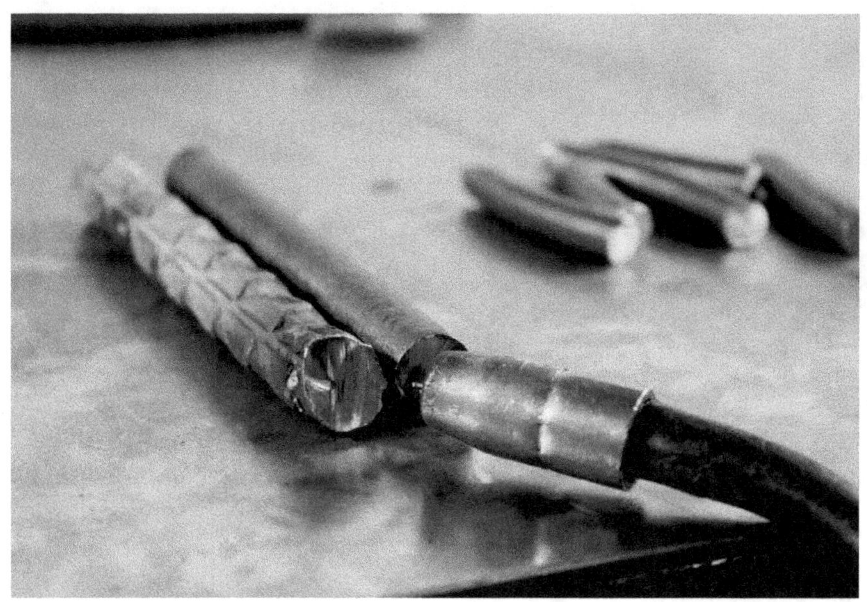

Weld the arm bones together at one end.

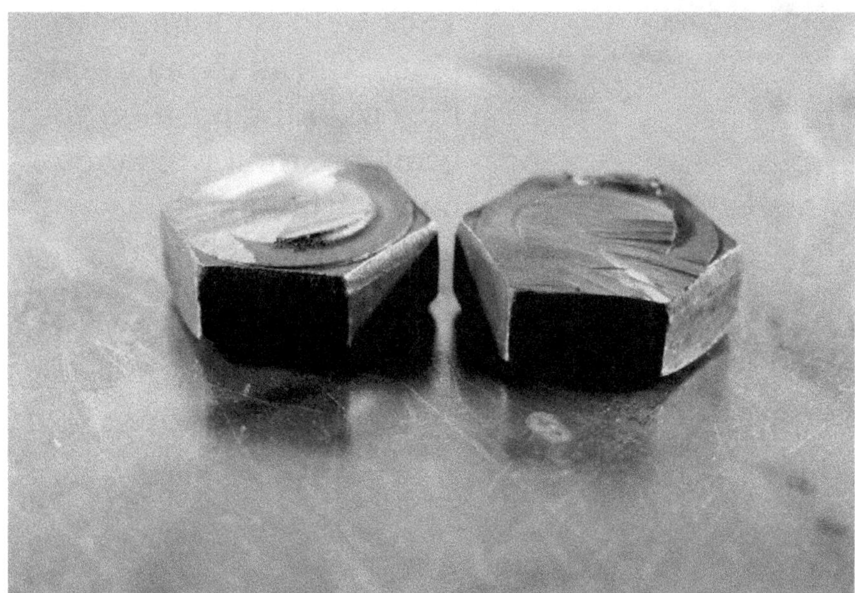

Cut the heads off the two bolts and grind them smooth.

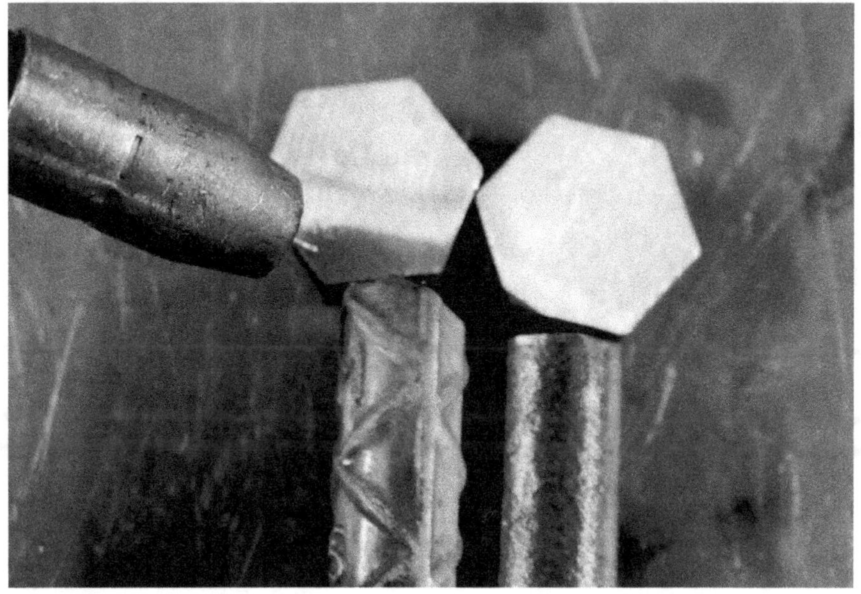

Weld the two bolt heads on the end of the arm bones that has not been welded.

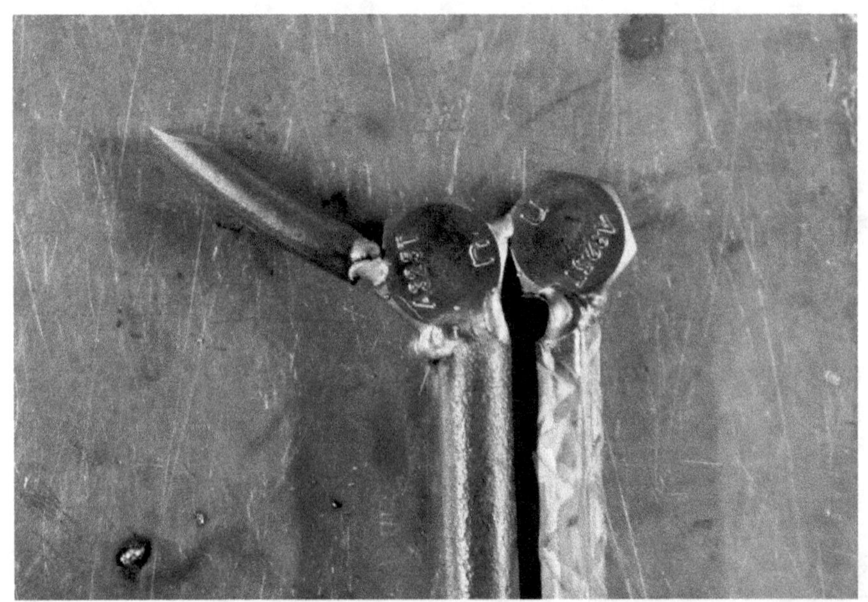

Use your hand as a guide to position the thumb and tack weld it to the bolt head.

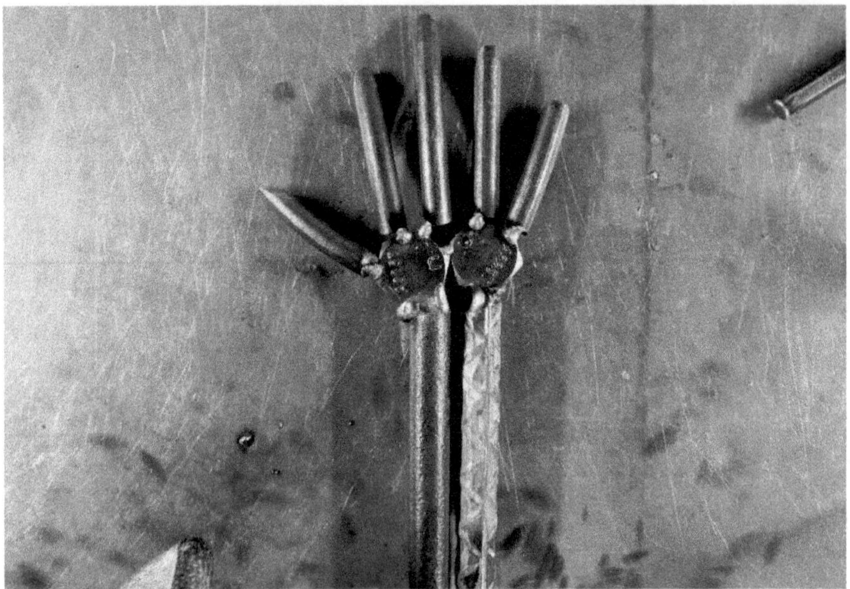

Tack weld each finger in place. Check to make sure they're in the position you want and then weld them on the front and back. Clean any weld spatter and discoloration.

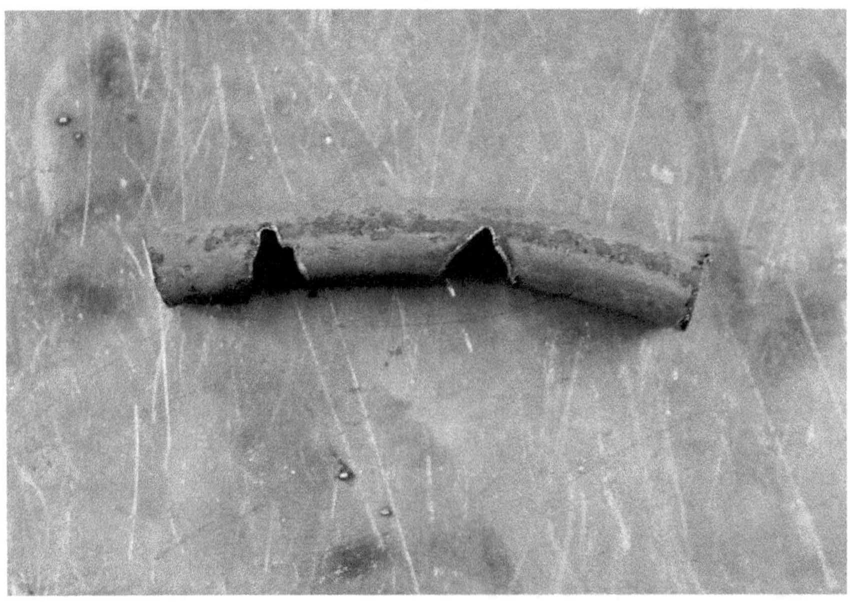

To give your skeleton hand more details bend fingers to point or hold something. Cut triangles into the fingers as shown The wider the triangles the more you can bend the fingers.

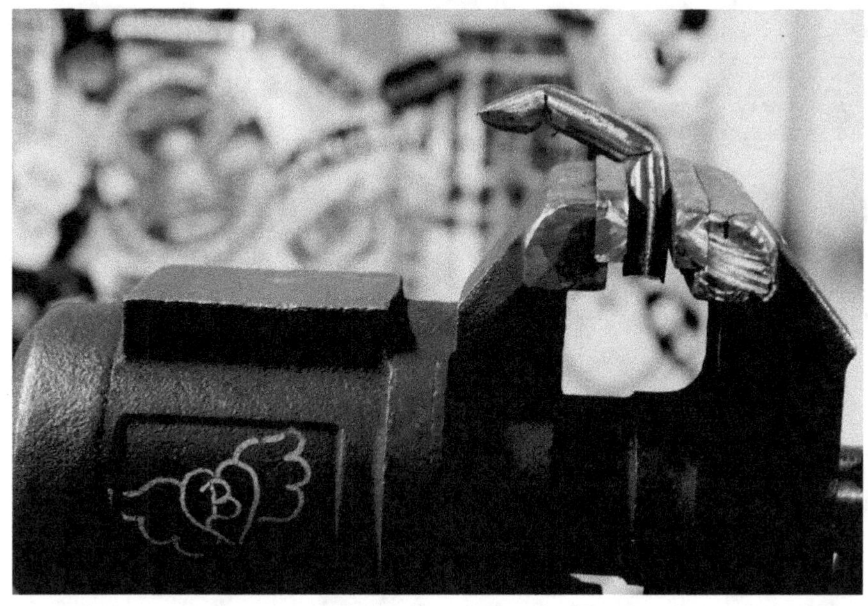

Clamp the finger into the vise and hammer to bend to the shape you want.

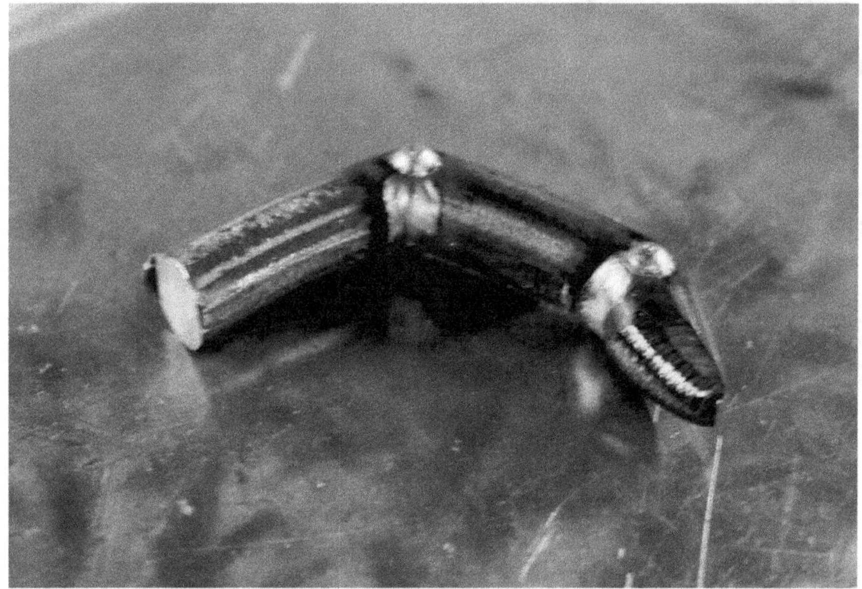

Weld the cuts.

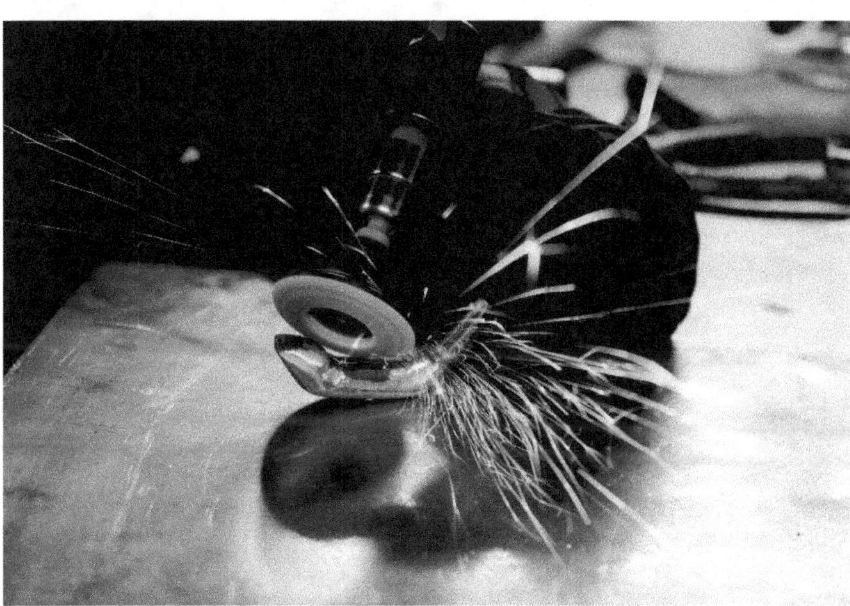

Grind the welds with a small die grinder and sanding disk.

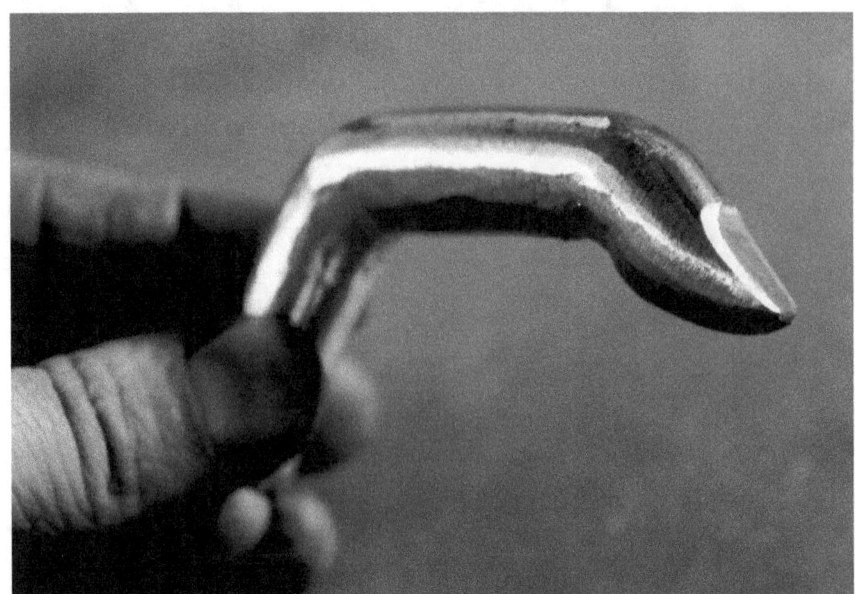

Grind a fingernail into the finger.

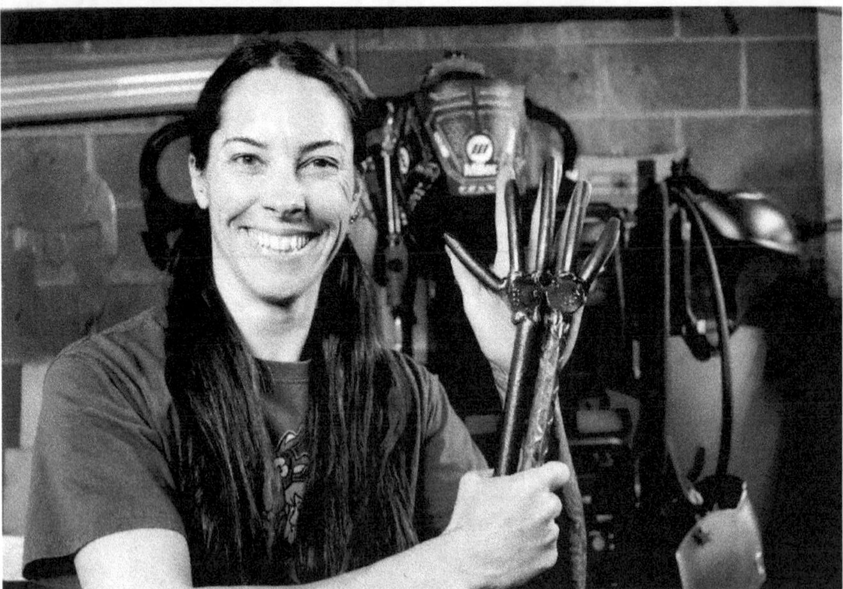

High five yourself forajob well done!

About Barbie The Welder

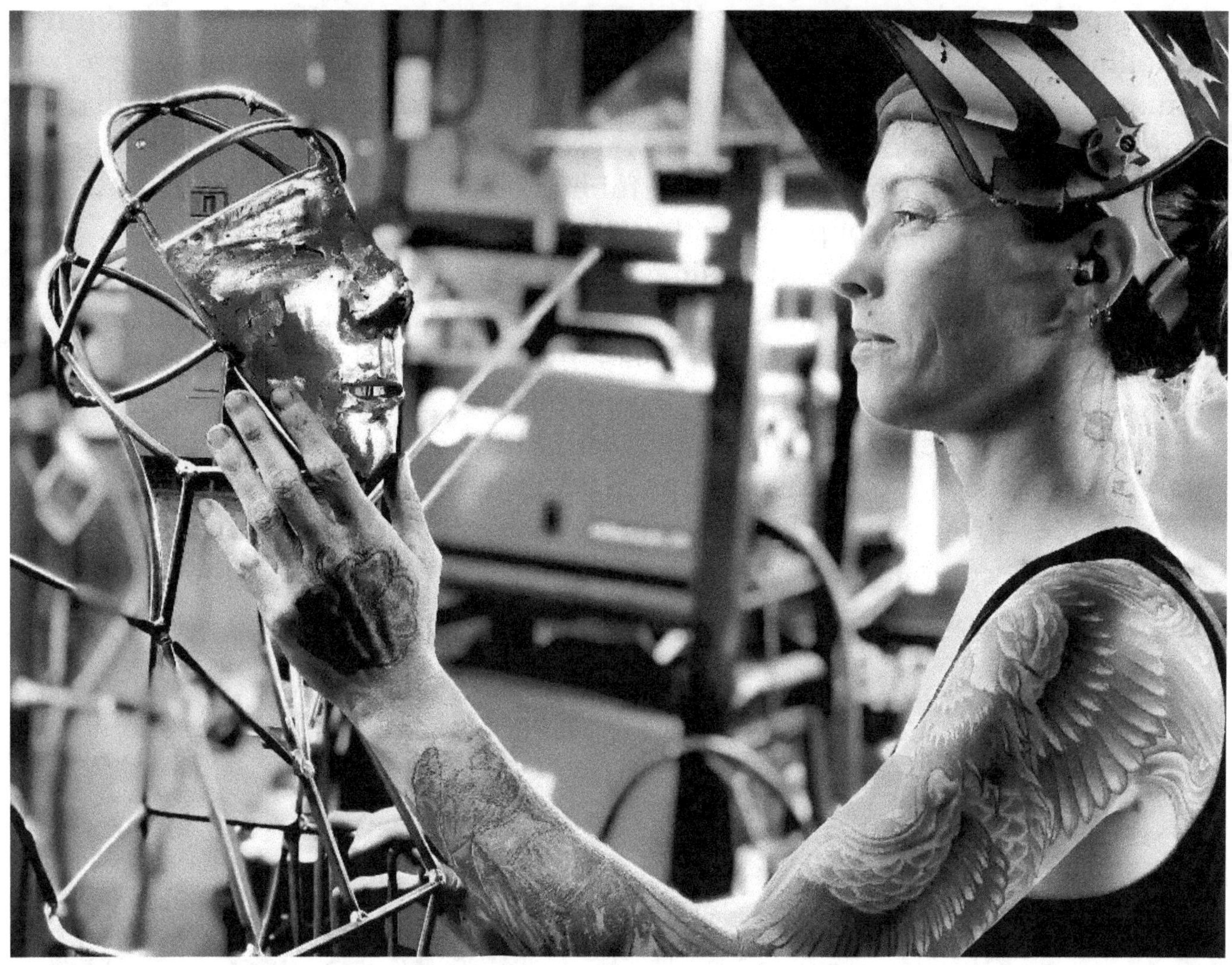

I took a 6 month welding program in 2007 after seeing the woman welding giant angel wings in the movie Cast Away starring Tom Hanks. The scene just spoke to my soul and I immediately knew I **needed** to be a metal sculptor. I was hired at a custom fabrication shop in 2008 after I graduated and worked there 4 years before I was able to save enough for a down payment to purchase a home, for the garage. It took me 9 more months of working and saving before I had enough to purchase the machines and tools I needed for my home studio, my 1 car garage. I quickly went to work designing and creating anything I could think of after work every day and on the weekends. I left the fabricating job I loved to create sculpture full time September 1, 2014.

Since that time I have failed my way to success! I knew nothing about selling, marketing, branding, or social media, all the things that make a business successful in today's marketplace. It took me almost a year of working full time and failing before I realized I needed to learn how to run my business like a business. I started spending hours each night, after working in the shop all day, reading business books and watching YouTube videos to teach myself all the important aspects of running a successful business. I started attending a business mastermind group locally that gave me support and priceless knowledge helping me take my business to another level! I tirelessly worked to improve myself and my business in any area I saw was weak and my business and my brand began to grow. Over the last five years I've been a full time artist I've sculpted a life for myself that is beyond my wildest dreams! So far, I have had the honor of designing and creating sculptures for major corporations, small businesses, and exclusive clients in 15 different countries, including Miller Welders, Harley Davidson, Weiler Abrasives, Chicago Pneumatic, and Carolina Shoe Company. I have welded sculptures live in front of thousands of

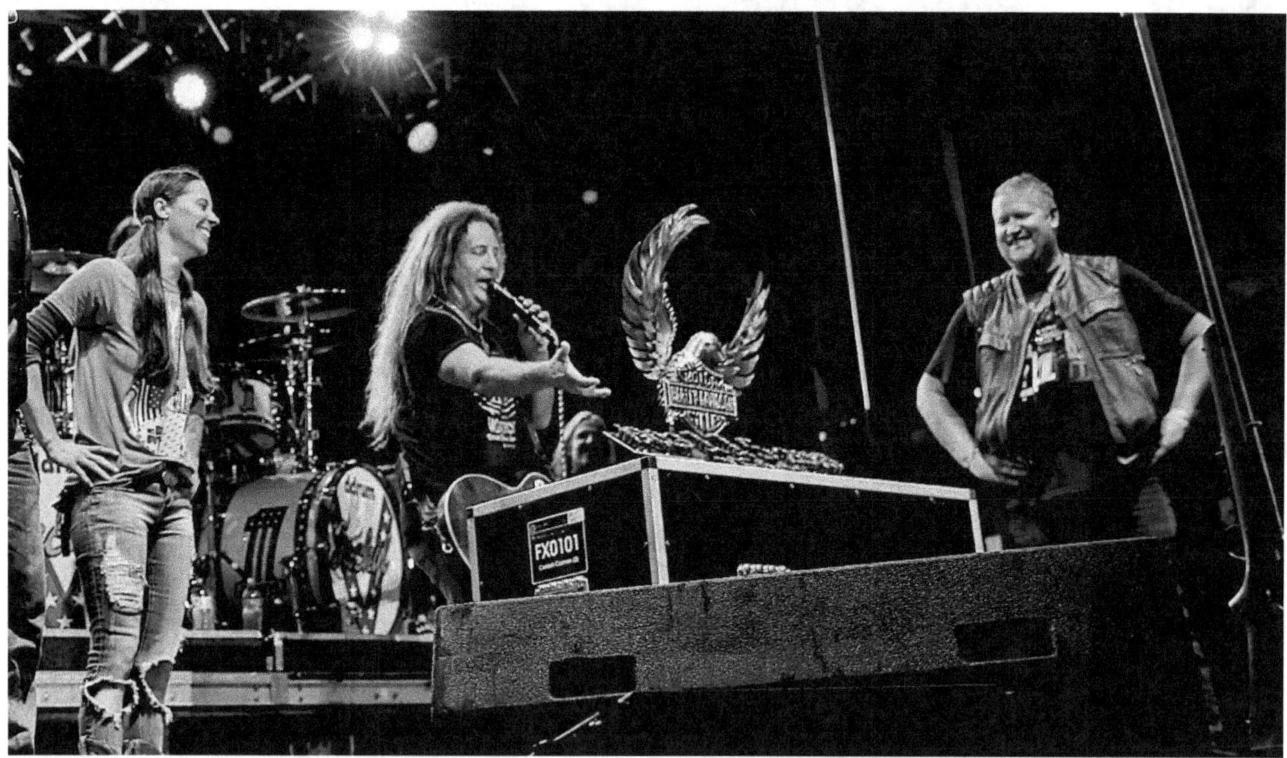

people at Sturgis Motorcycle Rally, Americade Motorcycle Rally, SEMA in Las Vegas, and have even presented sculptures to my clients live on stage at concerts! Each month my YouTube channel draws viewers from more than 50 countries, and so far, including this one I have written six books!

There's no telling what I will do next so make sure you connect with me on social media @barbiethewelder to see my most recent sculptures and shenanigans! You will not want to miss what I do next! View my YouTube channel, Barbie The Welder, where I teach you how to weld art, share my creation process of my masterpiece sculptures, and have no BS advice for entrepreneurs.

View my current project, available sculptures, and merch on my website. BarbieTheWelder.com

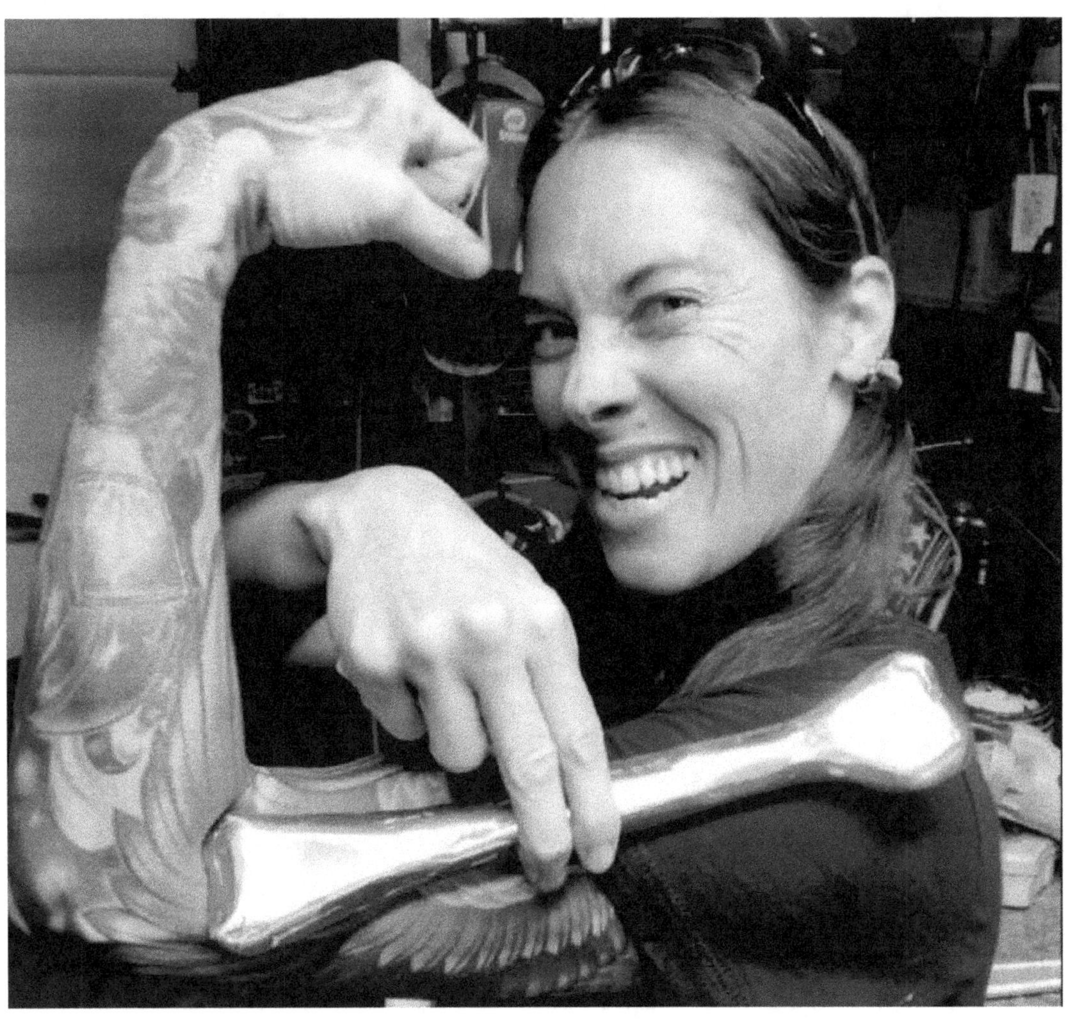

www.ingramcontent.com/pod-product-compliance
Lightning Source LLC
LaVergne TN
LVHW061203120826
845149LV00011B/1896

* 9 7 9 8 9 9 4 8 2 4 8 0 1 *